AF655514

Morality and Social Justice

Morality and Social Justice

Edited by
Abha Singh

Decent Books
New Delhi

Cataloging in Publication Data — DK
[Courtesy: D.K. Agencies (P) Ltd. <docinfo@dkagencies.com>]

Morality and social justice / edited by Abha Singh.
p. cm.
Contributed articles and lectures.
Includes bibliographical references.
Includes index.
ISBN 13: 9788186921531
ISBN 10: 8186921532

1. Ethics. 2. Ethics — India. 3. Social justice. 4. Social justice — India. 5. Human rights. 6. Human rights — India. 7. Reverse discrimination. 8. Reverse discrimination — India. 9. Social justice — Religious aspects. 10. Religious ethics. I. Singh, Abha, 1958-

DDC 303.372 22

© Author
First published in India, 2010
ISBN 13: 978-81-86921-53-1 (Hb) ISBN 10: 81-86921-53-2

All rights reserved. No part of this publication may be reproduced or transmitted in any form or by any means, electronic or mechanical, including photocopying, recording, or any information storage or retrieval system, without prior written permission of the copyright holder, indicated above, and the publishers.

Published and printed by:
Decent Books
D-36/A-1, Mohan Garden
Najafgarh Road
New Delhi - 110 059
Ph. (011) 2535-3435

Distributed by:
D.K. Printworld (P) Ltd.
Regd. office : *'Srikunj,'* F-52, Bali Nagar
Ramesh Nagar Metro Station
New Delhi – 110 015
Phones : (011) 2545 3975; 2546 6019; *Fax* : (011) 2546 5926
E-mail: indology@dkprintworld.com
Web: www.dkprintworld.com

Contents

Part III : Issues Concerning Rights

Part IV : Reservation and Reverse Discrimination

Part V : Socio-Centric Morality

Introduction

Abha Singh

A DEMOCRATIC set-up assumes that by granting political rights to all and by establishing equality before law, social differences would be conquered. The bottomline of such presumption is that in the distribution of political privileges and civil rights, the considerations of class, race, religion and gender are set aside. It is believed that political empowerment would provide new instruments for seeking equality in every walk of social life. However, when equal rights are granted to all citizens within the nation state, the ideal of formal equality appears to be less satisfactory. Equal accesses to public arena provided by law emerge to be insufficient because the issues of formal equality do not legitimately apply in the informal spheres of life. Since the informal aspect of (wo)man's life plays a vital role in building his personality, the concepts of "morality" and "social justice" acquire paramount importance.

Both morality and social justice are multidimensional concepts. The modern concept of social justice is complex. It includes a meritarian and egalitarian element as well. It recognizes the merits of persons as well as respect for personality as such.

The highly stratified Indian society with centuries of domination by a few on all the sections of the society is going through a crisis. In spite of many giant thinkers the country has produced the condition, instead of ameliorating, is gradually deteriorating. There is chaos in the matter of distribution of goods and services in the society. Indian society is lacking in moral energy and social imagination to understand the principles of a new society on the basis of peace and ordered liberty. Social progress cannot be achieved by external means. It is determined by man's intimate transcendent experiences. We must look for the renewal of the heart and the transformation of values which appear to be fast decaying in our society. At present, Indian society is on the verge of disintegration as each group is trying to garner positions in the society through shorter routes. Hence, a serious debate on the issues concerning social justice is essential so that no one grabs another's bite. In these circumstances, it appears to be essential to deliberate on the issues, taking in view the moral aspects that make (wo)man a human. In view of this, the topic *Morality and Social Justice* is at par with the demand of the day.

The volume explores the various possibilities for moral energy and social imagination in order to have a society comprising peace and ordered liberty as well. Some of the chapters included in it were delivered at the Indian Council of Philosophical Research, New Delhi, sponsored national seminar on Morality and Social Justice, when it met in Patna from 27-29 January 2008.

The explorations have been divided into six Parts. Part I of the volume deals with the basic concepts of twin issues clubbed together, i.e. morality and social justice. In the next part, one moves from the said concepts in general to justice in particular, as various theories are taken into account in the context of justice. Part III takes up the right-based issues. It has been felt that when rights of citizenship are granted to all citizens, social differences re-enter the discourse of democracy through social policies. Social policies try to overcome the effects of such social differences that were the initial source of discrimination and arbitrary exclusion. Thus this section contains chapters that deal with the issues concerning the third sex, capital punishment, language rights in a multilingual ethos, rights of children and rights of the subalterns in historical perspective. The issue of reservation and reverse discrimination appears to be unclinching in Indian society. Part IV discusses the issue from various angles. Part V takes up the issue of socio-centric morality in individual religious traditions of Hinduism, Islam, Buddhism and Jainism in that order. The sixth and the final part covers general themes, such as *niṣkāma-karma*, development and education.

Part I
Basic Concepts

CHAPTER 1

Morality and Social Justice

Nityananda Mishra

THE very first question that arises while discussing a topic is: Why should that topic be discussed at all? In other words, what after all is the relevance of the topic? Well, the fact that we have at present gathered here for discussing the above topic is a hard reality. We cannot deny it. And this fact clearly implies that there are beings on earth who can discuss things, that is, who can "think." And, it is also a hard fact that whatever it is, it tries to persist and preserve itself. I would also like to say that "what is endemically characteristic of any existence is that it 'covets' to preserve itself." At the consciousness level this coveting is nothing else but "instinct" or "desire." And we human beings are the very examples of such coveting consciousness. And, we must never be sorry for possessing such desires for self-preservation. They are our best hallmarks, so to say. It is not without reason that suicide is regarded as a crime.

Now, this self-preservation instinct must not be confused with selfishness. For, functionally they do not serve the same end. If you are cent per cent selfish you will never share things with others. And if suppose all the resources of the world are under your control, then you alone will use them and all others will remain deprived of them. The result will be that all others will die out of existence. Now, will you really be happy by remaining alone in the world keeping with you all its resources as your exclusive property? Surely, not. Even a diehard miser needs others for becoming a target of their envy. If you remain all alone it is likely that you will die out of existence sooner than later.

Now, from what we have argued out above it is quite clear that "Live and let live" is the very cardinal principle of living. And it is this very principle that is known as the principle of morality. Well, this morality must not be confused with spirituality. If, however, spirituality is taken as an aptitude or proclivity for promoting the realization of higher values, then, of course, morality may very well be regarded as spirituality.

I think it is also very clear from the above that morality is an inter-personal or social affair. And a social transaction must have to be taken as a transaction between at least two persons. Now, whatever a person does to any other person must either be constructive or destructive of social harmony. And only that social harmony is worth its name which is totally comprehensive both spatially and temporally. When a social action is constructive in the most comprehensive way, it is desirable and hence is moral; and when destructive it is undesirable and hence immoral. So morality and immorality are opposites of each other. But there is another sense of "morality" wherein the opposite of "morality" is not "immorality," but "a-morality." This sense of morality is wider than the one present in the above-mentioned distinction of "morality" and "immorality." The flow of a river is an a-moral movement. You can neither accuse nor praise the river for its flowing along the river bed.

Now, a very moot question arises here. Let us grant that all that is said above is quite in order. But why after all a person ought to be constructive in his actions? Usually the necessity of acting constructively is explained by linking morality with spirituality of the divine type. If you will not act constructively, that is, morally, God will punish you by sending you to the hell. Thus, it is on account of fear of punishment that people behave morally. Well it is indeed very strange that even the arch rationalist Hegel of Germany (eighteenth and nineteenth centuries) linked morality with the spirituality of the Absolute spirit (*Geist*).

But then, a genuinely rational account of anything cannot be connected with any spirituality of the supernatural type. The account that I have given at the very outset of this essay does not have any truck with any supernaturalism whatsoever.

We all know that a very close disciple of Hegel, Karl Marx, downright rejected any linkage between morality and spirituality or divinity. He said that his teacher was standing on his head with his legs high up, and so he set him stand normally by rejecting his dialectical idealism and establishing in its place dialectical materialism. I shall not go into the details of Marxism here. Very surely there are things in Marxism that I do not accept. But then, even the devil must have to be given his due. It was indeed very creditable on the part of Marx that he totally delinked morality from supernaturalism or divinity. Did he not say that "religion is the very opium of life?"

Even so as I have already said, we cannot see eye to eye with him in every way. For example, we cannot accept his method of the implementation of social morality. But before discussing this point any further let us clarify the notion of social morality. Well, social morality is not morality if it does not involve social justice. Let us suppose that the miser about whom we talked above becomes a bit liberal and shares the resources with his wife and children and not with the rest of human beings. In this way he does indeed behave morally at least with his wife and children. This is good so far as it goes. But is what he does enough? Must all the rest of humanity starve and die out of existence? Well, self-consistency, which is a logical principle, demands that if Mr X, along with his family, has a right to live, so has Mr Y with his own family. And not only Mr X and Mr Y, but also all other human beings do have the same right. All human beings *qua* human beings have equal logical, therefore, equal moral status. And this principle of the equality of human beings is at the source of morality. And it has been cognized as far back as the Ṛgvedic period. The very last *sūkta* of the *Ṛgveda* says:

samānī va ākūtiḥ samānā hṛdayāni vaḥ ।
samānamastu vo mano yathā vaḥ susahāsati ।।

The gist of this *sūkta* is that all our willings should be equality-oriented, so that we all may attain goodness.

Thus, we see that it is the demand of logic and, therefore, of morality that the entire existence including all humanity be treated as one single family (*vasudhaiva kuṭumbakam*). And such a morality is altogether mundane and it has nothing to do with any supernatural spirituality. I have argued elsewhere that "Morality must not culminate in spirituality of the supernatural type." Well, the *Gītā*, too, suffers from the same defect as that from which Hegelianism suffers. Not that the *Gītā* has no moral teachings in it. It is full of them, but they are all virtually rejected when the Lord says, *sarvadharmān parityajya māmekam śaraṇam vraja.*

It is, indeed, a pity that nobody so far has distinguished and "separated" the moral contents of the *Gītā* from its supernatural elements. Not even Lokmanya Bal Gangadhar Tilak of the *Gītā Rahasya* fame and S. Radhakrishnan have done this. In the West, Hegel, as we have said, was overturned by his own disciple Marx. Well, I would not go here into any details for earmarking the richness of the *Gītā*-morality. I have tried to do this elsewhere. Here I shall just point out as to how the *Gītā* has given enough emphasis on the very cardinal principle of equality about which we have already talked enough before. The *Gītā* (verse V.18) says:

> *vidyā vinaya saṁpanne brāhmaṇe gavi hastini* ।
> *śuni caiva śvapāke ca paṇḍitāḥ sama-darśinaḥ* ॥

Now, let us come to the most important question of the execution of social justice. The great apostle of dialectical materialism, Karl Marx, was extremely grieved to see that social justice was not being meted out to the general mass of humanity of his times. So, he, along with his friend Friedrick Engels chalked out a programme for its implementation. But it is here that I disagree with Marx. He recommended the method of violence for the implementation of social justice. He said, "Workers of the world unite. You have nothing to lose but your chains, and have a world to win!" And he also said:

> Yet, we must not forget that a sixth power [meaning by this, revolution] exists in Europe, maintaining at certain moments its domination over all five so-called "great powers," and causing them all to tremble. This power is revolution. After having long dwelt in quiet long retirement, it is now again summoned to the field of battle by crises and starvation. . . . There is needed only a signal and the sixth and greatest European power [revolution] will step forth in shining armour, sword in hand, like Minerva from the brow of the Olympian. The impending European war will give the signal.

But then, Marx's prophecy has been belied. The reason is that no "shining armour" can ever prove effective in bringing peace and prosperity in the world. Peace can never come from an armed struggle. And here comes in the great grand principle of *ahiṁsā* practised much too effectively by Mahatma Gandhi of our own country. He used this method of *ahiṁsā* in his fight against the British administration first in South Africa and then in India, and he succeeded in no small measure in both the countries. But then, it is surely very difficult to use this weapon of *ahiṁsā* in the way the Mahatma wanted it to be used. The user needs to undergo much too severe a training before he uses it.

Now, if we compare the Marxian method of violence with the Gandhian method of non-violence in the context of the execution of social justice or for that matter in the realization of world peace, we can very easily see that Mahatma's method far outweighs Marx's. Well, even if per chance Marx's method succeeds, the success must have to be the result of the sacrifice of at least some precious human lives. Precious because even an oppressor harbours within himself the logical possibility of being reformed. So, why kill him and not reform him? And surely the Mahatma's method results in what he called *sarvodaya*. Even our scriptures have said,

> *sarve bhavantu sukhinaḥ, sarve santu nirāmayāḥ* ।
> *sarve bhadrāṇi paśyantu, na kaścit duḥkhabhāgbhavet* ॥

If *na kaścit duḥkhabhāgbhavet,* why then kill anybody?

On account of many such solid reasons, I, on my part, would like to go with the Mahatma, rather than with Marx insofar as the implementation of social justice is concerned. But then, before I conclude, I must emphasize the point that no amount of theoretical emphasis can be effective after all. What is needed most is your and mine and everyone else's actual participation in the work of effecting social justice. Such participation is, in fact, the real price which must be paid for being an authentic man.

CHAPTER 2

Moral Considerations in a Democratic Polity

Vinod Kumari

BEFORE deliberating on the relationship between morality and politics in a democratic set-up it is imperative that these terms are analysed and understood properly. Moral questions arise when we pass beyond the stage in which we are directed by traditional rules prevalent in society. These traditional rules are generally so internalized that we can be said to be inner-directed. At moral level we think in critical and general terms and achieve a kind of autonomy as moral agents. Different kinds of thinking may be considered related to morality in one way or another. Descriptive or empirical inquiry about phenomena of morality, asserting normative judgements about morality and engaging in debate with oneself or the others about the nature of good or right in particular case or as a general rule, the analytical critical or meta-ethical thinking about the nature of moral expressions are examples of some of the varying types in which morality may be understood. For our present purpose we need not be concerned about all these usages of morality. We can take morality to be primarily concerned with providing the general outlines of a normative theory. Morality has an individual as well as a social dimension. The questions about the relationship of morality and law, morality and politics and morality and religion indicate to the social dimensions of morality. Some thinkers call it "the moral institutions of life." In this sense, morality is a social enterprise existing before the individual who is inducted into it and becomes a participant in it. It goes on existing even after the individual ceases to exist. The origin, sanction and functions of morality are social. Morality is an instrument of society as a whole for the guidance of individuals and smaller groups. It makes demands on individuals that are initially external to them. If they come to disagree with demands, they must still do so from the moral point of view that has somehow been inculcated into them. Conception of society with a supernatural dimension and including a given divine law is ascribing social character to morality.

Considered as a social system of regulation, morality is like convention or etiquette. Convention does not deal with matters of such crucial social importance as dealt with by law and morality. Morality is distinct from law in certain features that it shares with convention. It is not created or changeable by anything like legislative, executive or judicial act. It does not have its sanction from physical force or threat of it but from praise, blame, and appreciation and other such verbal signs of favour and disfavour.

Morality, as Western thinkers have been stressing, fosters or even calls for the use of reason. It implies a kind of autonomy on the part of individual. Considered even as a social institution of life, morality is supposed to aim at rational self-guidance or self-determination in its members. Moral thinkers have distinguished stages of morality. David Reisman portrays the following moral types:

1. The tradition-directed individual and/or society.
2. The other-directed individual and/or society.
3. The autonomous individual and/or society.

The general idea is that morality starts as a set of culturally defined goals and rules governing achievements of the goals, which are more or less external to the individual. These are imposed on him or inculcated as habits. These goals and rules become internalized. As a result the individual develops a "conscience" or "superego" in psychological terminology. It is this conscience which guides and checks the actions of an individual. Collectively the social morality too develops a mechanism of censor for the actions of its members and proclaims individual acts of its members, right or wrong.

The term politics carries with it a group of concepts, i.e. government, citizen, state, sovereignty, administration constitution, and election. Aristotle in his book *Politics* uses Greek terminology presenting a system of morality, which is based on the rational principle of a trained and discerning mind. In his *Ethics* he defines "virtue" as "a state of character, concerned with choice, which consists in a mean . . . determined by a rational principle."

State as a political institution exists with society. It regulates the outstanding external relationships of men in society. It supports or exploits, curbs or liberates, fulfils or even destroys the social life over which it is invested with control. In modern political world the ideal of democracy aims to abolish the distinction between the dominant will of the government that imposes state institutions and the common will that creates them. Sovereignty and law are the two great engines of political control exercised by the state governments. The ultimate sovereign is the name of the power which determines the policy or directions of the state. The will of the state is rarely attained, as on all questions of policy there is division. The "will of the people" is rarely the will of the people. In no democratic state is the active government the choice of all the citizens. It is at most a fluctuating majority that sits upon the throne.

If the sovereign, the will of the people, seems a poor and precarious thing in contrast with the grandeur of the state we shall have to reflect that policy is merely the concern of the hour. Underneath it is the deeper agreement of will. Every policy, every decision of authority and power is achieved through difference, but as time passes the slow play of criticism revises or affirms it, and a sense of the integrity of the state is built-up making such differences insignificant.

In a democracy, the legislature is sovereign in the form of the government. The legislature makes laws of universal validity within its own sphere whether defined or undefined. It has also the right to the exercise of force in the maintenance of such laws and of the authority, executive and judicial by which they are administered. One who exercises these rights constitutes a political government. It is only the legal aspect, the form of the sovereignty.

The substance of power falls far short of the title, within the limits set by the Constitution. There are nearer limits established by the very nature of political law, by the ever-present sense of the ultimate sovereign and finally by the pressure of the great body of tradition whose support is the general will. The government in itself is not one and indivisible.

Sovereign power is an attribute of common will made common by community of purpose. The government has power as the guardian of the Constitution, as the executor of law, not in its own right. It is due to political sovereignty that the laws of the state are unique unlike those of other associations. The law of the state alone is coercive. The laws of the state have universal and formal character and this limits the sphere of the state. Not only because of its universality but still more because of its coercive sanction, the law of the state has a limited competence. The root of the obedience to law is not coercion but the will to obey. But the law takes the form of an imperative. It can, therefore, regulate the external order of society. Some other sanctions within society are applied with greater persuasion. Custom and tradition, mode and fashion have influences on society. The sense of spiritual values — the most compelling to the sensitive and the creative mind — is capable of stirring the hearts of people.

The Constitutional law is binding on the government and the legislature. Behind the legislature lies the ultimate sovereign, the citizen, who has vested in the government certain powers, including the execution of the laws, but it has made the government its trustee and not its master. If the government were to violate Constitutional conditions of trusteeship, which are partly formulated as Constitutional law, it would destroy the support on which it rests. Thus the government has only a lease of authority revocable by the sovereign, which granted it. Government applies the compulsion of law against individuals but it would be powerless to do so unless the governed as a whole willed to obey the law.

Law cannot prescribe morality. It can prescribe only external sanctions. The government should prescribe those actions, which it adjudges to be conducive to welfare, e.g. promotion of the physical and social conditions requisite for the expression and development of free — or moral — personality. Law does not and cannot cover all the grounds of morality. Turning all moral obligations into legal ones would be to destroy morality. The party system in a democratic policy is another significant aspect. A political party is an association organized in support of some principle or policy.

The party system implies an elective and representative government. Party is the only means by which the ultimate political sovereign, the voters, can definitely control government. Party attains fruition only in democracy, otherwise the right of election, as itself a guarded privilege, is fulfilled in the spirit of class and not of party. As a result the control of the government becomes the prize of the factional strife, not the result of an orderly appeal. The party system is based on the contrary theory that men are rational beings, insofar as, at least, they admit principle to be a better ground of government than force, persuasion more desirable than compulsion, and the conflict of idea more creative than the clash of arms. Party system in spite of its defects and shortcomings should not be suffered to obscure. The original or the natural party is that organized in protest against privilege and class. Political parties are driven by the logic of the system to new positions. The "appeal to the people" obscures and modifies the claims of class-interest. Further, certain agencies of communications have been instrumental in the evolution of party system; of the agencies the most important are the press and media. These are "vehicles of publicity" and seek to influence as well as register opinion. But they have their limitations, as they are utterly dependent on the goodwill of the readers and the audience.

Now, we have to relate the political institutions to human intentions and social consequences. Though these institutions have purposive character, their establishment in the practice of men outstrips their reflection. Political understanding lags behind the political actuality.

Certain conflicting facts present challenge in the practice of democratic policy. The elected leaders represent the aspirations of those who elect them. The candidates in elections make elaborate and varying promises with a view to enticing the electorate. The voters expect that their representatives, to whom they are delegating authority, should have certain virtues at the least. We may reflect upon the requisite virtues in leaders in a democracy. First of all, the representative has to be committed to the social interest. They should rise above individual selfish interests as their interests have to be identified with the state and/or political organization to which they belong. They have correspondence in their thinking and actions. No dual character of the leader will be acceptable to the electorate. Rising above biases or expansion of vision on the part of the representatives requires a knowledge base and discerning mind which has clarity about the interest of self and society. His actions have to be based on the principle of transparency having no hidden agenda. Certain mental attitude and openness to new ideas are must in contemporary environment. Only those leaders can take the state or society ahead who can think over the viability of new inventions and polities. The basic characteristic of the reason-governed behaviour of a representative has to be simplicity and sensitivity to all.

But since in democracy it is the majority that elects the representatives, these representatives reflect the nature of the majority in a state. On the part of the electorate the people have to be well informed, reason-governed and unbiased. Such a state of mind is achieved only through proper purposive educational pattern (which is available to all land) — an environment wherein the voters feel their concern and accountability to the state. They have to realize the grave nature of the delegation of authority to representatives who will make policies for them, execute these policies and the consequences will have to be borne by all the members of the state. Ultimately, it is they who are going to be the sufferers.

Expectations from leaders in a democracy are sometimes frustrated due to some problems in the practice of virtues. Individuals have their own visions and aspirations. Sometimes party convictions clash with individual views. One has to sacrifice individual opinions in order to be a member of a party. Though democracy is called the government by the people, in fact so many pressure groups function in the political realm apart from the political parties. The business organizations, the minority groups, and the other associations having strong alliances due to common interests, always have great influence in elections. Sometimes these influences function under the surface and after the parties are elected and form the government they make pressure in making policies in their favour. The influence of capitalists is one such phenomenon, which ultimately makes democracy unobligatory.

Thinkers like De Tocquelle have indicated towards the drawbacks and dangers of democracy. One such danger is the dictatorship of the majority for which safeguards are taken in constitutions for minorities and disadvantaged groups. But sometimes the benefits are taken only by a selected section of that class who in turn wish to continue the same safeguards indefinitely and make pressure on the governments to continue with these. As a matter of fact, a large section of that class still is without those benefits and those who are making pressure no more need these privileges, yet they keep on pressing for policies so that their coming generations keep on getting those benefits.

In a constitutional democracy the provision of independent judiciary is made with a view to check the functioning of the constitutional provisions. It is also a safeguard against the dictatorship of the majority.

Democracy, in its present representative parliamentary form seems to be an ideal towards which all the existing democratic states are aiming. The ideals guide the realities. Democratic ideal requires first of all an aware, well-informed and reasonable electorate because it is from these that the elected representatives and the leaders come. The quality of the electorate will ultimately decide the level of the democratization of a political unit.

CHAPTER 3

Morality and Social Justice

A Review

D.A. Gangadhar

To talk about "Morality and Social Justice" certainly prompts one to seek clarification: "can morality be a basis for 'Social Justice'?" There may be similar questions. I begin to think about "morality" first. Morality as understood is the rule of life, the code of conduct. But who frames these rules and who prescribes these codes? In our Indian situation, we have seen that these rules and codes were framed by the ancient thinkers like Manu, Parāśara and many others. Also we have seen that these oriental idealists could perceive the needs of their period and to formulate some guidelines to construct "Society." Society is a place where individuals are the basic unit. So, in India, in order to maintain a regulated society, each individual has been assigned certain duty and responsibility.

Here let me quote the views of Dr B.R. Ambedkar who could comprehend these basic concepts. What does the word "society" connote? To put it briefly, when we speak of "society," we conceive of it as one by its very nature. The qualities, which accompany this unity, are praiseworthy community of purpose and desire for welfare, loyalty to public ends and mutuality of sympathy and co-operation.

Are these ideals to be found in Indian society? The Indian society does not consist of individuals. It consists of an innumerable collection of castes, which are exclusive in their life and have no common experience to share and have no bond of sympathy. Given this fact it is not necessary to argue the point. The existence of the caste system is a standing denial of the existence of those ideals of society and, therefore, of democracy.

Indian society is so embedded in the caste system that everything is organized on the basis of caste. Enter Indian society and you would see caste in its glaring form. An Indian cannot eat or marry with an Indian simply because he/she does not belong to his/her caste. An Indian would not touch an Indian because he/she does not belong to his/her caste. Go and enter politics and you would see caste reflected therein. How does an Indian vote in an election? He votes for a candidate who belongs to his own caste and no other. In other words, an Indian, by and large, votes his caste and not casts his vote. Even the Indian National Congress exploits the caste system for election purpose as no other political party in India does. Examine the lists of its candidates in relation to the social composition of the constituencies and it will be found that the candidate belongs to the caste, which is the largest one in that constituency. The Congress, as a matter of fact, is upholding the caste system against which it is outwardly raising an outcry.

The above view of Dr Ambedkar is the vivid picture of the concept "society" in the Indian context. There may be people who may differ to some extent with such views but an experience at the deep root may be taken to be self-explanatory. These views bring out the problem of "Social Justice."

India is a democratic country, but this democracy is dependent on the election pattern of governance to maintain the society. The fact should be that we should differentiate between democracy and government. The concept "democracy" is a word concept, which propounds the ideal of equality and justice in a society. Let me quote a few words of K.M. Panikkar who has been a recognized thinker of his time on the topic.

> The first postulate of democracy, therefore, is that the state represents, not symbolically, but in reality, the organized energy of the whole community — the people. Political power as well as social authority rest not in individuals, families or groups, but in the community as a whole. Democracy, then, would mean a state of society, an organization of government, a system of

> social relationship in which no single individual has inherent authority over his fellow creatures.[1]

It would be clear then that the definition of democracy as "the Government of the People" is only partially true. It is more than that. Democracy is the realization of the unquestionable and fundamental doctrine that man is an end in himself, and that the organization of society ought to have as its basic principle the generation of the utmost dynamic force in society as an aggregate of men, in union with the least restriction on each man as an individual.

When this fact is clearly recognized, the idea of human equality, which is the basis of democracy, will become clearer. The equality of man is not a new doctrine. From the beginning of human race it has found expression in some form in all religious creeds. Indeed, Jean Jacques Rousseau maintained with some truth and great exaggeration that human inequality has been the result of civilization. To him belongs the credit of enunciating the principle of equality as the great doctrine on which to base all ideas of social progress. Rousseau, in fact, is the father of modern democracy.

Equality has still its opponents: its cheap critics who say that it is the cry of the weak for the privileges of the strong. Scientists tell us that equality is physically impossible since each man is merely the result of his antecedents, of heredity, surroundings and natural gifts. Others tell us that the inequality between individuals, nations and races is so great that the idea of equality, if it means that men are of equal capacity or of equal character, or that they ought to be so, is manifestly absurd. No one denies these obvious truths. The idea of human equality does not deny the importance of heredity, character and all those incalculable factors that mould the lives of men. It only insists that the subjective valuation of each man is the same or ought to be the

1. K.M. Panikkar, *Caste and Democracy* (New Delhi: Critical Quest, 2nd Impression, 2007), p. 28.

same if human society is to attain its fullest development. It denies the inequality of classes, castes and professions, the inequality based on birth, or unalterable vocations. What democracy asserts are equality of rights, privileges and opportunities and not the equality of talent or character.[2]

Thus, I find enough to conclude, very briefly, that there is one morality for individual and another for society. What I mean by saying so is that an individual is a free being to live his life according to his ability, aptitude and temper, but he finds himself in chains where social restrictions are imposed on the way of life of an individual. For example, when a man feels to choose a partner of his life, i.e. marrying with some, he is free to choose, but he cannot do so as a part of a society where certain rules are given to choosing. Similarly social equality is also based on certain rules of the society. Therefore, there cannot be a standard factor for maintaining morality for social justice. To sum up, I may propose that there is need for purification at the mental and behavioural level of man. This purification is the moral concept which can play the role of a guide to bring out the best possible society. If this be admitted then one is right to propose that social justice as a slogan for democracy is based upon moral virtues as it is stated correctly that equality is its cardinal doctrine and its main principles are based on the unquestionable ethical formula that every man is an end in himself and the state itself is desirable only insofar as it affords to the individual the best chance of self-realization. It recognizes no principle of difference based on birth or possessions. It stands for equal opportunity for all, and its main social tendency is to breakdown the barriers of groups and weld them progressively into larger communities; in effect, to widen continuously the symbiotic circle of the individual.

---

2. Panikkar, p. 17

CHAPTER 4

Justice, Social Justice and Moral Values

Presuppositions and Connections

Indoo Pandey Khanduri

THE conceptual analysis of justice as well as moral values in separation would be impractical and merely theoretical without any practical implication for human beings living in the society. Practical implications of justice, social justice and moral values reveal that the concepts of justice and social justice are deeply rooted in the understanding of moral values and ways of life on the one hand and are directed towards making and enhancing the conditions of well-being in the society on the other; thus they are interconnected. In the present scenario justice and social justice are considered to be in the arena of legal aspects, and moral values are taken to be the subject matter of moral studies and their connections are hardly taken into account. This article aims at exploring the connections between moral values and social justice in general and development of the concept of social justice from the pure conceptual and legal connotations of the term "justice" in particular. There is an interconnection between justice, social justice and moral values in practice as well as in theory. For clarity and preciseness the structure of this article is divided into three parts. In the first part, we shall try to examine the conceptual analysis of the concept of justice and social justice. For this purpose we shall rely on the definition and examinations of the concept as taken by Plato and Aristotle on the one hand and John Rawls and Christianity on the other. The second section will focus attention on exploring the presuppositions in terms of need, development and elements of social justice, with specific reference to discrimination, exploitation and conflicts. The third section will try to answer the question: what kinds of moral values would be helpful in achieving the goal of social justice and which values would be detrimental to it? Is there any connection between pursuing the objective of social justice and advocacy of certain moral values? In the concluding part we shall try to argue that practical adherence to pragmatic moral values will enhance the conditions for the possibility of social justice. But before we take up the above tasks let us first reflect upon the conceptual analysis as given by Plato, Aristotle and John Rawls.

I

Justice and Social Justice: The Theoretical Foundations

It is a factual truth that no concept could be developed and formulated without its contextual reference and historical development of the society, so it would be better to understand the crux of any concept through its historical explanation and procedural development. And when it is the question of understanding conceptual implications of justice and social justice, Plato would be the first and foremost thinker to deal with. This is so because our concern is to review and explore the connection between justice, social and moral values, and Plato is the one philosopher who explored and explained justice itself as one of "cardinal virtue" along with wisdom, courage and discipline. For Plato any state must have wisdom because of the knowledge of the ruler, courage because of the courage of the auxiliaries and self-discipline because of the harmony between all and common agreement about the decision of the ruler. Justice as the principle seems to be followed throughout the principles of "one man, one job," of "minding one's own business," in the sense of doing the job for which one is naturally fitted and not interfering with other people. All the elements which are required to explain the concept of justice have been stated by Plato as follows:

> Justice, therefore, we may say, is a principle of this kind: its real concern is not with external actions, but with a man's inward self, his true concern and interest. The just man will not allow

> the three elements[1] as which make up his inward self to trespass on each other's functions or interfere with each other, but, by keeping all three in tune, like the notes of a scale (high, middle, and low, and any others there be), will, in the truest sense, set his house right, attain self-mastery and order, and live on good terms with himself. When he has bound these elements into a disciplined and harmonious whole, and so become fully one instead of many, he will be ready for action of any kind, whether it concerns his personal or financial welfare, whether it is political or private; and he will reckon and call any of these actions just and honourable if it contributes to and helps to maintain this disposition of mind, and will call the knowledge which controls such action wisdom. Similarly, he will call unjust action destructive of this disposition, and the opinions which control such action ignorance.[2]

For Plato, justice is the virtue of individual and it has to be developed through the realization of inner self and it will be reflected in the external self. Mere modifications in the external action would be only an apparent attempt. In accordance with his metaphysical commitment — as ideas are the only reality and ontological assertion that reason is the ultimate source of knowledge — Plato was consistent in accepting justice as cardinal virtue and concerned with inner self of the individual. But for practical purpose justice is reflected, required and practised in the external action of human being on the ground level of the society, and it is difficult to understand the Platonic concept of implementing justice in the real society, though it is fascinating at individual as well as social levels.

---

1. Plato describes three elements, the first is reason, the faculty that calculates and decides: second there is appetite, in the sense of bare physical and instinctive craving. There is also a third type of motive, covering such characteristics as pugnacity, enterprise, ambition, indignation, which are often found in conflict with unthinking mind – see Plato, *The Republic*, Eng. tr. Desmond Lee (Harmondsworth: Penguin Books Ltd., 1955, rev. edn. 1987), p. 207.
2. Ibid., p. 221.

Shifting the focus from internal to external, Aristotle defines justice and relates it to distributive justice in the following words:

> . . . when people speak of justice we see that they all mean that of character that disposes them to perform just acts, and behave in a just manner; and wish for what is just; and in the same way they mean by injustice the state that makes them act unjustly and wish for unjust things.[3]

He further clarifies, "So, just means lawful and fair; and unjust means both unlawful and unfair."[4] Since Aristotle puts the stress on the external focus while describing the concept of justice, he divides justice into political justice and family justice where the ruler of the state and family are responsible for imparting justice to the members of the state or family. Both Plato and Aristotle define the concept of justice within the framework of their epistemological, ontological and the persisting situations of the society. They may be criticized for their assertion and theoretical commitment but our concern here is to have a general idea of justice as reflected by Plato and Aristotle and prepare the background for the understanding of the concept of social justice.

The term "social justice" was coined by the Jesuit Luigi Taparelli in the 1840s, based on the teachings of Thomas Aquinas. As a matter of fact, the concept of social justice is a complex one and may be understood through the theoretical as well as religious connotations of it because humanitarian religions do talk about social justice. Social justice, when taken as civil justice, refers to the concept of a society in which justice is achieved in every aspect of society, rather than merely the administration of law. It is generally supposed as a society which affords individuals and groups fair treatment and an impartial share of the benefits of society. (Different proponents of social justice have developed different interpretations of what constitutes *fair treatment* and an *impartial share.*) It can also refer to the distribution of advantages

3. Aristotle, *The Nichomachean Ethics*, Eng. tr. J.A.K. Thomson (Harmondsworth: Penguin Books Ltd, 1953, rev. edn. 1976), p. 171.
4. Ibid., p. 172.

and disadvantages within a society. Social justice is both a philosophical problem and an important issue in religion and civil society. The term "social justice" is often employed by the political left leaning to describe a society with a greater degree of economic egalitarianism, which may be achieved through progressive taxation, income redistribution, or even property redistribution, policies aimed towards achieving that which developmental economists refer to as equality of opportunity and equality of outcome. Since our main concern in this article is to reflect upon the connections between justice, social justice and moral values, we shall try to understand Rawls' concept of social justice and religious social justice from the Western and Indian perspectives.

The political philosopher John Rawls draws on the utilitarian insights of Bentham, Mill, the social contract ideas of Locke and the categorical imperative ideas of Kant. In *A Theory of Justice* he proposed that, "Each person possesses an inviolability founded on justice that even the welfare of society as a whole cannot override. For this reason justice denies that the loss of freedom for some is made right by a greater good shared by others."[5] For him society is seen, "as a fair system of co-operation over time, from one generation to the next."[6] All societies have a basic structure of social, economic, and political institutions, both formal and informal. In testing how well these elements fit and work together, Rawls introduced a litmus test of legitimacy in addition to the theories of social contract of John Locke. To determine whether any particular system of collectively enforced social arrangements is legitimate, he argued that one must look for agreement by the people who are subject to it. But it faces a difficulty because not every citizen can be asked to participate in a poll to determine his or her consent to every proposal in which some degree of coercion is involved, so one has to assume that all citizens are reasonable.

---

5. John Rawls, *A Theory of Justice* (Harward: Belknap Press of Harvard University, 1971), p. 3.

6. Ibid., p. 14.

Kanchan Mahadevan[7] makes it clear that the individuals engaged in the reflective exercise, as narrated in the process, require two principles of justice. These are, firstly the right of all individuals to the maximum amount of freedom that **is** compatible with the like freedom of others, and secondly any inequality in society should promote the interest of people in the society.[8] To emphasize the general principle that justice should rise from the people and not be dictated by the law-making powers of governments, Rawls asserted that, "There is . . . a general presumption against imposing legal and other restrictions on conduct without sufficient reason. But this presumption creates no special priority for any particular liberty."[9] This is support for an unranked set of liberties that reasonable citizens in all states should respect and uphold — to some extent, the list proposed by Rawls matches the normative human rights that have international recognition and direct enforcement in some nation states where the citizens need encouragement to act in a more objectively just way. The views of John Rawls may be criticized for the following points: firstly that the existence of an objective standard of social justice itself is questionable, and secondly many other people accept some of the basic principles of social justice, such as the idea that all human beings have a basic level of value, but disagree with the elaborate conclusions that may or may not follow from this, and thirdly that in pursuance of establishing criteria of fairness in justice, Rawls seems to overlook the criteria of eligibility and mainly have focus on the criteria of needs.

After dealing with the theoretical foundation of justice and social justice in the perspective of traditional philosophers let us understand the concept of social justice in the religious tradition of Christianity. Catholic social teaching comprises those aspects

---

7. Kanchan Mahadevan, "Justice, Community and Selfhood", *Journal of Indian Council of Philosophical Research*, New Delhi, vol. XIV, no. 3, 1997, p. 5.

8. Rawls, pp. 60-61.

9. Rawls, pp. 291-92.

of Roman Catholic doctrine which relate to matters dealing with the collective aspect of humanity. A distinctive feature of Catholic social teaching is its concern for the poorest members of society. The prominent principles which could be taken as the basis of social justice are the focus on the life and dignity of human beings and preferential option for the poor and vulnerable. The foundational principle of all Catholic social teaching is the sanctity of all human life and the inherent dignity of every human being. Human life must be valued above all material possessions, with preferential option for the poor and vulnerable. Jesus taught that on the Day of Judgement God will ask what each person did to help the poor and needy: "Amen, I say to you, whatever you did for one of these least brothers of mine, you did for me." The Catholic Church teaches that through words, prayers and deeds one must show solidarity with, and compassion for, the poor. When instituting public policy the "preferential option for the poor" should always be kept at the forefront. The moral test of any society is how it treats its most vulnerable members." The poor have the most urgent moral claim on the conscience of the nation. People are called to look at public policy decisions in terms of how they affect the poor. Even before it was propounded in the Catholic social teachings, social justice appeared regularly in the history of the Catholic Church. After presenting the views of Plato, Aristotle, Rawls and Christian theology, we may state that justice and social justice either related with inward self and thinking or external actions, from beginning itself it has seeds of social justice but got exposed in the later period with emerging reality of changing society and its values, and, thereupon, it presupposes certain theoretical foundations which we shall deal in the next section.

II

Justice and Social Justice: The Presuppositions

The above analysis of justice and social justice clarifies that justice is the concept used for individuals without giving any preference or weight to economic, social or aristocratic positions, and social justice is the concept which takes into consideration the conditions of the persons as well as of the social situations compelling towards discriminations and exploitations of the particular individual or class. Plato and Aristotle reflected justice in this particular reference though their philosophical background and commitment made them hold different views. Plato considers justice to be the internal virtue of human being in terms of giving opportunity to everybody to avail their dues, while Aristotle talks about the distributive justice and exposes the complex concept to be the subject of external behaviours in terms of imparting justice by the superiors — either ruler or head of the family — and accordingly designated justice in terms of political and domestic justice. John Rawls and Catholic religion explained the concept of justice from the point of view of common people as well as refer to judges and thus become nearer to social justice. As a matter of fact social justice presupposes the conditions of discrimination and exploitation, criteria of social justice, equality, freedom, and well-being and a society divided into at least two groups, i.e. weaker and stronger. Apart from the above, social justice also presupposes the moral values and its inculcations in human behaviour. In the following discussion we shall focus our attention on these presuppositions, and first of all we shall take into account the criterion of social justice which has to be related with the concept of justice.

For Rawls, to be fair is the criterion of justice. While in most of the religions as well as in Christianity humanity becomes the litmus test of justice to maintain a healthy society, it incorporated not only the interest of the two but of the entire society and thus developed the concept of social justice. Barker[10] writes that society is a world comprising individual persons, each having intrinsic value. He feels that the end of any national society is to foster and encourage, in and through partnership, the highest possible development of all the capacities of personalities in all of its

---

10. Ernest Barker, *Principles of Social and Political Theory* [Oxford: Clarendon Press, 1956 (2nd impression), p. 123.

members; and this end is the justice or "right ordering" of such a society, and may accordingly be ruled by the name of social justice.

On the basis of the above analysis we may say that the conceptual analysis of social justice may not be possible without taking the foundation of justice, but they are not the one and the same as social justice incorporates not only "just" and "fair" as the criteria of justice, rather it keeps in the centre the welfare of all. And the very concept and acceptance of the need of social justice in the society presupposes that there is a division, discrimination and constant exploitation of the weaker section by the stronger group, and it anticipates the conflicts between them. It is on the basis of assumption that constant exploitation of the weaker section by the stronger group has made them incapable of protecting their interest. Thus special provision should be made to provide the facility and preference over the common people to enable to claim their dues under legal provision and it becomes the essence of social justice.

Social justice was intensively required by the legal experts as they were aware that for years the society has been under the illusion of three kinds of metaphysical thinking as follows:

- The value hierarchal thinking or mindset has focused attention on up and down categories that confer value, status and prestige on what is up than what is down. For example, the way human beings enjoy higher value and status than other species of the biotic communities or the superior class counterparts enjoy the higher value and status in comparison to their weaker counterparts. Thus, the way human beings are morally allowed to oppress or subjugate other species, similarly stronger groups are allowed to oppress or subjugate weaker sections. Nevertheless, we must keep in mind while applying the same thinking that there is a difference between the two. The argument of superiority conferred on the human being is based on the rationality, but in the case of stronger and weaker both have the rationality, and the same yardstick cannot be applied.

- The second distinctive feature of the oppressive conceptual framework is value dualism[11] that admits disjunctive pairs in which the disjunctions are seen as oppositional rather than complementary, exclusive rather than inclusive. Accordingly, one disjunction enjoys superiority over the other. To be clearer, if human beings are classified into stronger and weaker, the disjunctive value-dualism bestows higher value and status to the stronger that are considered similar to mind and reason than to the weaker identified as bodies and emotions. The *varṇa vyavasthā* of Vedic period reflects a similar case.
- The third theoretical feature of exploitative trend is the logic of domination that justifies subordination or domination of one species by the others. Here we must clarify that the logic of domination,[12] however, is not just a logical structure; it does involve a substantive value system. Justification of domination is based on some alleged characteristics possessed by the upper group. For example, in case of human beings, the alleged characteristic of superior class is rationality and, therefore, his domination over the weaker, lacking this special alleged characteristic, i.e. rationality, is wrongly justified.

The above division of common human beings creates apperception that weaker people are in the society to serve the stronger ones and in due course of time discrimination developed and education, health and nutrition were not available to them. This particular thinking makes a vicious circle for the weaker to be in the clutches of poverty, illiteracy, physically weak and subject to economic exploitation for their basic requirements. In order to protect the human dignity and social rights of the weaker section

11. Arpana Dhar Das, "Eco-feminism", *Indian Philosophical Quarterly*, vol. XXII, nos. 1-2, January–April, 2005, p. 92.
12. Ibid.

the concept of social justice captured the attention of the civil society. Social justice enhances the conditions and motivates the general personal development of the people. As a matter of fact, it is a balance between the individual's right and social control. It ensures the fulfilment of the legitimate expectations of the individual under the existing laws. It also ensures to provide benefits and protection in case of any violation or encroachment of one's right.[13]

Here we may point out that though the concept of justice is taken by Plato as one of the cardinal virtues out of four to ensure freedom, equality and fraternity when it comes to the concept of social justice it presupposes some other humanitarian qualities like care, concern and co-operation. Maybe for these reasons recent researches in value orientation have focused attention on such value. Even from the perspective of value education, Janet Powney draws the attention of the researchers towards the linguistic ambiguity and suggests: "We are now coming to the conclusion that it may be easier for people to make explicit their values if they are asked "What do you value?" rather than, "What are values?". The former question allows respondents to ground their answers firmly in their own experience and beliefs, whilst the latter seems to look for a more abstract reply."[14] In his survey-based study, he listed the values to be taught as consideration for others, respect for others, and for property and authority, religious values, a religious community, a school community work, pupil self-esteem, self-discipline, caring/concern for others, honesty/integrity, self-esteem, good manners, and co-operate/be helpful.[15] For E.G. Parameswaran, in this reference explains:

---

13. Abha Singh, "Varṇadharma through the Prism of Social Justice", *Indian Philosophical Quarterly*, vol. XXVII, no. 2, April, 2001, p. 169.
14. Janet Powney, *The Complexities of Researching Value* (The Scottish Council for Research in Education, http://www.scre.ac.uk), p. 4.
15. Janet Powney, p. 4.

> In the context of value education, we may describe a value as an acquired tendency or predisposition to work for certain goals or ends and also prefer certain means of reaching such goals in preference to other means and also exclude or avoid others.[16]

Parameswaran here describes the very nature and process of acquisitions of values and he lists these values which he thinks need to be inculcated to face the contemporary challenges in a healthy manner — respect, work-related culture, professionalism and concern for others and nature.[17] These values could be instrumental in framing and enhancing the condition favourable for providing social justice. In the absence of such values the concept of social justice may remain only instrumental in pulling and pushing, but will not improve the welfare of the society.

In brief, apart from the persisting inequality, discrimination, exploitation, the inculcation of the value of care, concern and co-operation becomes the important presupposition of social justice. Without going into controversy of subjective and objective nature of values required for this purpose we prefer pragmatic acceptance of the required values by the common people of both the groups.

III

Justice, Social Justice and Moral Values: The Connections

Once upon a time, legal and moral ideals were set to be similar. In the present scenario legal procedures and moral practices have been distinguished, since apparently the focus is on addressing the issue of just and unjust action and enhancing the human welfare scenario by inculcating moral values. But whatever be the situation and social reality persisting, legalities and judgements have to follow certain moral codes, have to presuppose moral values for the welfare of the society and enhancement of human capacities

---

16. E.G. Parameswaran, "Value-centered Education", *Journal of Value Education*, NCERT, New Delhi, vol. II, no. 1, January 2002, p. 34.
17. Ibid., pp. 34-37.

for overall development. Thus there is an intricate connection between justice, social justice and moral values. Fairness, equality and freedom are the values which provide instrumental foundation in the determination of justice in general and justice itself is supposed to be exercise for the sake of goodness. This particular connection between justice and goodness has been well explained by Aristotle and the essence can be understood in the following words as narrated by Barker,

> General justice is the same as goodness; it is our righteousness; it is in Aristotle's words, the justice which answers to the whole of goodness . . . being exercise as a whole . . . towards one's neighbour.[18]

The distinction between general and particular justice is relevant and important for our purpose, thus it becomes essential to understand particular justice and its further division between distributive and certificatory justice as they have different moral values and objectives, as Barker writes while describing the relation between justice, law and ethics. Explaining the division of particular justice into distributive and certificatory justice he writes,

> The first is distributive justice, which is justice shown by the whole state in distributing offices, honours, and other benefits among its members . . . and the other kind is certificatory justice, or the justice which the state seeks to maintain between one member and another.[19]

When we talk about social justice as a concept to describe the movement towards a socially just world it is based on the concepts of human rights, freedom and equality of all members and thus requires a fair treatment by the judging authority either at the state level or at the family level. And it directly provides the

---

18. Ernest Barker, *The Politics of Aristotle* (Oxford: Oxford University Press, 1986, rpt.), p. 362.
19. Ibid., p. 363.

foundational value for social justice in terms of the presupposition of equal distribution of the resources of the state among its members and if it has been overlooked, the certificatory measures are required to be taken into account while addressing the issues of discrimination, exploitation causing the vicious circle of human rights violation, economic disparity, government avoidance to the issue of minority's right to live a quality life through education and health facility. The concept of rectifying justice is not only meant to correct the mistakes and blunders committed in the past but also it is instrumental in achieving a socially just world and pursuing the goal of wider and greater goodness.

Apart from other legal procedures, the constitutional provision of reservation in education and jobs is emerging as one of the strongest tools to obtain social justice in the present society, but this has led to the theoretical controversy and conflicts between ability and need of the society members and it further requires the historical analysis of the fact to judge the matter in black and white. Since we are concerned directly with the relation between justice and social justice with reference to the connection with moral values, we will not take the controversy for it will divert the issue in a different direction, but we find that whenever the concept of social justice is taken into account the issues of ability and eligibility are kept aside, as Peter Singer says, " . . . it is against the basic principle of equality." Intelligence is irrelevant to the consideration of interests: for all that counts are the interests themselves.[20] This view also has been stated by John Rawls as "Justice can be ensured if an equal treatment is meted out to the people irrespective of the fact, whether they inherit certain abilities or not."[21] The concept of fairness, according to John Rawls is fundamental to justice.

---

20. Peter Singer, *Practical Ethics* (Cambridge: Cambridge University Press, 1991), p. 21.
21. John Rawls, "Justice as Fairness", *The Philosophical Review*, vol. LXVII, April, 1958.

On the basis of the above account we may say that all the legal and constitutional procedure have foundation of the moral value of common goodness through virtues for the well-being of the entire society and happiness for all, because there is relation between happiness and virtue as it has been said, "Virtue is fundamentally a matter of having right desire, towards the right objects and in the right degree."[22] He asserts that since right desire, right object in right degree is the source of happiness, a just person who is virtuous by action and character will definitely have pleasure and happiness both. Thus there is connection between justice, social justice and moral values of goodness in twofold manner — there are cardinal virtues and general virtues, and secondly, the values of fairness, equality, freedom and neutrality — as foundational values to pursue both justice and social justice for humanitarian face of the society. Any thinking about justice concentrates in a mechanical way to see right and wrong and starts with the individual complaints by one against another and requires particular proofs in support of the complainer or against him. Thus, it is said that justice is blind and absolute justice, which takes into consideration only temporal reality without considering the capacities and eligibilities into account, is going to impart mechanical kind of justice. But justice has to be done and achieved in the society, thus it has to take social conditions into account.

Consequently social justice claims to take into account the social conditions of the persons who suffer due to discrimination made either by particular individual, economic weakness or adverse socio-religious traditions to exploit the weaker section. Social justice presupposes the understanding of human values of care, concern and co-operation. Unfortunately, this particular aspect has been thoroughly ignored in any kind of study whether legal, social or economic planning or even scientific development as has been pointed out by Walter P. Reuther in his address:

---

22. Benn Pierce, *Ethics* (London: Routledge Publishers, 2003), p. 167.

> To begin with, I believe that the crisis in the world is not essentially political nor do I believe that it is economic. I think essentially it is moral. We face a moral crisis because mankind has made much greater progress in the physical sciences than he has made in the human and social sciences. We know much better how to work with machines than we do with men. There is developing a great moral and cultural gap between the progress that we continue to make in the physical sciences and our lack of comparable progress in the human and social sciences. I believe we need to give greater and greater attention to see to it that with our developing scientific, technical and production "know-how" we develop a comparable human and social and moral "know-why." Material wealth, economic power without vision or morality is wealth and power without a purpose. We need to equate these economic factors, these great material resources, with basic human problems.[23]

Apart from having foundations from moral values and objectives in its core, justice and social justice both have been considered as values in themselves, not the common values but Plato called them cardinal or intrinsic values which are values in themselves without any further justification. Thus we may state that justice and social justice both have moral foundation for its implications as well as for the objective set to be achieved in society through it whether it be providing one's, dues or maintaining equality, peace as well as ensuring genuine freedom clubbed with the sense of responsibility for each one of us.

Conclusion

The present scenario of discrimination and disparity demands that attempt should be made to achieve justice for each one in the society with the greater objective of achieving happiness and well-being of each member in the society. But it is true that a human being dwells between positive as well as negative desires, he is not ready to distinguish between his needs and greed. As need is

---

23. Walter P. Reuther, *The Empire Club of Canada Speeches 1955-1956* (Toronto, Canada: The Empire Club Foundation, 1956), pp. 26-42.

fulfilled in a natural way like hunger is satisfied when food is taken, thirst is quenched when water is drunk and it has another restriction of not accepting more than what is required. But greed is a never-ending impulse causing discrimination, disparity and exploitation, and, consequently, demanding the need of social justice for prolonged injustice done to a particular section of society. No doubt, in the name of social justice, many educational, health and rehabilitation programmes are launched by several countries, but how far are they meaningful in achieving the set targets? Since these programmes lack fundamental moral insight of care, concern and co-operation in the genuine manner these programmes may not be instrumental in achieving social justice. As it has been anticipated, "our narrow and selfish preoccupation with rights is a moral, spiritual health warning that all is not well with our society. In earlier ages, people focused on their moral and social *responsibilities* rather than complaining about their lack of rights. They also expected others to behave in the best interests of society. It worked because there was a clearer understanding that responsibility before God and man for one's own actions trumped rights every time. And peer pressure (not to mention legal enforcement) strengthened that concept."[24] Problems always have solutions with them and effective social justice for the needy can be obtained only by enhancing human being's sensitivity to other human and creating favourable conditions as it has been believed, quite rightly, by Walter P. Reuther:

> I believe we can begin to get people working and marching and building in the image of their hopes and their common faith and their common aspirations. If we do that I believe that peace and freedom and social justice, these indivisible values, can be made secure, and together with free people, together with men of goodwill everywhere we can build a better tomorrow, we can shape that better tomorrow in the image of peace and freedom and social justice and human brotherhood.[25]

---

24. David F. Lloyd, "Responsibility" in *Vision Journal Organization* , net. org. p. 4.
25. Reuther, p. 26ff.

On the basis of the above analysis we may conclude that the concept of social justice is a complex notion in itself and requires the theoretical foundations with clarity and referential context, criteria slightly different from the mechanical justice which takes into account the situation of the person as well as social conditions and covers a long period of generations to impart the justice if it considers the justice and injustice for a community. Social justice requires, apart from freedom, equality and democracy, the care, concern and co-operation. And, all these require a sense of responsibility of the individual, as well as institutions for taking up the task of social justice with moral insights, otherwise, like many other schemes of reforming and developing the conditions for welfare of the suppressed community, the objective of social justice will also remain a political gimmick in the immature democratic set-up.

CHAPTER 5

Revisiting Morality and Social Justice

Abha Singh

THE word "morality" has been derived from the Latin word *mores* meaning customs or habits. Every society has a system of constraint on behaviour different from legal ones, which is called "moral code of a society." Social moral code is true of individuals in the group. In a given society, generally, individuals' moral code is largely the same. For example, in the Indian context, individuals disagree about the propriety of smoking and drinking but do not disagree about a list of central things such as murder, armed robbery, kidnapping, assault, rape, infanticide, child abuse, breach of promise, etc. The key to such motivations is primarily just basic desires and aversions directed at certain forms of behaviour. But the question is: how does an individual acquire his moral code? Such acquisition depends upon the basic motivations and tendencies to have guilt feelings. Since these are, after all, desires and aversions, the account of their genesis incorporates principles in the development of desires and aversions, in general, and, in particular, the principles of classical and social conditioning. All moral motives are not acquired in the same way as they vary with difference in social strata and family background of the agent. Nevertheless, individual morality, which is customary in nature, precedes that which is based on law or on reflection. Gradually, in the life of an agent, definite rules of action are established.

Hence, it would be proper to say that morality is simply the best way of living under existing conditions. This is for the simple reason that the moral codes of the day need to be revised to meet the present needs of life. Thus, morality is not mere inheritance of convention. It is a rational application of naturalness and desirability of a moral code to the facts of life and human experience.

Obviously, when one deals with morality, one has to take into account the individual conduct in relation to the others. Every individual always modifies his behaviour in relation to nature as well as other individuals. Such behaviour, in turn, gives rise to the concept of value and ideal. The social values, which constitute the principles of customary morality, are relative in nature. They vary with time, situations and persons. Hence, the notion of vice and virtue based on these social values are bound to be relative. A practice considered to be vice in one set-up may pass as a veritable virtue in the other. Hence, there is the necessity of formulating the customary morality by an appeal to the basic human values.

We recognize a number of human values as necessary to an organized system of human relations. Liberty, equality, fraternity and co-operation are the crux of human values. All these values are present in any system, though in different degrees at different periods of time, and there is constant process of adjustment and readjustment between their claims. The claims of liberty have to be adjusted to the claims of equality; and the claims of both have also to be adjusted to those of co-operation. The moral standard of the community, precipitated in and enforced by the general conscience, is the source of a notion of justice that is a system of synthesis of values.

Values impart rhythm to the social dynamism, whereby the individuals get opportunity and inspiration to tend towards the state of perfection. Nonetheless, values constitute social morality, which is regulative in nature. They guide man along the path of righteousness. Hence, morality is bound with the problem of social progress or social good. But, what does the social goodness consist in? Obviously, it consists in the well-being of individuals.

Therefore, one may infer that morality provides the ideal and inspiration to the collective life of individuals. Morality itself needs no extrinsic justification, but from a social perspective, its purpose is to promote reduction of conflict.

Justice is a moral concept, that is to say, justice as fairness in the treatment of persons is one aspect of morality as practical consideration of others' interests. The root idea of the word justice is the idea of a bond or a tie for joining or fitting. Primarily the idea of joining or fitting implied in this root is that between man and man in an organized system of human relations. But justice may also be conceived as synthesis of individual and social values.

Hence, both justice and morality are concerned with what should be, and they speak in the imperative mood. Both the terms, in a way, deal with identical areas of life, its sanctions, the keeping of faith and honouring of pledges, the duty of consideration for others, and (wo)man's general duty to his neighbour. The subtle difference is that, while justice is a rule of outward life, morality is governed by the conscience of the individual. However, the rule of outward life of relations is vitally concerned with the inward moral life. Hence, it would not be an exaggeration to state that although justice is itself not morality, it is based upon it. If its code is not of ethics, it is a code that is ultimately deprived of morality. The moral standard of a community, precipitated in and enforced by the general moral conscience, is the source of a notion of justice, containing a system or synthesis of values, which, in turn, becomes the impersonal source of positive law.

In the Indian context, the problem of justice and morality has been considered under such terms as *ṛta*, *ṛṇa*, *bhavya*, *dharma*, etc. We find detailed deliberations as to how should one behave with others. It has been said that first of all one must have an impulse to do that which must be directed towards others. The urge of "I must do" (*codana*) comes from within. When it is an expression of oneself it takes the form of "ought." It is not an order from others. When the expression is in the form of "you must do it" it becomes an order imposed from outside. Orders imposed from outside do not lead to social order. The orders from outside must be chiselled and smoothened, and must be a free expression of what I do for others. "My doing something for others gives me a right to expect that others would be doing similar thing for me." Only then the concept of *dharma* would be realized. *Dharma* is supposed to uphold the society as a whole, and social justice is supposed to be ensured by the strict adherence to the principles of *dharma* in a society. The violation of the principle of *dharma* leads to the annihilation of the very social structure (*dharma eva hato hanti*). However, Indian thinkers developed a flexible approach towards *dharma*, and held the view that it plays a major role in social system and may, in that sense, be regarded as essential for the society, but it may undergo change and be replaced by new and better *dharma*s as well. The myth of *dharma*, in the sense of something of a permanent value in all possible circumstances, is doomed at the very outset in view of a changing system of values relevant to a certain context only.

The ordinary and traditional view is that a society is just when it dispenses justice to its members considering everyone's due. But it is difficult to decide what exactly one's due is. Should we take into account the worth and capacity of the individual, or should justice be meted out considering the need of the individual members ignoring their merits, or should we take into account the principle of equality, i.e. equal opportunity for all members? Each consideration is crucial and yet controversial. It may be held that man's due or right is that which is his by virtue of valid moral principles, and not merely of law or the prevailing principles. Thus, a society is just if it accords its members what are their valid moral deserts. According to this view, social justice consists in the balance of good and evil, rewards and punishments, jobs and other privileges in accordance with the valid moral principles. This argument sounds quite plausible for what could be more obvious than that a society is just, if it dispenses what is just to its members? But the difficulty lies in deciding what constitutes the justness in the society. It has to be made clear whether there are universally just principles for all societies. Moreover, whether justice is to be defined, distributively or retributively, in accordance with the valid moral principles seems to depend on the moral principles, which turn out to be valid. What exactly is the basis of these moral principles that can regulate social justice? The difficulty with this criterion is that it might lead to a confusion of right-making and just-making principles. This might coerce one to accept what is right (morally valid) as always socially just, or at least just.

But society is not an artificial creation of a group of individuals. In fact, we can find our selves already in a society or in a civilization just as we find a family into which we are born. Thus, our selves are already encumbered in many ways. Our loyalties, attachment and plain relations with other humans make it obligatory for us to seek moral and political life in the society itself. But this itself does not cancel the fact that the individual persons matter so far as their basic liberties are concerned. The basic liberties have a moral primacy, and so the principles of justice arise out of a moral necessity. Besides, the civilization, in which we are born, does not create the moral necessity itself. It only acknowledges the a priori character of the principle of justice. John Rawls holds that a well-ordered society is regulated by its public conception of justice. The members of a well-ordered society have a strong and effective desire to act according to the principles of justice. For Rawls, when institutions are just, those taking part in those arrangements acquire the corresponding sense of justice and desire to do their part in maintaining them.[1] The desire to act justly is also regulative of a rational plan of life. Hence, acting justly is part of our good (the goodness of individuals).[2] In a well-ordered society realizing the principles of justice as fairness Rawls has sketched the course of moral development of its individuals. For Rawls a person

1. John Rawls, *A Theory of Justice* (Oxford: Oxford University Press, paperback, 1973), p. 454.
2. Ibid., p. 456.

acquires an understanding of and an attachment to the principles of justice as one grows up in a particular well-ordered society. Elucidating it he makes a distinction between the morality of authority, morality of association and morality of principles. We shall not ponder over its details as the space does not permit us.

However, the well-being of the society depends on the co-ordination and reconciliation in the individual rights and the demands and needs of the society. Hence, the concept of society is based on two principles, viz. the principle of social liberty (where forced labour is not necessary) and the governing principles of social justice (applied to the system of forced co-operation). "But the society does not consist merely of the law of the state; it also has an informal aspect comprising of cultural institutions, conventions, moral rules and moral sanctions. In order for a society to be fully just it must be just in its informal as well as a formal aspect."[3] Social justice presupposes the following moral facts:

(a) The individuals constituting the social order are moral persons.

(b) The just social order is basically a moral order enjoining upon the participants to respect each other's freedom and equality in respect of all the basic or primary goods of the society.

In the broad framework, social justice confers rights and assigns responsibilities to its individual members. In an initial position, if and when equality is the fundamental condition for the association of individuals, free and rational persons accept these principles to further their own interests. If these principles are reflected in any social or political arrangement of a society, it can be termed as just.

The above discussion leads us to assume that both "morality" and "justice" are slippery concepts because no straightforward

---

3. W.K. Frankena, "The Concept of Social Justice", in *Social Justice*, ed. Richard B. Brandt (Prientice Hall Inc.), p. 2

analysis of the two appears to be possible. Again, the concept of social justice leads us to multiple conceptions of justice, which are, by no means, identical or even harmonious with each other advocated in different social systems, and even in the same social system at different times. When we come to deal with justice in a legal framework, we find something queer about it. Justice in the eyes of law may not be justice at all. It may even be regarded as injustice in a broader perspective and social reforms bring about reforms in our conceptions of justice in a legal framework. And in a day-to-day life, in a system that seems to be binding on all of us, or when the reforms begin to appear in the social set-up either slowly or on account of a revolution, we can never be sure that justice has been meted out in a more or less uniform manner to the people. In a democratic society, law tends to follow the growing moral consciousness and the opinion of the majority or the most vocal group of the society. While the law tends to follow the growing moral consciousness of many persons in the society, it also tends to lag behind it. Moreover, the law does not cover all cases of conflict, i.e. personal or social. In a rapidly changing society, law very often becomes antiquated and reform is needed. If the court interprets and decides new cases on the basis of precedent, mature judgements cannot be expected. In this context the concepts of morality and social justice appear as a saviour.

The great historic struggles for social justice have been centred around demands of equal rights. The struggle against slavery, political absolutism and economic exploitation, all these are related to the three components of social structure, i.e. legal, political and economic system. Nevertheless, a conception of "morality" and "social justice," which is acceptable under all circumstances, appears to be a chimera. Societies all over the globe seem to be split and stratified due to various reasons. In the Indian context, such stratification is clearly visible. People are born into a caste and a sub-caste, resulting into various kinds of social discrimination, which paves the way to various disabilities. The traditionally backward and deprived sections of the society are so weak that they have not been able to take advantage of opportunities as compared to educationally and socially stronger castes and classes. The social status of a person largely depends upon his caste. The enduring solutions to all the problems of the deprived classes can be possible through the amendment in growth model. This inequitable system has been responsible for inequality and unemployment in our society. Political leadership should mount their assault on this inequitable system.

Our short-sighted political leadership conceived of reservation as a means of creating social equality. Myth of social justice through reservation is based on a different concept of justice. This is a notion of caste balance in arbitrary selected sectors of the economy. As a result, meritocracy is being sacrificed at the altar of reservocracy. Since Independence, the reservation problem has been in focus. Added to the said problem, the problem of communalism has also been in limelight. These dual problems put adverse impact on our social and national integrity. In particular, in the last two decades, the politicians have been using the twin problems as a centripetal force to garner maximum votes. As a result, our social fabric is being destroyed, and tension, mistrust and hatred are prevailing between the communal and caste groups. Political parties thrive on a spirit of competition. The new buzzword is "social justice," and social integration and unity have been victims of neglect.

In a nutshell, the modern concept of social justice is complex. It includes meritarian and egalitarian element as well. It recognizes the merits of persons, as well as respect for personality as such. Still, there is chaos in the matter of distribution of goods and services in the society. At present, Indian society is on the verge of disintegration as each group is trying to garner positions in the society through shorter routes. Hence, a serious debate on the issues concerning social justice is essential. Nonetheless, such debate would be fruitful taking in view the moral aspects that make (wo)man a person. As so, no one would grab other's bite.

Part II
On Justice

CHAPTER 6

Justice and Secularism

A Conceptual and Cross-Cultural Analysis

R.P. Singh

In this article, I'll conceptually clarify the term "secularism" with reference to the cultural realities of India and Europe. For the sake of clarity and precision, I will divide this article into three parts. In Part I, I will furnish a conceptual analysis of justice. In Part II, I will explain the meanings of the terms like secular, secularization and secularism in its European potentiality. In Part III, I will try to apply secularism as a concept to appreciate two aspects of Indian reality, i.e. India as a state and India as a nation. Before I come to Part I, I would like to clarify that all "ism" words with two or three exceptions are of nineteenth century origin. Before that we would not find any "ism." Before nineteenth century, nobody talked of Hinduism, Buddhism, Jainism, Mohammedanism and all that. And the reason for that is that in the nineteenth century, thinkers wanted to classify everything in the world as systems or doctrines or dogmas or ideologies — a set of interconnected ideas. That is, what "ism" really means — a set of ideas and a programme of action based on it.

I

JUSTICE is concerned with the proper ordering of things and relation among persons within a society. As a concept it has been subject to philosophical, legal, and theological reflection and debate throughout history. A number of important questions surrounding justice have been fiercely debated over the course of Western history: What is justice? What does it demand of individuals and societies? What is the proper distribution of wealth and resources in society: equal, meritocratic, according to status, or some other arrangement? There are myriad possible answers to these questions from divergent perspectives on the political and philosophical spectrum. According to most theories of justice, it is overwhelmingly important: John Rawls, for instance, claims that "Justice is the first virtue of social institutions, as truth is of systems of thought."[1] Justice can be thought of as distinct from and more fundamental than benevolence, charity, mercy, generosity or compassion. John Rawls used a social contract argument to show that justice, and especially distributive justice, is a form of fairness: an *impartial* distribution of goods. Rawls asks us to imagine ourselves behind a *veil of ignorance* which denies us all knowledge of our personalities, social statuses, moral characters, wealth, talents and life plans, and then asks what theory of justice we would choose to govern our society when the veil is lifted, if we wanted to do the best that we could for ourselves. We don't know who in particular we are, and therefore can't bias the decision in our own favour. So, the decision-in-ignorance models fairness, because it excludes selfish bias. Rawls argues that each of us would reject the utilitarian theory of justice that we should maximize welfare because of the risk that we might turn out to be someone whose own good is sacrificed for greater benefits for others. Instead, we would endorse Rawls's *two principles of justice:*[2]

1. Each person is to have an equal right to the most extensive total system of equal basic liberties compatible with a similar system of liberty for all.

2. Social and economic inequalities are to be arranged so that they are both to the greatest benefit of the least advantaged, consistent with the just savings principle, and attached to offices and positions open to all under conditions of fair equality of opportunity.

---

1. John Rawls, *A Theory of Justice* (Oxford: Oxford University Press, rev. edn., 1999), p. 3.
2. Ibid., p. 266.

This imagined choice justifies these principles as the principles of justice for us, because we would agree to them in a fair decision procedure. Rawls' theory distinguishes two kinds of goods: (1) liberties, (2) social and economic goods, i.e. wealth, income and power — and applies different distributions to them — equality between citizens for (1), equality unless inequality improves the position of the worst off for (2).

There are variations of justice; for instance, *Utilitarianism* is a form of consequentialism, where punishment is forward-looking. Justified by the ability to achieve future social benefits resulting in crime reduction, the moral worth of an action is determined by its outcome. According to Mill, justice is not as fundamental as we often think. Rather, it is derived from the more basic standard of rightness, i.e. consequentialism: what is right is what has the best consequences (usually measured by the total or average welfare caused). So, the proper principles of justice are those which tend to have the best consequences. These rules may turn out to be familiar ones such as keeping contracts, etc.[3]

Retributive justice regulates proportionate response to crime proven by lawful evidence, so that punishment is justly imposed and considered as morally correct and fully deserved. The law of *retaliation* (*lex talionis*) is a military theory of retributive justice, which says that reciprocity should be equal to the wrong suffered; "life for life, wound for wound, stripe for stripe."[4]

Restorative justice is concerned not so much with retribution and punishment as with (a) making the victim whole, and (b) reintegrating the offender into society. This approach frequently brings an offender and a victim together, so that the offender can better understand the effect his/her offence had on the victim.

Distributive justice is directed at the proper allocation of things — wealth, power, reward, respect — between different people.

---

3. John Stuart Mill, "Utilitarianism", in *On Liberty and Other Essays*, ed. John Gray (Oxford: Oxford University Press, 1991), ch. 5.

4. *Exodus* 21, xxiii-xxv.

Oppressive Law exercises an authoritarian approach to legislation which is "totally unrelated to justice," a tyrannical interpretation of law is one in which the population lives under restriction from unlawful legislation.

Some theorists, such as the classical Greeks, conceive of justice as a virtue — a property of people and only derivatively of their actions and the institutions they create. Others emphasize actions or institutions, and only derivatively the people who bring them about. The source of justice has variously been attributed to harmony, divine command, natural law, or human creation. It may not be possible for me to go into all the details of these theories of justice evolved at different stages of the social development. Instead, I wish to focus my discussion on secularism and analyse the notion of justice in that framework especially with reference to India.

II

On secularism, let us first clarify three terms with their different meanings — secular, secularization and secularism. The word "secular" has a very old origin, "secularization" originated in the sixteenth century and "secularism" in the nineteenth century. The word "secular" as an adjective goes back to the Latin culture. It is a Latin word *saecularis* and it comes as an adjective after the word *saeculum* which in pre-Christian Latin meant "a long period of time" almost something like our *yugam* which means "world structure" but not the world as "basically conceived" but as "time conceived." Likewise a long period is called saeculum. Then it came to be, *saeculum* meant "century" or "a hundred years." Already in the time of Julius Caesar, that is 44 BCE, at the end of every century, they had *saeculum* games, once in one hundred years, celebrating the century that is passing and welcoming the new century that is coming. But then *saeculum* meant "belonging to the century." After the beginning of the Christian era, the word secular takes on a new meaning. It is distinguished from *saecularis* and religious. What does it mean? Religious means "monastic," i.e. attached to a monastery, i.e. community under a given set of rules. This is the meaning of religious till the eighteenth century. Opposed to it was the word secular.

The word "secularization" came up during seventeenth century. The word was first used in the Peace of Westphalia in Germany in 1648.[5] It was signed by the European nations fighting for the Thirty-Year War. The drafters of the treaty had used the word "secularization." What does it mean? It was a period of transition from feudalism to capitalism. In European feudalism, religion had a rigid control over every walk of human life. The ideologues of capitalism propagated the view that "unless we defeat religion, we cannot defeat feudalism." To defeat religion means to take away the two ways through which religion was having control over the society. These two ways were "the property" and "the ideas/values." The first phase was to take away property that belonged to the Catholic Church and to give it to the public. This was known as "secularization." Then "secularization" meant that not only property but also the institutions and the ideas should be taken away from the control of the church and be given to public openness. That is the way "secularization" came into being.

Secularism is a peculiar nineteenth-century word like all other "isms" and it has a specific meaning. Around the beginning of nineteenth century, a man called G.J. Holiock in England started a view called "secularism." It was very popular, promoted by some of the highest scientists of the time. What he said is this: "All the religions belonged to the immature past of humanity. Now we are at the stage of science and positive thought." In the beginning, it was very popular in England and America. But it

---

5. Paul Kennedy, *The Rise and Fall of the Great Powers, Economic Change and Military Conflict from 1500-2000* (Fontana Press, 1989), pp. 45-51. For details, see Paulos Mar Gregorios "On Humanism, Secularism, and Socialism", *Journal of Indian Council of Philosophical Research*, vol. XIV, no. 3, May–August 1997, pp. 75-89.

collapsed in the 1930s. When Hitler came up, people said "this is what secularism has produced." There was a reaction against Fascism and in that reaction secularism was also more or less abandoned by a large number of people.

Indian secularism is a peculiar thing. In India, we confuse secular, secularization and secularism with one another. At the time of partition, Jinnah said that Pakistan would be a religious country. In reaction to that, Jawaharlal Nehru said that India would be a secular state. There was no other word available that time as non-religious state or something. Therefore, Nehru chose the word "secular state." I have no intention of questioning that decision. That was a period of big crisis in which Nehru had to take the decision very quickly and he took over this word for his liberal education. But it moves away from the Western model and makes certain basic principles. One of them is that India as a state is secular but as a nation it is communal. The other principles are — state is not religious and that all religions are equal before the state and so on. This is one of the guiding and regulating principles of justice in India.

III

Like other democratic constitutions of the world, the Constitution of India also begins with a Preamble which outlines the main objectives of our Constitution in these words:

> WE THE PEOPLE OF INDIA, having solemnly resolved to constitute india in a SOVEREIGN SOCIALIST *SECULAR*[6] DEMOCRATIC REPUBLIC and to secure to all its citizens:
>
> JUSTICE — social, economic and political;
>
> LIBERTY of thought, expression, belief, faith and worship;
>
> EQUALITY of status and of opportunity;
>
> FRATERNITY assuring the dignity of the individual and the unity and integrity of the nation.

---

6. The Forty-Second Amendment Act, 1976, added the word "Secular" in the above Preamble.

The Preamble is considered as the key to the Indian Constitution. The term secular was the most comprehensive amendment made in the Constitution so far and has been described as a mini-Constitution. It asserted parliament's supremacy regarding amendment of the Constitution; primacy of Directive Principles over Fundamental Rights; curtailed the powers of the High Courts and the Supreme Court with regard to issue of *writs* and judicial review; provided administrative tribunals for speedy and substantial justice; made amendments in the preamble; and made it obligatory for the President to accept the advice of the Council of Ministers. It also made certain changes in the centre-state relations of which I cannot go into the details. Let me offer an analysis of Indian secularism with reference to Indian society and culture.

The initial characteristics of Indian society are that it is diverse, liberal, democratic and pluralistic in regulating and restructuring the features of secularism. As a matter of fact, Indian experience of democracy is in post-colonial and anti-contractarian society.[7] The pluralistic nature of Indian society is manifested in various ethnic identities, community structure, linguistic identities, different nationalities, languages and so on. Because of these features India as a nation is communal. But as a state, India is secular. So there is an antinomy between India as a state and India as a nation. In the last 60 years of our Independence, this antinomy has come out very strongly. Even the electoral process through which people's representatives are brought into power is under debate. If for five years these leaders are elected, do they remain responsible to the needs and aspirations of the people for even all these five years? In most cases they are not. This is

7. Social contract theory was introduced by Hobbes, Locke and Rousseau. It was criticized by Hume on its historical grounds. It was revived by Kant for its methodological and philosophical reasons. It was finally rejected by Hegel for its methodological and philosophic reasons. For details, see R.P. Singh, *Freedom and Causation* (Faridabad: Om Publication, 2000), pp. 64-91.

not only a problem in India, but it is also a global problem. Let us go into the origin of this antinomy. This implies going back to people and search for their identities — the local identities.

In search of our local identities, we have to go into the details of our tradition. Indian tradition could be divided into a two kinds, namely, the Brāhmnical tradition and the Śramaṇa tradition. The former is the textual, the written, the intellectual tradition or the *Śāstrīya paramparā* consisting of the Dharmaśastras, Puruṣārthas, Āśramas etc. And the latter is the oral tradition, the folk tradition, the tradition of the people or the *Loka-paramparā*. Fortunately, we have had both the traditions as equally strong. However, it is the oral tradition, which has a stronger social base. It consists of three pillars — family, community and the economy. Around these activities there developed idioms, symbols, proverbs, riddles and *sūtras*. This was the corpus of knowledge.

It is this oral tradition of our country that is the driving force behind our experience of justice, democracy and secularism. Indians have always had political management and even justice at local level with consensus or the *Panchayat* tradition. In fact, in the last 60 years we have survived with democracy precisely because of consensus and the *panchayat* tradition. In India, there are 327 languages, but more than 3000 communities out of 5000 speak in 33 languages. Despite these diversities, Indians have a participatory habit, we are not neutrals, and we have audience participation. We are very talkative people. Traditional factor of India is its community structure. It is highly segmentary. It is a multiple society. Caste structure gives India regional identity from 20 to 300 miles. And there are above 5000 castes in India. So, India is a land of very diversified and segmented social structure. It is in this rather complex situation that we have to assess our response to secularization and justice. If we wish to secularize our religious institutions and ethnic identities, we will have problems. But at the level of our philosophic heritage, we are not so weakly placed. Our philosophy has always been conducive to secular ideas and justice as fairness. I can illustrate this point with certain examples of Indian habits of mind different from European habits of mind. First of all, Indian mind has perpetually been cosmo-centric. There is an organic unity between humanity and the rest of cosmic reality. And this is expressed in holistic values and attitudes of Indians. On the other hand, Europeans have an anthropocentric world–view. The early Greeks, particularly, Thales, Heraclitus, Democritus and others were cosmo-centric. With Sophists particularly with Protagoras the dictum came up — "Man is the measure of all things." In modern times, particularly with liberal humanism, human being is regarded as "given" and nature is regarded as another "given" and nature is something for you to "use." One of the founders of modern thinking, Immanuel Kant has said, "The order and regularity in the appearances, which we entitle nature, we ourselves introduce. We could never find them in appearances; had not we ourselves, or the nature of our mind, originally set them there."[8] This was Kant's Copernican Revolution which quite literally shifted the direction of both epistemology and morality from the nature of reality, outside there, to the essential structure of human mind. These are some of the ways of our thinking through which we fundamentally differ from Europeans.

In conclusion, we can say that we have to secularize our local identities, ethnic groups, linguistic barriers and religious dogmas in order to attain justice as fairness. For this purpose, we have to take recourse to our rich philosophic heritage as justified insight and vision to combat the ritualistic and mythological religious fanaticism. We have to develop our philosophy of tolerance by accepting other identities, other cultures and languages. This will be our contribution to the conceptual scheme of justice and secularism and we have to revive and revitalize it.

---

8. Immanuel Kant, *Critique of Pure Reason*, Eng. trans. N.K. Smith (London: The MacMillan Press Ltd., 1973), p. 147.

CHAPTER 7

Capability Approach
Theory and Practice

Asha Mukherjee

Aims and Objectives of Capability Approach

> For two decades and more, Martha Nussbaum has been elaborating a distinctive political philosophy: welfarist, without being utilitarian; Aristotelian, without being perfectionist; universalist, without being altogether essentialist; feminist, without forsaking liberalism.[1]

MARTHA Nussbaum's thinking has undergone many changes between 1980 and now. The increasing emphasis on threshold level of each of the central capabilities and the specificity of the capabilities list itself are the visible changes in her position. So we have to take her theory as work in progress rather than at a fixed point. The most recent and synthesized overview we find in *Women and Human Development: The Capabilities Approach*.[2] But this overview is also "far from being complete."

A number of theories of justice have been developed in the history starting from Aristotle to John Rawls and Nozick. But they were also being discussed and found to be partially satisfactory. Nussbaum develops a theory of justice which is distinctive to provide gender justice as well as it is sufficiently "practical" which she calls as capability approach. It is the

---

1. Introduction, Symposium on Martha Nussbaum's Political Philosophy, *Ethics*, October 2000.
2. Martha Nussbaum, *Women and Human Development: The Capabilities Approach* (Cambridge: Cambridge University Press, 2000).

systematization and theorization of women's thoughts and plans. It is sufficiently general as women strive for distinctive goals. It focuses on capability or empowerment as opportunities and choices, rather than on imposing on any individual a mode of functioning. Underlying idea in the capability approach is the idea of human dignity which is linked with political theory — the relation between state and citizen. The issues of development, gender, justice, oppression, multi-culturalism, international feminism, etc. are discussed and developed by Nussbaum in utmost detail and with care. She presents a list of "central capabilities" which would serve as universal standards alternative to GNP per capita and utility, for assessing social progress towards meeting basic needs. The GNP model was based on development economics relying on narrow economic-utilitarian tradition produced by philosophy. The crude measure of GNP, though quite handy measure of quality of life, neither asks questions about the distribution of wealth and income nor about the related matters such as infant mortality rate, life expectancy, educational opportunities, the quality of gender, political and religious liberty etc. The capability approach gives us better ways to handle the problems about quality of life of human beings. This list of "central capabilities" can be adapted appropriately to local circumstances. Nussbaum argues that "international political and economic thought should be feminist, attentive (among other things) to the special problems women face because of sex in more or less every nation in the world, problems without understanding of which general issues of poverty and development cannot be well confronted."[3]

The guiding thought behind her approach is the "one that lies at the heart of Rawls' project, the idea of the citizen as a free and

---

3. Martha Nussbaum, "Women Capabilities and Social Justice", in Asha Mukherjee and Kumkum Bhattacharya (eds.) *Conditioning and Empowerment of Women: A Multidimensional Approach* (New Delhi: Gyan Publication, 2003).

dignified human being."[4] for her, Rawls' political conception of justice involves a commitment. Her approach to women's issues is "part of a systematic and justifiable programme that addresses hierarchy across the board in the name of human dignity." Her view is that political theory should be based on "the conception of human beings as essentially rational agents. The key type of reason to be emphasized is practical, moral and political."[5] She agrees with neo-Aristotelians that (i) accumulation of wealth cannot be the only end of politics, (ii) that each person should be treated as an end, and none as a mere means to the ends of others, and (iii) the proper goal of politics is to support a rich "plurality of human life-activities."[6] This neo-Aristotelian notion of human dignity, as an end in itself, comes very close to Kant; and Marx's reading of Aristotle was mainly shaped by the Kantian idea of humanity as an end. John Rawls being a Kantian starts with the intuitive idea that every person has an "inviolability founded upon justice." This is precisely the reason Nussbaum draws her insights from Aristotle in many respects and with Rawls as well, but she also differs from them on many important points. She differs with Aristotle on slavery, women, equality and citizenship.

Amartya Sen and Nussbaum[7] both advocate capability approach but the roots are different. "Sen's capabilities approach, though not directly inspired by a reading of Aristotle, clearly owes a good deal to Marx's reading of Aristotle, which focuses on the importance of making "truly human functioning," rather than the distribution of commodities in and of itself, the central political goal. Before talking of just distribution, we have to decide on a dimension whose relative value is important. Equal

---

4. Martha Nussbaum, *Sex and Social Justice* (New York: Oxford University Press, 1999), p. 46.
5. *Sex and Social Justice,* p. 71.
6. Martha Nussbaum, "Aristotle, Politics and Human Capabilities", *Ethics*, October 2000, pp. 105-06.
7. Martha Nussbaum and A. Sen (eds.), *The Quality of Life* (Oxford: Clarendon Press, 1993).

distribution of what? In case of poverty, we must know what we should be striving to increase. The capabilities approach has been used as a measure of the quality of life in a nation; it is also used to articulate a view of the proper goal of politics[8]. The approach claims that when we ask how people are doing in a nation or a region we must look at what they are actually able to do and to be rather just at their satisfaction or the resources distribution. "We should focus on what a group or country in question is actually able to do and to be."[9] The approach looks not at actual functioning, since individuals in a liberal society may choose not to avail themselves of opportunities to function but at the opportunities or "capabilities" they have. These are not just formal understandings but involve a set of material pre-conditions, which must be met before one can say that a person is genuinely capable of going to school or taking a job. The central claim is that these capabilities of persons are the measure of quality of life, and that the central goal of politics should be to provide all citizens with at least basic level of these capabilities. Importantly, "The capability approach considers people one by one." For instance, it does not lump individuals into families and ignore the relations and unequal distribution of powers within families. Sen and Nussbaum both are advocates of capability approach but there are differences between them. Sen has not committed himself to a definite list or the Aristotelian mode of justification, but he commits himself to universal norms of several sorts, in the areas such as bodily well-being, education, and the political liberties. Both agree on cultural relativism leaving enough room for plural specification of major capabilities; both stress on the point that the goal is capability, and not functioning. This allows freedom to individuals to choose the functions they want actually to perform. Sen has concentrated on the normative critique of utilitarianism while Nussbaum has focused more on the critique of relativism and the notion of "truly

8. Martha Nussbaum, "Public Philosophy and Feminism", *Ethics,* July 1998, p. 769.

9. *Sex and Social Justice*, p. 34.

human functioning." Although they both "continue to differ" on some important issues, they agree in allying the capability approach quite closely with Rawls' liberalism. Nussbaum interprets central capabilities in the spirit of a Rawlsian "political liberalism" as a core of basic goods about which citizens can agree; still they may differ on the more comprehensive conception of good.[10] There are three distinct types of capabilities: basic capabilities or the innate equipment of human beings that enables them, with sufficient support and care, so that people can attain the higher capabilities; internal capabilities, or state of persons which would be sufficient for exercise of relevant functionings; and combined capabilities, or the internal state combined with suitable external circumstances for the exercise of the function. For example, a woman who has some education and training but due to fear of physical violence does not leave the house for work has the internal but not the combined capability to seek employment outside the house. Politics should aim at production of combined capabilities.[11] A policy aimed at women's internal capability for employment outside the home would need to focus only on education and skills training; a policy aimed at women's combined capability would need to focus, as well, on non-discrimination in hiring, on sexual harrassment and on protecting women from threat which are highly practical issues.

International Feminism

Unequal social and political circumstances give women unequal human capabilities. Women are not treated as ends in themselves. They are treated as mere means or instruments of the ends of others — reproducers, caregivers, sexual outlets, and agents of a family's general prosperity. Traditionally they are not treated as persons with dignity, either by law or by the social institutions. This instrumental value may be positive or negative. Her natal

---

10. Martha Nussbaum, "Women and Cultural Universals", in *Sex and Social Justice*.

11. Martha Nussbaum's article, *Ethics*, 108, 1998, p. 775.

family treats her as an extra member of the family whose departure is inevitable, and, thereby, do not care for her health, education or general well-being as she would be gone in any case — either death or to her husband's house. Her marital home also hardly provides any respect for her ends — she is treated as means for grandchildren, extracting money as dowry payments from her parents, even if her education is cared for, it is only for the extra income to the family or creating an image of the family as part of the status symbol in society. For some reason if her husband dies she has no place to be, given the stigmas attached to widowhood. She is supposed to lose all interests in life and live the life of "living dead."

If women had equal nutrition and health care, they would live slightly longer than men and the sex ratio would be 102.2 women for 100 men (the actual sex ratio of sub-Saharan Africa). The actual sex ratio in India is 92.7 women for 100 men as Amartya Sen uses the term the number of "missing women" in India is 9.5 per cent. The basic reason for this is the lack of essential support for leading lives that are fully human and it is mostly due to the fact of being women. The general problems of poverty and development at national and international level cannot be addressed without paying a special attention towards women problem. Nussbaum suggests an approach which in her opinion is better than other alternatives. Capability approach, she suggests, "treats each person as an end and none as mere tools of the ends of others." She adopts a principle of each person's capability, based on a principle of each person as end. Her approach also "uses the idea of a threshold level of each capability, in a nation beneath which it is held that truly human functioning is not available to citizens; the social goal should be understood in terms of getting citizens above this capability threshold."[12] It is worth noticing that the comparative use of capabilities would not have much use if we do not have a normative conception that would tell us what to

12. *Conditioning and Empowerment of Women: A Multidimensional Approach*, p. 33.

make of what we find in our comparative study. We must move beyond the merely comparative use of capabilities in terms of wealth maximization and utility maximization, etc. to the construction of a normative political proposal, otherwise, it would provide us only a partial theory of justice. The capability approach is fully universal; it is important for each and every citizen, in each nation and each is treated as an end. Women in developing countries like India are important for this approach as they suffer from acute capability failure and they need to be attended by development economics.

With regard to women, both empowerment-related capabilities and sex-related capabilities are fundamental to human capabilities and, therefore, they complement each other. The capability approach tells us that none of the two capabilities should be subordinated to the other, and that public action on both fronts is a legitimate way of promoting both sexual and economic freedom. "The capability approach is the systematization and theorization of thoughts that women are pursuing all over the world, when they ask how their lives might be improved and what the government should be doing about that."[13]

Capability and not *Functioning*

The basic political goal is capability and not functioning and the reason for this is the respect of *choice*. The distinction between capability and *functioning* is of greatest practical importance. A policy which aims at a single desired mode of functioning would have no room for choice. But the policy which tries to promote opportunities for citizens to choose or not to choose some function would respect the individual choice or collective choice. A policy urging all the women to work outside home would be different from the policy providing all women the choice to work outside the home or not to do so.

Capability approach can be used for comparisons of life quality; it can serve as the measuring tool. But comparison use of capability

13. Martha Nussbaum's article, *Ethics*, October 2000, p. 139.

would not help us much if it does not rest on some determinate normative conception, which would tell us what to make of what we find in comparison. But Nussbaum is opposed to any *comprehensive* theory of human good as giving a set of appropriate goals for politics. The reason is that individuals have and pursue many different reasonable comprehensive conceptions of what has value. Respect for individuals and persons, therefore, entails that we respect these spaces for different conceptions. Thus, choice has been attached to the central importance. This leads us to the distinction between capability and functioning. We prefer capability as goal rather than functioning. The reason is not for any comprehensive liberal ideal of autonomy as would be for Rawls but an idea of respect for the diversity of persons and their conceptions. Many countries make voting compulsory or make public state functions religious — this is not acceptable to Nussbaum. There could be some mandatory functioning for children, if it is the only way to develop an adult capability. Sometimes, we may feel some capabilities are so fundamental that they may be justified in promoting as functioning, such as health and safety but this could only be permitted within an appropriate concern for liberty. It is the actual function not simply the capability that makes a life fully human. We want to make sure that all citizens have the ability to make their own plans of life and to use their own reason in making choices. (Regulating norms for smoking, mountain climbing, suicide etc.).

Capability: Theory and Practice

Why a philosopher is concerned with women in slums of Trivandrum and whether a philosopher has anything to contribute in this regard? Answering these questions Nussbaum argues at length that philosophy has something highly important to contribute to the guidance of public life which can guide in shaping policies that influence these women's lives.[14] The role of philosophy is very important in articulating and debating norms of "the

14. Ibid., July 1998, p. 765.

quality of life" and offering policies for distributive justice in connection with women's inequality. This can only be done when a philosopher is well informed by facts and experience. Neither the field worker nor a politician would be in a position to do this job. In fact, Nussbaum worked on a proposal for a project bringing philosophy together with economics, focusing on the articulation of the concept of the "quality of life." The philosophical arguments about relativism and universalism and about utilitarianism and the critique of utilitarianism had a valuable contribution to make to the further development and defence of the capabilities approach.[15] The capability approach may be taken as a friendly amendment to liberalism. Political liberalism of Rawls provides a platform for human capabilities. Philosophical discussion on cultural relativism would generally draw considerations from philosophy of science, philosophy of language and philosophy of mind and would illuminate the complex issues of culture, ideally by the use of Socratic Method. We find debates in other social sciences on these issues but they often seem "sloppy by comparison." Philosophers ask questions due to the nature of the discipline itself. Conceptual analysis as well as refinement of theories with sufficient attention to empirical facts is one of the central tasks of philosophy. The notion of "good life," "freedom and responsibility" which are of concern for many disciplines, are quite obscure and it is the task of the philosopher to remove the obscurities. Economists and political scientists often discuss the concepts of preference, choice and desire but it is the job of a philosopher to ask, investigate, distinguish and work out the relationship of these concepts and provide foundation for these disciplines. It is the task of a philosopher to distinguish between the functionings and capabilities and related distinctions between different types of human capabilities. "*The Human Development Reports* offer one device through which philosophy is already influencing practice in a good way."[16] Since 1991 United Nations

15. Ibid., July 1998, p. 771.

16. Ibid., p. 792.

Development Program (UNDP) in New York is using a theoretical approach designed by Sen, Sudhir Anand, and other economists sympathetic to capability approach.

There was a need to think about the inadequacy of utilitarian criteria of well-being, the relationship between well-being and agency, the structure of political liberalism and the role of the ideas of good played, the relationship between resources and human functioning, cultural relativism and its critique all need philosophers' attention. John Stuart Mill, William James and Bertrand Russell's writings were for general educated public and for many public debates. But the commitment to reality does not mean that philosophy need not be abstract, conceptual and theoretical. It is only by retaining these concerns it can make its distinctive practical contributions.[17]

Some Comments

1. It is obvious that in Nussbaum's theory the concept of human being is fundamental and the question arises whether this is a biological concept or a thoroughly evaluative concept. B. William's reading of Aristotle is that it is a biological concept. Nussbaum's reading of Aristotle is that it is thoroughly evaluative concept and, therefore, very much is a part of ethics in its broad sense of a search for good life. Her idea of human being has been very close to the idea of Rawlsian idea of a concept of the person. To settle the ethical questions we need to have a concept of human being or person which itself is evaluative. Whatever kind of human life it is if it is human life it is extremely important from normative perspective. According to capability approach the concept of human being plays role at a very general level having some non-negotiable points

17. Martha Nussbaum, "Why Practice Needs Ethical Theory: Particularism, Principle, and Bad Behaviour", in *The Path of the Law in Twentieth Century*, ed. S. Burton (Cambridge: Cambridge University Press, 1998).

in our judgements. These fixed points are practical reason and sociability, which are extremely important aspects of an existence that is truly human.

2. The other question which arises is that can such internal, evaluative concept of person or human being settle troublesome ethical disputes? Answering this question Nussbaum is of the view that the ethical arguments have to proceed from ethical premises.[18] And Aristotle was quite aware of this move; he was deriving ethical norms from some more basic generally shared ethical norms. But then what happens to the biology? The concept of person itself has normativity; its animality and its rationality both together are valuable. "Our dignity and rationality just are those of a certain sort of animal." In some respects Kant is responsible for distorting our relation with animals.

3. Nussbaum uses the idea of threshold level of each capability beneath which it is held that truly human functioning is not available to citizens; the social goal should be understood in terms of getting citizens above this capability threshold. But this does not mean that once the capabilities are above the threshold then we do not care about inequalities. As "a list of central capabilities is not a complete theory of justice. Such a list gives us the basis for determining a decent social minimum in a variety of areas. . . . But the provision of a threshold level of capability, exigent though that goal is, may not suffice for justice."[19] She does not tell us much about what to be done when the citizens are above the threshold. Perhaps many distributive principles should be entertained at this point.

---

18. Martha Nussbaum, *Women and Human Development: The Capability Approach* (Cambridge and New York: Cambridge University Press, 2000), p. 119.

19. Ibid., p. 75.

In this sense the whole enterprise is so far incomplete. Still the question remains how we get a threshold level in a non-arbitrary way. In *Women and Human Development* Nussbaum suggests that this would best be done by internal process of each liberal democracy. This is, perhaps, the only reasonable way to get universal norms in a culture and country to make a place for cross cultural dialogue and international attention. It would always be difficult to say what legitimate local interpretation of a capability is and what is not. When we set the threshold level of capability "we must attend to current possibilities but not too much." For example, in India at present right to a college education could not be included as fundamental right where only 35 per cent of its women and 65 per cent men are literate whereas right to primary education to all children is. The level should be high enough but not so high that it is discredited later.

4. What happens if there is a potential clash between two capabilities, for example, religion and education? Answering this Nussbaum tells us we must not fear but keep the threshold level as if there were no clash. Although this is a tragic situation as we are asking them to forgo something to which they have an entitlement based upon justice, this is a tragic clash of right with right, which is morally wrong if the reason we do this is to get them above the threshold on another capability. But we may have a consolation that after all we are preparing ourselves to a better future where such tragic clashes would not be there.

CHAPTER 8

Alterity Concept and Ethicality of Human Actions

Mritunjay Narayan Sinha

ALTERITY concept is one of the important concepts of post–modern thought. It is a complex, multifaceted and ambiguous concept, difficult to define and not even easy to describe. It covers within its ambit the largest chunk of people, "the others." "Of becoming "different," or "making somebody different," or "captivating others," or "performative subjectivity," which is unfair, terrible and without hope, is its essence. It is both the state and quality of becoming other. The interchangeability of "alterity" and "the other" is sometimes preferred. It wraps up within itself infamous feelings of otherness and exclusion.

Alterity concept outgrows from subjectivity more so when one does not keep up with knowledge, feeling and action of other or when one is only subjective towards oneself. It is the principle of exchanging one's own perspective for that of the other. Institutionalized racial prejudice, gender prejudice and class prejudice are some of its important examples. These examples along with innumerable examples of becoming excluded to an uncomfortable position such as privileged and unprivileged or victimizer and victimized are seen cropping up in future course of cultural and civilizational interplays. Naturally, the people excluded or often victimized within a predominantly liberal humanistic view of the subject are also covered under alterity concept. A formulaic way is:

Other than ourselves = Less than ourselves

The said formula succinctly reveals understanding of this alterity concept.

Alterity concept is relational and context bound. The world process reflects that a person who is privileged today may become unprivileged in course of time and vice versa. Similar is the case with the victimizer and the victimized. Alterity is a lack within the whole, holding that the other is present only as absent from the whole. It is the excluded or the suppressed in any system. Though alterity concept sparks exclusion, its inclusion allows wholeness or totality to take shape. Alterity entails exclusion which percolates from it. Differentiation between white and black, male and female, majority and minority, master and slave and even east and west marks this exclusion. Openness to the other, respect for differences and cautions against insensitivity towards the other are also included in alterity concept. It is inherently articulated and is different without being opposed. It is a fact about the world where one lives among particular kind of others. It conditions our existence as human beings. The ethical relationship between an individual and the other marks the movement of alterity.

In this age of globalization and consumerism, the importance of diversity and concern to love "the other" have become fashionable and that too within a particular context. It could come to such an extent on the level of lived realities that the concrete others are intentionally evaded whereas concern for otherness on a rhetorical level is talked about. It reflects that people in society are unanimously like "abstract floating othernesses." This is why prominent thinkers like Levinas and Derrida along with many post-modernists go for alterity ethics and its role in resolving a state of conflict and sincerely project to achieve or build a more just world, a world ethically centred and alterity–sensitive. These post-modernists go for projecting "alterity concept" and its ethics that is coming up as "a central theoretical-ethical tenet."

The sharp end of the expression "ethicality of human actions" is ultimately relevant to human conduct that is adjudgeable within the ambit ultima, the world process. Human actions are always purposive and are open to judgement, evaluation or determination of their worth or desirability in a dualistic continuant of right and wrong, virtue and vice, good and bad and some more such dichotomies which provide base for a search for judgement, the ethical judgement on human actions, the end-product of which is a moral progress from the actual towards the ideal. The extent of this lies in the attainment of individual, as well as social virtuosity, value/values. The search for value/values is always reasoned which repels what sensory methods or physical measurements do not validate. The choosing rightly of one action and avoiding the wrong one comes in course of such validation. The decision regarding ethicality of human actions is always parental to rational evaluation with reference to human nature, the satisfaction with reference to human nature, and of human interests even in terms of logical synthesis or appeal to experience. The setting up of value of human actions is straightaway related to their ethicality or to the analysis about what we have to do in order not to downgrade our way of life, a natural hint towards attainment of moral goodness. The ethicality of human actions with regard to rightness and wrongness in the context of alterity concept may be viewed in situations stated below:

(i) The person or persons might be clear about the standard/standards of conduct, and actions to be performed rightly are sharply defined and understood. They are done according to reason behind them or according to some guiding principles. In this case ethicality of such actions performed is proved as they conform to and are in harmony with the standard/norm.

(ii) The person/persons might not be clear about the standards of behaviour (what is right or wrong, about what constitutes virtue in human action) and without knowing the norm, one performs the action/actions. Actions performed here are blind. They are thus beyond evaluation, justification or decision regarding their ethicality.

(iii) Persons might be clear about the norm of conduct but do not hesitate in violating it in performance of their actions. At times they put pleas for such violations.

In the light of these three positions, actions creating differentiation/otherness/alterity can be judged. Viewed in the light of the first, the persons performing their actions according to norm of behaviour do not create crisis of becoming different (alterity), maintain balance, display individual as well as social responsibilities and contribute to the moral progress and social goodness. Their actions, therefore, are normal, rational, desirable and value-neutral. Evaluated in the light of the second, the person's action can be said to be blind, actuated by involuntary impulses, affected by unreason, and therefore, a-moral. The third position, in turn, is important and relevant with reference to the present problem, i.e. the ethicality of human actions involved in reasoned exclusion of the other and naturally stops or even retards moral progress. When the person in his attitude, motivation and even in wrong justification of one's actions with respect to one's share in degradation of ethical environment, causes abrasion and destruction of the system, he negates its maintenance, and ultimately impedes moral progress and social wellness. Such action of the person can be judged as undesirable, individually and, socially irresponsible, ethically not permissible and, therefore, immoral. These actions do not help the evolutionary path and thus are not ethically good or virtuous. They partake in retardation and, therefore, are evil acts. Abject subjectivity resulting from this situation gives rise to inequality, injustice, frustration and all sorts of disquieting no-win situation.

The history recording evolutionary process is filled with a series of struggles involving opposed systems of ethics. Individualism, Socialism, Utilitarianism, Psychological Hedonism, and Rationalism do try to address such ethical problems partially and not wholly. It is true that man is made by circumstances but he also makes them. If human freedom is limited by certain realities, it is also free to work upon those realities and modify them. Ethical evaluations are not advanced in vacuum. Actions are judged to be morally worthy because they lead to desired moral ends. The relation of ends and means is a unity. Each is meaningful only in the context of the other. The prevailing cultural relativism always hinders discovery of a universally acceptable norm for evaluating human action/actions. The ethically not permissible actions are to be prevented for overcoming moral crisis. Moral progress is the result. This is why credibility instrument is to be evolved not only by intellectual understanding of the magnitude of the problem involved but with the chisel of commitment to right action in hands with more courage than conviction. Moral responsibility of individuals and groups should be encouraged, promoted and evaluated through compliance at all levels of cognition, conation and affection. It will enable people to build strong quality consciousness to convey right message to reach across individuals living in every society. The Self-Other relationships are paradigms in which the alterity concept takes its birth as "of becoming different" or "of making somebody different" creating exclusion, abjection, otherness and performative subjectivity of differentiation, distinction and denigration.

It is true that the process of living transforms the human beings and their actions both profoundly and lastingly. It imposes on them such characteristics that reflect their own biological and social nature. What they perceive and the way they perceive are conditioned by (i) evolutionary, and (ii) each person's existential experiences. So individual conduct, and in most of the time, social conduct can never be objective completely. But the interplay between human beings and their settings goes on from which result both good and bad or right and wrong actions in one's life span. The bounden duty of the person as a free and responsible agent is to perform good or right action/actions and to prevent performance of bad or wrong action/actions. It is also true that moral progress is a function of behaviour arising, on the one hand, from continuous introspection and reappraisal and, on the other, from critical analysis of changing social realities.

The balance lies in scratching from the mind of both the Self and the Others in their relationships, all sorts of evil like exploitation, victimization, denigration or repression or denial of any right which creates a deprived lot of people (the others) who always encounter absurdity, ignobility, negativity and are open to abuse. Thus, alterity becomes the product of impulse, impatience and untampered power. Ethicality of human actions naturally produces positive, right, good, and noble results even by facing uncomfortable and absurd situations. The alterity hypothesis would have had radically tangible effects on our everyday lived realities had it been into practices where ethicality of human actions would have prevailed and is prevailing. Ethically doused human actions would have worked like golden syrup that alone could have cured the ills hidden within alterity concept. This is the path which can be trodden quietly, steadily but cautiously towards building alterity ethics rationally and freely for creation of a good society in which good persons are igniting good deeds, where justice becomes most common and every citizen cares even for those who cannot care for themselves. They possess refined aesthetic sensibilities, sense of fairness and equality, the two central features of justice.

CHAPTER 9

The Greek Reversal of Justice

An Interpretation of the Philosophy of the Age of Sophists

Binod Kumar Agarwala

NOBODY can deny that sophists like Protagoras of Abdera, Gorgias of Leontini and Prodicus of Iulis played a significant role in the intellectual revolution in fifth-century BCE Greece. Yet what significance they hold in this intellectual revolution is a matter of dispute among the historians of philosophy. Plato presents them as self-important materialistic and even violent. Aristotle seconds this moral censure and defines them as orators who rely completely on tricky emotional appeals rather than on a methodological investigation of the types of argument required for a case at hand.[1] Hegel in his *Lectures in the History of Philosophy* gives a further push to the negative evaluation of sophists. But positivist Lewes and banker George Grote valuing the sophists' philosophical scepticism and their practical ability to effect agreement among members of social groups reversed this negative reading of the sophists. W.K.C. Guthrie also self-consciously tries to restore sophists to respectability as serious thinkers in the first half of Volume III of his history of Greek philosophy lifting the veil of opprobrium from the sophists through historical and textual research. The classicist Eric Havelock's *Preface to Plato*[2] presents sophists as performers from the angle of communications skill. Even in literacy sophists exhibit the mesmerism of orally recited poetry used as a means of transmitting cultural information,

1. Aristotle, *Rhetoric*, 1355b, 11–12.
2. Eric A. Havelock, *Preface to Plato* (Cambridge, Mass.: Belknap Press of Harvard University Press; Toronto: S. J. Reginald Saunders, 1963), pp. xiv, 328.

customs and habits. Havelock's *Liberal Temper*[3] also resurrects sophists as the earliest liberal politicians. Finding in their materialistic explanations of human species the foundation of liberal temper, he attributes to sophists a view of man characterized by ability to solve problems through creation and continuing readjustment of flexible social arrangements, the fifth-century Greek *polis* being only the manifestation of that ability. According to Havelock sophists see the art of verbal persuasion as the mechanism allowing for the smooth functioning of social organizations and group values as a matter of custom and habit, i.e. pragmatic solutions to temporal and historical needs. With this brief history of evaluation of sophists we have to face the questions now: Are Plato, Aristotle and Hegel wrong in their negative assessment of sophists? Are Lewes, Grote, Guthrie and Havelock correct in their positive reassessment of sophists? To answer these questions is very important as the thought of sophists lies close to the modern theory of the state. If we look at the history of the development of modern theories of state which are based on the concept of power, we find that sophists' kind of thinking having come down to us via Plato and Thucydides has been of prime importance in shaping this history.[4] Regarding sophists' thinking Gadamer writes,

---

3. Eric A. Havelock, *The Liberal Temper in Greek Politics* (New Haven: Yale University Press, 1957), p. 443.

4. Relevance of the thought of sophists to our own times has been noted by many thinkers. For example, W.K.C. Guthrie, *The Sophists* (Cambridge: Cambridge University Press, 1971), p. 3, "With the change that came over philosophy in the fifth-century [BCE Greece], we are plunged into a discussion of questions which are as relevant now as they were when first raised by the Sophists. Whatever we may think of the Sophistic movement, we must all agree that . . . no intellectual movement can be compared with it in the permanence of its results, and that the questions which the Sophists posed have never been allowed to lapse in the history of Western thought down to our own day." See also A. Lesky, *A History of Greek Literature*, 2nd edn., Eng. tr. J. Willis and C. de Heer (London, 1966), p. 341; Wilhelm Schmid and O. Stählin, *Geschichte der griechischen Literature*, I. Teil, Die →

> If viewed historically this kind of thinking, as it has come down to us via Plato himself and Thucydides, can be seen to have been of decisive importance in shaping modern theories of the state insofar as the latter are founded on the concept of power.[5]

The present study is an interpretation of the philosophical thought of sophists taking into consideration the wider circle of writers of Greece of the fifth century BCE The phrase "the Philosophy of the Age of Sophists" in the subtitle indicates this aspect of the present study. This interpretation is undertaken with the belief that the climate of thought of any recognized historical age shows some kind of unity and coherence. Different thinkers coming from the same age articulate from their own perspective and interest different aspects of the same one climate of thought which is a kind of interdependent unity of diverse elements. Take for example Descartes and Hobbes developing their philosophies in the climate of thought of modern age. Descartes in his epistemological metaphysics articulated a duality of mutually independent substances: mind and body. Hobbes articulated his political philosophy of individualism starting from state of nature. These two thinkers, in fact, articulated two aspects of the same

---

→ Classische Periode, 3. Band, I. Hälfte (Munich, 1940), p. 216, "The questions and controversies of that time have lost nothing of their actuality"; M. Gigante, *Nomos Basileus* (Naples, 1936), p. 15, "The theoretical foundation of the general doctrine of law in the twentieth century recapitulates the speculation of fifth-century Greek Sophistic." The effect of thought of sophists on the Enlightenment of the eighteenth century is vividly portrayed in Ernest Cassirer, *Philosophy of the Enlightenment*, Eng. tr. FCA Koelln and J.P. Pettegrove [Princeton University Press, 1951 (Beacon Pressrepr. 1962.)] especially ch. 6, wherein he justifies his statement (p. 285) that "after more than two thousand years the eighteenth century establishes direct contact with the thinking of antiquity. . . . The two fundamental theses represented in Plato's *Republic* by Socrates and Thrasymachus oppose each other again." They still stand opposed today.

5. Gadamer, "Plato's Educational State", *Dialogue and Dialectic: Eight Hermeneutical Studies on Plato*, Eng. tr. P. Christopher Smith, (New Haven and London: Yale University Press, 1980), p. 78.

climate of thought. Descartes was trying to get at what will be recognized later as the metaphysical distinction between subject and object, as only that experience has cognitive function where the distinction between subject and object is available. If in the context of an experience the distinction between subject and object is not available, then that experience has no cognitive role and is treated as mere feeling. Hence this distinction can be said to define, distinguish, and identify the cognitive experience from other experiences in modern philosophy. The entire modern metaphysical tradition, which began with Cartesian distinction between mind and body, tried to clarify the nature of subject and object and the epistemic relation between the two. It is interesting to note that in spite of their differences both empiricism and rationalism analysed experience at length in its epistemic role. Locke, Berkeley, Hume, Spinoza, and Leibnitz grappled with this problem of Cartesian dualism, but the tradition reached its zenith and culmination in Kant's *Critique of Pure Reason* where he tried to determine the transcendental condition of maintaining the distinction between subject and object. Precisely at a time when the subject-object distinction was being articulated by Descartes (1596–1650) another master of modernity, Hobbes (1588–1679) was also developing the conception of civil society commensurate with the articulation of the cognitive experience. He was developing the idea of individual in the state of nature from which society is constructed artificially through individual's will and contract. When any member of the society takes the stance of the subject, i.e. conceives himself as the subject to get knowledge of society, i.e. conceives the society as the object of knowledge, then he must reflect himself out of the society, out of all social relations so that the duality of subject and object can be maintained. Hence, that person must conceive himself as an individual who can exist independently of society. Any person who, by taking the stance of subject, reflects himself out of all social relations also, when he conceives each member of society as a subject he reflects them each out of all social relations and hence conceives them all as individuals. So, the society is reflected out of existence, since each member is conceived as an individual. This is the reason why modernity cannot admit the ontological autonomy of society and admits only the primacy of existence of individuals and thereby begets metaphysical individualism in philosophy. Together with society, by similar arguments, both tradition and history also get dissolved as no one belongs to tradition and history. The concept of individuals standing in no social relations to each other, and also without tradition and history, is the concept of state of nature of political philosophy. So, clearly both Descartes and Hobbes articulated two aspects of the climate of thought of the same age. To take one more example, this time from the post-modern age, consider Gadamer and Rawls. What unites the two thinkers is their understanding of how they are undertaking their investigations. Rawls calls his way of proceeding as the way of wide reflective equilibrium, while Gadamer's way is the way of hermeneutic circle. The idea of wide reflective equilibrium is nothing but his version of the hermeneutic circle of Gadamer. While Gadamer is articulating the ontology of the post-modern climate of thought through his metaphor of play, festival, symbol, etc. Rawls is articulating the liberal political thought commensurate with the advocacy and existence of multiple traditions in the post-modern age.

Similarly for us the sophists like Protagoras and Georgias, historians like Thucydides, and tragedians like Aeschylus, Euripides and Sophocles are articulating different aspects of the same climate of thought prevalent in the fifth-century BCE Greece. The climate of thought of the age of sophists according to the present study is based around transformation of man into *homo faber*. Greeks of fifth century BCE experienced this transformation not as fall but as tragedy. This experience of the Greeks is articulated in the myth of Prometheus. According to Greek mythology Prometheus stole fire from Olympus and gave it to men. It symbolizes that man is introduced to a mode of action called "making." Prometheus is the God who taught mankind all the arts and crafts. So man is a victim of an external deed, this learning is involuntary, and so is the accompanying suffering, symbolized by the anger of Zeus who took revenge on man through Pandora, who opened the box from which sprang all the evils and diseases which beset man. But hope could not escape before the lid was shut so man is left without hope. Hence, the experience of learning art, i.e. "making" is a tragic experience for Greeks, unlike the Hebrew account. So both the fall of Adam and the myth of Prometheus articulate in different ways the transition of man into *homo faber*. It is experienced as evil by Hebrews because, in their account, by this change the blessedness of harmony and order of God was lost which man enjoyed by voluntarily doing the bidding of the natural order of God. In Greek mythology Zeus seeing the plight of man sends Hermes to teach man justice (*dike*). Both Plato and Aristotle elaborated this justice not in terms of the mode of action called "making" and mode of reason called "art," rather in terms of mode of action called "acting" or "doing" and mode of reason called *phronesis*.

In this essay an attempt is made to show that the sophist movement was a tragic experience for ancient Greek civilization. The tragic experience takes the form it does in any society by virtue of the values in terms of which that society looks at the world. Learning of *techne* and consequent emergence of the *homo faber* personality of man was an unmitigated disaster for Greeks. It produced not only confusion of but also a complete reversal of moral values in Greek civilization leading to the mentality that nobody is just voluntarily and will be just only if compelled by power and force. Aristophanes lamented that due to sophists all values were being abandoned and distinction of right and wrong was being obliterated and where apparently people were claiming to uphold standards, there they were upholding the wrong and despising the right. Once this mentality took hold of people, it hastened the decline of the civilization and within a short span of time the unity of *polis* was lost irrevocably.

I explained the biblical concept of fall of Adam and the Christian concept of "original sin" as involving two perspectives in an earlier essay[6] of mine. It is one and the same experience, which is experience of the involuntary happening and experience of wilful action without any contradiction. The experience under consideration is the experience of transformation of man into *homo faber*. This experience of transformation is an experience of an involuntary happening when looked at from the perspective of "doing" [*prattein*]. Yet the same experience of change is the experience of wilful action when looked at from the perspective of "making"(*poien*). Hence there is no contradiction here. It appears as contradictory if we overlook the fact that here two different perspectives are involved and think that the experience is being analysed from a single perspective.

Are these two perspectives in transition available in Greek antiquity? Speaking about Greek antiquity Gadamer writes,

> We too are familiar with darkness, perplexity, madness, catastrophe, sickness and death, love and hate, jubilation, arrogance and ambition, the whole vast range of human sufferings and passions that the Greeks experienced as the real presence of their gods. Greek myth speaks about this fundamental experience which we all have of the way in which such things befall us. One may well ask whether this experience of being overwhelmed is all that is involved here. For are we not really agents? What about conflict, decision, error, and guilt? Are not all these to be found in Greek epic and drama as well? This is certainly true. . . .[7]

But are these two perspectives — of involuntary happening and of agency — involved in the same action? Let us listen to the findings of Gadamer once again:

---

6. Cf. B.K. Agarwal, "Meditations on Experience of Evil And Will: A Solution of Ricoeur's Paradox of Experience of Evil", in *Sandhan*, Journal of Center for Studies in Civilizations, vol. II, no. I, January-June 2002.
7. Gadamer, *The Relevance of the Beautiful and the Other Essays*, Eng. tr. Nicholas Walker (Cambridge: Cambridge University Press, 1986), p. 77.

> . . . one of the most fruitful insights to be gained from the study of antiquity lies in the quite new perspective it offers us upon the nature of "action" in dramatic and particularly in epic literature. . . . When we find in Homer descriptions in which the gods themselves inspire the decisions of men juxtaposed with other more subjective, more reflective and self-conscious descriptions in which we see the hero making his own decisions in an agony of doubt, we are no longer tempted to refer them to different stages of epic composition, ascribing the passage to authors of a different date, for example. We now realize from a closer observation of reality, and that means also a closer observation of ourselves, that Homer is quite justified in combining both kinds of account in one and the same passage. When a character makes his decision and Athena also inspires him to it, that does not imply two contradictory claims of which only one can be true, so that either the hero makes the decision or the decision was inspired by Athena. On the contrary, we have one and the same event seen from different perspectives.[8]

Philologists like Bruno Snell and Albin Lesky[9] have shown in connection with the epic and the drama of Greek antiquity that "our concept of action represents an extremely one-sided self-interpretation on the part of modern man."[10] According to Lesky, human reflexion and freedom of decision though opposed to the divine intervention, there was a mutual and often indissoluble fusion of these two aspects in Aeschylus' tragedy. In the dramas of Aeschylus, the personal decisions of the human agent within the framework of a basically God-governed "Welt-bild" are presented. Freedom of decision and compulsion of gods are united in a genuinely tragic way in the actions of agents. Eric A Havelock also notices in the *Hippolytus* of Euripides that

> (a)t the human level . . . moral decision is dramatized as complicated, uncertain and difficult, liable to produce results

8. Gadamer, *The Relevance of the Beautiful and the Other Essays*, p. 77.
9. Cf. Albin Lesky, *Göttlichen und menschliche Motivation im homerischen Epos, Sitzungsberichte der Heidelberger Akademie der Wissenschaften* (Heidelberg: Carl Winter, 1961).
10. Gadamer, *The Relevance of the Beautiful and the Other Essays*, p. 77.

> which are self-defeating if carried to extremes. The same decision-making process is then portrayed as taking place within an arena marked out by superior powers that set the rules for what takes place and in effect control the results of the decisions, directly or indirectly. . . . May there be logical connection between these two — between the complexity of human decision on the one hand and the control exercised by the external divine apparatus on the other! If in the course of human life choices are forced on us which are difficult to make and involve results which are uncertain and possibly disastrous . . . or which are made with righteous moral conviction and resolutely pursued, only to end in moral and physical collapse . . . then the conclusion follows that influences, causes or forces of some kind, external to our decision-making process, exist and weigh on us in order to produce the said results. We think we are free, but our freedom is conditioned.[11]

It was only during the heyday of sophists and the period when *nomos-physis* antithesis was played out that the full impact of the transformation of man into *homo faber* is felt and experienced by the Greek mind.

The writers who were supporters of *nomos* attest that it was the period when the *homo faber* personality of man was strikingly visible. Let us first hear what Prometheus taught mankind as described by Aeschylus in his *Prometheus Vinctus*. Aeschylus died in 546 BCE. In lines 442-68 and 478-506 Aeschylus makes Prometheus say,

> But hear the sufferings of mortals, how aforetime they were witless but I gave them sense and made them masters of their minds. At first they had eyes but saw to no purpose, heard but took no heed. Like dream-shape they lived their long lives in utter confusion. They knew no houses of break to face the sun, nor working of timber, but lived like crawling ants deep in the sunless recesses of caverns. They had no sure sign of winter or flowery spring or fruitful summer but acted all without judgement until I showed them the risings and obscure settings

11. Eric A. Havelock, "The Double Vision of Greek Tragedy", *The Hudson Review*, vol. 37, no. 2 (Summer 1984), p. 268.

> of the starts. I discovered for them also number, that supreme device, and writing which is the universal memory and mother of culture. I first brought beasts under the yoke, that with bodies bowed to the collar they might relieve mortals of their greatest toil, and brought horses to the chariot, obedient to the reins, to be the glory of wealth and luxury. None but I invented the sea borne, canvas-winged craft of sailors. . . . If one fell ill, there was no healing food, unguent or draught, but for want of remedies they pined away until I taught them to mix soothing remedies to drive away all diseases. I devised many systems of prophecy, I first judged which dreams were true visions and made known to them the secrets of omens and chance-met portents, I explained clearly the flight of crook-clawed birds, those on the right and on the left, the habits of each and their mutual hates, loves and gatherings; the smoothness of entrails also, what colour of gall-bladder is most pleasing to the gods, the subtle formation of the liver; and burning the limbs wrapped in fat, and the long loins, I brought men to a difficult art, and made plain the dim tokens of fire. So much for that. But as for those buried aids to human life, copper and iron, silver and gold, who could claim to have discovered them before myself? None, I well know, unless in vain talk. In one short word you may know all at once: all arts men owe to Prometheus.

What is striking in the above passage is that Prometheus taught man to control the external world but there is no trace of any kind of teaching of self-control or virtue. He is teaching men art and skill (*tehne*) only. He is making man *homo faber*. Havelock should have no objection to our reading of these lines as he himself basing on 445ff lines has ingenuously tried to show that *homo faber* and not Prometheus is the protagonist of Aeschylus' play *Prometheus Vinctus*. In his view neither Zeus nor Prometheus is presented as the vehicle of any power above that of Man. They are transparent and secular symbols: Zeus for the fears and superstitions of man's outmoded past; Prometheus for man himself in his autonomous and splendidly successful effort to employ scientific, technological "forethought" in the winning of a richer cultural life. Havelock has also subjected Sophocles' famous *stasimon* on Man (Antigone 332ff.) to a comparable analysis.

So, now let us hear Sophocles' famous *stasimon* on Man telling us what man has learnt. Sophocles in Antigone lines 332-71 describes around 44 BCE the capacities of man:

> *There is much that is strange, but nothing*
> *that surpasses man in strangeness.*
> *He sets sail on the frothing waters*
> *amid the south winds of winter*
> *tacking through the mountains*
> *and furious chasms of the waves.*
> *He wearies even the noblest*
> *of the gods, the Earth,*
> *indestructible and untiring,*
> *overturning her from year to year,*
> *driving the plows this way and that*
> *with horses.*
>
> *And man, pondering and plotting,*
> *snares the light-gliding birds*
> *and hunts the beasts of the wilderness*
> *and the native creatures of the sea.*
> *With guile he overpowers the beast*
> *that roams the mountains by night as by day,*
> *he yokes the hirsute neck of the stallion*
> *and the undaunted bull.*
>
> *And he has found his way*
> *To the resonance of the word,*
> *And to wind-swift all-understanding,*
> *and to the courage of rule over cities.*
> *He has considered also how to flee*
> *from exposure to the arrows*
> *of unpropitious weather and frost.*
>
> *Everywhere journeying, inexperienced and without issue,*
> *he comes to nothingness.*
> *Through no flight can he resist*
> *the one assault of death,*

even if he has succeeded in cleverly evading
painful sickness.

Clever indeed, mastering
the ways of skill beyond all hope,
he sometimes accomplishes evil,
sometimes achieves brave deeds.
He wends his way between the laws of the earth
and the adjured justice of the gods.
Rising high above his place,
he who for the sake of adventure
consorts with wickedness loses
his place in the end.

Clearly man is learning arts and crafts from Prometheus to become *homo faber*. According to Hans Jonas this is an awestruck homage to man's powers. This tells us "of his violent and violating irruption into the cosmic order, the self-assertive invasion of nature's various domains by his restless cleverness; but also of his building — through the self-taught powers of speech and thought and social sentiment — the home for his very humanity, the artifact of the city." In his view,

> The raping of nature and the civilizing of man go hand in hand. Both are in defiance of the elements, the one by venturing into them and overpowering their creatures, the other by securing an enclave against them in the shelter of the city and its laws. Man is the maker of his life *qua* human, bending circumstances to his will and needs, and except against death he is never helpless.[12]

Yet in this immodest bragging about the marvel that is man there is also a subdued and even anxious anxiety about him. This crafty inventive creature is capable now of both good and evil. If he honours the laws and the decree of heaven his city is exalted but

12. Hans Jonas, *The Imperative of Responsibility: In Search of an Ethics for the Technological Age* (Chicago & London: The University of Chicago Press, 1984), pp. 2-3.

if he does what is shameful and wicked to which he may be led by his reckless spirit he becomes outlaw and hence stateless.

It will be the burden of our argument that the first possibility remains only a fond hope but never a real possibility once man has become *homo faber*. It is only the second possibility which fructifies in reality as claimed by the upholders of (*physis*) once man has become *homo faber*. So the Greek mind never approves of the man as *homo faber*. It is attested by the concluding lines (lines 372-75) of the chorus reproduced above which run as follows:

> *May such a man never frequent my hearth;*
> *May my mind never share the presumption*
> *of him who does this.*

So here Sophocles is neither praising nor giving his avowal to the "inventive skills," rather he is rejecting both the man with such skills as well as such skills. Traditionally the chorus has been described variously as "awestruck homage to man's powers" or "Ode to Man," etc. This is done by neglecting the concluding lines. The tradition has failed to integrate the conclusion of the chorus (*Antigone* 365-75) with the apparent praise of skills of man (*Antigone* 332-64).

The word *techne* of the sophists includes both *art* and *craft* of present-day usage. Words like "skill," "cunning," "ingenuity," etc. do not capture the meaning of *techne* as they refer only to individual proficiency in the whole endeavour. But although sophists talked about *techne* and claimed to teach various kinds of *techne*, yet they did not elaborate in clear terms what was the structure of *techne* in general. It was left to Plato to elaborate it. According to Plato there are five essential factors belonging to the structure of *techne* as such: (1) the useful end, *on account of which* the art exists; (2) the work or concrete achievement of the art, which can serve this purpose; (3) the general form or structure which every such work must exemplify if it is to meet the end; (4) the technical procedure by *which* this form is imposed on the matter; and finally, (5) the concrete matter, *on which* the form is imposed.

The act of making or production, i.e. the act with which *techne* is concerned requires the idea of empty space and empty time contrasted with the fulfilled space and time of festive activity. As the *homo faber* personality emerged the Greeks had to introduce the empty space and time within the fulfilled space and time of festive activities. The essence of the effect of theatrical phenomenon was to change the nature of space and time in the experience of the theatre public. The theatre of Dionysius at Athens was one of the first matrices of empty space conceived by the Western world. The "Theatron" is both the place "to see" and the place "from where one can see." In terms of the life of the archaic Greek community, the major shift effected by the theatre was to play down the audio-tactile involvement and promote a new understanding of space under the governing of the eye. In his article of 1935 on "the Invention of Space" F.M. Cornford makes one point very clear on textual evidence that the notion of infinite space was just baffling to common sense in fifth-century BCE Athens. He even detects a growing confusion of terms between physical space and geometrical space which is purely theoretical. If this idea is extrapolated to the theatre of Athens, it becomes clear that the theatre of Athens was a place where under the gaze of the public, practical, physical space and a theoretical one, that of the stage, coincided. Since the spectators were gradually being deprived of a direct and immediate bodily involvement with the action, a point which will be clarified later in this essay, and that their response was being re-channelled in a visually dominant subjective synthesis, their ordinary environmental references were being gradually emptied of their content and that a new spatial condition was being created for them. It was a neutral, abstract container for programmed activities, a spectacle created by *homo fabers*. Another development also points in the direction of acceptance of the conception of empty space. The public of Athens accepted the daring reforms of Kleisthenes at the end of the sixth century, reforms which transformed the space of Athens from the close-knit allegiances of the *phratries* into the artificial geometrical divisions of municipalities. Acceptance of this desacralization of the homeland by the population indicates towards a substitution in place of a sense of space which was governed by organic relationships with one which posited space as a given, absolute dimension of experience. In Solon's time, *Ge*, mother Earth, was still a divine being, "a mother to the Olympian gods." Even before a century later it became real estate. It was a move from fullness to emptiness, from presence to absence. Such a change was internalized by a population most of which was illiterate as a full-scale model was available in the whole theatrical set-up in the city.

The *nomos-physis* controversy is related to the emergence of *homo faber* personality during the sophist movement. It is interesting to note that supporters of "*nomos*" describe what the man as *homo faber* makes and aspires to make but the supporters of *physis* describe what actually happens or gets done through man, the *homo faber*, and the two descriptions diverge. Be it noted that the word "sophist" itself also points to the perspective of *homo faber* or maker or artist since at first the words "*sophos*", "*sophia*" — although translated as "wise" and "wisdom" — connoted primarily "skill" in a particular craft or art. When *homo faber* personality of man comes to the fore the idea of cosmos and ordered change breaks into its two contrasting aspects: *physis* and *nomos*. *Physis* is that aspect of the ordered change and cosmos, which is amenable to the control of *homo faber*, and *nomos* is the constraining aspect of necessity of the ordered change and cosmos that is being felt by the *homo faber*. This constraining aspect of the cosmic order is first conceived as "usage or custom based on traditional or conventional beliefs as to what is right and true." But when this idea is coupled with what the men of classical time thought about *nomos*, it acquired the sense of "laws formally drawn up and passed, which codify "right usage" and elevate it into an obligatory norm backed by the authority of the state." For the men of classical times according to Guthrie, "*Nomos* . . . is something that *nomizetai*, is believed in, practised or held to be right; originally, something that *nemetai*, is apportioned, distributed or dispensed. That is to say, it presupposes an acting subject — believer, practitioner, or apportioner — a mind from which *nomos* emanates."[13] When the *homo faber* personality came to the fore, constraint of necessity of the ethos involved in the cosmic order appeared as the law imposed by external authority — first by the authority of external God and subsequently by the authority of the leaders of *polis* — to the Greeks. Once the idea of necessity imposed by constraining powers of leaders for regulation of persons is crystallized out as *nomos* from the cosmic ordered change, the idea of *physis* is also crystallized out of cosmic ordered change as nature, growth, the natural necessity operating out there in the reality by itself without needing help from the power of men, and yet in which man can intervene. It was the order of things that shows itself out of itself and regulates itself and yet leaves some space to allow human intervention within this pre-given ordered whole. According to Guthrie,

> We have now reached the point where a new generation has divorced *nomos* from *physis*, as what is artificially contrived from what is natural, and sometimes what is false (though commonly believed) from what is true.[14]

Be it noted that to the fifth and fourth-century Greeks it became clear that what is "by *nomos*" is not "by *physis*" and vice versa, i.e. *nomos* and *physis* were mutually exclusive.

Homo faber personality and individualism are related concepts. As the *homo faber* personality emerged in the sophistic movement, individualism also emerged with it. In fact, we find one of the most extreme versions of individualism in Protagoras, one of the prominent sophists. He said, in fr. 1, *panton chrematon metron estin anthropos, ton men onton hos estin, ton de ouk onton hos ouk estin*. This statement of Protagoras is generally translated as, "*Man is the measure of all things, of those that are that they are, of those that are not that they are not.*" But this translation is not correct, since *panton chrematon* are correctly translated not as "*all things*" but as "*all*

13. Guthrie, p. 55.

14. Ibid., p. 56.

things insofar as they are in use." It is interesting to note that *chrema* is etymologically connected with *chresthai*. If this etymology is taken into account the meaning of *chrema* is "something one uses." So it is something in close relationship to man according to Nestle.[15] According to Untersteiner, it means "the totality of things understood as action or experience."[16] It is also interesting to note that *chremata* belongs to a group of words in the Classical Greek language in which it is distinguished from other words in the following manner:

1. *Ta physica*: The things insofar as they originate and come forth from themselves.

2. *Ta poioumena*: The things insofar as they are produced by the human hand and stand as such.

3. *Ta pragmata*: The things insofar as we have to do with them at all, whether we work on them, use them, transform them, or only look at and examine them, *pragmata* being related to *praxis*: Here *praxis* is taken in a truly wide sense, neither in the narrow meaning of practical use (*chresthai*) nor in the sense of *praxis* as ethical action; *praxis* is all doing, pursuing, and sustaining, which also includes *poiesis*.

4. *Ta mathemata*: the things insofar as we take cognizance of them as what we already know them to be in advance, the body as the bodily, the plant-like of the plant, the animal-like of the animal, the thingness of the thing, and so on. And lastly,

5. *Ta chremata*: The things insofar as they are in use and therefore stand at our constant disposal — they may be either *physica*, rocks and so on, or *poioumena*, something specially made.

---

15. W. Nestle, *Vom Mythos zum Logos*, 2nd edn. (Stuttgart, 1941), p. 271.
16. M. Untersteiner, *The Sophists*, Eng. tr. K. Freeman (London, 1957), p. 79.

So the correct translation of Protagoras' saying is

> Man is the measure of all things [insofar as they are] in use, of those that are that they are, of those that are not that they are not.

But what is the sense in which Protagoras uses the term "*anthropos*" (man)? He is taking man (*anthropos*), in the sense of an individual and not in a universal sense of "mankind" in general. Guthrie gives the following three passages from those who have commented on the sentence above, as confirmation of individualism of Protagoras.

In the Theaetetus (152a) Socrates asks Theaetetus if he has read this sentence. "Often," is the reply. "Then you know that he puts it something like this that as every single thing appears to me, so it is to me, and as it appears to you, so it is to you — you and I being men." The emphasis on the separate identity of "I" and "you" confirms individualist reading of "man."[17]

Aristotle in *Metaphysics* (1062b13) writes,

> Protagoras said that man is the measure of all things, meaning simply and solely that what appears to each man assuredly also is. If this is so, it follows that the same thing both is and is not, and is both bad and good, and whatever else is asserted in contrary statements, since often a particular thing appears good (or beautiful, *kalon*) to some and the opposite to others; and the criterion (με'τρον) is what appears to each individual.

Aristotle's understanding of the Protagoras' sentence also confirms Protagoras' individualism.[18]

Lastly, let us hear the common sense of a historian of Greek literature, Lesky, who says in his *History of Greek Literature*:[19]

> Certainly the sentence refers to the individual. Anyone who doubts it must hold that Plato is lying or mistaken. . . . If we are

17. W.K.C. Guthrie, *A History of Greek Philosophy*, vol. III (Cambridge: Cambridge University Press, 1969), p. 171.
18. Guthrie, *A History of Greek Philosophy*, vol. III, p. 171.
19. Lesky, p. 345.

> determined to disbelieve Plato, we have still to reckon with other authors [Aristotle, Sextus] whose use of the word ε'καστς shows that they also took the sentence as referring to the individual.[20]

The conception of man as individual endowed with *homo faber* personality is also related with the idea of state of nature, i.e. the condition of men without any social organization and full of violence as shown in "The Foundations of Modern Liberalism: Inscription of Art And Morality in the Perspective of Modern Metaphysics."[21] This is also confirmed by Protagoras. He wrote a piece called, "On the Original State of Man," (περίτηςε'ν άρχη κατασετασες, D.L. 9.55).[22] It is generally believed that when Plato puts a speech in his mouth on that topic probably he is reproducing Protagoras' own views. The passage in question is Protagoras 320c ff. Protagoras says that from the very beginning man is endowed with technical sagacity (ἔντεχνος σοφία). According to the myth, Prometheus, stealing from heaven fire and the knowledge of industrial arts, bestows them on the first men who see the light.

Using their own skill, men soon provided themselves with food, houses and clothing and learned to speak; but they still lived "scattered," without cities, because although they had the "craftsman's art" [δημιουργικη τεχνη, 322b] they lacked the 'political art." In this original state skill of men was not enough to secure them against their animal competitors. The only defence lay in the combined action of men. This attempt to associate themselves in "cities" gave rise to all kinds of aggression and violence on one another.

Be it noted that unlike Hobbes's state of nature where men were to reckon with mutual violence, in the original state of

---

20. Lesky, quoted in Guthrie, *A History of Greek Philosophy*, vol. III, p. 189.
21. *Journal of Indian Council of Philosophical Research*. vol. XVIII, no. 4, October–December 2001.
22. Protagoras, cited in Guthrie, *A History of Greek Philosophy*, vol. III, p. 63.

Protagoras men had to deal with not only mutual violence but also natural calamities symbolized by the attack of beasts of nature.

Man cannot rest without being there at home in the world. But once man became the craftsman, the expert, the creator of new shapes and forms, the technites, the man who masters a technique he is an alienated being both alienated from his fellow beings as he becomes individual and alienated from the world as he becomes a subject distinct from the object a point which we will discuss below. Hence thinking of "being there at home" becomes a task of "coming to be at home" which for the *homo faber* further becomes a task of "making oneself at home" in the world. One aspect of this was to discover a free space for creative production in the middle of a pre-given nature, a problem solved conceptually by *nomos-physis* distinction as outlined above. The second aspect of this problem was to look for basis of social unity. Sophists like Protagoras tried to solve this problem too.

Protagoras once again refers to the myth of Zeus. Fearing that the whole race of mankind would be wiped out, Zeus sent Hermes, the messenger of gods, to bestow on men two moral virtues, *aidos* and *dike*, "to make political order possible and create a bond of friendship and union" (322c). According to Guthrie, "*Dike* is a sense of right or justice, *aidos* a more complicated quality combining roughly a sense of shame, modesty, and respect for others. It is not far from "conscience."[23] According to Protagoras' account these gifts are not to be bestowed on selected individuals as it happened with arts and crafts when Prometheus bestowed them on mankind. Every man must have a share in them, because "there could never be cities if only a few shared in these virtues as in the arts." But not even Zeus can make everyone learn these virtues for they were no part of the original nature of men. So he adds the proviso that, if anyone proves incapable of acquiring them, he must be put to death as a cancerous growth in the body politic.

---

23. Guthrie, *A History of Greek Philosophy*, vol. III, p. 66.

So Protagoras must face the problem of making man conform to the *aidos* and *dike*. The perspective of art or the *homo faber* personality bestowed by Prometheus on men confounds the problem.

"Man is the measure of all things . . ." and the interpretation put on it confirms that each man has his own idea of good and tries to achieve that good in Protagoras's philosophy. But that will make no society. So each man's pursuit of his own conception of good must be restricted and this can be done only externally. *Dike*, which is "bond of friendship" becomes *dikaion,* i.e. morality of rules and which in turn becomes *nomimon,* i.e. the positive law in Protagoras.

So the problem of social organization can be turned into how to make the *homo fabers* pursuing their own conception of good conform to positive law.

It is generally believed that the problem of establishing positive law is solved by social contract by the sophists including Protagoras. But this belief is unfounded. Greeks had no notion of social contract. The idea of social contract or compact that moderns accepted comes from the reinterpretation of Hebrew idea of covenant (*berit*). Hobbes, the first full-fledged contract social theorist, gave a hint of this in the very introduction to his *Leviathan,* where he writes, "Lastly, the pacts and covenants, by which the parts of this body politic were at first made, set together, and united, resemble that fiat, or the 'let us make man,' pronounced by God in the creation." That is to say Hobbes explicitly admits that his conception of social contract is nothing but reinterpretation of God's covenant of creation in the Genesis.

The idea of contract is essentially related to culpability of breach of contract and hence it presupposes free will through which contract is made. Greeks had no notion of free will. Civilization had to wait for the elaboration of free will till Augustine, who elaborated it to defend the culpability of sin an idea inherited from Adam's fall.

In the theory of punishment that is stated immediately after the myth of Zeus mentioned above, Protagoras has explicitly rejected the idea of culpability of wrongdoing. The passage needs to be quoted in full (324 a-c):

> In punishing wrongdoers, no one concentrates on the fact that a man has done wrong in the past, or punishes him on that account, unless taking blind vengeance like a beast. No, punishment is not inflicted by a rational man for the sake of the crime that has been committed (after all one cannot undo what is past), but for the sake of the future, to prevent either the same man or, by the spectacle of his punishment, someone else, from doing wrong again. But to hold such a view amounts to holding that virtue can be instilled by education; at all events the punishment is inflicted as a deterrent.

This follows from the myth itself when Zeus sends Hermes with the message with the proviso that, if anyone proves incapable of acquiring them, he must be put to death as a cancerous growth in the body politic. That is to say the punishment does not follow from the culpability of wrongdoing but follows from the incapability of learning otherwise.

If society or law were an outcome of a covenant then the above theory of punishment will make the contract meaningless for it is no more the basis of obligation and unity of society. Since Protagoras explicitly rejects culpability of crime he rejects contract theory as well. Protagoras has nowhere in his theories used the contract idea.

In fact, the very original idea of tragedy was based on the idea of non-culpability of wrongdoing. The experience of learning *techne* was experienced as tragic due to the revenge of Zeus through Pandora precisely because that learning of *techne*, which was wrongdoing, was not culpable in their eyes. Greeks never experienced it as sin, which is culpable. Aristotle elaborated this discrepancy between act which was nonculpable and the revenge that Zeus took as disproportionate between guilt and punishment because he took the wrongdoing to be culpable. So the experience of tragedy became disproportionality of culpable guilt and the punishment inflicted, while the original Greek idea of tragedy was based on the idea that Zeus took revenge for an act that was not-culpable. The clearest example of the non-culpable act being treated as culpable is provided by the Oresteia of Aeschylus. Clemenstra has slain her husband Agamemnon, just returned from the Trojan War, for the sake of her lover Aegisthus. This was an expiable act and not a culpable act according to the earlier ethos as Erinyes argues, "Unrelated by blood was she to the man that she slew." But in the changed conditions of fifth-century BCE Greece it was treated as a culpable act as testified by the vote of Athena and Athenian jurors, the Areopagites. The "gods of junior lineage," as they are descried by the Erinyes themselves, are victorious over the Erinyes, and the latter allow themselves finally to be persuaded to assume a new office in the service of the new order based on the *homo faber* personality of man.

Socrates and Plato elaborated the reason for non-culpability of wrongdoing; all wrongdoing is due to ignorance and hence involuntary. Since Greeks lacked the idea of voluntary wrongdoing Greek mind failed to elaborate any idea of free will. It is only when Aristotle rejected the idea that all wrongdoing is involuntary and argued for the fact that people can do wrong knowingly and hence voluntarily due to ακρασία (incontinence, literally "lack of mastery"). Ακρασία is generally translated as "weakness of the will" also thereby giving hint to the idea that probably Aristotle had inkling of "free will," but he failed to elaborate any idea of free will. Be it noted that the structure of Aristotle's ακρασία is similar to the structure of the fault in the will or nature of man according to Augustine. But Augustine elaborated this fault into a theory of free will whereas Aristotle failed to do so.

Greeks, including sophists, had no notion of free will and, hence, lacked the idea of social contract. Even though one is convinced by my argument that Protagoras had no notion of social contract it may be difficult to accept the fact that other sophists also had no notion of contract only on the ground that Greeks had no notion of free will.

One may argue like Guthrie:

> When . . . the view was gaining ground that law is purely human institution designed to meet particular needs, nothing permanent or sacred about it, it could be contrasted with either a divine or a natural order or both. In drawing this contrast the act of legislation is usually said to be outcome of an agreement or compact (συνθήκη) between members of a community, who have "put together," composed, or agreed upon certain articles.[24]

He even can give actual statements like Hippias (Plato, *Prot.* 337d) explicitly defining law as "covenants made by citizens whereby they have enacted in writing what ought to be done and what not,"[25] or Antiphon saying, (fr. 44A DK/OP1364, fr.1) "Laws are artificial compacts, they lack the inevitability of natural growth." Aristotle in his *Politics* (1280b10), arguing for the view that aim of state is to promote good life, writes,

> ". . . otherwise the political society becomes a mere alliance, differing only in respect of locality from alliances between distant countries, and law becomes a compact, and as Lycophron the Sophist said, a guarantor of men's right against one another, not a means of making the citizens good and just."

So Lycophron is also given the credit for social contract theory in its earliest form.[26]

Even Plato's *Crito* is interpreted as description of Socrates expounding "in the prison cell the doctrine of an agreement between himself and the laws of his city as an argument against attempting to evade the judgement which those laws have passed

---

24. Guthrie, *A History of Greek Philosophy*, vol. III, p.136.
25. Ibid., p. 138.
26. Ibid., p. 139.

upon him."[27] According to Guthrie, "in Plato's works . . . the conception of law as a compact put forward by witnesses hostile to it."[28]

On the face of such massive evidence given by Guthrie can we maintain that Classical Greeks had no notion of social contract? The answer is in the affirmative for the evidence given is not conclusive.

It is generally the Greek word 'συνθήκη' which is translated as an "agreement" or "compact." This is done on the ground that

> ". . . the prefix συν– in compound verbs has two uses: (a) objective, as in συντίθημι (act.), to put two or more things together, thus constructing a composite whole; (b) subjective, to do something conjointly or in harmony with someone else, as inσύμφημι, which does not mean to say two or more things together or at the same time, but to say something in unison with another person, i.e. to agree with him. The middle voice of συντίθημι was used in both ways. It meant, first, "to put together for oneself," or organize, and also hear and understand ("put two or two together"); secondly to agree with others, and (with an infinitive) to agree to do something. When the object was laws, a treaty or the like, it is probable that both meanings were present: the constituent articles are composed or put together, and they are mutually agreed upon (the reflexive force of the middle assisting)."[29]

Our contention is that the above account of meaning of συν– is dependent upon a more fundamental sense of συν– ; which we must understand to settle the question whether συνθήκη is contract or not. For understanding that sense of συν– we have to first understand the function of λόγος in early Greek thought.

Λόγος in early Greek thought means "discourse." Λόγος as

---

27. Guthrie, *A History of Greek Philosophy*, vol. III., p. 140.

28. Ibid.

29. Ibid., p. 136 note 3.

discourse has the function of δηλουν : "to make manifest what one is 'talking about' in one's discourse." Aristotle has explicated this function of discourse more precisely as αποφαίνεσθι [*De Interpretatione* 1-6, also *Metaphysica* z4, and *Ethica Nicomachea* z]. The λόγος lets something be seen (φαίνεσθι), namely, what the discourse is about; and it does so either *for* the one who is doing the talking . . . or for persons who are talking with one another, as the case may be."[30] Heidegger further explains,

> And only *because* the function of the λόγος as αποφανσις lies in letting something be seen by pointing it out, can the λόγος have the structural form of σύνθεσις? Here "synthesis" does not mean a binding and linking together of representations, a manipulation of psychical occurrences where the "problem" arises of how these bindings, as something inside, agree with something physical outside. Here the συν has a purely apophantical signification and means letting something be seen as its *togetherness* [*Beisammen*] with something — letting it be seen *as* something.[31]

This finds confirmation in Gadamer's studies also. He writes,

> We live in the *logos*, and the *logos*, the linguistic dimension of human being-in-the-world, fulfils itself by making something visible so that the other sees it. The Aristotelian word for this is *deloun*, which contains the "de" root of the deictic comportment or showing.[32]

He also writes at another place,

> "It seems to me that Aristotle had already indicated the true character of the being of language when he freed the concept of *syntheke* from its naïve meaning as "convention."

---

30. Heidegger, *Being and Time*, 56/32.

31. Ibid., 56/33.

32. Gadamer, *The Relevance of the Beautiful and the Other Essays*, Eng. tr. Nicholas Walker (Cambridge: Cambridge University Press, 1986), p. 160.

He then explains,

> By excluding every sense of founding or originating from the concept of *syntheke*, he pointed in the direction of that correspondence of soul and world that comes to light in the phenomenon of language as such and is independent of the forceful extrapolation of an infinite mind by which metaphysics provided this correspondence with the theological foundation. The agreement about things that take place in language means neither a priority of things nor a priority of the human mind that avails itself of the instrument of linguistic understanding. Rather, the correspondence that finds its concretion in the linguistic experience of the world is as such what is absolutely prior.[33]

This idea of λόγος is associated with ἀλήθεια "Here the 'being true' of the λόγος as ἀλήθεύειν means that in λέγειν as αποφαίνεσθι the entities *of which* one is talking must be taken out of their hiddenness; one must let them be seen as something unhidden (ἀλήθες); that is, they must be *discovered*."[34]

At another place also Heidegger explains,

> Laying, λέγειν, concerns what lies there. To lay is to let lie there before us. When we say something about something, we make it lie there before us, which means at the same time we make it appear. This making-to-appear, and letting-lie-before-us is, in Greek thought, the essence of λέγειν and λόγος.[35]

At this stage of Greek thought λόγος is in intimate unity with the entity since it is only λόγος that lets the entity seen in its unhiddenness. The language, object and thought belonged together as one. This idea is formulated by Permenides in fr.8, 34ff " ταυτον δ' έστι νοειν τε και ουνεκεν έστι νόημα. ου γαρ άνευ

33. Gadamer, *Philosophical Hermeneutics*, Eng. tr. David E. Linge (California: University of California Press, 1976), p. 78.

34. Heidegger, *Being and Time*, 56-7/33.

35. Heideggar, *What is Called Thinking*? (Harper & Row Publishers, 1968), p. 202.

του εοντος, εν ω πεφατισμένον εστίν, ευρήσεις το νοειν", i.e. "The same thing is there to be thought and is why there is thought. For you will not find thinking without what is, in all that has been said [Or: in which thinking is expressed."[36] These lines have been translated by W.K.C. Guthrie as:

> What can be thought . . . and the thought that "it is" are the same; for without that which is, in which . . . it is expressed . . . thou shalt not find thought.[37]

What we let lie before us in language is the essential community between thinking and being. What we let lie in language is expressed also by the Permenides's principle: " το γαρ αυτο νοειν εστίν τε και ειναι,"[38] which is generally translated as "for it is the same thing to think and to be." The idea is further formulated by Parmenides in fr. 6 which begins with the words, " χρη το λέγειν τε νοειν τ϶ εον 'εμμεϖαι" which means "it is useful what is there to be said and thought must be."

But this intimate unity of language and object and thought was broken and the question became paramount how language relates to object, during the sophist movement. The problem of correctness of words or names, i.e. how they relate to objects was debated very keenly. For our purposes it is not important whether words are conventionally or naturally related to objects, but the very fact that the issue is debated is important for us as it shows that the intimate unity of word and object was broken. What hastened the breakdown of the unity of name and object was the spread of the writing and literacy. In the pre-literate people when language is only spoken the unity of name and the object obtains as the two are not distinguished. With the written language the

---

36. G.S. Kirk, J.E. Raven, and M. Schofield, *The Pre-Socratic Philosophers: A Critical History with a Selection of Texts*, 2nd edn. (Cambridge: Cambridge University Press, 1983), p. 252.
37. Guthrie, *A History of Greek Philosophy*, vol. II (Cambridge: Cambridge University Press, 1965), p. 39.
38. Permenides, quoted in Heidegger, *What is Called Thinking?*, p. 240.

difference between the name and the object can be seen and hence under the gaze of the eye the unity of word and object breaks down. Word is what the subjective self speaks (or writes and reads), and the object is out there in reality. The *Antigone* (I 76) Kreon couples *psyche* with *phronema* and *gnome* and the three mean "courage and wisdom and eloquence," whereas Haimon of fifth-century BCE Greece in a passage couples *psyche* with the organ *glossa*.[39]

With the advent of literacy, according to Havelock's *Preface to Plato,* the Greek ego frees itself from the tradition and begins to think independently of it.[40] "This amounts to accepting the premise that there is a 'me,' a 'self,' a 'soul,' a consciousness which is self-governing and which discovers the reason for action in itself rather than in imitation of the poetic experience. The doctrine of the autonomous psyche is the counterpart of the rejection of the oral culture."[41] Along with the discovery of the soul Greece of the last quarter of the fifth-century discovers intellection, the activity of thinking. "It now became possible to identify the 'subject' in relation to that 'object' which the 'subject' knows."[42] The Greek stage helped in the acquisition of subjective consciousness, distinguished from objective reality according to Eric Havelock in his *Preface to Plato.* Whereas the performance of epic poetry would involve the whole body of the performer as well as the whole body of his audience without implying that there be a strict distinction of subjective mental processes over objective physical ones, the act of writing knowledge down would liberate the memorizer from all objective mnemonic devices and leave him dependent only on subjective mental devices. From the point of view of communication, as speech gave way to writing at personal

39. T.B.L. Webster, "Some Psychological Terms in Greek Tragedy", *The Journal of Hellenic Studies*, vol. 77, part 1, 1957, p. 151.
40. Havelock, *Preface to Plato*, p. 200.
41. Ibid.
42. Ibid., p. 201.

level, so also oral epic poetry gave way to theatre at social level in Greek civilization. One of the most interesting insights of classical scholarship into the nature of chorus dancing is H.C. Baldry's opinion that it probably "was the sort of physical reaction to the play which the audience might have shown if they had risen from their seats."[43] This is likely but ultimately the theatrical situation led to a repression of all overt bodily responses to the action on the stage. Charles R. Beye reminds us that heavy fines and sometimes ejection from the theatre were imposed on those who created disturbances during the day-long performances. It is probable that the experience of theatrical performances, even for the short duration of their occurrence during the year, would introduce a new distinction in the relationships between body and mind. As the public was exposed to highly involved actions based on common knowledge and yet prevented from responding physically by the seating arrangement and the distance between the orchestra and itself, the need to control and convert physical impulses into mental ones must have arisen leading to the distinction of subject and object even without any theoretical articulation of the two. Even the tragedy reinforced the distinction. For example, the figure of Aeschylus' Prometheus tied and bound to his rock is the very image of the spectator bound to his uncomfortable seat in the theatre rows. The title of the play and the elaborate enactment of Prometheus' binding in the very first scene indicate that this bodily immobilization of the central figure should be granted the utmost attention. In such a situation Prometheus can only respond by speech. Thus divorced from bodily action, this speech is the closest theatrical approximation of subjective thought. The first speech of Prometheus is in fact a monologue and it expresses in thought-like patterns the tensions and frustrations endured through the bodily repression. We can infer that the age is struggling to get at the distinction of subject and object which will be articulated clearly much later in history. Webster has noted several instances where psyche means a

43. H.C. Baldry, *The Greek Tragic Theatre* (London: London C&W, 1974).

particular soul, feeling, enduring, or planning and so stands for the person in his psychical aspects, distinguished from his physical aspects or body or *soma*.[44]

Even though the subject-object distinction was emerging and to that extent man was being alienated from the world, in the age of sophists it did not go to the extent of modern notion of "object" or "objectivity." They did not have a term for "object" and they could barely speak of even a "thing." The word they used in this sphere was *pragma*, which refers to that within which men are entangled in the praxis of living. It refers not to that which stands over against subject or opposed to subject which he has to overcome, but rather refers to that within which men move and that with which men have to do. Since the distinction was emerging via *psyche* and *soma* distinction there was limit to which it could be carried as man's body is inaccessible to objectification in an essential way. Similarly, the Greek *psyche* also never rose to take the form of modern self-conscious ego. And because of this, even though word and object were distinguished in Greek thought, they did not go to the extent of thematization of language and did not see it as an instrument, a system of signs for communication. They had no word for language, but had the word *glotta* which means tongue which calls forth sounds and a word for that which is communicated in language: *logos*.

As the subject and object precipitated out from original unity the apophantic signification of συν–, which it had when object and language belonged together, was also broken into two apophantic significations, i.e. συν– was interpreted as having two apophantic significations — objective and subjective respectively. In objective apophantic sense συν– meant putting two things together thus construing a whole not in the sense of fabricating but in the sense of seeing an entity as something. In the subjective sense it meant in agreement with others but this is not agreement in the sense of promise or vow but agreement in the sense of

44. T.B.L. Webster's article in, *The Journal of Hellenic Studies*, vol. 77, part 1 , 1957, p. 151.

assenting to a fact, a judgement. Heraclitus, in fragment 2, laments about the lack of this second apophantic significations, i.e. συν– in language, "One must follow what is common; but although the *Logos* is common, most men live as if they had a private understanding of their own." Further Heraclitus says in fr. 50, "Listening not to me but the *Logos* it is wise to agree that all things are one." The notion of "the common" and the unity is elaborated in fr. 114:

> One must speak with intelligence and trust in what is common to all, as a city in its law and much more firmly; for all human laws are nourished by one, the divine, which extends its sway as far as it will and is sufficient for all and more than sufficient.

So in the legislation during the sophist movement συνθήκη did not have the sense of fabricating the terms through/of mutual promise, which is a contract, rather it meant agreeing together in letting the order of society be seen in its togetherness as this such and such *nomos*. For Greeks legislation was never a making or fabricating of a law; rather it meant only codification of the discovered law which exists already. The acting subject presupposed from which *nomos* emanates is not a fabricator of *nomos* but the believer, practitioner or apportioner, who discovers the *nomos* from the ethos of the *polis*.

Be it noted that συνθήκη in its apophantic sense presupposes the existence of law and hence the existence of *polis* a fact which the sophists cannot account for within their scheme of things. So συνθήκη of *nomos* was never proposed to explain the existence of the unity of polity, even though Greeks talked about συνθήκη of *nomos*, sophists like Protagoras tried to solve the problem of social unity from the state of nature and the state of disunity in a different way. Similarly since the συνθήκη of *nomos* presupposed prior existence of *nomos* they tried to solve this problem of pre-existence of *nomos* in a different way, i.e. without presupposing prior existence of social unity. We will see now how far the sophists succeeded in their attempt.

Be it noted that during the sophist movement in spite of the fact that *homo faber* personality had come to the fore and *nomos* was conceived as positive law laid down by the legislator or lawgiver, since they had no notion of *free will*, they could not see *nomos* as something that is fabricated by exercise of free will. So for them it is neither fabricated by the lawgiver nor made by the contractual agreement of citizens. When sophists conceived of the lawgiver they were merely the discoverer of the *nomos* and codifier of it. When they talked of agreement of citizens on *nomos* they had apophantic agreement in mind, not the contractual agreement. Why did the sophists conceive of the lawgiver to be a discoverer of law? Why did they conceive of the agreement of citizens to be an apophantic agreement? Before we answer these questions let us first see how the society is made out of the state of nature according to Protagoras.

Protagoras tried to solve the problem of establishing social unity from the state of nature by educating man in political art and *arete*. It is not only for Protagoras but also for sophists in general, education was the basis of social unity. The discussion whether virtue can be taught occupies a central place in the sophistic discussion, they supporting the claim that "virtue" can be taught and also eking out a livelihood by teaching "virtue" so that social unity can be established.

Greeks during the sophist movement saw a close connection between *arete* and the special skills and crafts (*technai*). "Protagoras' references in Plato to "craftsman's *techne*" and "craftsman's *arete*" show that for Protagoras they meant more or less the same."[45] But he considered the instruction in the special *technai*, which some sophists offered, to be beneath him because for establishing social unity none of the special *technai* is needed. A social unity can be established even if people lacked the special *technai* and even if only some had them. "Political art" or "political *arête*," which is

---

45. Guthrie, *A History of Greek Philosophy*, vol. III, p. 255.

his own speciality, is needed universally for organized society to be possible.

But this educational solution of the political unity proposed by Protagoras was marred from the very beginning, since he modelled "political art" and "political *arête*" on the model of special *technai* and their *arête*. His solution was flawed because he tried to solve the problem of social unity from the perspective of *homo faber* act or making. Hence the political art, which he claimed to teach, turns out to be "prudence in personal affairs and the best way to manage one's own household, and also in the affairs of the state, so as to become a most powerful speaker and man of action."[46] Since the political actor is an individual *homo faber* this conception of political *arête* turns out to be an advice to successfully advance one's own power, since ultimately only external control of others, who are also *homo fabers*, by establishing the power of one *homo faber* (the political actor himself) can solve the problem of social unity in Protagoras' scheme of things. His education, therefore, turns out to be coupled with use of violence or force, i.e. control of men by external force. This aspect comes out in the famous passage on the punishment, quoted above, in which he discusses the educational solution to the problem of social unity starting from the state of nature. Let me quote the relevant portions of it once again:

> No, punishment is not inflicted by a rational man for the sake of the crime that has been committed (after all one cannot undo what is past), but for the sake of the future, to prevent either the same man or, by the spectacle of his punishment, someone else, from doing wrong again. But to hold such a view amounts to holding that virtue can be instilled by education; at all events the punishment is inflicted as a deterrent.[47]

As the last sentence makes it clear, Protagorean education is

46. Plato, *Protagoras*, 318-d-e, cited in Guthrie, *A History of Greek Philosophy*, vol. III, p. 255.

47. *Protagoras*, 324 a-c.

nothing but external violent (i.e. involving use of force) shaping (making virtuous) of matter (the men without political art) to produce intended result (i.e. the social unity). That is to say Protagoras' education in political art is nothing but a *homo faber* forging a social unity by force. So Protagorean educator also turns out to be the forerunner of Prince of Machiavelli.

So even though Protagoras does not solve the problem of social unity by contract like the moderns yet ultimately his solution also led to the supreme power of one man, the educator, who is the statesman. He gives the law and enforces them.

Only Socrates, Plato and Aristotle solved the educational way to the problem of social unity, for only they understood what the education was for. But the credit must go to Protagoras for throwing in an idea of how to build society from the state of nature, which culminated via Socrates and Plato into the Aristotelian theory of community based on non-*homo faber* personality of man, an idea, which was not available to the sophists.

No doubt, Protagoras knows that virtue of self-restraint and a sense of justice are necessary for making a society, and *nomoi* are the guidelines laid down to teach people the limits within which they move so that social unity is possible, yet when it came to teaching the political *arête* or political art he advocated personal success in acquiring power as the goal of education. The inconsistency between the two, i.e. on the one hand, education in success, in acquiring power and, on the other, education in *nomos*, *arête* of self-restraint and *dike* will be resolved only in renaissance in Europe when Machiavelli will make a distinction between the virtue of rulers and the civic virtue of the citizens. If we use Machiavelli's distinction then it turns out that Protagoras himself is the educator of rulers who will use supreme violence — if need be the violence, may be in the form of killing — but the rulers will be the educators of people to teach them *nomos* and *arete* in self-restraint and *dike* through use of force if need be.

But how does Havelock see Protagoras as a liberal? According to Havelock, if historians of philosophy are to interpret the writings of sophists correctly, they must overcome their prejudice against the sophists, especially against those of the first generation at any rate, of seeing them as primarily rhetoricians owning no principle other than commitment to their own cleverness or advantage. For Havelock, this prejudice is due to a caricature of sophists of Aristophanes' imagination, which is further reinforced by the broad farce with which, in some of his dialogues, Plato has sought to reduce them to the absurd. He exhorts interpreters to understand the true inwardness of the *dissoi logoi* of which Protagoras was reputedly the earliest practitioner. According to Havelock, far from contravening the first principles of logic and morals, the *dissoi logoi* are merely a legitimate and practical device subservient to a tolerant and democratic ideal, that of discussing every issue pro and contra.

His argument is based on his interpretation of Protagoras, Prodicus, and Hippias, in Plato's dialogue the *Protagoras*, as political liberals devoted to the democratic ideal. But he does not arrive at this view after giving an interpretation of Plato's *Protagoras*, rather he reads the Platonic dialogue with the assumption that Protagoras is a thoroughgoing naturalist and liberal. In consequence, all deviations from the approved and admired norm ascribed to him in the dialogue are due to Platonic misrepresentation.[48] Thus, Havelock takes Protagoras' promise, as reported in the dialogue, to make his pupils better able to attend their own and the city's interest, not as an ill-founded and extravagant claim, for that is only Plato's devaluation of sophists' claim, but as the general statement of a responsible programme of education for democracy, which, when placed in the context of the liberal tradition, reveals an unexpected depth.[49]

---

48. Havelock, *The Liberal Temper in Greek Politics*, p. 165.
49. Ibid., pp. 166-67.

Similarly where Platonic Socrates charge Protagoras with employing long and digressive speeches, Havelock assumes that the accusation must be false, since it is out of line with the liberal programme, which seeks to improve opinion by eliciting and combining alternative views. Protagoras must have been equipped with an irreproachably liberal technique of leading group discussions and an active interest in developing the most fruitful parliamentary procedure to govern discussion. So, to present Protagoras in the role of shifty rhetorician was again just one of Plato's defamatory tricks.

More fundamentally Havelock's understanding of liberalism is not without problems. According to Havelock, Greek liberalism is characterized by a pragmatic and empirical approach to knowledge, a "historical" (i.e. evolutionary) view of society, a contract theory of the state, a measured commitment to equalitarianism, and a claim for "philanthropy and goodwill as instinctual principles of social order." When one investigates the particular analysis of some of the liberals' positions doubts begin to surface. We have already examined the contract theory of state. Maybe Havelock himself is in doubt for the claims that liberalism views society as "natural."[50] An interpretation of liberalism that views society as "natural" will dismay those students of political theory who view the tradition, from Hobbes and Locke forward, as being based on an interpretation of society and government as artificial creations of men. Havelock's suggestion that the Sophistic argument posits a "common mind" or "common judgement,"[51] that liberal democracy implies a "meeting of minds" on the substance of public policy,[52] that it emphasizes fundamental goodwill among men[53] goes counter to the liberal understanding that the locus of rationality is the individual, and as rational

50. Havelock, *The Liberal Temper in Greek Politics*, p. 401.

51. Ibid., pp. 201, 247.

52. Ibid., pp. 236, 313.

53. Ibid., pp. 343, 349.

individuals come inevitably into conflict and this is the inevitable reason for the establishment of the institutions of political authority by individuals. Havelock here fails to appreciate that as a political theory liberalism is not only a theory of freedom but also a theory of authority as well. Havelock's claim that the liberal position cannot accept any social form as "theoretically final, complete, or correct" because "if such existed, it would represent the completion of man's hedonist drives; but these are still evolving"[54] goes against the attempt of liberal thinkers from Hobbes to Rawls to arrive at such final visions.

Vijay Tankha also sees Sophists' interest in rhetoric related to democracy. He writes,

> The founders of rhetoric are said to be Corax and Tisias of Sicily who invented a system designed to aid in civil litigation. Notice that from its very inception rhetoric, or forensic rhetoric as it later came to be called, is designed to fulfil democratic needs.[55]

It may be noted Tankha here is confusing civil litigation with democratic needs. Similarly, he elaborates,

> Newly constituted democracies with written codes and procedures gave to the citizenry a voice that was likely to have been muffled if not entirely smothered by both the monarchies and aristocracies that proceeded and competed with the new democratic forms of government. This new freedom of speech permitted a wholescale questioning of traditional values and norms on the one hand while demanding skills in debate and argument on the other. We find both these features in thought and practice of individual Sophists. The Sophists are sometimes grouped on the basis of whether they are ethical theorists or whether they teach political oratory or rhetoric as a means to practical success. These two features were used by their contemporaries to distinguish them. We might see Protagoras

54. Havelock, *The Liberal Temper in Greek Politics*, p. 379.

55. Vijay Tankha, *Ancient Greek Philosophy: Thales to Gorgias* (Dorling Kindersley (India) Pvt. Ltd. 2006), pp. 295-96.

> as an example of the former, Gorgias as an example of the latter. . . .[56]

But in the very next paragraph he further clarifies why the democracies needed rhetoric.

> . . . Litigation seemed to be part of the body politic in most of the democratic city-states. The ability to persuade a jury or a mass of citizens in these theatres was, therefore, essential to success in the political life of the city. Skilled speech or argument . . . was thus viewed as the single most valuable asset a young man could acquire. This is the skill these thinkers offered to teach. . . ."[57]

In these two passages there is no disentangling of democracy and litigation. Protagoras's *Dissoi Logoi* and Gorgias' *Economium of Helen* and *Defence of Palamedes* as models of rhetorical style of speeches are more suitable for the context of litigation than the context of arriving at a consensus in assemblies of democracies. Similarly, sophists' technique of argumentation on the basis of probabilities or likelihood is more relevant to the context of litigation than building consensus in democratic assemblies. Emotional appeal in large assemblies, for example, tearful speeches to arouse pity for old age and poverty refer not to democratic assemblies to arrive at consensus but large assembly of people in the context of litigation. So unless one is confusing democracy with litigation the rhetoric of the Sophists cannot be taken as exhibiting the liberal democratic spirit of the Sophists. We must keep in mind the fact that the word *demokratia* after the fifth century changed its meaning so that it could be applied ultimately to any republican government, no matter how oligarchic. When the word *"demos"* was adopted to designate the sovereign people in the records of votes in the assembly as early as the middle of the fifth century, Athens undoubtedly had manhood suffrage giving the vote to all adult male citizens. But it was not the case that all states in which

---

56. Vijay Tankha, op. cit., p. 296.

57. Ibid.

the government was a *demokratia* and in which the sovereign people was called the *demos* possessed manhood suffrage. Undoubtedly, the "reforming" of democracy by limiting the rights of the lower classes directly or indirectly was common and began at Athens very soon after the restoration of democracy in 403 BCE. A result was that *demokratia* ultimately was applied to any republican government. The change in the meaning of *demokratia* is not very difficult to understand if it is borne in mind that the word means rule by the *demos* and that such rule need not necessarily involve manhood suffrage. The early meaning of *demos* was "country" or "land," but afterwards *demos* was applied to the people of the countryside, and, since the people of the countryside were largely poor, the word came to mean the people of the lower classes and this meaning was prevalent even in the fifth-century BCE Greece. Not only the meaning of democracy in Greece but also the common understanding of freedom prevalent in Greece needs to be taken into account before declaring the early Sophists as liberal democrats. The common Greek view of freedom prevalent in Greece was such that freedom for oneself tended to include the right to dominate others. It was this spirit of freedom for oneself but not for others which was largely responsible for the failure of Greek movements for unity. This conception of freedom is quite consistent with *homo faber* conception of man of Sophists, but it can hardly make them liberal.

Despite talk of *nomos, arête* of self-restraint and *dike* what the sophists were advocating was education in success in acquiring power without any scruples regarding virtue of justice, self control, etc. The best example of Sophist morality is given by Thrasymachus, the sophist *rhetor*, in the *Republic* of Plato when he blurts out the undisguized thesis that justice is the advantage of the stronger, i.e. of those who rule.[58] He explains that whatever be the form of government — tyranny, aristocracy or democracy — the ruling

58. Plato, *The Republic*, 338c.

power legislates laws with a view to their own benefit. By legislating these laws, they declare that to be right for their subjects which is beneficial to themselves, and punish whoever departs from them as law-breaker and wrongdoer. Justice in all states is the same, namely what benefits the established government. Since the government holds the power, justice everywhere is what benefits the strong.

In the refutation of this thesis of Thrasymachus by Socrates, however, it becomes apparent that if this means that the ruler seeks his advantage by using that which he sets up as just as a means, the possibility indeed remains that he can be mistaken about what is truly to his advantage. The gap between the ends and means opens up the possibility of having chosen the wrong means harming the ends. Hence, in the present instance, since justice is the means, justice would become something, which harms the one who rules.[59] To remove this possibility the gap between the means and end has to be closed. Hence, if the ruler really understands how to rule, he does not at all understand his *own* advantage but only what is advantageous for ruling. [60]

The deeper truth that this discussion discloses is that if the virtue of justice for those who *are ruled* is to be the advantage of those *who do the ruling* then for those who are ruled it is an alien advantage, the advantage of someone else who himself does not hold to what is just. Justice is what is to the advantage of the unjust. So the definition of justice as the advantage of the stronger provides no answer at all to the question of what justice is in essence and what justice means to the one who tries to live according to it. This definition says only that it is to the advantage of the tyrant, i.e. the one who violates what is just with impunity and that everybody else continues to adhere to the code of justice. This means, however, that justice amounts to *naiveté*.[61] The

---

59. Ploto, The Rebublic, 339b-e.

60. Gadamer, pp. 80-81.

61. *The Republic*, 341c.

hollowness of this position is now clear. What is said to be just, the advantage of the stronger, is only just when it is not taken to be what it really is, i.e. not taken to be the advantage of the stronger but taken to be "just." Hence, a justice which is postulated and advocated using mere power as its rationalization cannot suffice to explain why what is based on power is valid as *just* and not merely as what is coerced. One may add that the founding of justice in power would be conceivable only if what was so founded was just for the one who rules as well as for those ruled, and if his power was thus not his but the rightful power of the state to enforce what is just for all.[62]

What Thrasymachus develops as justice thus contains no real answer to the question of what the essence of justice is. Rather it is only an implicit declaration of his rejection of justice. At this stage of discussion the argument that justice is true prudence and virtue, genuine strength and real happiness[63] also evades the question of what justice is in essence. A failure to define its essence, in spite of this glorification of merits of justice, gives this first conclusion of the discussion a negative and tentative character.[64] According to Gadamer,

> And the very failure of the discussion to define justice shows us how accurate Plato was in his characterization of the existing state as decadent. What began as mere ignorance of the just order in society and ignorance of justice as the power in the soul which sustains that social order, has now developed into a total perversion of justice.[65]

Or is this the sovereign instance of Plato's tendentious distortion of sophistic thought, which Havelock thinks he has discovered in the contrast between the brutal cynicism of the Platonic Thrasymachus[66] and the sweet reasonableness and democratic

---

62. Gadamer, pp. 80-81.
63. *The Republic*, 349-54.
64. Ibid., 354a ff.
65. Gadamer, p. 81.
66. *The Republic*, book I.

liberalism of the Thrasymachus who presents himself "without the aid of Plato's ventriloquism" in a substantial surviving fragment of a "parliamentary discourse"?[67] Does Havelock succeed in his redemption of Thrasymachus, on the grounds that he was in reality a profound and liberal advocate of the basic reasonableness of the common mind? Is Havelock's interpretation of the speech which has come down to us as fragment of Thrasymachus correct? In Havelock's interpretation the speech in question is meant for use in an actual debate in the Athenian Assembly. But one can equally plausibly argue that it is just a model designed for disciples. But Havelock denies it without any evidence. Havelock also assumes that the views expressed in the speech are Thrasymachus' own. But this in itself is a quite dubious assumption. Anyhow Havelock gives high honour to the sophist on the ground that the speech is calling upon a bitterly divided Assembly to "come to terms with itself by a negotiation of opinion," and that it embodies the "assumption that beneath the division and confusion . . . there exists a common mind waiting to be evoked by the processes of reasoned inquiry and careful debate." Thrasymachus, he says, in clinging "to the belief in the capacity of a democratic assembly . . . to find agreement even on the most perilous issues," gives "precise testimony" to those "parliamentary postulates" with which he believes the sophists are to be credited. But when one reads the speech, it is disappointing as one fails to find such high parliamentary liberal democratic views in it. Only by very special pleading can one discover an appeal to what Havelock is meaning by a "negotiation of opinion" and the "parliamentary postulates." What one finds there is that only a speaker is advocating the adoption of the famous "Constitution of our Fathers," a form of "democracy." But, Havelock knows, that "democracy" in Athens was popular in oligarchic circles. So, in advocating it, the speaker can hardly be said, as Havelock does say, to be turning "his back on the past." True, the speaker commends his proposal as the rational means for achieving that

67. Thrasymachus, *The Liberal Temper in Greek Politics*, p. 231.

"concord" which both democrats and oligarchs desire, even as the unconscious common aims of both. But this is only a mere dogmatic claim. There is no suggestion that agreements on specific constitutional points of difference are to be reached by mutual concession and equitable compromise. Only a readymade suit is presented, together with a solemn assertion that it will fit the shoulders of two very different men. If this is democracy, it is that form of it which demagogues and supersalesmen most frequently accept. Havelock believes in Thrasymachus almost instinctively, repelling, for example, the suggestion that the speech at a deeper level may harbour oligarchic sympathies by the untroubled assertion that it "does not fit . . . with . . . [the] non-partisan quality [of the speech], its air of objectivity, its plea for clarity of thinking." But the fact is that we cannot know from this speech what were the real views of its author, and that it cannot be used, therefore, to measure the correctness of Plato's picture of Thrasymachus. Havelock's supposed independent source of knowledge of the sophists' views appears to fail.

I have tried to show in my essay, "The Foundations of Modern Liberalism: Inscription of Art and Morality in the Perspective of Modern Metaphysics"[68] that the liberal vision of society is based on the *homo faber* conception of man, yet the liberal vision cannot be made actual by *homo faber*. That is to say, liberalism harbours a contradiction. Thinkers like Havelock are guided unconsciously by the first part of this thesis in their interpretation of sophists but remain oblivious of the second part. It was the second aspect of liberalism which was actually operating in the sophist thought as brought out by Plato's dialogues. It was this contradiction which played itself out subverting the first through the overworking of the second in the sophist minds. Even if Havelock is granted his premise that there existed in Athens during the fifth and fourth centuries a highly defensible and influential liberal-naturalistic

68. See B.K. Agarawal, "The Foundations of Modern Liberalism: Inscription of Art And Morality in the Perspective of Modern Metaphysics", *Journal of Indian Council of Philosophical Research*, vol. XVIII, no. 4, October–December 2001.

political vision; one cannot agree with his view that Plato's and Aristotle's political theories, through distortions and misdescriptions and after they had capitalized on certain aspects of the liberal tradition, choked it with the subtleties of critical assimilation. Rather they brought out what was inherent in the sophist temper.

With the entry of two brothers of Plato into the dialogue at the beginning of book 2 of the *Republic* the questioning moves to another level setting off from what has preceded it. Even someone who does not consider justice good in itself but, given his fear of suffering injustice, holds it to be lesser of two evils, can see in practice justice is preferable to injustice. Thus out of prudence and the knowledge of how weak he is by himself, each individual may enter into an agreement or contract with others which will establish what is right and assure that injustice is valued (358e).[69]

Even though this theory of justice seems to be both politically and pedagogically realistic and even appeals to the modern mind, the positive evaluation of justice is only conditional, for it obviously depends on correctly assessing how the conflict between powers will be resolved. Hence, it is not valid in itself but only relative to what might emerge in that conflict.[70]

Plato's Socratic insight was that a binding political ethos, which would assure the proper application and interpretation of poetry, no longer existed once sophism had come to define the sprit of education. Although the sophists' education sought to inculcate justice and the virtue of the political man, Socrates succeeded in uncovering the real content and dogma of their new ethos. For the sophists, justice is only the conventions of the weak which protect the interests of the latter. For the sophists, ethical principles are no longer valid in themselves. Rather they became the only form of our mutual "keeping an eye" on one another. In Gadamer's words, "The 'just' is that by means of which one person can assert

69. Gadamer, pp. 81-82.

70. Ibid., p. 82.

himself against another with help from everyone else and, as such, it is adhered to only out of mutual distrust and fear. It is not the justice intrinsic and internal to me myself. All the many variations of the sophists' theory of justice are alike in providing a "foundation" for justice. And whether the sophists conceive of themselves as conservative or revolutionary, indeed even when the sophists think that they are giving a foundation to the authority of civil law, in principle they have already perverted the sense of justice. As judges of justice they fail to acknowledge it even if they "acquit" it. Thus Callicles' and Thrasymachus' declaration that might make right only serves to disclose the mentality which prevails in all sophism: *No one does what is right voluntarily.*"[71]

Not only "*No one does what is right voluntarily*" came to be believed but it also became a reality in sophist movement. Realists like Thucydides, Antiphon and others testify the amorality of power struggle through which tyranny came to be based. They were not only advocating their own amorality but also describing the prevailing mentality at the time of sophist movement. According to Guthrie,

> Thucydides had an impressive insight into the minds of his fellow-Greeks" and "it is remarkable how seldom his orators, aiming at persuasion, see any point in appealing to considerations of right, justice or other normally accepted moral standards: it is taken for granted that only an appeal to self-interest is likely to succeed.[72]

Let us listen to the emerging traits of Greek personality in the words of Thucydides himself (3.82):

> War, destroying the ease of everyday life, is a violent schoolmaster, and assimilates most men's tempers to the conditions around them . . . the customary values of words were

---

71. Gadamer, "Plato and the Poets", *Dialogue and Dialectic: Eight Hermeneutical Studies on Plato*, Eng. trans. P. Christopher Smith, (New Haven and London: Yale University Press, 1980), p. 50.

72. Guthrie, *A History of Greek Philosophy*, vol. III, p. 85.

> changed as men claimed the right to use them as they pleased to justify their actions: an unreasoning daring was called courage and loyalty to party, a prudent delay specious cowardice; moderation and self-control came to be reckoned but the cloak of timidity, to have an understanding of the whole to be everywhere unwilling to act. . . . Applause, in a word, went to one who got in first with some evil act, and to him who cheered on another to attempt some crime that he was not thinking of.[73]

Machiavellian perspective — that only success in obtaining the wished for outcome matters and morality of actions is irrelevant or is only a means to a desired outcome — for the emerging *homo faber* personality of Greeks is best illustrated by what Guthrie calls "the most famous example" of the discussion which Thucydides represents as being held between Athenian envoys and the small island of Melos, which the Athenian wished to force into their confederacy (5.85-III). According to Guthrie's account of the discussion reported by Thucydides:

> The Athenians begin by saying that they will neither use moral arguments nor expect them from the Melians, because both sides know that by human standards *justice* depends on equality of power: the strong do what they can and the weak submit. Very well, say the Melians (ch.90). To confine ourselves, as you wish, to considerations of *interest* (το ένμφέρον) rather than *justice*, we claim that it is useful (χρήστμον) as a general principle that those in danger should meet with fairness and justice (τα εικότα και δίκατα) — a principle that you yourselves may need to invoke some time . . . (98). Since you forbid us to talk of *justice*, and bid us give in to your *interest* (ένμφόρω), we will tell you what is good (χρήστμον) for us, and, if it agrees with your interests, try to persuade you.[74]

That a tyrannical solution, based on pure power, to the problem of social unity among *homo faber*s was emerging in the sophist

---

73. Thucydides, quoted by Guthrie, *A History of Greek Philosophy*, vol. III, pp. 84-85.

74. Guthrie, *A History of Greek Philosophy*, vol. III, pp. 85-86.

period is testified by realists as well as the supporters of *physis*. The story of the Athenians persuading the Melians continues:

> Later however (ch. 104) the Melians do venture to introduce moral considerations, claiming that in spite of their weakness they may hope for divine favour because they stand for right against injustice (όσιοι προς ον δικαίονς). The Athenians retort that this is unrealistic:
>
> Our belief about the gods, and certain knowledge about men, is that universally, by *natural* necessity (νπο φνσεως αναγκαίας), he who is superior rules. We did not make this law (νόμον). . . . We merely use it and shall leave it to exist for ever. You would do the same in our position. . . . Nor will the Spartans help you. More than any others they equate pleasant with good and *interest* with *justice*.[75]

It is interesting to note that the essence of sophism, which Thucydides reported and Plato wanted to overcome in his dialogues, has shaped the modern perspective more than the views of Plato himself.

Even Pericles told the Athenians frankly that they held their empire "like a tyranny."[76] Be it noted that since Greeks had no notion of free will, they did not elaborate any idea of absolute will or sovereignty. But the people felt the absolute power that was emerging purportedly to unite the society and they called it "tyranny."

Sophist Gorgias says (*Hel*. 6, DK, II, 290):

> It is not in nature for the strong to be thwarted by the weaker, but for the weaker to be ruled and led by the stronger, for the strong to lead and the weak to follow.[77]

Similarly upholders of *physis* declare what is the nature that has grown now that man has turned into *homo faber* and social unity is

---

75. Guthrie, *A History of Greek Philosophy*, vol. III, p. 86.

76. Ibid.

77. Ibid., p. 99.

broken. Plato in his *Gorgias* attributes the view to Callicles which he summarizes in the *Laws* in the words (890a):

> These views are held by men who say that the height of justice is a conquest won by force. Hence young men fall into irreligion, as if there were no gods such as the law enjoins us to believe in. Hence, too, outbreaks of civil discord as men are attracted to the "right life according to nature," which plainly expressed means a life of domination over one's fellows and refusal to serve others as law and custom (*nomos*) demand.[78]

It is fairly a good account of what is the condition that prevails when men become *homo fabers*. No doubt, Plato wants to decry this. But it is an accurate account of what was happening at that time in Greek world and of course Callicles was convinced that rule of the stronger and hence tyranny is the only solution to the problem of social unity in such condition.

When *homo faber* personality of man came to the fore during sophist period and consistent with *homo faber* personality tyrannical solution to the problem of social unity — i.e. shaping a social unity by the strength and power of one man — was emerging, Greek mind was uneasy with this solution. Theseus in Euripides' Suppl. 429ff, says:

> A city has no greater enemy than a tyrant, under whom in the first place there are no common laws, but one man rules having taken the law into his own possession. There is no fairness in this. But under written laws justice is meted out impartially to the feeble and wealthy, the weaker if slandered may speak on equal terms with the prosperous, and the lesser man prevails against the greater if his cause is just.

Here the Greek mind is trying to solve the problem of controlling the tyrant by written laws. The solution was that the ruler himself, discovering the law with apophantic agreement of the people, write it down for the city. But it must be kept in mind that he is

78. Guthrie, *A History of Greek Philosophy*, vol. III, pp. 101-102.

not making laws in contractual agreement with the public. This explains the question raised earlier why the sophists elaborated a theory of discovery and legislation of laws by rulers and apophantic agreement on law by public.

The solution of the problem of control of tyrannical power presupposes the prior existence of social order from whose ethos the law is discovered by apophantic agreement of people, but sophists had no conceptual tool to account for the prior belongingness of man to city. Be it noted the solution proposed undercuts the very premise on which tyranny is erected. Tyranny came into being starting from the fact that there was no social unity as *homo fabers* cannot make a social unity without being tyrannized by one man.

Similarly, no doubt, sophists tried to theorize about the unwritten laws, which existed to be discovered by rulers in apophantic agreement of citizens to write them down, yet they had no proper conceptual tools to account for them. Since the being of the laws presupposes prior belongingness to society it is inconsistent with their main philosophical idea that man is a *homo faber* and society is constructed from the state of nature by the supreme power of one man, the tyrant.

So the sophists had to account for prior existence of unwritten laws in a different way without presupposing prior belongingness to society. According to Guthrie, "In the tragic poets . . . the unwritten laws are unequivocally of divine origin, the 'unwritten ordinances of the gods' in whose name Antigone defies the power of King Creon." In Sophocles again, a chorus of the *Oedipus Tyrannus* (863ff.) speaks of holiness in words and deeds "for which laws are appointed on high, brought to life in the clear air of heaven, whose father is Olympus alone, fem, nor will forgetfulness ever put them to sleep." Metaphorically, these unwritten laws may be said to have been "written by the gods," as when Ion in Euripides's play rebukes Apollo for his sin against a mortal woman (440ff.): how can it be right for the gods, who have written the laws for mortals, themselves to disobey them? In Aeschylus, respect for parents (cited as one of the unwritten laws in the conversation between Socrates and Hippias) is described by a chorus as "written in the statutes (θεσμίοτς) of Diké (Justice) highest in honour."[79]

Both Kant and Hobbes had to fall back on the idea of God to limit the sovereign, and they had to admit, in spite of their secular outlook, the existence of God on moral grounds. The same thing now we see happening much earlier in the age of Sophists. Sophists, by and large, were either agnostic like Protagoras or atheist like Diagoras, Prodicus, and Critias. So this falling back on gods to account for the unwritten laws invited some such remark of Critias in his Sisyphus (fr. 25.9 ff.):

> Then when the laws prevented men from open deeds of violence, but they continued to commit them in secret, I believe that a man of shrewd and subtle mind invented for men the fear of the gods, so that there might be something to frighten the wicked even if they acted, spoke or thought in secret. From this motive he introduced the conception of divinity. There is, he said, a spirit enjoying endless life, hearing and seeing with his mind, exceedingly wise and all-observing, bearer of divine nature. He will hear everything spoken among men and can see everything that is done. If you are silently plotting evil, it will not be hidden from the gods, so clever are they. With this story he presented the most seductive of teachings, concealing the truth with lying words. For a dwelling he gave them the place whose mention would most powerfully strike the hearts of men, whence, as he knew, fears come to mortals and help for their wretched lives; that is, the vault above, where he perceived the lightnings and the dread roars of thunder, and the starry face and form of heaven fair-wrought by the cunning craftsmanship of time; whence too the burning meteor makes its way, and the liquid rain descends on the earth. With such fears did he surround mankind, and so by his story give the godhead a fair home in a fitting place, and extinguished lawlessness by his ordinances. . . . So, I

79. Guthrie, *A History of Greek Philosophy*, vol. III, pp. 120-21.

> think, first of all, did someone persuade men to believe that there exists a race of gods.[80]

Religion as a political invention to ensure good behaviour was the Machiavellian solution of political religion. This Machiavellian solution was presented in a little less Machiavellian way by Hobbes in his *Leviathan*, and in a completely sanitized way — so that no trace of Machiavellianism is visible — by Kant. But this solution fails, as there was no place for god in a metaphysics which is the basis of man's *homo faber* personality, yet God is needed for good behaviour so it remains a mere fiction (or Ideal according to Kant) without any reality.

So the problem of the existence of unwritten laws had to be solved not by God but by bringing in the idea of prior belongingness to the city, an idea that eluded sophists. Plato realized it in his *Laws*. He writes,

> All that we are now discussing [says the Athenian (793a)] is what people in general call "unwritten laws" [αγραφα νόμιμα], and all such injunctions amount to what they call the "laws of our ancestors" [πατρίους νόμους]. And what we said recently, that one should neither call them laws nor yet pass them over, was well said. They are the bonds that hold a political society together, links between laws already on the statute book and those still to be enacted, in truth a body of ancestral and age-old precepts which if rightly conceived and put into practice protect and safeguard the written laws of the time, but if they swerve from the right path they cause everything to collapse like a building when the builder's supports give way. With this in mind we must bind your new city together with everything possible that goes by the name of law, custom or usage.[81]

So the unwritten laws turn out to be customs or usages of ancestors

---

80. Critias, cited in Guthrie, *A History of Greek Philosophy*, vol. III , 199, pp. 243-44.

81. Plato, cited in Guthrie, *A History of Greek Philosophy*, vol. III, 199, p. 122.

which presuppose a continued unity of society in time for Plato. It is the bond of society that appears as *nomos* for Plato. But to account for this prior belongingness Plato had to dismantle the entire sophist's edifice of philosophy based on *homo faber* personality. He had to turn man into a non-*homo faber* person.

Aristotle solved the problem of what it means for the unwritten laws to exist. In Guthrie's words, "Aristotle first equates unwritten with universal laws, and then calls universal laws 'according to nature' (*Rhet*. 1368b7, 1373b6, 1375a32)."[82] But to solve the problem of existence of unwritten laws Aristotle had to take man as essentially a political and social animal so that he is not a subjective individual. For this he had to dismantle the basis of sophistic philosophy. The ground for this was prepared by Socrates, which Aristotle received through the teachings of Plato.

The ground for answering the question: What it means to belong to society? is prepared by Socrates, on which both Plato and Aristotle built their political philosophies. But they also failed to stem the tide unleashed by the sophists and the Greek *polis* declined irrevocably.

---

82. Guthrie, *A History of Greek Philosophy*, vol. III, p. 118.

CHAPTER 10

The Needs Principle

Tariq Islam

BRIAN Barry refers to a recent sociological study on twelve American families in his polemical work *Why Social Justice Matters*. The study expectantly shows that social class position of parents determines the school success of children and consequently their ultimate life chances. He then goes on to point out that,

> . . . people's chances of falling and rising from their location at birth in the social order have declined in the last twenty years to such a degree that some sociologists have begun to talk about "social closure."[1]

We in India have a longer experience of the phenomena with the caste system with virtually no social mobility. The American experience has been intensified by the lack of debate on social and political philosophy and therefore the lack of pre-emptive steps. It was as recent as 1966 when Richard Wollheim wrote an article defending the possibility of political philosophy as a serious intellectual discipline.[2] Wollheim stressed that no major work in the dominant analytic Anglo-American tradition of political philosophy has been produced since 1930s due to the prevalent opinion that work in the traditional area of political philosophy was not possible. Political philosophers hailed a revival of their subject with the publication in 1971 of John Rawls' *A Theory of Justice*. The revival re-orientated political philosophy and the

---

1. Brian Barry, *Why Social Justice Matters, Polity* (2005), p. 15.
2. Richard Wollheim, "On the theory of democracy", in Bernard Williams and Alan Montefiore (eds.), *British Analytical Philosophy*, (London: Routledge and Kegan Paul, 1967), pp. 247-66.

contemporary parameters of liberty, equality, welfare, and social justice, that are primarily the conceptual tools used to assess government policies, entered the discourse. The major shift was towards consideration of social justice as a major concern of political and social philosophy. The reactions were many and varied, even to the extent that the very notion of social justice was rejected as being meaningless, religious, self-contradictory, and ideological. It was contended that realization of any degree of social justice is not feasible and that an attempt to do so may destroy all liberty. It has been argued that the purported goal of social justice is to eliminate economic inequities, which are largely due to individual choices and as such can only be managed by imposing controls. One such example, if not entirely so, is Hayek. In fact, under the influence of Hayek's thesis and the adoption of neo-liberal policies the effort to install this new discourse was blunted and resisted in practice. There was a complete rejection of the notion of "social justice" by Hayek, who asserted that "social justice" is simply a semantic fraud originating from the same discourse from where the phrase "People's Democracy" has come.

This article is a modest attempt to initially offer some brief introductory remarks on the issue. It will then proceed with outlining the Marxist perspective on the notion of "rights," which that tradition understands as bourgeois. The essay will pass on to Marx's criticism of the notion of fairness as being confined to a mode of production. It then will present in an intertwined manner the needs principle found in Marx, the solitary problem in the popular imagination with regard to the principle together with a very brief conclusion of the advantage in adopting the principle.

The notion of distributive justice concerned with allocation of goods in a society has been around since antiquity, which can be contrasted with juridical procedures that concentrate on maintenance of juridical relations. Rawls rightly assesses the problem encountered with juridical procedures,

> There is . . . a general presumption against imposing legal and other restrictions on conduct without sufficient reason. But this

> presumption creates no special priority for any particular liberty.[3]

However, the liberties, Rawls emphasizes, are freedom of thought; liberty of conscience, affecting social relationships instilled through philosophy, morality and religion; political liberties, constituting representative democratic institutions and freedom of expression, including the press; freedom of association; all liberties required to maintain liberty, dignity and integrity of persons, such as freedom to choose one's occupation, etc.; and finally all the rights and liberties enshrined under rule of law. The view is not restricted to Rawls alone; many others, like H.G. Wells, presume that human beings have a value system that has as its basis the equal entitlement to the respect of their fellow-men — the implication is that what we witness today is a distorted version of the actual value system.

Rawls echoing Kant proposes that,

> Each person possesses an inviolability founded on justice that even the welfare of society as a whole cannot override. For this reason justice denies that the loss of freedom for some is made right by a greater good shared by others.[4]

He re-emphasizes his views to see the society,

> . . . as a fair system of co-operation over time, from one generation to the next.[5]

However, this overrides the criteria of need as a principle of social justice and simply prefers liberties to sharing the goods produced by the society on the basis of needs.

The notion of social justice is primarily concerned with the concept of society which is just in all respects. The concern is not

---

3. J. Rawls, *A Theory of Justice* (Harward: Harvard Press, 1971), pp. 291-92.
4. Ibid., p. 3.
5. J. Rawls, *Political Liberalism* (New York: Columbia University Press, 1993), p. 14.

simply with distribution but with the principles of a just society where distribution would follow in a just manner that affords individuals and groups a fair treatment and just share of the benefits and burdens of society. The sharing of the burden of society is important to ensure that no preferential treatment is afforded to any individual or group. The recent assertions of Hayekian neo-liberal polices with its lack of welfare measures, dismantling of public service sectors and stress on free market economy have in a dialectical process brought the notion of social justice to focus resulting in an upsurge of interest in it. The growing awareness of social and economic factors has pushed distributive justice to the peripheries and social justice has captured the centrestage of moral political discourse. Adam Swift dates this shift to have started around 1850 and remarks,

> It developed only as philosophers came to see society's key social and economic institutions, which critically determine the distribution of benefits and burdens as a proper object for moral and political investigation.[6]

It should not be lost sight of that the basic societal structures differ in social, economic, and political institutions, both at the formal and informal level, from society to society. The requirements of social justice therefore vary too, for instance a religiously homogeneous society may not require enshrining freedom of religion. Any theory of social justice is a negotiation between three clearly demarcated criteria — rights, deserts (fairness — the most popularly held view), and needs. The three criteria compete for the moral ground of constructing the just basis of society. However, no serious philosopher has ever denied anyone of these elements; they have only differed on the stress or juxtaposed different combinations of the criteria related to their ideological bents, but primarily within a democratic norm of governance. The Right and the conservatives have stressed the notion of free market economy with equality of opportunity,

6. Adam Swift, *Political Philosophy*, 2nd edn. (Polity Press, 2006), p. 9.

philanthropy and charity. The post-modernists have argued that there cannot be a universal principle of reason. The Left has talked of economic egalitarianism with the adoption of a policy of progressive taxation, income and property redistribution. The commonality between philosophers of different bent is that they all tend to ignore the needs principle or at best attach the principle as dependent on some other principle. David Miller in his book, *Social Justice*, has rightly pointed out:

> To claim that the concepts of rights and deserts form conceptually legitimate criteria for applying the idea of justice is hardly controversial. Although some thinkers have adopted, as a substantive moral view, the position that needs and needs alone should form the basis for a just distribution of resources, these thinkers have not (to my knowledge) ever claimed that other views were conceptually improper. In the case of the concept of need, however, matters are different. *An influential minority view* in political philosophy is that, conceptually speaking, needs have nothing to do with the concept of justice. To use needs as a basis for just distribution is not so much morally reprehensible as conceptually confused. (Italics in the original.)[7]

The reason for ignoring the needs principle is because primarily it is identified with the Marxian outlook. The dominant allergy to Marxism takes a precedence to form the basis of rejection of the needs principle. The criticism of justice present in Marx leads to the requirement of the needs principle as the principle which will be the basis of the possible form of society. The envisaged society will not be based on scarcity and therefore not on competitiveness prevalent in any capitalist mode of production. However, this should not be understood to mean the ignoring of other criteria. Marx and Marxists are identified with a struggle to protect and demand workers' rights, the free press, universal suffrage, etc. which form the corpus of basic civil rights. But beyond this Marx criticizes the concept of right in the context of justice and refers to

---

7. David Miller, *Social Justice* (Oxford: Clarendon Press, 1979), p. 122.

it as ". . . ideological nonsense . . . so common among the democrats and French socialists." In his essay "On the Jewish Question" he condemns rights as,

> . . . nothing but the rights of a member of civil society, i.e. the rights of egoistic man, of man separated from other men and the community.[8]

The theme is further emphasized in "The Holy Family,"

> It was shown that the recognition of the rights of man by the modern state has no other meaning than the recognition of slavery by the state of antiquity. . . .[9]

Marx is clear in his specifications and elaborates his stand,

> It is, therefore, right of inequality, in its content, like every right. Right by its very nature can consist only in the application of an equal standard; but unequal individuals (and they would not be different individuals if they were not unequal) are measurable only by an equal standard insofar as they are brought under an equal point of view, are considered in one particular aspect only, for instance, in the present case, are regarded only as workers and nothing more is seen in them, everything else being ignored. . . . To avoid all these defects, rights instead of being equal would have to be unequal.[10]

Marxian analysis of right depicts it basically as the bourgeois right based on abstraction and perpetuation of inequality in the guise of equality in law. The abstraction and the effort to universalize the right of the individual by liberal philosophy ignore the differences of individuals — a complaint not registered only by the Marxists but for different reasons also by post-modernists

---

8. Karl Marx, "On the Jewish Question", *Marx and Engels Collected Works* vol. III, p. 162.
9. Karl Marx and Fredrick Engels, "The Holy Family", *Marx and Engels Collected Works*, vol. IV, p. 133.
10. Karl Marx, "Critique of the Gotha Programme", *Selected Works*, vol. II, p. 24.

and feminists. Moore has rightly pointed out that a social system is inequitable to the extent that it regulates through general rules which cannot ". . . consider all the aspects in which individuals differ from one another. To apply such rules entails applying the same standard to different cases."[11]

The needs principle, however, is as old as 1850, when, as mentioned by Adam Swift, awareness of social and economic factors of society started to surface. Marx had argued for determining the distribution of the benefits of the society on the basis of this principle. Miller rightly assumes that

> . . . egalitarians [primarily Marxists] are committed to the view that justice consists (minimally) in a distribution of resources according to need, and that this forms a primary part of their conception of equality."[12]

However, the Marxian analysis of justice has been wrought with controversies within and outside the tradition. The Marxists tradition has sharp differences on whether Marx held a concept of justice for the analysis and evaluation of the capitalist society. There are defendants of the view that Marx's criticism is not based on any normative content, judgement or influence. However, we do not have the time here to go into the niceties of these arguments. For our purpose it is sufficient to note that Marx maintained that there can be no trans-historical concept of justice by insisting that ". . . there cannot be an independent standard of justice, external to capitalism, yet appropriate to assessing it."[13] The criterion of assessment has to spring from the very mode of production from which arises the concept of justice. Marx, therefore, contends that any notion of fairness is bound to be confined to the prevalent mode of production:

---

11. S. Moore, *Marx on the Choice between Socialism and Communism* (Harward: Harward University Press, 1980), pp. 48-49.
12. Miller, p. 149.
13. Norman Geras, "The Controversy about Marx and Justice", in *Marxists Theory*, ed. A Callinicos (OUP, 1989, www.marxists.org), p. 2.

> Do not bourgeois assert that the present-day distribution is "fair"? And is not, in fact, the only "fair" distribution on the basis of the present-day mode of production? Are economic relations regulated by legal conceptions, or do not, on the contrary, legal relations arise from economic ones?[14]

Marx was of the very clear view that fairness can only be restricted to a particular mode of production and therefore in a letter of 1877 writes rather condescendingly of the Socialists' attempt to explicate it as the most desirable principle,

> . . . a whole gang of half-mature students and superwise diplomaed doctors who want to give socialism a "higher, idealistic" orientation, that is to say, to replace its materialistic basis (which demands serious objective study from anyone who tries to use it) by modern mythology with its goddesses of Justice, Liberty, Equality, and Fraternity.[15]

For Marx the notion of fairness therefore can only be judged from within and determined by the specific mode of production and he therefore asserts there is no *injustice* in the wages paid to the labourer for he says,

> To clamour for equal or even equitable retribution on the basis of wages system is the same as to clamour for freedom on the basis of the slavery system. What you think just or equitable is irrelevant. The question is: what is necessary and unavoidable within a given system of production?[16]

The point is expressed slightly differently by Miller when he says,

> If we consider what we have in mind when we ascribe needs to a person, we shall, I believe, recognize that we are thinking not of the person's wants, whether actual or hypothetical, but rather

---

14. Karl Marx, "Critique of the Gotha Programme", *Selected Works*, vol. II, p. 21.
15. Karl Marx, "Letter to F.A. Sorge, 19 October 1877", *Selected Correspondence*, p. 376.
16. Karl Marx, "Wages, Price and Profit", *Selected Works*, vol. 1, pp. 426.

> of the consequences for the person of not having what is needed. We are thinking of the harm which the person will suffer through not being given what we say he needs.[17]

There can be a detailed argument whether Marx relativizes the concept of justice or the concept is relativised to the extent of being objective for a mode of production. The argument may hold ground but we lack space here for such a discussion; it will suffice our purpose just to mention the controversy. The issue may be illumined by quoting Wood,

> . . . as Marx interprets it, the justice of capitalist transactions consists merely in their being essentially capitalist, in the correspondence of capitalist appropriation and distribution to those standards of justice which serve the system itself.[18]

For Marx the injustice is not in the labour as commodity exchanged for wages since there is no cheating involved; the market operates openly and the labourer knowingly sells his labour for the settled price. The injustice is in the distribution of the produce of labour when it is realized that the exchange for labour power is only illusory and a mere semblance or form. It is the surplus value generated and usurped by the capitalist which is criticized by Marx. Young has rightly pointed out,

> . . . in Marx's view, the worker is treated justly as seller in the exchange of labour power for wages, but is then robbed in the production process, during which the capitalist extracts surplus value from the worker.[19]

However, for Marx it is not a matter of undoing injustice but the development of society which will ensure the operation of principles, it is therefore corollary for him that justice should be

---

17. Miller, p. 130.
18. A. Wood, "Marx on Right and Justice: A reply to Husami", *Philosophy and Public Affairs*, vol. VIII (3), Spring, p. 108.
19. G. Young, "Doing Marx Justice", in K. Nielsen and S.C. Patten (eds.), *Marx and Morality* (Ontario: Canadian Association for Publishing in Philosophy, Guelph, 1981), p. 252.

viewed as development of society. In fact, Marx, it is contended by some, not being absolutely clear in his articulation of the concept of justice can be read coherently to be proposing a developing concept of justice linked to the progress in society. Therefore, he proposes that there will be different phases of post-capitalist society with different principles which are referred to by Norman Geras as ". . . the *contribution principle* and the *needs principle*" (the italics in the original).[20] These principles arise out of the realisation of the exploitation of and, in the literal sense, "robbing" the labour of his produce.

The former for Marx is a principle where each will, after some deduction required for overall maintenance of the society, get an amount equal to his labour contribution. He argues that this principle is ". . . still stamped with the birth marks of the old society from whose womb it emerges."[21] However, it is a necessary step leading to the second principle where,

> . . . after the enslaving subordination of the individual to the division of labour, and therewith also the antithesis between mental and physical labour, has vanished; after labour has become not only a means of life but life's prime want; *after the productive forces have also increased* with the all-round development of the individual, and all the springs of co-operative *wealth flow more abundantly* — only then can the narrow horizon of bourgeois right be crossed in its entirety and society inscribe on banners: From each according to his ability, to each according to his needs! (Italics added).[22]

The envisaged society is expected to be beyond scarcity where wealth will flow abundantly and as such the principle, "From each according to his ability, to each according to his needs" would not ignore the differences between individuals but will operate with those differences. Lukes has rightly depicted the issue when he points out that the differences would be material in the

20. Norman, www.marxists.org, p. 3.
21. Karl Marx, "Critique of the Gotha Programme", *Selected Works*, vol. II, p. 23.
22. Ibid., p. 24.

envisaged society of abundance for,

> (1) those abilities and needs would be infinite, that is, unlimited in advance, and unspecifiable by any rule; (2) the former would be harnessed to "the common interest of all individuals who have intercourse with one another". . . ; and (3) the latter would all be satisfiable without conflicting claims because of those relations and because of material abundance.[23]

There are philosophers who have disagreed with the needs principle having an independent status. It has been argued that needs principle can only be significant in combination with rights and deserts. For instance, I take out medical insurance which will provide me with assistance with my health as and when the need arises but this is part of the right I have accrued according to the earlier terms of contract. It is from this that Lucas concludes that needs form a basis for justice if and only if they are also rights, deriving from a prior agreement or an established set of rules.[24] It will suffice here to show the fallaciousness of the argument proposed that in a welfare state there might be expectations not covered by any rule or contract accruing rights which if not met may still be considered injustice.

Nathan, on the other hand, ties up need with deserts. The example he enumerates is of two children reaching equal academic standards but one of them comes from a deprived background and therefore finds the achievement to be harder than his privileged classmate and therefore the need of the child coincides with his deserving more resources as his need.[25] The argument can easily be countered if we take the example of a famine where food is to be distributed, when it is not necessary that the neediest is the most deserving.

---

23. Steven Lukes, *Marxism and Morality* (Oxford: Clarendon Press, 1985), p. 57.
24. J.R. Lucas, "Justice", *Philosophy*, vol. XLVII, 1972.
25. N.M.L. Nathan, *The Concept of Justice* (London: 1971), pp. 35-36.

The only lesson to be learned from the two theorists according to Miller is the difficulty to simply analyse need in conceptual terms and

> People who use need claims to ground their judgements of justice mean what they say. To show that they are misguided, one must engage in substantive moral argument, not rely on conceptual analysis alone.[26]

The needs principle has essentially an empirical character.

However, it can be further argued that needs change with changing society and Marx himself acknowledged this when he said that man produces his needs and in turn his needs are produced. The changing needs as we know now are created by media and advertisements. The needs principle being empirical in character is expected to be able to cope with particular concrete situations. For example, the needs of a worker and an ascetic will be dire opposites and therefore the question arises as to how the society will assess these needs and provide for them. I will mention here as a possibility, a notion presented by David Miller, who argues that the principle is to be viewed from the perspective of developing one's plan of life, which actualizes one's identity. He argues that there are two forms of activities involved in any plan of life — the essential and the non-essential. The essential establishing one's identity would be the activities that make up the plan of life, say for example music if one has the plans to be a musician and the activities which support these activities, such as getting sufficient food. The essential activities are identified as those the cessation of which will create a hindrance in the plan of life. The non-essential activities would be those the cessation of which will not hinder the plan of life, such as consuming superfluous food. It is in this sense that Marx is talking of abundance and the needs principle. I may conclude finally by pointing out the advantage of the needs principle — the advantage of being concrete in its universalism.

---

26. Miller, p. 126.

CHAPTER 11

Some Ethical Questions in Social Justice

Debashis Guha

I

WITH the phenomenal increment in our interest in social, political, legal, economic and business ethics, we are now churning out a number of issues of ethical interest. One such issue is to consider whether the different aspects of "social justice" should be analysed in the broad context of "social ethics" that covers inquiries concerning political and legal justice for sure, and with some extended reason, distributive justice as an important aspect of economic justice. If we accept the inclusion of discussions concerning "social justice" in the broad fold of social ethics, we may be tending to take "justice" in "social justice" in its narrow sense because in this case "justice" conveys normative and value-related sense. However, "justice" in "social justice" conveys other non-normative sense particularly when we are concerned with the *macro-level justice* in society or what may be called, the engineering in social justice — the nitty-gritty of the same. In this sense, macro features or engineering of social justice demands *positivistic* discussions of engineering *methodologies*, something which often ethicists take up as a passion or fashion but wrongfully so, as I think. There is least doubt however that ethicists should take interest in the "second order" discussions about whether "social justice" forms a part of "social ethics," whether "justice" in "social justice" is merely normative-evaluative and whether the engineering methodologies are of ethicists' concern. Further, ethicists should take part in a "first order" inquiry, that is, which *standard ethical norm or norms* justify the right and good (or value) of an engineering methodology. This is very interesting as the macro-level social justice and its methodologies cannot overlook the latest *micro-level* questions of social justice, which are the questions of the ethical or the *desirable* ends or objectives of engineering. The moot point is, why at all a model for positivistic justice be accepted even if all touted macro-level judgements of good has been taken care of. The point is, despite all *desired goods* of macro-level model for social justice, what *should* be or *ought* to be the *desirable goal* of those models and their application? The answer cannot be as simple as, "the desirable end being social justice, which is good itself, models of engineering as desired are justified" because in many cases than not models of engineering are *unethical models* of pseudo-social justice because the desired positivistic goal or ends are merely means to maximization of physical pleasures correlative to exploitation, alienation and ecological disasters. Therefore, to call any positivistic methodology well, the evaluative inquiries at the micro-level take precedence. This article thus tries to analyse some ethical questions in social justice, not the engineering ones rather those latent in them at the micro-level, that is, the ethical rumblings in social justice. In doing so, it shows how "justice" in "social justice" covers both the normative and value-related (or ethical) aspects and the non-normative, procedural aspects.

II

Lucius Garvin succinctly puts that there is no social ethics without individual or personal ethics, and there is no personal ethics if social ethics is not conceived because there is no conception of individual good and well-being if individuals live all alone, and there is no social good or well-being if none of the individual members have attained their well-being. Similarly, rights, duties, and justice are individual as well as public virtues. One important aspect of social ethics is to discuss about these social virtues, among which "justice" plays an important role. We have already seen that the concept of "rights" is closely related to those of duties, obligations and justice. If there is a claim to right to wages out of the labour we invest, it is just for a competent party to distribute the wage in equitable manner in due proportions and in time. We know that just distribution of wealth or property is related to what is someone's duty or obligation and related to the right a party holds to have some wealth or property and another party who holds the right to distribute it equitably. Among the ethically relevant discussion of social issues, therefore, the issue of justice is extremely important, but that is a sweeping remark because we can speak of social, economic, political and legal justice in the social context. However, in the social context, when we are concerned more about *procedural fairness* on the part of some responsible parties such as the executive and the legislature (the two organs of government), who seek fairness and equitability in the distribution of goods and benefits, social and political, we say that we are concerned with "social justice," covering thereby "personal justice." It appears that "social justice" is a very broad conception of "justice" in which the socio-political benefits of individuals and the community they constitute are fairly and equitably distributed by agencies responsible to do so, thus making us believe that social justice is no "justice done to oneself" or justice done to one's own family, groups and so on. It is justice done to one and all as far as practicable, though ideally probable. We tend to come nearer to such justice, which does not happen suddenly, or with a stroke of decision. Clearly, such justice conceives of "other than my own decisions and actions, fair towards me" though "I may be equally decisive and active in all fairness towards others." This is so because given our nature and position in societies, we tend to be best judge of ourselves, that is, best to judge our good, which often neglect those of others, which is detrimental to social good at large. Hence, we need competent persons and institutions to do *our* good, which is the pathway to social justice. Obviously, individuals disagree on doing good by others, but they agree too, which is basic to social justice. In any way social justice is highly *relative* as what is good for persons of a society and when is good done to them, is variable. Such an evaluation of good is thus context dependent. It is very difficult, therefore, to conceive of universal or international justice. In fact, with differences in political ideals, social goals and moral perceptions, the conception of justice done to people differs. It differs in a society even with the fleeting time.

An important aspect of social ethics is that ethical scrutiny of social matters naturally drags us to the matter of justice done to all the sections of a society though "inequality" appears to be the natural course when it comes to social distribution of material goods, educational opportunities and leading a civil life enjoying benefits due to that life. Social justice is thus a basic issue to reflect on the ethicality of human conditions that has been created out of unjust decisions, actions and schemes of the responsible legislature and the executive. The point becomes ethically so relevant because society is looked upon as a personal and comprehensible entity that imposes necessary moral burden on its members to not only legitimately enjoy the benefits given to them but to act consciously and morally charged to rectify the wrongs that have permeated the masses and thus the society. Social justice, ethically speaking, is some sort of correlative measure on the part of the members of the society to see whether wanton wrongdoings have been taken care of. To take care of the legislative inaction, malfunction and wrongness that cause injustice in society, we need to go for legal justice because such injustice cannot be corrected without an institutional intervention. Truly, the institutions being parts of the social superstructure, their interventions should be treated indirectly at least as social intervention, but not in an unorganized, uncivil and unmethodical manner. Hence, in social ethics, we discuss the ethical aspects of nature, purpose and limits of legal justice in the context of social justice, taking it to be a truism that both are neither mutually exclusive nor necessarily correlative. In the words of Wojciech Sadurski,

> They (social and legal justice) apply to different phases of the social process. Social justice applies to work done by a legislator,

> legal justice is work done by a judge (or any person acting authoritatively in applying rules).[1]

What is of great theoretical interest having far–reaching practical implication is whether the legislative and the judicial grounds (or rules) for justice are different because social and legal justice are, in fact, different forms of justice? Well, the debate drags us further to the deeper *ethical* issue whether it is desirable or *ethically just* (on ethical grounds available to us) to imagine that what law enacts in society as just will be good enough to settle any issue of social injustice. Or, other way round, is it ethically just to say that what the legislature enacts in society as just will be good enough to settle issues of social justice? The questions are really about the ethical validity of the assured unilateral just acts of the "judiciary" *vis-à-vis* those of the "legislature." The point is who *constitutes* judicial laws in the society for justice? If the institution or the authority is a sovereign social authority or institution, not a person or group or association, it represents by and large the ethical approval of the masses through moral churnings and practical repercussions, the focus of which is to maximize social good or social well-being. In this sense, though laws are constituted by the people, for the people that aims at well-being through broad spectrum justice to the people, the judiciary as an organ of the government enacts the law, they are the trustees or custodians to these sovereign laws (because they are just and good). Hence, the function of the judiciary that does "legal justice" though relies heavily on the just laws that have been constituted for social good and thus on what *bases of justice* legislators provide them, they try to *enforce* laws in the real hard life case for ensuring social justice depending on many things that are beyond what the legislators provide. They rely on facts, evidences, justifications, instances and many other things. This way it is ethically just that the judiciary enforces laws for social justice being free from the

---

1. Wojiech Sadurski, *Giving Desert Its Due: Social Justice and Legal Theory* (Dordrecht: J. Riedel Publishing Co., 1950), p. 36.

bindings of the legislators though not overlooking the spirit of the law enacted and hard facts available. In another way, it is ethically just that the legislature constitutes law to ensure social justice being free from intervention of the judiciary though not overlooking the aspects of legality and pragmatics of the law when enforced. In yet another way, it is ethically just that the executive enforces what the legislature and the judiciary demand for ensuring social justice. The moot point is that for all the three organs of the government, "social justice" is vital and such justice is to maximize social benefits or goods in the quantitative and qualitative sense. It is important, therefore, to note that though *functions* of legislature, executive and judiciary are mutually exclusive, non-interfering and unique, they nevertheless, in close relation, act in unison because they guarantee social justice only in doing things that way and they keep in view that in doing so they have strong ethical grounds available to them. It may well be that all of these organs of social governance do not agree on all issues in practice. But if they do not lose sight of social, distributive, legal and political justice as what is ethically just as well because they are conducive to the maximization of social well-being, they realize that though differently they "function" and independently they "decide and act," they are in unison (and this idea of acting in unison than conflict) must be ethical itself.

However, in social ethics, interesting ethical questions about the above-mentioned simplistic view of justice (social and legal) are further put for deeper ethical inquiry. The central point of the debate is whether any law that assumes to do social justice should be really taken *ethical as such* because in any case, non-arbitrarily framed laws are for social good, constituted by the people, for the people. If it be true, "all laws are intrinsically ethical or just." In the "simplistic" opinion, "all laws are intrinsically moral and not immoral or unjust" and for that matter it is ethical on the part of the legislature to see that the laws are framed for social good, and for the judiciary to see that the laws are enforced as and when necessary for social good. Hence, the "unison" opinion has nothing to offer in terms of the possibilities of either (a) the framed laws are unjust though legal justice begs them or (b) the laws are just though legal justice is stupefied in individual cases. In any case, we have to conceive of non-sacred laws which fail from within for many reasons and thus cannot be intrinsically just in all cases, and we need to conceive of non-sacred legal justice that fails owing to many reasons to do legal justice in the individual cases and thus cannot be ethical as such. In the view of Lon L. Fuller[2] a truly intrinsically ethical law need not be a failure in any of the two ways because laws are for him, much like the "sacred optimum," intrinsically ethical, and do not fail in any case. This must be right in favour of the *logical possibility* of laws assuming to do justice, but fails to do so or are *formally* so constituted that they fail to be cogently ethical, foolproof ethical, so to say, and yet are "laws." Such laws are "ineffective" and to a great extent unethical, not inherently but when evaluated for value from a perspective other than the *positivistic perspective* seen above. Hence, to "have a law" does not necessarily and sufficiently beg to "have a law that never fails to do justice substantially and individually." "Having a law" does not imply "having an intrinsically ethical law," though it is expected of a law that it is *judged for its ethical value* on the given *teleos* of assuming social well-being. This appears to disparage the *deontic* view that among many things of intrinsic value, we must conceive of "law", but tragically, all *constituted laws* are on ground reality not intrinsically good though ideally we have been expecting laws to be intrinsically good. This may be refuted by a *deontic* argument that though laws constituted by *us* are contingent on *our* wisdom and severely dependent on *teleos* of the law, if they were not intrinsically good, we would have not bothered for any law that is in principle ideal or unfailing. Laws being bereft of inherent value are thus not deemed to have any purpose (*teleos*) whatever. Our urge "to have laws" in society shows that among other good things, laws are good even if they failed in some cases

---

2. Lon. L. Fuller, *The Morality of Law* (New Haven: Yale University Press, 1972).

or they did not. But even in that case, "to have laws" is not to have "just laws" always. Having just laws always is contingent on so many things that do not depend on abstract laws but on concrete factors. It may well be that our wisdom takes us to the "conception of law" that is just intrinsically and the conception of "a law" or "laws" which are judged for ethical value teleologically. However, to forget the truth that legal justice can be valued for ethical worth, on deontic and teleological grounds is to forget that such justice often conflict with social justice. And in many cases of social justice, particularly when we come to justice done to individuals in society, the conflict is too sharp, unredeemable or rather not to be redeemed at all because such "injustice" on the part of the legal system is demanded for "substantive social justice." Sadurski writes,

> Impartial and strict implementation of legal rules may lead to injustice in individual cases, but the magnitude and diversity of social situations cannot be grasped by legal rules in such a way that their application will always lead to socially just solutions.[3]

Hence,

> Avoiding injustice requires sometimes departure from rigid rules: to prevent a situation where social justice demands legal injustice, various legal systems "open themselves" towards moral considerations and include direct appeals to moral judgements in the legitimate operation of the application of legal rules.[4]

Such a view of social and legal justice amounts to conflict with the thesis advocated by Ronald Dworkin[5] because Dworkin seems to suggest that social justice is an *integral aspect* of judicial justice, and as such cannot be the basis for the value-judgement of legal rules, and that Dworkin seems to argue that social justice is not an evocation of the moral perception of a person because for a judge in the court of justice, social justice is within the legal system, and

---

3. Sadurski, p. 43.
4. Ibid.
5. Ronald Dworkin, *Taking Rights Seriously* (London: Duckworth, 1978).

for that matter does not beg any moral basis beyond it. It is important in social ethics to evaluate this con-view about moral basis to social and legal justice. On the simplistic unison thesis, the thesis of Fuller and Sadurski, it may be extremely difficult to agree with what Dworkin says because it may be argued that both social and legal justice *involve* moral perceptions of persons in society. In other words, the talks of justice, social and legal, involve *cases* of social and legal justice, "justice" conveys the sense of "procedure"; whereas moral justice conveys the sense of "desirable" or "good"; nevertheless, "procedural justice" does involve questions of "desirability" because "procedural justice" is not mere evocation of persons involved in such justice, those are well thought out and planned methods in giving certain things due to us in society, which asks for evaluation of *worth* on basis that is not limited to legality and legislation. In fact, the legal and the legislative decisions, principles, rules and actions are never beyond moral scrutiny, for which interesting moral theses such as the teleological and the deontological have already surfaced.

III

Social ethics as a meaningful ethical enterprise takes us to consider the *methodological* issues in distributive, social, political and legal justice. The way in which different forms of justice opens for ethical inquiry is whether such forms of justice follows a "method" that is ethically "just." If the forms of justice have a definite aim for them, that is, if procedural justice in many conceivable ways aims at doing what is "just" in the society, it must not be ambiguous. The ways in which justice is done cannot simply state that all of them aim at "doing what is just" because we need to clarify what it is to "do what is just." It may be said that all forms of justice aims at ensuring the due *benefits to its optimum* to the public that constitutes the society or in ensuring the rightful claims or goods to the optimum. If this be true, all forms of justice do not merely aim at doing what is just, they aim at maximization of rightful benefits to the public. It would be a little awkward to say that justice in any form must not be linked to an explanation of benefits because losses cannot count as just for humans. However, it may be said that "benefits maximization" is a *physical* concept, involving mostly the criterion of "quantitative" benefits and associated calculus. This may be true in case of distributive or economic justice to a large extent. Social and political justice cannot be said to be completely beyond the physical or quantitative conception of justice, for which definite "scientific methods" are deemed to be most suited, which are still as elusive as the ideal of justice in any form. No amount of Nobel prizes till date to economists has given us at this point a method of physical or quantitative economic justice. The sociologists and the political scientists are in a similar situation, but all of them are after the ideal. However, not all among us would agree to this idea that "benefit maximization" is purely physical or quantitative because more often than not justice is taken as distributive justice in which fairness and equity rules supreme, but this is only one aspect of justice, not the whole of it. In the recent times, there have been important ethical discussions among economists about the validity of measuring benefits on purely quantitative terms. Many of them have argued that holistic justice apart, even economic justice is done when "well-being" of individuals in society, which is a way to look at what are the benefits, is attained. The "well-being" or a "happiness" index that does not merely count on physical or quantitative benefits has become a point of discussion though what amounts to such a benefit is more or less ambiguous to many of us. Some Western economists are at awe when they find that people in abject poverty in India as so "happy," some of them are not happy owing to physical conditions, resources, money, wealth and so on but many of them are happy on queer "qualitative" grounds such as the metaphysical, spiritual and so on. Is it important to inquire into such qualitative forms of benefits? If at all they are important, how do we maximize them? Or, are these benefits non-optimal, they are intrinsically valuable or optimally good *per se*? More important in social ethics is to inquire whether such intrinsically valuable benefits for humans are of greater worth or do they not make any sense? No doubt there have been quantum shifts in the utilitarian conception of physical or quantitative conception of benefit maximization as justice done in the society right from Hume, through Bentham to Mill. J.S. Mill does not only recognize the value of quantitative benefit maximization as just action, he, nevertheless, does not lose sight of quality of benefits thus maximized. This must be particularly inspiring for the ethico-spiritual thinkers of the East but not for the mainstream ethicists of the West or even for the mainstream economists of the East and West, particularly those of the Freidman *gharānā*. Anyway, despite ethical imbroglio over which benefits *should* be maximized and/or encouraged and why, the point of *methodology* remains stiff, and its stiffness is owing to the ethical imbroglio over *why should* such and such methodology take precedence over others.

It is very difficult to keep aloof from the Indian ethical conception of overall justice done in the society that considers seriously the quantitative-qualitative aspects of benefit maximization in society. It speaks of the ethical view of justice done at the "social level" and at the "personal level" through quantitative and qualitative benefits, the latter taking us to the ethico-spiritual ideal realization in life, which gives some solace to ethicists who do not equate any form of justice to the purely physical. However, the method of doing all these things is not so pronounced at one place. Some important thinkers have contributed immensely with regard to the models of procedural justice in society that is ethically deemed to be stronger than pure physicalism and metaphysicalism, as they combine the spirits of physicalism, Aristotelian eudemonism, contractarianism of Locke and Kantian deontology. Most of these models do not blindly work on justice as maximization on utilitarian benefits, they move "beyond" utilitarian benefits or goods in society that combines the spirits of the above, though it does not in principle prevent our welfarist to combine some points of metaphysicalism that are awestruck as to why hungry people in India should still smile. Thinkers like John Rawls, Robert Nozick, Amartya Sen and many others have contributed in this field. We need not enter into the details of these models here; what is of our interest is that among other socially relevant issues that open for ethical critique, justice — social, economic, legal and so on — make good cases for their nature analysis, justification and methodology. In short, we can say that most models of justice invite us for the ethical critique of the conceptions of procedural fairness and equality in society by the government and its several institutions and organizations particularly in view of the rights and aspirations of individuals and the positions they enjoy by virtue of the advantages they have in life. This also brings in the ethical scrutiny of the advantages, aspirations, rights, and obligations the distributors of advantages enjoy in society. Another point is to rank the benefits of the masses for maximization at the priority basis; this is also linked with the idea of quantity and quality of goods to be distributed on priority basis.

CHAPTER 12

Subaltern Morality and Social Justice

Ramesh Chandra Sinha

THE term "subaltern morality" requires explanation especially in its relations with social justice. The term 'subaltern' was popularized by Antonio Gramsci, an Italian Marxist writer. He attempted to counter Fascism in the 1920s and 1930s. He submitted it for the much-in-use proletarian class. In India, the term has been brought to the centre of Critical Philosophy by a group of thinkers referred to as the Subaltern Studies Collective. From 1982 to 1996, the subaltern collective has published substantial volumes on South Asian History and Society from a "subaltern perspective." The subaltern morality attempts to redefine moral behaviour. The subaltern Indian philosophy attempts to rethink and rewrite Indian philosophy afresh. I have interpreted the subaltern in Indian context. I put the inferior gender and lower caste under subaltern. By the expression "subaltern," I mean awareness of *dalit* and women. In the Preface to *Subaltern Studies*, volume I, Ranjit Guha proposes the following definition:

> The word "subaltern" stands for the meaning as given in the *Concise Oxford Dictionary*, that is, "of inferior rank." It will be used as a name for the general attitude of subordination in South Asian society whether this is expressed in terms of class, caste, age, gender and office or in any other way.[1]

---

1. Ranjit Guha, "Preface", in *Subaltern Studies*, vol. I : *Writings on South Asian History and Society*, ed. Ranjit Guha (New Delhi: Oxford University Press, 1978), p. viii.

In a clarificatory note, at the end of this same preface, he further states,

> The term "people" and "subaltern classes" have been used synonymous throughout this note. The social groups and elements included in this category represent the demographic difference between the total Indian population and all those whom we have described as the elite.[2]

I think that the subaltern philosophy is to rewrite philosophy, and, in the process, write about society from a people's viewpoint. The subaltern philosophy contemplates to bring the marginalized people in the mainstream.

First, we move away from a homogenization of the subaltern by clubbing together all categories of differentiation, i.e. class, caste, age, gender and office and any other way. At one level many groups share in a multiplicity of handicaps and oppressions. However, to unify collectives that preserve and struggle to maintain their own particularity is to fall prey to the fallacy of hasty and unwarranted generalization. Spivak, an eminent historian, appropriately warns those involved in the subaltern studies project in India not to essentialize the multiple identities of the subaltern as if it is "a single underlying consciousness." In keeping with this, we have tried to concentrate on fleshing out the caste dimension of subalternity. The subordination and subjection that marks the life of *dalit*s and women in India bring them into the centres of a particularly contextual assembly of subalternity.

> Untouchables (*dalit*s) have retained their identity as a subordinated people within Indian society, and by this we mean to identify a condition hierarchy.[3]

---

2. Guha, p. 8.
3. Oliver Mendelsohn and Upendra Baxi (eds.), *"The Untouchables" in the Rights of Subordinated Peoples* (New Delhi: Oxford University Press, 1996), p. 115.

This is not to deny that collectivities held together by commonalities of age, gender, class and office do share in the state of subalternity. Rather, this article takes seriously the specific manner by which the institution and ideology of caste engenders a contextual manifestation of subalternity, which is intrinsically tied-up to social justice in India. The subaltern, thus, are the communities (the *dalit* and women) that are cumulatively and comprehensively disadvantaged and subordinated through the caste and gender system, which operates to benefit the dominant caste communities and male perception. The words of Partha Chatterjee are relevant here:

> . . . no matter how we choose to characterize it, subaltern consciousness in the specific cultural context of India cannot but contain caste as a central element in its Constitution.[4]

Subaltern consciousness is concerned with the justice to subordinate or deprived people. The subaltern justice postulates that subaltern communities are not entirely controlled by the dominant communities. The term "subaltern" in Aristotelian logic denotes the relationship between two propositions. The proposition is subaltern to another if it is implied but does not imply. In this relationship, if the universal proposition is true then particular must be true but not vice versa. It means universal implies particular but particular does not imply universal. So subaltern is implied but does not imply any other proposition. Aristotle does not consider the relationship of subalternation as the relationship of opposition. In this relationship, two propositions can be true together and also false together. Subalternation is the relation between two propositions having the same subject and the predicate but differing in quantity and not in quality. Resistance to the elite class and emancipation of subordinate class may be considered as subaltern social justice.

---

4. Partha Chatterjee, "Caste and Subaltern Consciousness", in *Subaltern Studies*, vol. VI: *Writings on South Asian History and Society*, ed. Ranjit Guha, p. 169.

In Indian context, the upper caste and subordinate caste may be symbolized as A and I. A stands for upper caste and I stands for subordinate caste. A implies I, but I does not imply A. If A is true, I must be true but not vice versa. This rationale is best exemplified in the following excerpts from the German Ideology:

> The ideas of the ruling class are in every epoch the ruling class, i.e. the class which is the ruling material free of society, is at the same time its ruling intellectual force. The class which has the means of material production at its disposal has control at the same time over the means of mental production at its disposal, so and thereby, generally speaking, the ideas of those who lack the means of mental production are subject to it.[5]

The emerging school of "Cultural Marxism" seems more relevant framework within which to interpret subaltern social justice as encountered among Ambedkar and Periyar. This complex interweaving of domination and subordination, on the one hand, and compliance and resistance, on the other, is capable of realistically holding together both the camouflage of submissiveness, which characterizes the overt behaviour of subaltern class. *Dalit* and women are trying to come in the centre of power. According to traditional system, *dalit* and women were given subordinate position. The idioms of domination, subordination and revolt, are often inextricably linked together. If this is true, it follows that subordination and domination is seldom complete. The process is marked by struggle and resistance.

Our topic is "Subaltern Morality and Social Justice." As D.D. Raphael puts,

> Justice and liberty are the two basic ideas of all political thought. Every society needs some sort of concept concerning that structure. Justice is the basic concept of social values, it is what holds a society together.[6]

---

5. D.D. Raphael, *Moral Philosophy* (New Delhi: Oxford University Press, 1986), p. 68.
6. Ibid., p. 67.

Most of the social philosophers think in ethical terms — the public interest, social justice, freedom from oppression or freedom from want. Differences of ideology crystallize especially around the two concepts of justice and liberty. Everybody is in favour of justice, but not the same interpretation of it. Raphael further observes,

> Left-wingers give priority to "social justice" with an intention to reform society in the direction of greater equality and the removal of poverty. A right-winger's concept of justice (he is unlikely to use the phrase "social justice") sets more store by the virtues of law and order, of stability, of reward for enterprise and merit.[7]

This contention of Raphael is partially acceptable to me. It is true that left-wingers attach less importance to liberty but it is not true that right-wingers attach less importance to social justice. A democrat whether he is a right winger or left winger attaches equal importance to "social justice." I strongly contend that for Indians it is a fundamental value. We want to retain it as a social goal. The contention of Raphael may be true to people who do not believe in democracy. For a democrat, justice is a social virtue. It appears both in law and in ethics. But the morality of a society is distinct from its legality. However, I contend that principles of social justice are akin to principles of morality. Social justice becomes the meeting point between morality and legality. The administration of social justice in that case becomes the administration of a morality accepted by that society. The administration of social justice, within this context, need not evidently be identified with the administration of law, for law may or may not be in conformity with the concept of social justice. Justice is a complex concept. It appears both in law and in ethics. Justice in law and justice in ethics are distinct but not completely separate concepts. Raphael upholds,

---

7. Raphael, op. cit., p. 68.

> The idea of justice always has an ethical tinge and when it is used in law or is applied to the legal system as a whole, it is a reminder that law, as commonly understood is not simply a set of any old rules subject to enforcement, law has an ethical purpose and is normally expected to use ethical methods.[8]

However, the principles of social justice are nothing but principles generated by human reason in its application to social context.

Justice, for Plato, is one of the four virtues, the others being wisdom, temperance and courage. Justice is the practice of virtues. Virtue is the right condition which enables each man to do his own job. He is free to follow that activity for which he is best qualified by his nature. Justice contemplates that the rulers, the guardians, and the artisans in a state must be in their proper order and practice of their particular virtues: wisdom for the rulers, courage for the guardians and temperance for the artisans.

Here justice has a purely metaphysical connotation implying a life of people conforming to the rule of functional specialization. The original principle underlying it is that one man should practise one thing only and the thing to which his nature is best adapted. Plato pinpoints that each individual should be put to the use for which nature "intended him, one to one work, and then everyman would do his own business, and the one and not many.[9]

From the above, it may be inferred that justice, as conceived by Plato, has both individual and social aspects. It asks the individual to take only that office to which his nature is best suited. It is also required that the society must assign that office to him that is in conformity with his natural aptitude. The highest good of both the individual and the society is conserved if we take it for granted that there is nothing better for a man than to do a work that he is best suited to do.

The philosophical interpretation of justice takes an empirical

---

8. Plato, *Republic*, vol. IV, p. 423.
9. John Rawls, *A Theory of Justice* (New Delhi: Oxford University Press, 1971), p. 3.

direction at the hands of Aristotle who says that injustice arises when equals are treated unequally and also when unequals are treated equally. Aristotle came to lay down the foundation of, what is now called, the doctrine of "distributive justice." The implication of Aristotle's explanation is that justice is either "distributive" or "corrective," the former requiring equal distribution among the equals, the latter applying wherein remedy for a wrong is provided. With the penetration of democracy into social and economic spheres, the meaning of justice has expanded itself into social justice. A new subaltern consciousness has developed. It urges that the rights of an individual should be reasonably restricted in the wider interest of subaltern community, namely *dalits*, backwards and women so that the ends of social justice are properly achieved. In other words, it is widely recognized that the well-being of society depends on the co-ordination and reconciliation between the rights of the individual and interests of subaltern community. John Rawls in his book, *A Theory of Justice,* contemplates that justice is well-off of the worst-off. Social justice relates to the balance between an individual's rights and social control ensuring the fulfilment of the legitimate expectations of the individual under the existing laws and to assure him benefits thereunder and protection in case of any violation or encroachment of his rights. Social justice must be consistent with the unity of nation and needs of the society. It is evident that the context of social justice is very wide. It covers within its fold everything pertaining to the norms of "general interest" ranging from the protection of the interests of the subaltern to the eradication of poverty and illiteracy. In India, the idea of social justice enjoins upon the state to make effort for the improvement of the conditions of the downtrodden and weaker section. A dichotomy that needs to be noted is that between justice as a conservative and as a reformative principle. Conservative justice protects the established order of society with its established distribution of rights, and in the event of breaches it requires restitution of the *status quo* so far as that is possible. Reformative justice calls for revisions of the social order and a redistribution of rights to suit current ideas of fairness. The second of these concepts is, I think, what people usually have in mind when they speak of "social justice." The term "social justice" tends to issue from the mouths of reformers, and to be looked upon with suspicion by those who are satisfied with the existing order. In my opinion, it is not pertinent to say that reformative justice is social while conservative justice is not. Justice always has a social reference because it concerns the order of society as a whole.

Legal and moral justice are each concerned both with an equitable order of society and with protecting the rights of individuals against the demands of society, if need be, as well as against other individuals. Each of the two again has its conservative and its reformative aspects: both law and morals regard it as unjust to violate expectations based on long-standing arrangements; yet both recognize that an established order is always liable to ossify conceptions which have become out of date, and that change in the character of human life, both national and spiritual, requires change of the social structure. It is obvious, finally, that the distinction between conservative and reformative justice is quite different from that between justice of the social order and justice for individuals. Conservative justice is concerned both with the preservation of established social norms and with the protection of the freedom, person, and property of individuals. Reformative justice is undoubtedly intended to produce a more equitable society, as the common term "social justice" implies, but it is equally intended to secure for needy or meritorious individuals the rights to which it thinks they are entitled.

Undoubtedly, the idea of social justice requires the sacrifice of certain rights of an individual at the altar of the general interest. However, viewed in a wider perspective, the idea of social justice not only aims at the proper reconciliation of the interest of an individual with the over-all interest of the community. It also stipulates prevalence of the community interest over the individual interest in the event of any conflict. It also constitutes an essential part of the great complex of social change, for which something may have to be sacrificed for greater good. The concept of social justice covers within its fold everything pertaining to the norm of general interest. It protects the interest of the subaltern which comprises *dalit*, women and downtrodden. It also relates to the eradication of poverty and inequality. It also relates to the liquidation of the vested interest of elites. The idea of social justice enjoins upon the state to make effort for the improvement of the lot of the downtrodden and weaker sections of the society. John Rawls conceives social justice as fairness. Rawls observes:

> I then present the main idea of justice as fairness, a theory of justice that generalizes and carries to a higher level of abstraction the traditional conception of the social contract.[10]

The aim of Rawls is to work out a theory of justice that is a viable alternative to the doctrine which has long dominated our philosophical tradition. Although a society is a co-operative venture for mutual advantage, it is typically marked by a conflict as well as by an identity of interest. There is an identity of interest since social co-operation makes possible a better life for all. There is a conflict of interest since persons are not indifferent as to how the greater benefits produced by their collaboration are distributed, for in order to pursue their end they prefer a larger to a less share. Rawls further observes:

> A set of principles is required for choosing among the various social arrangements which determine their division of advantages and for underwriting an agreement on the proper distributive shares. These principles are the principles of social justice: they provide a way of assigning rights and duties in the basic institutions of society and they define the appropriate distribution of the benefits and burdens of social co-operation.[11]

In the post-modern society, the subaltern morality and social justice

---

10. Rawls, p. 4.
11. Ibid., p. 10.

are interconnected. The marginalized *dalit* and deprived women are trying to come in the centre. Moreover, feminism has also upset the entire male dominated social structure. Post-modernism is an attempt to de-construct the old social structure. In Indian context, Brāhmanical social system is under threat. Here by Brāhminical social structure, I do not mean any particular caste like brāhmaṇa but it denotes "elitism" prevailing in Indian society. Subaltern are subordinate and deprived. The marginalized class can be termed as the "other." The "other" is on the margin. They are struggling for their rightful place in social structure. As a matter of fact, it is said that in modernity project, the subaltern was not restive to come in the mainstream. In post-modern project the subalterns are trying to be liberated. The Western social philosophers pinpointed the concept "othernesses." The "other" is part and parcel of social development. The feminist movement and *dalit* consciousness are chief marks of post-modern society. The subaltern consciousness is growing and marginalized people demand fair share and equal treatment. The "other" is the main agenda of post-modern society. Post-modernism highlights differences. The hallmark of post-modernism is plurality. It attempts to de-construct the established social structure. It is a project relating to subaltern morality and social justice, in which *dalit*s and women, in the scheme of social justice, get their fair share of benefits and burdens.

Part III
Issues Concerning Rights

CHAPTER 13

The Third Sex and Social Justice

Ashok Kumar Verma

A VERY pertinent question arose in my mind while selecting this topic. Why should this problem be discussed at all? To put it in a bit simpler form: What kind of relevance be assigned to the topic under review?

In order to be able to answer the problem raised above, I am tempted to quote A.J. Ayer who said, "the ordinary system of ethics . . . is very far from being a homogeneous whole."[1] This is a pointer to the fact that history of moral philosophy is a record of various transitions. We notice that ethics roughly began with Casuistry, then passed to theoretical ethics and then came a long period of meta-ethical discussions with two major thrust areas, the language of ethics and ethical methodology dealing with arguments used in ethical life.[2] But after some time an impasse in the field was seen and yet another change on focus of ethical problem became important. This took the form of distributive justice and applied ethics. The problem concerning the third sex and social justice belongs to these particular areas and can be classed together with the problems of distributive justice and women, distributive justice and down-trodden, distributive justice and the *dalit*s and so on and so forth. Thus, the topic has multidimensional importance as a point of view of applied ethics and distributive justice.

"The Third Sex and Social Justice" combines in itself two phrases, "The Third Sex" and "Social Justice," and can be

1. A.J. Ayer, *Language, Truth and Logic* (London: Victor Gollanez, 1936), p. 103.
2. C.L. Stevenson, *Ethics and Language* (Yale University Press, 1945), p. 1.

understood as social justice for a class of persons to be called persons of the third sex. Very naturally, the starting point of discussion will centre around the third sex.

The class of *homo sapiens*, called humans, is divided into two sub-classes, male and female, and this is prevalent in almost every part of the world — be it Indian census or railway reservation requisition slip. But this classification of humans is never complete for a simple reason that a sizeable portion of human population is of a type that does not exclusively belong to either of the categories, male and female, and I have preferred to classify them as persons belonging to third sex. There are several nouns for them, such as *kinnara*, eunuch, *khojā*, *hījaḍā*, "impotent," etc. — since some of them carry a derogatory meaning and are used as abuses, I use the term "the third sex." The problem of their nomenclature appears to me of lesser importance.

The Status of the Persons of Third Sex: Then and Now

THE THEN

We get various pictures of the status of the persons of this category. The two most important mythological books, the *Rāmacaritamānasa* by Tulsīdāsa and the *Mahābhārata* by Vedavyāsa present a picture of their lifestyle. In the *Rāmacaritamānasa*,[3] particulary in Uttara–Kāṇḍa, on the occasion of coronation of Rāma, we find;

> *nabha dundubhiṅ bajāhiṅ gandharva kinnara gāvahiṅ* ।

This shows that even at that time their primary source of earning was by way of singing and dancing for entertainment purpose and collecting the rewards, maybe that this one was sufficient earning to them.

In the *Mahābhārata*[4] we get a somewhat different picture. It should be said that the *Mahābhārata* is claimed to be a victory of

3. Tulsīdāsa, *Rāmacaritamānasa*, "Uttara–Kāṇḍa".
4. Vyāsa, *Mahābhārata*, "Bhiṣma-Parva".

righteous (*dharma*) over unrighteous (*adharma*). But the way and purpose for which a character like Śikhaṇḍī, an eunuch, is used very much show that instead of following the canon of *dharma–yuddha*, a very prudent maxim was followed, "Nothing is wrong in love and war." But at least one thing is clear that they have been a privileged community, in the sense that it was an accepted practice for a normal man not to raise arms and weapons against them. Arjuna too made an appearance as eunuch while in hiding, but this has nothing to do with the status of eunuch-like persons.

During the middle period, particularly in the Mughal Empire, the *khojās* used to amuse the kings and the courtiers. They had a role like that of court jesters almost akin to some characters of the Shakespearian dramas, etc.

We have hitherto confined ourselves to, under the caption of the third sex, the then, someones from Indian mythology and a bit of history. We get a somewhat similar account of living and lifestyle in other countries. *Britannica Ready Reference Encyclopaedia*[5] provides us the following information:

> Eunuch castrated human male. From remote antiquity on eunuchs were employed in the Middle East and China as guards and servants in harems or other women's quarters and as chamberlains to kings. The eunuchs' confidential position frequently enabled them to exercise an important influence over their royal masters. Many of the patriarchs of Constantinople during Byzantine times were eunuchs. Eunuch advisers disappeared as a class only with the end of Ottoman Empire.

The description that we have found above is that of those persons who enjoyed better positions as advisors to their royal masters. Some of them had the status of patriarchs and this is better than that of those who earned their breads by singing or dancing and, thereby, collecting monetary rewards. But they never enjoyed royal positions. Also, their performative side differed from those of clowns, who, from eighteenth century onwards, worked in

5. Britannica, *Ready Reference Encyclopaedia*, vol. IV.

circus and made facial expressions even with vulgarity and castrato who used to produce alto voice that had its greatest prominence in seventeenth- and eighteenth-century opera.[6]

THE NOW

The author is apologetic for his failure in providing a worldwide data and analysis based on empirical study. As an outsider to the community what has been felt and what ought to be done to the community have been attempted and he is sorry for any omission and commission.

In presenting an analysis of the status of the third sex *vis-à-vis* that of the normal, one finds himself bewildered actually as to what areas one should cover and indeed what is more important is the problem of their identity. The other areas, we shall see, such as the economic, the sociological and bio-ethical will also emerge as significant.

Due to the prevalent distinction and recognition of male-female dichotomy we fail to place them anywhere. Even in this respect if we look for determination of personhood for them, we see that be it Strawson's[7] criterion of person to which one can sensibly attribute both predicates p and m, p — predicates denoting states of consciousness and m — predicates denoting physical properties; Dr Davidson's[8] criterion for persons as agents who pursue goals and act as per their intentions, they are persons. As persons they have identity, what is lacking is their separate category. The Indian census mentions no wise data, literary, etc.; what it does about them, nothing. This is evident from the fact that it is not known in the census report as to what is their number, what profession they have. They are counted as males. The report varies so much that regarding their population in India the report varies from

6. *Britannica*, vol. III.
7. P.F. Strawson, *Individual* (London: Methuen, 1959), ch. III.
8. D. Davidson, "Agency" in R. Binkley et al., *Agent, Action and Reason* Oxford, 1971.

fifty thousand to fifty lakh. According to yet another version[9] their population in India is about twenty-five lakh, which includes two types of persons of eunuch-category, those who are by birth so and those who have been forcibly made eunuch. The second one is more disturbing because the number of them is on a decline in other countries, say in a city of the most populated country China, in Peking, as per internet report, has dwindled to twenty-six only, in India it has shown a rising trend.

The overall situation in regard to the identity problems even now does not present a radically different picture compared to then. This is, however, a good symptom that some of them are trying to prove their identity by their participation in those activities which make them closer to mainstream. For example, some of them have come forward for contesting and winning assembly seats or seats of local bodies. But this too is just a silver lining in the dark sky.

Under the caption "The Status of the Third Sex: The Now," we focused on the identity problems of persons of this category. Very naturally a question comes to our mind, as to what is the reason behind their seemingly lost identity. There can be many physical, sociological and psychological reasons but the foremost, I, consider is the behaviour pattern of them with other persons, thereby, an attitude of discarding by fellow beings. There is almost lack of social intercourse and if casually there occurs some occasion, they (the eunuchs) avoid interacting properly, evading to reply the questions put to them and behaving not in a dignified way, and the result is that they fail to get any sympathetic treatment. We too have developed a feeling of evading tendency. This is why one fails to get them properly recognized and one also finds them very shy of meeting the others.

---

9. Anjali Sinha, "Kinnara ke liye Insāf kā savāla", *Hindustan*, October, 2007.

The Economic Conditions

While presenting the economic conditions of the persons of this category in the remote or recent past, we saw that barring a few, the economic conditions they had were not good and they earned their bread by dancing, singing, creating amusement or working as servants or guards of harems of the royal persons. Nowadays their situation has worsened. One can still find them applying the same mode of earning, not better than previous ones.

The Social Conditions

The term "society" and "social" enjoy different meanings. R.M. MacIver and Charles H. Page point out,

> Society is a symptom of usages and procedures, of authority and mutual aid of many groupings and divisions, of controls of human behaviour and of liberties. This ever-changing complex system we call society. It is the web of social relationships. And it is always changing.[10]

Like the society, the term "social" can be understood to convey an idea of those pertaining to society and social relationship. It should be said that social relationship is differentiated from the physical or meta-physical. The relationship between the many objects on the table I am writing at is physical. Similarly, the relationship between one doctrine or one religious belief and the other, is metaphysical. But none of them is social. Social relationship includes mutual recognition and a prevailing sense of sharing something common.

When we observe the lifestyle of the persons of the third sex we see that most of them prefer or are compelled to lead a group life where the members are of the same category. Their behaviour pattern in their own group has some features that they like, but those who are said to be normal do not like it. They are, if not hated, treated as segregated category. This is evidenced by the

---

10. R.M. MacIver and Charles H. Page, *Society* (New Delhi: Macmillan India, 1987), p. 5.

fact that when they approach the other category of persons, they do not get a welcome, and a tendency to evade them is seen. Maybe that their mode of behaviour is not favoured by others. The overall picture is not very sound.

Social Justice

"Social Justice" is a combination of two terms "social" and "justice." The phenomena they refer to are not only manifold but are also much debatable. Better to begin with justice. When we look at the various concepts of justice, we find that they admit of three areas, viz. law, social morality and institutions of individual rights. Plato, one of the champions of justice, made a meta-ethical study of the term "justice" and raised a meta-ethical question: What is the meaning of justice? Before putting his reply through the mouth of an important character, Socrates, he examined[11] the various prevalent concepts of justice as those held by Cephalus, Polemarchus, Thrasymachus and Glancon, and for Plato, in the words of Irvin Edman,

> Justice is . . . the kind of individual life where every "part of the soul" does its own business, that life of the state where each individual and each class performs its appropriate function.[12]

Justice is regarded as excellence of soul, and the soul comprises the appetite, the spirit and the wisdom. Thus, it was wholly an ethical concept meant both for individual and the state equally. But contrary to this, Plato's pupil Aristotle[13] believed that justice is not among ethical virtues, it wholly belonged to state.

"Justice" had different meanings even in ancient times. Basically it has two applications, the recursive meant for awarding punishment and reward, and distributive having the modality of distribution of justice based on equality, merits and also needs. In

11. Plato, *Republic*, ch. I.
12. Irvin Edman, *Review of Republic*, back page.
13. W.T. Stace, *A Critical History of Greek Philosophy*, London: Macmillan & Co., 1964, p. 310.

this respect the Utilitarian principle of counting one unit for each member of the community was propagated by J.S. Mill[14] and was adhered to by John Rawls[15] and even by R.M. Hare[16] and many others. It is not intended to dwell upon this problem with much detail in a brief note like this, and we pass over to social justice.

Justice, we have seen, assumes different forms, social justice being one of them, especially an important modality of distributive justice. But from this one need not conclude that it has nothing to do with the prevailing social order, rather it comes out of some disorders of the society and in one or more ways it has recursive functions if the law has to be applied and changes brought about for removal of some prevailing evils. Social justice nowadays, is concerned with the social order as a whole. The basic principle involved herein is the distribution of benefits and burden equally. But in the context of contemporary Indian society, this seems to be an apportionment of some special benefits to persons belonging to a particular category who had but to suffer an utter neglect in the society both in the distribution of material benefits and also in recognition of their status as a social being.

There are many areas of social neglect and to my mind a most neglected lot among the whole neglected lots has been that of persons belonging to the category, the third sex. The persons of this category, we have seen, are not only physically handicapped but also economically backward and what is most disturbing is that they are ill treated as if they deserve segregation or a treatment of social outcaste resulting in their lost identity. No doubt, some ameliorative symptoms such as granting Rs. 300 (three hundred) per month pension to them and provision of free education by some NGOs have emerged but those too seem to be not enough. Under the situation some drastic measures need to

---

14. J.S. Mill, "How Connected with Justice", *Utilitarianism*, ch. V.
15. John Rawls, *A Theory of Justice*, Oxford: Oxford University Press, 1971.
16. R.M. Hare, *Freedom and Reason*, Oxford: Oxford University Press, 1963; R.M. Hare, *Moral Thinking*, Clarendon Press, 1981.

be taken for the betterment of their lot. To me, there can be two types of measures in this respect, those of temporary nature and those having enduring effects.

Among the measures of the first category attention is needed to be focused by the government and voluntary organizations on the following:

- As per their demand the persons of the category of third sex be treated as physically handicapped and thereby they be given consequential benefits in jobs and admission into educational institutions by way of reservation.
- They should be given free education by the government and efforts need to be made to bring them into the mainstream of society.
- They should be provided financial assistance by the governments to settle them in life and earn their bread by establishing their own small industries, etc.
- While doing census a proper account of their population be made available and for this the government should change its modality of procuring population data.
- A separate category of physically handicapped be made in railway reservation slips and they be allowed occupation in the railway compartments meant for physically disabled people.

We have made some suggestions for betterment of the lot of the people of the third sex and have listed them in the category of measures of temporary help. But to find out some kind of permanent solutions some drastic measures need to be adopted. We find that medical surgery and genetic engineering have achieved a new height. Now, it is a great challenge for the persons and professionals associated with these disciplines to find out ways and means to remove this abnormality. This may be now a dream but so many dreams have been changed into reality.

A less difficult way of improving their lot can be achieved by attitudinal change and behaviour patterns. The society we live in should realize that the persons of this category are part and parcel of the class homo sapiens. The nature has played a cruel joke with them. At least the normal ones should not adopt a hostile attitude and for this the sociologists, the philosophers and many others have a challenging job to bring an attitudinal change in the society.

CHAPTER 14

Justification of Capital Punishment
A Review

Girish Baruah

THE right to life is not only fundamental to human beings, but also to other animals and plants. All governments are, therefore, obliged to protect the life of all. A criminal has also the right to live as he possesses life like others. So the government is obliged to save his life also along with the protection of innocent people from the onslaughts of the criminals. From this standpoint there is no ground to justify capital punishment.

When someone is punished capitally he is put to death. To put to death means to kill and the killing of anyone is not the civilized practice. It is a different thing to kill a person when someone's life is in danger from that person, i.e. in self-defence. But cold-blooded murder can by no means be accepted.

Everybody admits that when a murderer is at large he threatens society. But when he is in confinement it is not so. Somebody may, however, argue that even in confinement he may murder his co-prisoner or a guard. But if proper vigilance is there then there is no possibility of such incidents. Moreover, he may be put in an isolated chamber if there is such a threat from him.

To inflict capital punishment is a revengeful activity on the part of a government or a society. The government may argue that for the sake of deterrence or retribution capital punishment is necessary. Legally it may sound well, but morally? Can we accept it morally? Yes, by awarding capital punishment we are doing justice to the victim. But what about the offender? Does he have no right to his life? These are some of the questions that arise while thinking of capital punishment and hence the review.

The advocates of capital punishment offer the argument that capital punishment is necessary as it is the best way to deter further crimes. It may be an example to others who are intent on doing mischief in society. Yes, the government has every right to protect society from the danger of criminal activities and it is also its duty to look to the good of society. It cannot allow that someone will perpetrate dreadful outrages in society. To prevent such outrages is its bounden duty. But let us think, can these be viable circumstances to retain capital punishment as the only antidote against criminality?

We have seen that day by day criminal activities are increasing even though capital punishment is in vogue. In the countries where it is not in vogue there also these activities are increasing, but not in greater number than in the countries where it is prevalent. The increase of capital punishments has not decreased criminal activities. So it cannot be a plausible argument in favour of capital punishment that it is necessary to do away with criminality.

To do away with criminality we have to undertake some other methods. We cannot make a few unfortunate criminals the scapegoats with a view to reforming society. If society takes their lives in the name of social good then it will amount to a joint murder of a criminal and it cannot evade responsibility for it. As a criminal has no right to take the life of a man similarly society has no right to take the life of the criminal. A man, either he be good or bad, should not sacrifice his precious life under compulsion. He has got every right to live. So the responsibility of society is to make him good if he is bad and it must find out ways and means to make all the criminals good instead of taking their lives.

Every man has the right to freedom, justice, etc. When a man is free, he can live honourably. A free man can only be responsible and if he is not responsible it is the duty of the society in which he lives to make him responsible. Again society has every right to prevent a government to act arbitrarily. A government is not supreme, what is supreme is society. So a responsible society can make its government and its people responsible. In the long run, therefore, society is ultimately responsible for whatever a man does, either good or bad.

We can understand the psychological position of a man waiting for the execution of his death sentence. It is true that the majority of the people want that a criminal undergoing death sentence be hanged. His vileness, his depravity, his baseness, his turpitude — all these are abhorred by the majority of people. But should majority always rule? Whatever is said or felt by the majority or even by almost all cannot be always true. Once, all men thought that the sun revolved round the earth. Was it correct to think so? So we are not to judge something by the majority opinion but by merit of the case.

A civilized society is maintained by the standard of decency. A society which is not decent cannot be civilized. Both criminal assaults and capital punishment mar his decency. Even a criminal also has no intention always to murder a man. We know the story of Ratnākara who indulged in robbery and when asked why he did so, he answered that he was to look after his family and his parents. He was turned to be a good man who could rise to the standard of a seer with sermons of divine personalities. Therefore, there is scope that we can convert a criminal into a good man with required education. But if his life is taken away this scope would not be there.

What we require, therefore, is the principle of civilized treatment. Any type of inhuman treatment cannot be regarded as civilized treatment. A civilized treatment means a dignified treatment. Every man in society wants to live in a dignified way. He does not want that his dignity be curtailed. In most of the cases a state fails to safeguard this dignity of its people. It acts in a barbaric way. But we cannot do away with the state before the proper time comes, because in that case there would be anarchism. Capital punishment is definitely an inhuman and uncivilized treatment. It is so because it is unusual, cruel and barbaric. When one of your children becomes unruly, do you kill him or her, or reform? Children are very delicate and they are to be treated so.

Capital punishment is based upon a judgement of a judge or jury, and a judge is obliged to follow the constitution of his land. He has to work within the limits of permissibility of it. He cannot surpass the jurisdiction or the boundary stipulated by the constitution concerned. So although it is said that the punishment is inflicted judiciously yet we have doubt about its moral viability, because the argument of judiciousness is based on the constitution made by parliamentarians, the qualification and wisdom of whom is well known.

Capital punishment has a tantalizing effect on the victim. The period which he has to undergo for long brings him untold suffering and pain, both mentally and physically. His whole personality is mutilated. This mutilation is done on the excuse of law which is framed by man with all limitations. The police and the guards are indulged in getting the upper hand over the victims and the latter are tortured like anything.

We should remember that human beings are not to be toyed with but to be honoured. A human being may be the vilest criminal, a mad person or a person suffering from AIDS or handicapped either physically or mentally; yet after all he is a human being and he is to be treated so. Every man, high or low, possesses a common human dignity and is entitled to the recognition as a human being. He expects and at the same time he deserves to be treated so. So when we behave with a man we should remember that he possesses a status of being a human being. Therefore, we should not do anything which will jeopardize his personality. Even a small child is conscious of his status as a human being and he does not like that somebody will toy with him.

Criminals are diseased persons. They are diseased persons of a diseased society. So instead of killing them they are to be treated medically. Of course, before their treatment we should treat the society itself either economically or socio-politically. We should not bear for ever the enormity of criminality. To bear it indefinitely will be a folly on the part of man. Yet we should act rationally without going back to our primitive stages in which men were killed for simple reasons.

We should create a shield to safeguard human dignity. An umbrella of protection should be created so that every human being can live by maintaining his individuality and as member of the human community. This shield and umbrella should be created to safeguard ourselves from either government or judicial onslaughts.

If we are not living in a civilized society at present then let us form a concept of it as was done by Plato of his ideal society. We will have to go a long way to such an ideal society as conceived by Plato, but we can very well form a concept of a civilized society, which, if we wish, we can establish with less effort. It is, however, not possible to build such a society unless we uplift our living standard. A high standard of living will create a high standard of judiciary and legislative functions in our country. To do this we have to surpass the past usages. History should not be the guide to us in this respect. Let us not repeat the history. That in the past there was capital punishment and, therefore, we should continue it is a bad argument. We are living in a new society and everything is to be looked from this standpoint. Old is not always gold if it brings suffering to humanity. Therefore, the present judiciary system is to be changed overwhelmingly and a new system be created. The same can be said with regard to the legislative functions of the state.

We are not against punishment, but are against punishment in excess. Excessive punishments are unnecessary and are to be avoided at any cost. In the name of punishment we never want degradation of humanity. The government has no right to terrorize its people in the name of punishment. Tit for tat formula in its extreme form cannot be accepted always.

So it is high time to review the processes of punishments. Let us do it before it becomes too late. Such a review will compel the government to reconsider its bad practices with regard to punishment. Society is above the government and a government cannot deny the will of the people. If the society feels that some kind of punishment is fatally offensive the government is bound to abandon it. The government cannot forego the principles of humanity and should act by following these principles. If the whole society does not come forward to take such a step then let some sane members of it start it without any hesitation. A time will come when the whole society will be behind them.

We understand the penal purpose behind punishments. We are not against this purpose. What we oppose is the extreme form of punishment. In the name of punishment we do not want a person to be thrown into an unusual situation. Hasty and drastic action should not be the motto of a government. It should act with the utmost tolerance and patience. It should act in such a manner that the sanctity of human life is not jeopardized. Let us follow the ideals of those countries where there is no capital punishment. Let us examine how they are maintaining law and order without resorting to it. I think their administering of criminal justice is not inferior to ours.

The ghastly scenes of the execution of death penalties are so disgusting that they are beyond description. I still remember the ghastly scene of the execution of Saddam Hussein when his head was thrown away from his body from the acute knot of the rope with which he was hanged. Thereby, I am not supporting Saddam's activities, but am reluctant to accept the way he was hanged; nay even the whole episode of sentencing him to death was wrong. This is only one instance among many. There are so many others to mention or to describe which our space here does not allow.

The execution scene has very bad psychological effects on man. It is very bad for children. Such ghastly scenes should not be shown on television. There is no doubt that the process of carrying out the verdict of death has brutalizing effect on all — the person hanged, the persons connected with the hanging process, the audience, etc. Such scenes degrade the human spirit. When I saw Sadddam Hussein being led to the gallows with chains around feet and hands, it seemed that a slave was being led so in the primitive period of Greece. Such an inhuman treatment cannot be accepted. Man should not be brought down to the level of beast.

Death is a phenomenon which negates existence. Man does not want death either natural or unnatural. We cannot escape natural death as it is inevitable. But we cannot accept man-made deaths; they are caused by accidents, natural calamities, murders, capital punishments, etc. and these are avoidable deaths. When the life of a man is taken away it forecloses all his future possibilities. All murders are not calculated killings, but capital punishment is definitely and invariably a calculated killing. It is rather a cold blooded murder. Such a killing robs all that a person possesses, his independent thinking, his feelings, his religion, his love and affection — all. Should we accept such a position being members of the so-called civilized society? Protection of some persons should not lead to the destruction of some others.

It becomes very dangerous when some innocent persons are hanged or killed otherwise as a result of capital punishment. But if a person is confined in jail even for the lifetime then he gets a chance to seek legal redress for his unlawful confinement, if he is not actually guilty. In this way, he can right a wrong. If he is successful then it will be a lesson to future judges who often pass wrong judgements.

Death sentence when carried out becomes irrevocable. But a life sentence can be revoked. A judge may make mistakes in passing a judgement. There are some inefficient lawyers who cannot plead well. In that case there is every possibility of committing mistakes. Nobody can escape human folly including the judges. Many judges indulge in corruption due to which they become biased to certain parties. Again, some genuine culprits escape conviction due to lack of proper evidence. Some convicted persons escape punishment due to appeal in higher courts. Mercy, parole, etc.

granted by higher authorities like the president or governors are very common. These practices make law unviable. So only a few persons have to suffer from the evil effects of the prevalence of capital punishment which can be very well avoided.

The practice of capital punishment is a pragmatic one. It is not guided by human principles. We are, therefore, waiting for the day when the public demand for the abolition of capital punishment will outstrip its support. Pragmatism alone cannot maintain public morality and human dignity. Unprincipled pragmatism may lead to many problems. It may arouse controversy, provoke public opinion and lead to the violation of human values. That certain things may lead to good practical results does not mean those things are good. So pragmatic solution of a problem is not enough, because such a solution may create further insoluble problems. An action should not be guided by practical wisdom alone; we are to reply on theoretical wisdom also. Anything that does not subscribe to the attainment of *summum bonum* may not be regarded as good. The action that leads to *summum bonum* is deemed to be right. When we follow higher moral principles then only we can expect better behaviour. To lead a virtuous life we need moral excellence. What is supreme is to be adopted. The lower values are to be abandoned or surpassed. Belief in retribution, continuance of ancient practices, atonement, etc. all these represent lower values. So in the assessment of capital punishment these cannot be standards. It requires a very close human behaviour. Buddha said that you cannot get rid of suffering unless you know its causes and try to do away with those causes. Similarly, we have to find out the real causes of man's criminal behaviour and try to do away with such behaviour by removing those causes.

Society needs a congenial atmosphere so that we may live in peace. Peace is the burning cry of the present world. Everybody needs peace. Primarily the common people need it very much. So let us try to establish peace. It is our first and foremost need. All the conditions that cause death are harmful to peace. So it is better to diminish the cases of death as far as practicable, especially accidental and man-made deaths. The abolition of capital punishment will help a step further to establish peace. Although there are many who may think that it will be a very insignificant step to this end, yet it will be rather a bold step to begin with.

We should not do anything which may prick the conscience of even a single person. If the practice of capital punishment is put to vote as to its agreeableness, majority of people, I think, will vote for its abolition. Although we have said before that majority opinion cannot always reveal truth, yet if somebody wants it to be decided through vote we may do so. Although many people find it difficult to stand against law yet there is a deep-seated reluctance to the practice of death sentence and its execution. We hope this practice should automatically wither away. But something withers away when the conditions nurturing it are nullified or negated. Karl Marx, for example, said that the state would wither away when class division would be nowhere. When universal societal doubts will arise in everyman's mind and when people will think that capital punishment will not serve any viable penal purpose then its days would be numbered.

The technique of isolation is better than that of death. A criminal, when proved that he is a real criminal, is to be confined away from mixing with other men. But only in rare cases it should be done. It is advised only in preference to death.

If we wish, we may change human nature. The basic human nature is instinctive and we do many things on instinct. Rationalization or sublimation of human instinct is very important to transform the animal man to the human. An animal man cannot be human until humanistic elements are infused in him. When a man will be completely human he will behave as a man and when he will behave as a man, criminality and other bad instincts will go away. For it we need the cultivation of good qualities and for it we need education in true sense of the term.

There are some thinkers who think that by keeping the present socio-economic system as it is, it is not possible to eradicate criminality and, thereby, capital punishment. Mostly in a capitalist system it cannot be eradicated. But we see in most of the European countries capital punishment is not there, while in countries where the so-called socialist system is prevalent it is there. But in both the set-ups criminality is there. So, those who urge that socialism or communism will lead to the end of criminality may be wrong in this respect. But if true communism would be set up or if we can achieve Gandhi's *Rāmarājya* or Plato's Ideal State, perhaps there may be the eradication of criminality and, thereby, capital punishment, because when criminal activities like murder or rape will not be there, consequently the question of capital punishment will not arise. As up till now all these have not been achieved, we cannot say at this moment whether the above possibility will materialize or not.

We can expect law abiding citizens in a state which is founded on human principles. A government which follows the moral codes and conducts can only expect such citizens. Under such a government everybody will respect the law of the land. The government must honour the value of life and dignity of man. The government should be a moral organization, not a legal one. It should not use its brute force to control the masses. While private blood feuds may be accepted to some extent, blood feuds let loose by the government can never be accepted. The condemnation of such types of feuds is a must on the part of all. Criminals, both governmental and public, should be brought to book and should be punished with a strong hand, but not with death penalty.

Justice is an equivocal term and its meaning has been changing from time to time, and society to society. What was just once may not be so at present. Similarly, what is just in one society may not be so in another. In reviewing capital punishment these facts are to be considered.

We are more interested in rehabilitation than in retaliation. A government with a welfare concept should try for rehabilitation.

The government is a much more powerful organ than an individual. So it should not deem an individual to be its rival. But the masses are more powerful than the government and, therefore, it bows down before public opinion. If public opinion is strong enough against capital punishment the government must abide by it and change its laws accordingly.

At present a new science like eugenics has been developed, the aim of which is to produce healthy intelligent children. We may try it with a view to improving the human genetic stock. Then we can diminish the number of recidivists or persistent offenders.

All of us may not be civilized. But we have a concept of civilized values. When we learn to honour these values then we advance in the path of civilization. We should learn more in the school of civilized values than in the school of penological justification.

It is true that the opposition to capital punishment creates some embarrassment in the minds of some people. Nay, it may also create uproar among men supporting capital punishment. It is true that always there will be supporters and opponents of a particular practice. Differences of opinion cannot be avoided. It is also true that everything has its merits and demerits. Every concept, every value is relative to time and space. Even then some human values have eternal import and we should try to safeguard and maintain them. In this respect I think we should abolish capital punishment with a view to respecting universal human values.

Our examination in this review is not based on statistics, but on the principle of evaluation, as it is mainly an ethical problem. We may show very many statistics both for and against capital punishment. Again, we have also logical arguments for and against the same. These will not help much. We are considering here only the human question. Our aim here is to safeguard human values from legal and political onslaughts. There are many other problems, but for the present we are selecting capital punishment, because we are very concerned with maintaining human dignity which we deem to be one of the important factors of human civilization. My arguments put forward here may seem to be precious to somebody. But I ascribe less value to anything that jeopardizes human dignity. Death penalty, in my view, cannot be consistent with human dignity. Humanism, human rights — all these high sounding words will be meaningless if human dignity is not maintained.

We are interested in eradicating criminality, not criminals, as Marx is interested in eradicating capitalism, not eradicating capitalists. If we eliminate one criminal, a second criminal will arise and so on. But if we are successful in eradicating criminality as a whole there will be no criminal at all. So, which should we prefer — the first alternative or the second one? The choice is ours, and whichever alternative we choose will indicate our wisdom. A positive effort will be a more acceptable phenomenon to others.

CHAPTER 15

Language Rights and Social Justice in a Multilingual Ethos

Imtiaz Husnain

> All language communities are entitled to have at their disposal all the human and material resources necessary to ensure that their language is present to the extent they desire at all levels of education within their territory: properly trained teachers, appropriate teaching methods, textbooks, finance, buildings and equipment, traditional and innovative technology.
>
> [Universal Declaration of Linguistic Rights (draft), 1996]

HOWEVER, we have only a few dozen language communities that are privileged to have these kinds of rights. There are many language communities, which do not have their languages at any level of education within their territory. Education is the key to all human advancement, including economic and social uplift, and, therefore, a potential site for contestation and struggle. Besides empowering and disempowering or enabling and constraining people, education is also an equally important tool for linguistic genocide. In fact, it is one of the most successful means of promoting or retarding, cultivating or destroying languages. Fate of any language largely depends upon its use in the domain of education. Is the democratic polity respecting the right of minorities to protect and promote the use of their language in the domain of education? Is our language policy all about upholding the rule of majority without caring to nurture and fulfil the aspirations of and providing social justice to minorities and their language rights in a multilingual ethos? Language is a contributing feature in many political conflicts at the regional, national and even international level and there is a significant relationship between language and politics. But what is surprising to note here is that much of the problems with regard to language and politics and particularly those with respect to language rights are simply overlooked and have not been much discussed within political theory. This gloss-over by the political theorists has assumed all the more importance because of the language diversity and infringement on language rights of the linguistic minorities. It may appear to be a startling revelation, but it is true that India is a country of linguistic minorities. Then how do we explain this remiss by the political theorists? Although instances of discussion on "the language of politics" can be seen in the writings of political theorists, very little has been said about "the politics of language." Why the issue regarding language rights, particularly with reference to minority language rights, has been given peripheral treatment? Perhaps some general answer can be seen from the way language, in general, and minority languages, in particular, have been perceived, and the kind of distinction made with regard to majority-minority languages. Some general answer can also be found in the ambivalence attached to the issue of language rights and the tendency to regard the ongoing promotion of ethnocultural and/or ethnolinguistic differences as problematic in and of itself. Joshua Fishman has aptly summarized this:

> Unlike "human rights" which strike Western and Westernized intellectuals as fostering wider participation in general societal benefits and interactions, "language rights" still are widely interpreted as regressive, since they would, most probably, prolong the existence of ethnolinguistic differences.[1]

Language–Species Equivalence

In the history of linguistic theorization, one can discernibly find a slant towards an organicist conception of language. This slant was

---

1. Fisman, cited in A.H.Y. Chen, "The Philosophy of Language Rights", *Language Sciences*, vol. XX, no. 1, 1998.

largely associated with the work of Schleicher, a nineteenth century comparativist, who viewed language as a natural object going through the same developmental stages as plants:

> . . . languages are natural organisms, which without being determinable by the will of man, grew and developed in accordance with fixed laws.[2]

The upshot of the organicist conception of language was the presupposition that "language equals species" whereby parallels were drawn between the social evolution of languages and the biological evolution of species. Both species and language face extinction or death in the course of time. We are all familiar with the events of extinction or death around us. These are not isolated events. They have occurred in the past and have significantly affected the cultural visions and lives of our indigenous people. Cultural invasion leading to loss of cultural heritage and language is being witnessed all over the world. It may be Narmadā for us or it may be destruction of forests in Malaysia. For the Penan, destruction of their forests represents far more than the loss of subsistence. It implies the death of a people and, anthropomorphically speaking, the death of a language. It also brings with it a sort of collective amnesia whereby generations of Penan have forgotten that the use of the word *thank you* is alien to their culture, for sharing in their culture is an obligation; they have six words for *we* and only one word for *he, she,* and *it* which underlines the solidarity and shared feeling among a people;[3] they have further forgotten that there existed over 2000 names for streams alone, each imbued with its own history, representing the cultural significance of the land.

---

2. Schleicher, cited in D. Holdcroft, *Saussure: Signs, System and Arbitrariness* (Cambridge: Cambridge University Press, 1993), p. 7.
3. See S. Imtiaz Hasnain, "Minority Rights and Education: Question of Survival of Minority Languages", in Joseph Benjamins (ed.), *Minorities in Indian Social Systems*, New Delhi; Gyan Publishing House, 2006. (Also in *Languages in India*, an online journal.)

The best measure of the crisis emanating from these events is the loss of languages. Throughout all of history something in the order of 10,000 spoken languages have existed. Today, it has been reduced to 6,000, but many of them are not being taught to children and more than a million people speak only 300. By some estimates, languages that do not have 100,000 speakers are condemned to die. According to Karttune and Crosby, 50 per cent of the languages of the world, including most of the Amerindian languages and languages of Oceania have fewer than 6,000 speakers, and around 90 per cent of the languages of the world are endangered.[4] Language extinction is witnessed all over. In India, Koi has disappeared. Irish and Scottish Gaelic are endangered, while Cornish, Norn, and Manx Gaelic have disappeared in Europe. Romany, the idiomatic language of the gypsies, is on the critical list, and the indigenous languages in Australia, which once boasted of 250 different languages, have now been reduced to about 20. The phenomenon continues even today, which is followed by an alarming forecast that approximately 90 per cent of the existing languages of the world will be threatened with extinction within the twenty-first century brought about by the forces of globalization, modernization and assimilation. Michael Krauss, an anthropologist from the University of Alaska, believes that modern technologies of communication are responsible for the strangulation of these languages. He refers to these modern technologies of communication as "cultural nerve gas."[5] Even the biological species are likely to be threatened by these forces. As Pinker points out:

> The wide-scale extinction of languages is reminiscent of the current (though less severe) wide-scale extinction of plant and

---

4. Karttune and Croshy, quoted by Douglas A Kibbee,. "Language Policy and Linguistic Theory", in Jacques Maurais and Michael A. Morris (eds.), *Languages in a Globalizing World*, Cambridge: Cambridge University Press, 2003.

5. Cf. M. Krauss, "The World Languages in Crisis", *Language*, 1992, 68.4.

> animal species. The causes overlap. Languages disappear by the destruction of the habitats of their speakers, as well as by genocide, forced assimilation and assimilatory education, demographic submersion, and bombardment of electronic media.[6]

Problematizing Language–Species Equivalence

Language-species equivalence needs to be problematized. It carries with it a sense of "natural." Flowing from the sense of "natural" is the Darwinian principle of the survival of the fittest. In this game what is most likely to survive is the dominant language. It is not only natural for the dominating language to survive but even the emergence of the dominant language is also quite inevitable, largely because of the cluster of economic, military, political and technological factors and the inherent linguistic characteristics that constitute a commonality and ecumenical acceptability, which only the dominant language happens to enforce. The notion of natural selection and the dictum of the survival of the fittest enable the dominant language to assume authority, commonality and evaluation, which are, according to Foucault, "central to the relations of power in society in which we live."[7]

Indispensability of Language

What makes us human is language, and it is the possession of language, more than any other attribute, that distinguishes man from other animals. To understand man's humanity one must understand the language that makes us human. According to the philosophy expressed in the myths and religions of many people, it is language, which is the source of human life and power. For example, the tradition among the people of Mali in West Africa is that a newborn child is a *kuntu*, a "thing," not yet a *muntu*, a

6. S. Pinker, cited in Chen's article, *Language Sciences*, vol. XX, no. 1, pp. 259–60.
7. G.L. Wickhman, "Power and Power Analysis: Beyond Foucault", in *Economy and Society*, 12.4, 1983, p. 475.

"person." Only by the act of learning language an inanimate becomes an animate — the child becomes a human being. Thus, we become "human" not just because we know a language but also use it. The use of language is, in fact, a universal feature of all human societies, and no case has ever been discovered by anthropologists suggesting that any human group, including group of hunters living a "primitive" lifestyle, has lacked a language. Language has always been with us.

Conceded that language has always been with the human group, what is required to understand is the nature of this language, i.e. what is the existing ideology with regard to language? Do languages differ in terms of development? Were the languages of the "primitive" societies undeveloped as compared to those of the "civilized" societies? Are some languages intrinsically inferior because they possess inherently simple structure as compared to others, which are superior because they have far more complex language structure? These developmental and emancipatory discourses have created a widely held perception and belief suggestive of backwardness and underdevelopment of language/culture. Categories like "desirable-undesirable," "economical-uneconomical," and "developed-undeveloped" are being created with a view to showing that these languages, because of their inherent backwardness, are coming in the way of development. Even existence of many languages is also seen as being detrimental to the growth and development. If we glean through the whole language planning and language policy paradigm in post-Independence India, we find that, contrary to its wide proclamation, it has created more diversities and inequalities than ever before. So much so that whereas we used to have the good old distinction between language-dialect (*bhāṣā*, the cultivated and standardized form and *bolī*, the natural, spontaneous and spoken form), now one gets, thanks to the strategy of naming or labelling, a whole set of distinctions, namely, "standard-non–standard," "major-minor," "majority-minority," "national-regional," "scheduled-unscheduled" and so on. This kind of nomenclature, we feel, contains the very seed of inequality. This inequality has become more pronounced as a consequence of conscious language policies, the very crux of which is to be found in the constitutional provisions and the Eighth Schedule, which, as of date, includes twenty-two languages that are further sub-categorized as national official, state official and other languages. This, when seen in conjunction with linguistic reorganization of states, has led to certain anomalies, for example, Sindhi and Kashmiri are not the official languages of any state, while Sanskrit, the pan-Indian classical language, enjoys a kind of supra schedule status. The case of English is still more curious — this ex-colonial, language is not only the associate national official language of India but also serves as an inter-state link language and is promoted, propagated and supported as the language of opportunity, the language of higher learning, the language of prestige and the language of power.

Human Language and Equality of Language

Although the existing ideologies have caused inequality among languages and differentiated languages in terms of development, the current linguistic theory, which has its foundation premised on Chomskyan formulation, has radically changed our perception regarding the nature of language. In an interesting debate between Noam Chomsky and Michel Foucault on the topic "Human Nature: Justice versus Power" some years ago on a Dutch television programme, anchored by Fons Elders (1974), Chomsky emphatically argued in favour of existence of some form of relatively fixed human nature — some guiding principle, which enables a person to acquire his own language despite being "faced with a very definite empirical problem" that surfaces as a result of his exposure to partial and fragmentary set of experiences. Not only that he acquires his own language but also acquires "an amazing range of abilities, which enable him in particular to say what he means, to understand what people say to him, and still able to say in a way which is novel or new [and which] doesn't bear any close resemblance to anything in your experience."[8] How is it that "varying individuals with very varied experience in a particular language nevertheless arrive at systems which are very much congruent to one another [in which] what one of them says, the other can understand?"[9] According to Chomsky, this can be understood only if we are able to specify in terms of "neural networks the properties of human cognitive structure that can make it possible for the child to acquire these complicated systems."[10] There must be, Chomsky insists, a "mass of schematisms, innate organizing principles, which guide our social, intellectual and individual behaviour."[11] This guiding principle forms the basis of the concept of human nature. In the absence of human nature neither any true scientific understanding is possible nor any struggle against the injustices of our current society in the name of justice. It is a guiding principle that enables us to judge the actions of others. Our understanding of what constitutes a better society will be lost if we do not have some fixed and rational standards.

Corollary to the notion of human nature is the conviction informed by the current linguistic theory that all languages, whether they are languages of "primitive" society or those of "civilized" society, are equally highly developed. There is nothing intrinsic about languages being superior or inferior; all languages have the equal potential to meet the needs of their users adequately. From linguistic point of view, neither it is possible to rate the excellence of different languages nor it is acceptable to value a language on the basis of the political or economic influence of its users. These are important considerations as they suggest that equality of all languages should be adopted in a theory of language rights.

---

8. Fons Elders, *Reflexive Water: The Basic Concerns of Mankind*, (London: Souvenir Press (Education and Academic) Ltd., 1994), p. 136.
9. Ibid.
10. Ibid., p. 140.
11. Ibid., p. 138.

I talk, therefore, I am. This connection along the line of "I" (as "human") — "talk" (as "language") — "am" (as "being" or "existence") can be traced to the philosophical hermeneutics of Gadamer. Expounding and elaborating the insights of the nineteenth-century German thinkers such as Wilhelm von Humboldt and Herder, Gadamer has reminded us that language and human existence are inseparable from each other. The use of language is part of the essence of human being: language is essentially human and the human being is an essentially linguistic being. According to Gadamer, language is indispensable to human beings' understanding of the world. The world that human beings experience, or the world that presents itself to human being, is constituted by language. Hence "language is a medium where I and world meet"[12] and language introduces its users to "a particular orientation and relationship to the world."[13]

The philosopher Charles Taylor (1994) has also established the connection between language and human existence. He points out that human identity is not constituted "monologically" but "dialogically" through the interactive relationships, contact, and dialogue with other persons. To quote Taylor:

> We become full human agents, capable of understanding ourselves, and hence of defining our identity, through our acquisition of rich human languages of expressions. . . . But we learn these modes of expression through exchanges with others. People do not acquire the languages needed for self-definition on their own. Rather, we are introduced to them through interaction with others who matter to us . . ..[14]

Gadamer has also given the idea of dialogicality for acquiring the language of human identity when he says:

---

12. H.G. Gadamer, *Truth and Method*, 2nd rev. edn., tr. and revised by J. Weinsheimer and D.G. Marshall (New York: Continuum, 1995), p. 474.

13. Ibid., p. 443.

14. Charles Taylor, cited in Chen's article, *Language Sciences*, vol. XX, no. 1, 1998.

> . . . language has its true being only in dialogue, *in coming to an understanding* [emphasis in original] . . . Coming to understanding . . . is a life process in which a community of life is lived out . . . human language must be thought of as a special and unique life process since, in linguistic communication "world" is disclosed. . . . Thus the world is the common ground — uniting all who talk to one another. All kinds of human community are kinds of linguistic community: even more, they form language. For language is by nature the language of conversation.[15]

If all kinds of human community are kinds of linguistic community, as Gadamer points out, then the diversity of language and cultures becomes a foregone conclusion. Since every language is a view of the world which is shaped by the historical tradition embodied in that language, the diversity of languages and cultures is to be celebrated as something which is intrinsically valuable and enriching to the world. Each person is justified in having a sense of pride in its history, culture, tradition and language. This sense of pride gives her an identity, destiny and the sense of being. And if the pride is snatched away from him, his identity will be lost.

Anthropologically speaking, language is not merely a cluster of words or a set of grammatical rules. Rather it is "a flash of the human spirit by which the soul of a culture reaches into the material world."[16] It is, according to Michael Krauss, an anthropologist from the University of Alaska, "as divine and mysterious as a living organism."[17] And if we feel strongly about and mourn the loss of a species, we should feel equally strongly about and mourn the loss of a language. What will be the significance of such diversity from Language Rights and Social Justice points of view?

---

15. Gadamer, p. 446.
16. W. Davis, "Vanishing Cultures", *National Geographic*, August, 1999, p. 65.
17. Michael Krauss, cited in Davis' article, *National Geographic*, August, 1999, p. 65.

Problematizing Language Rights

If the unique vision of life constituted through language and culture are being lost in a whirlwind of change brought about by linguistic hegemony and regimentation then there is a need to stem the tide of language loss. The eco-linguists fighting for the protection of all languages and particularly those concerned with the project of language endangerment, i.e. the process whereby a language loses grounds to another, look up for support from the principles of Linguistic Human Rights (LHRs), notwithstanding the fact that there are certain weaknesses and problems associated with the assertion of LHRs which are both theoretical and practical in nature.

The advocates of language rights have been preoccupied with the issue of language loss as they believed that any loss of language involves loss of traditional knowledge and elimination of linguistic diversity. Hence the strong imperatives to take up an approach to social justice, which not only recognizes diversity as constitutive of the reality of the human condition but also treats linguistic diversity as no less than other forms of diversity. Since individuals and groups have distinctively different language interests, these differences must be "addressed in different ways in public policy if social justice is to be served."[18] Certainly consequences of language loss are immense and, therefore, need to be addressed immediately, but equally important is the problematization of the issue of language loss and the means of achieving justice.

Anthropomorphically speaking, death of a language implies death of the speakers who speak it or when they cease to use it any more, and even though there may be a political economy of language and rational choice theory governing the maximal use of language, no individual can be treated as the means to the ends of language. Nor an individual alone can bring about linguistic and social justice on individual strength. To assume that

18. David Corson, "English Only and Social Justice", *TESOL Journal*, 8.3, 1999, p. 18.

individuals "who change languages [can] automatically alter all the distinctions that were important to them in their first language" anticipates that "languages have no flexibility"[19] and also rests on a belief that individuals have enormous power to cause language loss. On the contrary, not only languages have flexibility but also tremendous resilience to survive beyond the lifetime of an individual.

Even the concern of language rights advocates to achieve linguistic justice has the underlying ideology characterized by Western presupposition involved in the "language equals species" and the organicist conception of language, along with the Eurocentric biases verging on the notion of individualism, which derive its inspiration from the individualistic approach to social justice. Language as a feature of human collectivities located in the social institution is both an instrumental convenience given to individuals as well as a means by which individuals are socialized. This socialization brings in an individual an element of consciousness — a sense of identity — which reflects the culture of the social, ethnic, gender, and class groups who share the language. The individualistic approach fails to appreciate that in any attempt involved in the promotion of social justice in language policy matters, different language interests of the minority groups need to be addressed as much as those of the majority groups in a given setting. This is because it underplays the communitarian and critically realistic approach to justice obtained through the social conception of language, which views language as a social product or a "social fact." This "social fact," according to Saussure, is situated "outside the individual who can never create nor modify it by himself; it exists only by virtue of a sort of contract signed by the members of a community."[20]

Situating Agency of the Speakers

If an individual's ability to act as an agency is circumscribed by

19. Kibbee, p. 52.
20. Saussure, cited in Holdcroft, *Saussure: Signs, System and Arbitrariness*, p. 8.

the constraints of structure, how does the agency of the speakers articulate itself? Can the subalterns speak? What must the elites do to watch out for the continuing construction of the subaltern? Although Spivak (2001) has addressed these issues in terms of gender/sexual claims of identity, they hinge upon the question of whether individuals can freely and autonomously initiate action or whether the things they do are in some sense determined by the ways in which their identity has been constructed. Spivak's famous sentence, *White men are saving brown women from brown men*, discussed in terms of gender/sexual claims of identity, not only hints at displacement for describing the relationship between brown and white men and suggesting an attempt to accommodate the third world women with the first world, but also reminds us that it is not so easy to see the world from the point of view of most other people because both "Us" and "They" are positioned differently by their experiences. Neither "Us" and "They" position is compatible nor even mutually understandable. Not only that we are culturally removed from the interest groups that our decision may not affect their interests, but also we lack the necessary information required in the decision making. Hence, we cannot make fair and well-informed decision about anything on behalf of others. A fair treatment cannot be obtained in the absence of knowledge of the discursive practices of the context and cultural and historical influences that have shaped the context. This is particularly true in case of language policy matters and more so when there is a multilingual context in which variety of factors operate and influence the decision making. A critically realistic approach focuses on the justice needs of social groups "alongside and sometimes even ahead of the needs of individuals" and recognizes that "people are inevitably shaped by the social and the cultural, such that any conception of individualism that ignores the impact of these influences is impoverished for failing to see people the way they really are."[21] Critical realism as an ontological theory "seeks the most basic forms of existence in the

21. See Corson's article, *TESOL Journal*, 8.3, 1999, p. 18.

social world" which are the reasons and accounts that relevant individuals offer to describe."[22] Thus when viewed from language policy perspective it would amount to involving the reasons and accounts of all those participants having important interests at stake in the decision making. Since at every stage of policy making there is an involvement of the participants, the critically realistic approach to social justice will enable the language policy to acquire a devolutionary processual characteristic in the decision making and will also facilitate the precarious balance of structure and agency. Hence, the National Curriculum Framework's insistence on multilingual classroom, use of home language and local knowledge in the construction of knowledge, appropriateness, etc. which are suggestive of devolutionary approach to language policy obtained through critically realistic conception of social justice.

Social Justice, Constitution and Language

The Preamble, Directive Principles and the main body of our Constitution carry the idea of social justice. Despite the assurances of social justice guaranteed by the Constitution, the gulf between promise and performance, privileged and deprived, and oppressor and oppressed has widened. Several articles incorporated in the Indian Constitution deal with different aspects of language use. For instance, Articles 120, 343, 344, 210, 345, 346 and 347 deal with language use at the Union and State level, respectively; Articles 348, 349 deal with language use in the judiciary; Articles 29, 30, 350, 351 are regarding language use by the linguistic minorities. But the unfortunate aspect concerning these Articles is that they were not dictated by the multilingual reality of India We merely borrowed, lock, stock and barrel, the features of the Constitution from the monolingual set-up of the West through their tainted glasses. Much of the development of a mother tongue especially in the formal domains, takes place within the schoo

22. See Corson's article, *TESOL Journal*, 8.3, 1999, p. 20.

system. Notwithstanding the guarantees enshrined in the Constitution, in practice the language policy of India is overtly non-discriminatory and maintenance-oriented, especially with regard to the use of minority languages, as they are struggling hard for survival. From the perspective of a conflict paradigm, we can discern both the structural and ideological dimensions of the struggle.

- *Structural dimension*: It could be a state, an institution, laws and legislations, directives and issuance of certain orders concerning allocation of languages on time tables, budget allocation for teacher training, material production, etc.
- *Ideological dimension*: It is norms and values ascribed to different languages and their speakers which bring about certain positive or negative identification with the mother tongue, the sense of utility and worth of the minority language(s) and its speakers.

The Eighth Schedule is a "monolingual relic" of the Constitution, which is based on "an inadequate appreciation of the linguistic plurality in the country."[23] Through its selective recognition of languages, Eighth Schedule has generated lot of injustice by denying equal opportunity of growth to many unrecognized languages. Perhaps it may appear anachronistic to many, particularly in the age of globalization and technological boom, one possible solution that can be suggested here is the proposal of Gandhi's *Grām Swarāja*, "the autonomous village," and the four-pillar state marking the post-Gandhian political realities suggested by Lohia. Keeping the multilingual and pluri-cultural character of India, the four pillars — the *panchayat*, the district, the state and the Union "must draw sustenance both in terms of power and finance" for protecting the interest of diverse linguistic and cultural groups.

---

23. D.P. Pattanayak, "Language and Social Injustice", in Ajit Bhattacharjea (ed.), *Social justice and the Constitution*, Shimla: Indian Institute of Advanced Study, 1997, p. 220.

A degree of social justice can only be ensured by making the Constitution accept the fact that the deprived sections and the marginalized sector have a fighting chance of survival with justice only if grassroots are strengthened.[24]

Suggested Reading

Cameron, D., *Feminism and Linguistic Theory*, London: Macmillan, 1985.

Chaudhary, S., "Rights to the use of Mother Tongue", in O.N. Koul and S. Imtiaz Hasnain (eds.), *Linguistics: Theoretical and applied*, Festshrift in honor of Professor Ruqaiya Hasan, New Delhi: Indian Institute of Language Studies, 2004.

Chen, A.H.Y., "*The Philosophy of Language Rights*", *Language Sciences*, vol. 20, no. 1, 1998.

Corson, David, "English Only and Social Justice," *TESOL Journal*, 8.3: 18-22. 1999.

Davis, W., "Vanishing Cultures", *National Geographic*, August, 1999.

Elders, Fons, *Reflexive Water: The Basic Concerns of Mankind*, London: Souvenir Press (Education and Academic) Ltd., 1994.

Gadamer, H.G., *Truth and Method* (2nd rev. edn., tr. and revision by J. Weinsheimer and D.G. Marshall), New York: Continuum, 1995.

Imtiaz Hasnain, S., "Linguistice Human Rights and Language Planning", in A.P. Vijapur and Kumar Suresh (eds.), *Perspective on Human Rights*, New Delhi: Manak Publications, 1999.

Imtiaz Hasnain, S., "Minority Rights and Education: Question of Survival of Minority Languages", in Joseph Benjamins (ed.), *Minorities in Indian Social Systems*, New Delhi: Gyan Publishing House, 2006. (Also in *Languages in India*, an online journal.)

Imtiaz Hasnain, S., "New Economic Policy and the Fate of Minority Languages", in S. Ramakrishna (ed.), *Translation and Multilingualism: Post Colonial Contexts*, New Delhi: Pencraft International, 1997.

Imtiaz Hasnain, S., "Place of Minority Languages in Education", C.J. Daswani (ed.), *Language Education in Multilingual India*, UNESCO, India, 2001.

Imtiaz Hasnain, S. and R.S. Gupta, "Globalization, Language, Culture and Media: Some Reflections", in B.N. Patnaik and S. Imtiaz Hasnain (eds.),

---

24. D.P. Pattanayak, op. cit., p. 221.

Globalization, Language, Culture and Media, Shimla: Indian Institute of Advanced Study, 2006.

Holdcroft, D., *Saussure: Signs, System and Arbitrariness*, Cambridge: Cambridge University Press, 1993.

Kibbee, Douglas A, "Language Policy and Linguistic Theory", in Jacques Maurais and Michael A. Morris (eds.), *Languages in a Globalizing World*, Cambridge: Cambridge University Press, 2003.

Krauss, M., "The World Languages in Crisis", *Language*, 68.4, 1992.

May, Stephen, "Misconceiving Minority Language Rights : Implications for Liberal Political Theory", in Will Kymlicka and Alan Pattern (eds.), *Language Rights and Political Theory*, Oxford: Oxford University Press, 2003.

National Curriculum Framework, New Delhi: National Council of Educational Research and Training, 2005.

Pattanayak, D.P., "Language and Social Injustice", in Ajit Bhattacharjea (ed.), *Social justice and the Constitution*, Shimla: Indian Institute of Advanced Study, 1997.

Skutnabb-Kangas, T., *Bilingualism or Not: The Education of Minorities*, Multilingual Matters Ltd., 1981.

Wickham, G. L., "Power and Power Analysis: Beyond Foucault", in *Economy and Society*, 12.4, 1983.

CHAPTER 16

Subaltern Consciousness in Sixteenth-Seventeenth Centuries

Sensitizing Egalitarian Approach to Life

Damodar Singh

DELIBERATIONS on fraternity, equality and social justice often tend to be descriptive in Indian context, examining and evaluating the approach of unequal behaviour of different social groups and castes. Egalitarian indignation is expressed at the absence of equality in upper caste people held responsible for denial of justice to the majority. Attempts are also made at framing "normative" ethics, that is, what ought and what ought not to be done, by locating the traditional sources of egalitarianisms such as religious books, scriptures and ancient philosophical treaties. References are made to subaltern groups and marginalized voices, but it is hardly realized that in traditional sources egalitarianisms constitute the "grand" discourse of the dominant social groups, i.e. so-called upper castes, which subsumes the different and divergent aspirations of the subaltern[1] groups. What mars such deliberations are: an inadequacy to recognize the dynamism of social formation and emergence of new power-groups/castes; a tendency to gloss over incongruities, discrepancies and contradictions in social life

1. Subaltern is a late sixteenth-century word. It is derived from Latin "subalternus," from Latin sub-next below + alternus every other. According to the Concise Oxford Dictionary the word "subaltern" means "of inferior rank." It is used as a name for the general attitude of subordination whether this is expressed in terms of class, caste, age, gender and office or in any other way.

and fascination for grand abstractions in place of empirical evidence.

Right from the Vedic period — when the Indian/Hindu society was divided into four *varṇa*s, viz. brāhmaṇa, kṣatriya, vaiśya and śūdra — the people belonging to the fourth *varṇa,* i.e. śūdra, though constituting the majority, were treated as lowest strata in the society. They were constantly suppressed and marginalized by the dominant class; and with the passage of time the condition of this subaltern section went to the dogs. The indication of resurgence of the subaltern first became visible in sixteenth and seventeenth centuries, but during the course, they progressively estranged themselves from the orthodox brāhmaṇas and, resultantly, had to face their onslaughts. This article is an attempt to critically evaluate some of the activities of subalterns and the extent of their success in their endeavour during the period under review.

In the present context, "Subaltern Consciousness" is an inclusive term incorporating experiences of suppression, exploitation and denial of justice and equality to the low-caste people, i.e. śūdras. It was a revolutionary mentality that exhorted the suppressed to be aware of their "slavery" and inequality, and they, thereupon, actively participated in the process of social transformation that was taking place in the form of *bhakti* movement in sixteenth and seventeenth centuries. Rebelling against caste, creed, and sex, it sought to place "Man" as such within centre of existence. The active participation of the śūdras in the *bhakti* movement during the period under review sought to "deconstruct" the grand narratives of religion, culture and philosophy which conceal the "will of truth" and then the "will of power" of the dominant groups. Their activities, on the other hand, revealed the "felt" experiences of agony and suffering over deprivation and exploitation through their claims to have access to the religious text books and to be part and parcel of certain religious recourses that were denied earlier. They asserted for the right to have access to the scriptures like the *Bhagavad-Gītā* and the Purāṇas, to venerate the sacred *śāligrāma-śilā*[2] and to have acquaintance with Tāntric *mantra*s as well. Quite a few of them were elevated to such a position in the society that even the brāhmaṇas treated them as their spiritual preceptors.

There are a couple of evidences indicating to the fact that some śūdras during Mughal India acted as priests and taught spiritual initiation to the populace. A Tamil copper-plate inscription of 1596 bears testimony to the fact that during the sovereignty of Venkayapati Deva[3] (1586–1614), a śūdra cleric had become so strong that he, along with several śūdras, dared to enthrone Kandiya Deva as the king of Vṛddha-kāsī (modern Vṛddhācalam) in the presence of Butta Kṛṣṇappā Nāyaka.[4] Besides, some of the non-brāhmaṇa disciples of the famous saint Caitanya[5] became spiritual preceptors; and, in due course, turned out to be so popular that people of all the four *varṇa*s, including the brāhmaṇas, became their staunch cohorts. One of them was Narhari Sarkar of

2. *Śāligrāma-śilā* is one of the most important *pūjā* items of the Hindus. This is actually a black-coloured stone worshipped by the Hindus. Presently *śāligrāma-śilā* is worshipped in the worship chamber of almost every Hindu family as a manifestation of Lord Viṣṇu, alias Śāligrāma. As per Hindu mythology, in the *Padma Purāṇa*, Lord Śiva, a very powerful Hindu God declared that the merit that a devotee gets by seeing and worshiping idols of lord Śiva for a thousand times can be obtained by worshipping the *śāligrāma-śilā* just for one occasion.

3. Veṅkatapathi Rāya, *alias* Veṅkata II, the King of Vijayanagara Empire (1586-1614), was the fourth ruler of the Araviḍu dynasty. His reign of three decades saw a revival of strength and prosperity of the empire. For detailed information about him, see K.A. Nilakanta Sastry, *History of South India, From Prehistoric Times to Fall of Vijayanagara*, 1955, OUP (rpt. 2002).

4. Sewell, *Lists of Antiquities*, vol. II, Copper Plate List, no. 75, p. 9. Also see www.whatisindia.com.

5. The Beṅgālī saint and religious reformer Śrī Caitanya Mahāprabhu (1486–1533), whom devotees revere as a direct incarnation of Kṛṣṇa, gave a powerful impetus for a massive *bhakti* (devotional) movement throughout India. He made Vrindavan as his base, which soon turned

→

Śrīkhaṇḍa (in the district of Burdwan), who, in spite of belonging to *vaidya* caste, had several brāhmaṇa disciples, such as Gauraṅgadāsa Ghosal, Lokānanda Ācārya and Kaviratna Miśra.[6] Moreover, Kavivallabha has explicitly acknowledged in the *Rasakadamba* that he undertook to compose the illustrious work under the patronage of a brāhmaṇa disciple of Narhari Sarkar, namely Mukuṭa Rāya.[7]

In the closing years of the sixteenth century Narottama Ṭhākur (1531-87), a kāyastha by caste, became spiritual preceptor. Several brāhmaṇas became his ardent followers. One of the more important ones was Śrila Viśvanātha Cakravarti Ṭhākur,[8] who is arguably considered the most learned intellectual and poet in later half of seventeenth century. He had confessed, rather proudly, that the intellectual preceptor trait in him was instigated by the grand disciple of Gaṇgānārāyaṇa Cakravartī, who, in turn, was

---

→ into a reputed centre of Vaiṣṇava studies. Thereunder his direction hundreds of volumes on the philosophy of Kṛṣṇa consciousness were compiled. It may be noted that in the twentieth century one of his disciples, A.C. Bhaktivedānta Swāmī Prabhupāda, not only brought the teachings of Caitanya to the West, but also spearheaded a movement known as "The International Society for Krishna Consciousness" (ISKCON) — established in 1966 — to spread Caitanya's teachings throughout the world. For some interesting escapades about Caitanya, see A.K. Majumdar, "Vignettes of Decaying Buddhism", *Bulletin of Tibetology*, vol. VIII, no. 2, pp. 5-12.

6. Ramgopal Das, "Sakhā-nirvāṇa", in *Rasakalpavalliī* (Kolkata: Calcutta University), pp. 208-10.

7. See Kavivallabha, *Rasakadamba*, p. 83.

8. Śrīla Viśvanātha Cakravartī Ṭhākur (b. 1674) hailed from Naḍiyā district of West Bengal. He received initiation from Śrī Kṛṣṇacaraṇa Cakravartī, in whose house he lived for a long time and wrote many books. Later on, he shifted to Vrindavan in order to serve Lord Kṛṣṇa in the Lord's transcendental abode; and soon got wide acceptability as the leader of Lord Caitanya's followers. Some of his commendable literary works are *Śrī Gurvāṣṭakam: Eight Prayers Glorifying the Spiritual Master*, as well as commentaries on *Śrīmad-Bhāgavatam* and *Bhagavad-Gītā*.

initiated by the distinguished scholar Narottama Ṭhākur.[9] Similarly, there were many other brāhmaṇa disciples of the latter, such as Gopīramana Cakravartī, Ravirāya Pujārī Raghudeva Bhaṭṭācārya, Vasanta Rāya Dvija, Madhusūdana Cakravartī, Balarāma Pujārī, Rāmakṛṣṇa Ācārya, Śaṅkara Bhaṭṭācārya and so on and so forth.[10]

In the Deccan, too, was noticeable a similar phenomenon during the Mughal days. The famous poet-saint of the seventeenth-century Maharashtra, Tukārām[11] (1598–1650), was a śūdra. The venerated saint gave religious discourses to the populace of the area. Several people, not to exclude brāhmaṇa, became his ardent follower. His popularity made some of the brāhmaṇas jealous of him. One of them, namely Rāmeśwar Bhaṭṭa, considered to be a learned scholar, complained to the royal court that Tukārām, a śūdra, was not only studying the holy books, but also receiving salutes from the brāhmaṇas. In this way he was, on the one hand, making the scriptures impure and, on the other, turning the social hierarchy upside down. The district officer, thereupon, directed the *pāṭil* of Dehu to immediately give marching orders (from the village) to Tukārām. However, in due course, the complainant Rameśwar Bhaṭṭa, himself, became convinced of the saintliness of Tukārām. The resolution of difference of perception impelled the former to become one of the most ardent followers of the latter. Besides, one prominent brāhmaṇa woman saint, Bahinābāī, has also conceded about her devotion to the śūdra saint in her autobiography, and exclaims in one of her songs that "Jñānadeva

---

9. Cf. Viśvanātha Cakravartī, *Bhakti-Ratnākara*, p. 1018.

10. For more information about the followers of Narottama Ṭhākur, see *Narottama Vilāsa*, chapter XII.

11. Tukārām (1598–1650) is arguably considered the greatest poet in the Marāṭhī language. His genius partly lies in his ability to transform the external world into its spiritual analogue. Tukārām's stature in Marāṭhī literature is comparable to that of Shakespeare in English or Goethe in German. He could be called the quintessential Marāṭhī poet reflecting the genius on the language as well as its characteristic literary culture.

laid the foundation, and Tukārām became the pinnacle." Furthermore, she even acknowledged that her husband became infuriated on coming to know about her inclination towards the latter. This, however, did not deter her from the devotion, and she, along with many other upper caste people, remained the disciples of the great Marāṭhā saint. In an *Abhaṅga*, the great Marāṭhā saint said: "Our Lord knows nothing of high or low birth; he stops wherever he sees devotion and faith."[12] Again in another *Abhaṅga*, he has given similar message by stating: "Consider him as a brāhmaṇa, vile though his birth may be, who utters correctly the name of Rāma and Kṛṣṇa."[13]

In the Far East India also one comes across similar observable facts in the sixteenth century. The famous saint of Assam Śankaradeva[14] (1449–1568) was a kāyastha by caste, (i.e. śūdra *varṇa*) and he has mentioned that his father Kusumavara was "the famous chief of the feudal lords."[15] He existed in popular consciousness and had a number of brāhmaṇas as his staunch followers as well. A couple of them — Sārvabhauma Bhattacharya and Ananta Kandali — were considered the most prominent ones. The former starts the Svargakhaṇḍa of the *Padma Purāṇa* with

12. *Abhaṅga*, cited in J.F. Edwards, *Life and Teachings of Tukaram*, p. 162.
13. Ibid., p. 162.
14. Śaṅkaradeva, saint-scholar, playwright, social-religious reformer, is a colossal figure in the cultural and religious history of Assam, India. He is credited with providing a thread of unity to Assam straddling two major kingdoms (Ahom and Koch kingdoms), building on past literary activities to provide the bedrock of Assamese culture, and creating a religion that gave shape to a set of new values and social synthesis. The religion he started, Mahāpuruṣīya *dharma*, was part of the *bhakti* movement then raging in India, and he inspired *bhakti* in Assam just as Rāmānanda, Kabīr, Bāsava and Caitanya Mahāprabhu inspired it elsewhere. For recent valuable studies on Śaṅkaradeva, see Śivanāth Barman, *An Unsung Colossus: An Indroduction to the Life and Works of Śaṅkaradeva*, Guwahati: Forum for Shankaradeva Studies, 1999.
15. Śaṅkaradeva, *Bhāgavata, Dasama Skandha*, vv. 12001-02.

millions of obeisance at the feet of Śaṅkaradeva and, describing him in appreciable terms, he equated the saint with absolute incarnation, i.e. God. Another Śaṅkaradeva's principal, as well as equally gifted disciple was Mādhavadeva (1489–1596),[16] who was also kāyastha by caste. Both Śaṅkaradeva and Mādhavadeva were detested by the orthodox brāhmaṇas, and, in consequence, both of them were subjected to harsh hostility from some of them. But this did not deter Śaṅkaradeva, and he continued preaching his philosophy. Initially the topography of his religious sermon was Ahom kingdom. But the Ahom King, under the influence of the Śākta brāhmaṇas, is said to have created hindrance to such an extent that the śūdra saint was compelled to shift to Patbausi near Bārpeṭa first and then finally settle down at Bheladoṅga in Kochbehar.[17]

In the seventeenth century some of the brāhmaṇa disciples of Mādhavadeva, viz. Harideva, Dāmodaradeva and Gopāladeva, broke away from him and formed a separate community, distinguished as "Bamuniā Gosāiṅ." It was nothing but a wilful and conscious attempt of revival of orthodoxy in the society. These secessionists, once again, insisted on strict observance of the caste system and declared that only the brāhmaṇas could impart spiritual initiation. Thus, liberalization in the Hinduism initiated through the preaching of Śaṅkaradeva and Mādhavadeva in Assam, was contained within a century.

Meanwhile, several orthodox brāhmaṇas detested the meddling by the people of other castes/*varṇa*s into the religious

---

16. Mādhavadeva (1489–1596) was a saint, composer, poet, playwright and scholar. The chief disciple and apostolic successor of Śaṅkaradeva, he carried on the works of his *guru*. He was a religious reformer; and the Mahāpuruṣīya Vaiṣṇavism in Assam owes a great deal to his organising ability, foresight and exemplary conduct.
17. Charles N.E. Eliot, "Hinduism in Assam", *Journal of Royal Asiatic Society*, 1910, p. 1169.

functioning, which they considered to be their birthright. They were distinguished as *nibandhakāras*.[18] One of the more prominent ones was Raghunandan Bhaṭṭa,[19] who was considered the greatest *nibandhakāra* of sixteenth century. He viewed that in the Kali age a couple of *varṇas*, kṣatriyas and vaiśyas, had ceased to exist, and, consequently, the Hindu society was left with only two *varṇas* — brāhmaṇas and śūdras. In other words, he considered all the non-brāhmaṇas to be śūdras. He propagated an extreme form of orthodoxy presumably on the basis of the view provided in the religious textbooks, the *Matsya Purāṇa*, the *Viṣṇu Purāṇa* and the *Bhāgavata Purāṇa*.[20]

If the śūdra Kamalākara is believed, similar point-of-view was expressed by Kamalākara Bhaṭṭa[21] in western India.[22] The conservative brāhmaṇas even maintained that the Marāṭhā heroes Śāhjī and his son Śivājī were, in fact, śūdras. However, Śivājī has explicitly mentioned in one of his letters written in July 1556 that

18. *Nibandhkāras* are the authors who clear the doubts raised due to difference between one Smṛti and another, as well as give the details of some missing observations — assuming that some of the rites were commonly known to everybody — not mentioned in the Smṛtis. Their works are called *Dharmasastra Nibandhanas*.

19. Raghunanadan Bhaṭṭācārya (fifteenth-sixteenth centuries) was the chief of the writers of law-treatise of Bengal. According to *Malamāsatattva*, he wrote twenty-eight treatises on the law which regulated the Hindu society of Bengal for many years. Apart from writing critical analyses of the law, he also had a bent for social reform. He was the first to give recognition to Tāntric practice, which had been neglected till then and was looked down upon by the brāhmaṇas.

20. See *Matsya Purāṇa*, 272.4-5; *Viṣṇu Purāṇa*, IV.23.4-5; *Bhāgvata Purāṇa*, XII.1.6-9.

21 Kamalākara Bhatṭṭa wrote *nibandhana* under the title *Nirṇayasindhu* for Maharashtra region. The work has the force of law and is accepted as such by the law courts. It may be noted that each region follows its own *nibandhana*.

22. *Śūdra Kamalākara*, cited in Pandurang Vaman Kaṅe, *History of the Dharmaśātra* (Pune: Bhandarkar Oriental Research Institute, 1941), vol. II, p. 381 the work has been divided into five volumes, all of them

→

he belonged to rājpūt clan.[23] Reaffirming it, two decades later, on the occasion of his enthronement, Śivājī issued a royal decree on 28 January 1677 wherein he declared himself to be a kṣatriya.[24] Of course, he had to face stiff opposition from the orthodox brāhmaṇas of the area during the *rājatilaka* ceremony, for they considered him to be a śūdra, and, hence, not entitled for the coveted post. Ultimately, in order to prove his bonafides, Śivājī had to take the help of a brāhmaṇa from Varanasi, namely Gaṅgādhara Bhaṭṭa. The latter came to Maharashtra and formally justified the fact that Śivājī was, indeed, a kṣatriya and, therefore, rightful claimant to the throne. Later on, Chatrapati Śivājī secured the support of the said brāhmaṇa in getting the candrasenīya kāyasthas[25] the right to perform *ṣodaśa saṁskāras*.[26] In doing so, Śivājī was vehemently opposed, in particular, by an orthodox brāhmaṇa Raghunanadan Bhaṭṭa, who asserted that the śūdras were entitled for only one *saṁskāra*, namely marriage. Although the all-powerful Śivājī was successful in implementing his liberal views, mentioned above, he could not upgrade his caste on a permanent footing. Later on, the Madras High Court passed a judgement that the Marāṭhā princes of Tanjore, descedants from a step-brother of Śivājī, were śūdras and not kṣatriyas.[27]

→ have been published between 1930-62. The work is considered as Dr. Kane's *magnum opus* in English.

23. Sri Sampradyyachi Kagadapotra, *Lekhana*, cited in V.S. Bendrey, *Indroduction to Kesava Pandit's Dandaniti*, p. 62.

24. K.S. Thackarey, *Gramanyacha Sadyanta Itihasa*, pp. 154-55.

25. Nowadays they are commonly known as "*Candrāsni Kāyastha* Prabhu" or "CKP". The kāyasthas of Maharashtra have several surnames, viz. Deshmukh, Thakerey, etc.

26. That is sixteen *saṁskāras*. They are : *garbhādhāna saṁskāra, puṁsavana saṁskāra, sīmantonnayanam saṁskāra, jātakarma, nāmakaraṇa, niṣkramaṇa, annaprāśana, vapana, karṇavedha, upanayana, vedārambha, keśānta, samāvartanavedaśnāna, vivāha saṁskāra, vivāha gṛparigraha, tretāgni saṁgraha*. To know the details about the *samskāras*, see Swami Dayananda Saraswati, *Saṁskāra Vidhi*, Ajmer: Vedic Yantralaya.

27. Madras High Court verdict, cited in Kane, II.382. It may be noted that →

In the *Vallāla-carita*, Ānandabhaṭṭa[28] has briefed about some protests against the changed position of the *suvarṇavaṇika*s in the social hierarchy. According to the author, the *suvarṇavaṇika*s, an important trading class, protested against their degradation to the śūdra class[29] by the ruler Ballal Sen.[30] The author wrote the illustrious literary work at the behest of Buddhimanta Khan, the Rājā of Nabadwīp, in 1510. Interestingly, one year earlier, i.e. in 1509, the famous saint Nityānanda had also taken shelter in Nabadwīp. His liberalism was apparently so popular that soon after his arrival several important members belonging to the *suvarṇavaṇika* community, under the leadership of Uddharana Dutta, willingly became his followers.

The patron Buddhimanta Khan had exhibited his broad-mindedness on several occasions. It was he who had shouldered the financial burden during the marriage of Caitanya with Viṣṇupriyā.[31] He had, moreover, met all the expenses of the dresses and ornaments when Caitanya was staging a symbolic drama — expounding the issue of exploitation in the society — on the marriage of Rukmiṇī.[32] In the drama that was eventually staged,

→ a similar verdict was delivered by the Court of Allahabad regarding the kāyasthas of north India. The Allahabad bench declared the north Indian kāyasthas belonged to śūdra class.The judgement was, however, challenged by the great freedom fighter of Bihar, Sacchidanand Sinha, in the Calcutta High Court. The matter was referred to the Full Bench, which reverted the earlier judgement of the Allahabad Court and gave a ruling that the north Indian kāyasthas were not śūdras, but a constituent of the forward class.

28. Ānandabhaṭṭa was a sixteenth-century Beṅgālī Śaivaite commentator on Vedānta.

29. Ballal Sena (1159-79) was the king of the Sena dynasty (1070–1230) of Bengal, the third ruler of that dynasty. He was considered a staunch Hindu. He is said to have re-enacted the caste system as was prevalent in Kanuaj and pioneered the brāhmaṇa *kulina* rule.

30. It may be noted that the brāhmaṇas treated the śūdras so much inferior that they even did not accept drinking water from them.

31. Vrindavan Das, *Caitanya-Bhāgavata*, I.10.

32. Das, II.18.

Nityānanda appeared in the role of Badai or great-grandmother and Caitanya played the part of Lakṣmī. As a matter of fact the Khan was so much attached to Caitanya that he used to go to Purī every year during the car festival purposely to meet and get blessings from the latter. The information, stated above, is indicative of the fact that he was fully magnetized by the revolutionary spirit of Caitanya, as well as Nityānanda. Resultantly, Buddhimanta Khan, taking his cue of thought from the said legendary figures, directed Ānandabhaṭṭa to thoroughly expose Ballal Sen's inexcusable action of degrading the *suvarṇavaṇika* caste and bracketing them with the śūdras.

Ānandabhaṭṭa has recorded the reason behind the degradation of the *suvarṇavaṇika* castes at the hands of Ballal Sen. According to the author, the king had once taken a loan of Rs.100 lakh from a *suvarṇavaṇika* businessman, namely Vallabhananda, which he was unable to repay. Yet Ballal Sen asked for a fresh loan of Rs.150 lakh from the businessman. The latter's polite but firm refusal touched the vanity of the former. He, thereupon, ordered confiscation of the entire property of Vallabhananda and, in fit of anger, degraded all his caste men, i.e. the *suvarṇavaṇika*s, to śūdrahood, and thenceforth they were debarred from wearing the sacred thread. Suitable instructions were given to the brāhmaṇas as well. They were directed to stop taking teaching or priestly work from the *suvarṇavaṇika*s with immediate effect.

However, the narrative of Srimanta Sagar's education in different branches of learning, as well as description of the *śrāddha* ceremony of Dhanapati's father in the *Kavikaṅkaṇ-cani* makes us believe with high level of probability that the royal instructions were not complied with. Interestingly, during this troublesome period the sea trade in eastern India was primarily under the control of the *suvarṇavaṇika*s, and, seemingly, even the harsh royal decree (mentioned above) did not have any adverse effect on their maritime trade. They were, on the contrary, in a much advantageous position to undertake an economic warfare against the so-called upper castes, particularly brāhmaṇa. Exhibiting the dominance of their money power over the muscle power, they bought all the slaves, at a higher price, who could possibly become domestic servants of the rich populace belonging to these castes. The latter was ultimately compelled to plead to the king, who, as a way out, reportedly upgraded the *kaivartta, mālī* (gardeners), *lohāra* (blacksmith) and *kuṁbhāra*s (potters) as worthy of providing drinking water to the brāhmaṇas and other upper castes.[33]

It is quite difficult to ascertain the veracity of the said event because it is said to have taken place in twelfth century, during the reign of Ballal Sen (1159-79), that was reproduced by Ānandabhaṭṭa three centuries later in sixteenth century, particularly because we do not come across any contemporary or near-contemporary source confirming the episode. However, through this narrative, the author has certainly tried to drive home the message, quite successfully, of the antipathy shown by the *suvarṇavaṇika*s against the social injustice meted out to them in the early years of sixteenth century.[34]

Interestingly, Nityānanda declined to regard the *suvarṇavaṇika*s as lower caste. It is worth noting here that one of his closest

---

33. Devakinanadan, *Vaiṣṇava-Vandanā*, 105.
34. Some modern scholars have, however, doubted that Ballal Sen mentioned in the book is the twelfth century ruler of Bengal. Of course, their doubt does not appear to be without reason. The author has not mentioned any date in the book giving rise to doubt the period and, thereupon, the authenticity of the personality concerned. On the other hand, there seems to be some truth in their assumption that there was one Ballal Sen, an influential *zamīndāra*, who rose to prominence in Vikrampur towards the close of the fourteenth century. He belonged to the vaidya caste and he was a different person from Ballal Sena (of the Sena dynasty of Bengal), who flourished in the twelfth century. According to such scholars, it was at the instance of this Ballal Sen of the vaidya caste that Ānandabhaṭṭa wrote his book *Vallālacarita*. For more information, see Muhammad Enamul Haq, *A History of Sufism in Bengal*, Dhaka, 1975; A Karim, *Social History of the Muslims in Bengal*, Chittagong, 1985.

followers Uddharana Dutta was a *suvarṇavaṇika*, who travelled along with him during his second pilgrimage across India. and, at times, probably cooked his food as well. The *Śāligrāma-śilā* worshipped by Uddharana Dutta is still preserved at Bally, near Kolkata. Nityānanda and his disciples treated the *suvarṇavaṇika*s very generously. Its immediate impact was that each and every *suvarṇavaṇika* of the area became staunch devotee of the Vaiṣṇava faith. The overwhelming endorsement of Nityānanda's faith by the *suvarṇavaṇika*s, had the possible impact of unsettling the *varṇa*-based society in Bengal, while also indicating what possibly lay in store for the brāhmaṇas. Fearing the threat to their superior position in the social hierarchy, orthodox brāhmaṇas, vehemently opposed the liberal views propagated by the followers and successors of Nityānanda.

The consciousness of the śūdras in the sixteenth century was not appreciated even by the contemporary scholar Tulsīdāsa, who has been considered one of the greatest exponents of *bhakti* movement. Exhibiting his apparent displeasure at the śūdras being appointed as religious teachers, he sarcastically observed:

> In the Kali age those who are devoid of purity and are deserters from the Vedic path are known as *jñānī vairāgī*s. The śūdras now impart knowledge to the brāhmaṇas, . . . get their feet worshipped by the brāhmaṇas and thus destroy their prospects in this as well as in the other world. The śūdras presume to perform *japa, vrata*s and austerities and teach the Purāṇas from the seat of the teacher.[35]

Again, while briefing the conduct of the men of the Kali age,[36] he is found to be quite critical regarding the activities of the śūdras.

35. Tulsīdāsa, *Rāmacaritamānasa*, Nagari Pracarani Sabha edn., p. 483.

36. Kali age [lit. "Age of (the male demon) Kali", "age of vice"], is one of the four stages of development that the world goes through as part of the cycle of *yuga*s as described in Indian scriptures, the others being Satya Yuga, Tretā Yuga and Dvāpara Yuga. According to the *Sūrya Siddhānta*, an astronomical treatise that forms the basis of all Hindu →

Commenting on them, he said that the śūdras of the period are trying to compete with the brāhmaṇas and are claiming to be in no way inferior to the latter. They (i.e. the śūdras), moreover, reprove the brāhmaṇas by declaring only those who have knowledge of the *Brahman* should be accepted as legitimate brāhmaṇa. Such views were totally unacceptable by Tulsīdāsa, and he not only detested them, but also openly opposed them, tooth and nail.

Thus, we observe that, effectively, a sincere attempt was made by the śūdras to carve out an egalitarian society in sixteenth and seventeenth centuries.[37] It, however, received stiff opposition from the conservative classes, in particular by the brāhmaṇas, who were not ready to accept any change in the social hierarchy. Ballal Sena of Bengal, "Bamuniā Gosāiṅ" and *nibandhakāra*s under the leadership of Raghunandan Bhatt in the Far East India, Kamalākara

---

→ and Buddhist calendars, Kali Yuga began at midnight on 18 February 3102 BCE in the proleptic Julian calendar or 23 January 3102 BC in the proleptic Gregorian calendar, which is also considered by many Hindus to be the time that Kṛṣṇa, an incarnation of Viṣṇu, died as a result of a freak bow hunting accident. The Kali Yuga is traditionally thought to last 432,000 years. Most interpretations of Hindu scriptures believe that earth is currently in Kali Yuga. Hindus believe that human civilization degenerates spiritually throughout the Kali Yuga: it is mostly referred to as the Dark Age, mainly because people are the furthest possible from God.

37. It is worth noting that such liberal sentiments were also influencing the contemporary west. In England, the Tudor monarchs (1485–1603), particularly Henry VIII and Queen Elizabeth, gave patronage to such liberal views. Indeed, voices were being raised against superstitions, exploitation by the church, slavery, poverty and illiteracy. Creative writers, such as William Blake (fourteenth century), Chaucer (fifteenth century), Shakespeare (sixteenth century), and, above all, William Blake (eighteenth century) highlighted the exploitations, and, therefore, have been termed great subaltern writers of the West. William Blake is arguably considered the greatest subaltern writer the west has ever produced.

Bhaṭṭa in western India, and, more importantly, Tulsīdāsa in northern India were the main exponents of the orthodox section. The vehemence of their hostility and the intimate conservativism of the masses made the resurgence of the śūdra a short-lived one. Strictly speaking, the attempt for social space by the śūdras could not withstand virulent resistance by the brāhmaṇas who considered the whole venture to be an infringement of their birthright, which they were not ready to share at any cost. Meritocracy and social justice were, consequently, suppressed; and by the closing years of the seventeenth century the subaltern class, i.e. the śūdras were, once again, relegated to their inferior position in the social stratification. But the voice of the subaltern class could not be gagged for long, and after a lull of almost one century, they, once again, raised their heads during the socio-religious reform movement in late eighteenth and nineteenth centuries; and the baton was later taken over by B.R. Ambedkar,[38] who became the champion of the downtrodden, i.e. the *dalit*s, in the twentieth century.

---

38. Ambedkar vehemently fought that the *dalit*s should have rightful place under the sun. After Independence, on his recommendation, reservation in various sectors was implemented for a decade as one of the measures for the upliftment of *dalit*s. But the reservation policy became a tool in the hands of politicians, who not only broadened the base of reservation, but also made this policy a permanent feature of Indian polity for their vested interest. In the process Ambedkar's dream of upliftment of the *dalit*s seems to have been lost in the way; and meritocracy is being sacrificed at the altar of reservocracy.

CHAPTER 17

Issues Concerning Rights of Children

Ameeta Jaiswal

POLITICAL thinkers since earliest times have been trying to formulate the concept of justice. However, with the dawn of modern consciousness, especially under the influence of the principles of democracy and socialism, this concept has been greatly transformed. As a result, the traditional view of justice has given way to the concept of social justice. The ideal of social justice envisages promoting the welfare of the people especially the poor, needy and weaker sections of the society. This ideal can be attained only when there is no discrimination in the distribution of rights and privileges on the basis of caste, creed, class, age, race and the like. But it is a great irony that in spite of the inclusion of this ideal in the form of fundamental rights and directive principles of state policy, several sections of the society are still facing oppression and exploitation in the society and are subject to severe forms of injustice and violation of their rights. One such section is the children, the future leaders of our country. It has been learnt that nearly one billion children across the world are deprived of their basic rights of survival and growth. This article is an attempt to discuss the issues involved with the concept of social justice and that too keeping the rights of children as the centre of focus. With a genuine concern, an effort will be made here to define justice, especially social justice concerning children by tracing its historical development. Also, we shall discuss the rights of children, the ways in which they are abused and lastly the solutions from a philosophical point of view will be attempted at.

I

The issue of justice regarding children has assumed tremendous significance today in the wake of constant violation of children's rights of survival and total development of their personality. The children are the first and foremost foundation of the grown up man or as John Milton has said, "The child shows the man as morning shows the day." They are the future citizens of our country, the leaders and torch-bearers of the nation. Hence, for the balance of the whole social order their fundamental rights have to be preserved. Our Constitution also ensures to observe this most important aspect for the preservation and continuation of humanity. The Preamble of our Constitution reads,

> We, the people of India, having solemnly resolved to constitute India into a Sovereign, Secular, Democratic, Republic and to secure to all its citizens: Justice, social, economic and political;
>
> Liberty of thought, expression, belief, faith and worship;Equality of status and of opportunity; and to promote among them all;
>
> Fraternity, assuring the dignity of the individual and the unity and integrity of the Nation.

However, with the highly developed economic society, scientific advancements, materialistic outlook and pseudo-pragmatic approach the social reality has taken an entirely different shade and there are distortions in the name of social justice. It won't be an exaggeration, if we say that children are the most neglected part of the society because they are totally dependent on their parents who are busy since morning till night hoarding money with the distorted idea of comfort level.

Children worldwide are deprived of their childhood, dignity and rights since they are minor and cannot fight for their rights. We are harping on it much through workshops, seminars, talks, articles, etc. but the corresponding action level is totally absent. The result is almost zero and requires serious reflections and forceful will to achieve it. Philosophy offers the clue to all types of knowledge, concerning nature, society and values. Social philosophy covers that part of philosophy which seeks to make human life worth living. Hence, a solution from the side of philosophy for the problem of injustice to children is feasible.

II

We would start with a brief observation of the meaning tied up with the concept of justice. Justice is believed to be a condition of the ideal state of humanity, a morally correct state of things and persons. It concerns the order of society as a whole and is an expression of the rights of individuals. However, the concept of justice is a complex one. It is used both with law and social morality. On the one hand, justice is concerned with the order of society as a whole, and on the other, it is an expression of the right of individuals in contrast to the claims of general social order. Justice functions as a conservative and reformative principle.

> Conservative justice is concerned with the preservation of established social norms and with the protection of freedom as well as property of individuals. Reformative justice is undoubtedly intended to produce a more equitable society as the common term social justice implies, but it is equally intended to secure for needy or meritorious individual the rights to which it thinks they are entitled.[1]

Hence, the term "social justice" is generally associated with reformers. In his essay entitled "Justice as Fairness," John Rawls has said,

> One practicable aim of justice as fairness is to provide an acceptable and philosophical basis for democratic institutions and thus to address the question of how the claims of liberty and equality are to be understood.[2]

Ernest Barker has said that justice represents a synthesis of the

---

1. D.D. Raphael, *Problems of Political Philosophy* (Delhi: The Macmillan Company of India Ltd., 1977), p. 172.
2. Colin Farrelly, *An Introduction to Contemporary Political Theory* (Delhi: Sage Publications India Pvt Ltd., 2004), p. 13.

principles of liberty, equality and fraternity. Hence, justice is primarily a concept of moral philosophy, though it has to be implemented by a political order.

In the history of Western political thought, the best example of the theory of justice is to be found in Plato's *Republic*. Plato's concept of justice was focused on "just" man, where it was primarily concerned with the virtues befitting a man for enhancing his moral worth and consisted in performing his duties. Aristotle believed that justice consists in "treating equals equally and un-equals unequally." Justice, in India, had been identified with *dharma*, meaning righteousness and implies all that comes within the fold of a righteous way of life. The idea of justice is dynamic and under the influence of democracy and socialism, the traditional concept has been thoroughly transformed. Applying it to the concept of social justice, it means that justice is dispensed to all sections of the society without any discrimination of colour, caste, creed, sex, wealth, class and age. "Justice demands that each individual should be treated as an end in itself and not as a means to an end."[3] In this context, social justice is based on the concepts of human rights and equality. Naturally, injustice to any section of the society would lead to chaos and confusion.

A society is defined as a web of social relationships. It consists of individuals categorized into different sections based on certain criteria, one of which is "age." On the basis of age, we can broadly outline four classes in the society — children, youth, adult and the old aged people and obviously childhood is the first stage of this hierarchy. Children belong to that section of the society which has to be nurtured and taken care of for the progress of the society and the nation at large. Children are the gift of God. It is said that child is the father of man. A child is like wet clay which can be moulded in whatever shape we want. The childhood stage is greatly influenced and structured by the family, society, culture

---

3. O.P. Gauba, *Social and Political Philosophy* (Noida: Mayoor Paperbacks, 1976), p. 141.

and environment. Hence, utmost effort has to be made for their development. In other words, to do justice to them is the prime responsibility of the society.

III

Historically seen in the Indian context, we find that in the early Vedic society (1500–900 BCE), girls moved freely in society and were educated as boys. Later Vedic period (900–500 BCE) saw a gradual decline of the education of girl children and eventually Vedic education was reserved for the males of three upper classes. Gradually, sons came to be considered more useful than daughters, the reason being that they alone could serve their father in this world as well as in the next world (*piṇḍa-dāna*). The uselessness of daughters made them feel that female child was a burden and an unwelcome arrival in the family. The Mughal period proved further detrimental to children. Many vices like child-marriage, infanticide, prostitution and illiteracy were prevailing during the period. But, Akbar had passed orders prohibiting marriages of girl children before the age of fourteen and those of boys before sixteeen. The British period saw the period of renaissance. The British encouraged education for the girl child and women. They passed legislation for the remarriage of widows, abolished *satī-prathā*, restrained child marriages and permitted them to come out of *purdah* and share liberty with their counterparts. But social bias and religious injunctions worked against them and proved to be a hindrance in their emancipation. However, one is constrained to remark that during the British period, emancipation of the girl child remained minimal and improvement in their position was negligible. "In fact, the position of children since long has been pitiable in all aspects of life and subjugation of female children by males has been throughout the matter of history."[4] But the present scenario presents a totally different picture. Today children in general are victimized and their rights are abused.

---

4. Suman Lata and Anjani Kant, *Child and the Law* (Delhi: APH Publishing Co., 2007), p. 2.

Hence, we have started to emphasize the protection of the rights of children. They have to get justice as they have been the most neglected class, shaking the very foundation of the society. Philosophically speaking or in the larger perspective they have to be developed totally, that is physically, mentally, socially, morally and spiritually so that in the long run they would grow into a wholesome and aesthetic person. In other words, they would be enlightened persons and would enliven the society.

The *Taittirīya Upaniṣad* speaks of five *kośa*s inside a *jīva* — the *annamaya-kośa, prāṇamaya-kośa, manomaya-kośa, vijñānamaya-kośa* and *ānandamaya-kośa*.[5] The child at the infant stage has the right to survive. The first two *kośa*s are essential to preserve the fundamental rights of survival. When he grows up the other *kośa*s have to be developed. Hence, a child has to be given proper care, nourishment, education, and healthy environment for the healthy mind and body. For this, a joint effort is essential on the part of the government and the society.

IV

The Constitution of our country has left no stone unturned to protect the rights of children. Children are entitled to the wide range of fundamental rights provided under Article 19 of the Constitution. Apart from these, they have been accorded additional rights like "Right to Education" which is recognized as the fundamental right of children. Article 21A says: the state shall provide free and compulsory education to all children of the age six to fourteen years in such a manner as the state may, by law, determine. Such positive rights indicate the steps taken by the state to improve the quality of life of its citizens and to help them in their self-development.

The equality clause contained in Articles 14 and 15 of the Constitution prohibits discrimination on the basis of race, religion,

---

5. Surendranath Dasgupta, *A History of Indian Philosophy* (Delhi: Motilal Banarsidass, 2004), p. 46.

caste, colour, creed, sex, etc. Hence, the Constitution of India ensures equal status to male and female children. Employment of children below the age of fourteen is strictly prohibited under Article 24. Also, sections 366(a), 372 and 373 of IPC state that procuration of minor girl for the purposes of prostitution, selling, etc. are criminal acts carrying a penalty of up to ten years imprisonment. Juvenile Justice (Care and Protection of Children) Act, 2000 also aims at protecting the rights of children in conflict with law. Article 13, chapter 2 of the Act clearly states:

> No report in any newspaper, magazine, news sheet or visual media of any enquiry regarding a juvenile in conflict with law under this Act shall disclose the name, address or school or any other particulars calculated to lead to the identification of the juvenile, nor shall any picture of any such juvenile be published.

But the irony is that in spite of laws being prescribed by the Constitution, there are many children in our country who are deprived of their fundamental rights.

In a discourse on "Deprived and Repressed Child" organized in the memory of Pradhan Harishankar Prasad, noted economist and Professor Emeritus, Glasgow University, UK, Mr Radha Sinha said, "Around one billion children across the world are deprived of their basic rights and are victims of physical and mental torture in their own settings."[6] In India, several forms of injustice and criminality against children have become rampant. A few examples are:

- Employing children as child labour for hazardous works like making of crackers, *bīḍīs*, carpet weaving, etc.
- Child sexual abuse in India is on a higher scale compared to the rest of the world.
- Sexual abuse of girl children or child prostitution is increasing at an alarming rate in the country and in many cases the close relatives are found to be the culprits.

---

6. *The Hindustan Times*, Patna edition, 25 November 2007, p. 2.

- Due to fast lifestyle and competitive socio-economic structure, children are not receiving quality time from their parents.
- Child marriage is still1 prevalent in Bihar, Rajasthan and some other states and parents still prefer to get their daughters married between 10-14 years of age.
- Female foeticide is the most heinous crime in our country, especially because we worship goddesses and she is the epitome of recreation.
- Condition of children in remand home is also pitiable. These children are either abandoned by their parents or are lost children or bonded labourers released from metros or unfortunate children forced to live on railway platforms.
- In school, too, many children are subject to ill treatment and harsh punishment at the hands of teachers. "Hit by teacher, he may lose his eyes" read a news headline of *HT*, New Delhi, 13 December 2007.
- Nithari incident a year ago shocked the whole world when people came to know that skeletal remains of 15 children were unearthed from a drain in a rich businessman's backyard in Noida's up-scale Sector 31.
- Paedophilia: Paedophiles, especially from developed countries are getting children from developing countries like India for satiating their lust which they could not do in their own country due to social stigma attached to these acts and stringent laws.

Thus, there are numerous other ways in which children are being deprived of their rights and privileges.

Now, the question arises as to why such incidents are taking place in our society and how can this problem be solved. This will also give the true answer to the meaning of social justice regarding children.

If we reflect on the causes behind such incidents taking place in our society, we find that the socio-economic backwardness and poverty of the lower classes in the society; the rising demand of available goods of comfort in urban and metropolitan cities leading to immoral practices; the short-cut method of achieving material happiness; wide gap between the income and expenditure of the family; carelessness and negligence on the part of parents; and the negative impact of science and technology are some of the causes. Philosophically speaking, as *rajas* and *tamas guṇa*s are predominating human nature to the neglect of *sattva guṇa*, there has been imbalance in the personality of the individual leading to injustice in the society. Unfortunately, the "animality" in man is suppressing his rationality. Above all, lack of proper education to children is the most important cause for the abuse of their rights; for it is education alone that can acquaint them of their rights so that they do not become victims of injustice.

When we talk of education as an indispensable tool for providing children social justice, we want to empower the child with his basic right to lead a dignified life. "This creates the necessity of formal institutions like schools and professional groups like teachers. A person who fails to benefit is more likely to be left behind and pushed to the margins."[7] If proper education is not given to a child and he is left illiterate, he will not be able to understand, leave alone appeal against any injustice done to him. A child deprived in his childhood will prove disastrous to the society in the long run. The Right to Education has even been recognized by several international declarations — Universal Declaration of Human Rights (UDHR), 1948; the International Covenant on Economic, Social & Cultural Right (ICESCR), 1966 and the Convention on the Rights of the Child (CRC). Human rights determine the very source of all the rights of human beings. They provide for moral foundation of any system of rights. In a way, they are akin to the concept of justice. "World fit for children" an agenda for

7. Daisy Narain and Vinay K. Kantha, *Rights on Hold* (Patna: East & West Educational Society), p. 1.

improving health, education, and protection of children under the age of eighteen has been ratified by the UN General Assembly.

V

But, we see that in spite of numerous laws enacted for providing justice to children in India they are still being deprived of their basic rights and continue to live under the stress and strain of the society. Much of their problem is due to their lack of awareness of the laws and the indifferent and hostile attitude of the law enforcing agency. The most unfortunate part of the child's education is the implementation part of the educational policies. The recommendations of Sri Prakash Committee and Kothari Commission should have been forcefully implemented. Keeping in mind that children's rights are the responsibility of everyone, the state and central governments should devise effective means for the implementation of the laws concerning the education of the children and the society should build pressure on the parents to send their children to school. The initiatives of the government like "Sarva Shiksha Abhiyan" and "Common School System" are commendable programmes for the development of education but a lot more has to be done through innovative ways as the aim of social justice to children will not be fulfilled so long as a single child is deprived of elementary education. Still, children in villages of India are grazing cattle instead of receiving basic education. A century back Swami Vivekananda had remarked,

> A nation is advanced in proportion as education and intelligence spread among the masses. The chief cause of India's ruin has been the monopolizing of the whole education and intelligence of the land among a handful of men. If we are to rise again, we shall have to do it again by spreading education among the masses.[8]

The role of teachers is also very important. They should act as role models and facilitators for the all round development of the

---

8. N.L. Gupta, *Swami Vivekananda* (New Delhi: Anmol Publications Pvt. Ltd., 2003), p. 92.

students. Education imparted should be in accordance with what Gandhiji had visualized, that is, in such a way that it would help a child in the formation of his character, increase the strength of his mind, expand his intellect and help him to stand on his own feet.

Last but not the least is the role of parents. Those parents who do not allow their children to go to school should be explained about the benefits of education through awareness campaigns like door-to-door awareness programmes, advertisements in both electronic and print media, etc. School-going children should not be allowed to work in houses or factories. For the poor parents who send their children to work for earning money, the government should come out with some lucrative incentives like employment and some other support systems.

Hence, we conclude by saying that social justice cannot be conceived even if a small number of children are deprived of their basic rights. Children are the foundation of the edifice of the society and if the foundation is not strong, the structure is bound to collapse some day. Hence, to maintain the balance in society which is a part of cosmic moral order or *ṛta* in the Vedic terms, children should be given their due rights, especially their right to education. The challenge lies in making children the strength of the nation by evolving strategies for developing curriculum to educate them. Only then we shall be able to realize our dreams of a world where children will live with freedom and dignity and enjoy their innate rights.

LET US UNITE TO PLEDGE THAT NO CHILD IS
ROBBED OF HIS SMILE AND CHILDHOOD

Suggested Reading

Farrelly, Colin, *An Introduction to Contemporary Political Theory*, New Delhi: Sage Publication, 2004.

Gauba, O.P., *Social and Political Philosophy*, Noida: Mayoor Paperbacks, 1976.

Gupta, N.L., *Swami Vivekananda*, New Delhi: Anmol Publications Pvt. Ltd., 2003.

Johari, J.C., *Contemporary Political Theory*, New Delhi: Sterling Publisher Pvt. Ltd., 1979.

Kantha, Vinay K., and Madan M. Jha, *Search for Rights, Equity and Social Justice* (Right to Education Bill, 2005), Patna: East & West Educational Society.

Lata, Suman and Anjani Kant, *Child and the Law*, New Delhi: APH Publishing Co.

Narain, Daisy, and Vinay K. Kantha, *Rights on Hold*, New Delhi: East & West Educational Society.

Raphael, D.D., *Problems of Political Philosophy*, New Delhi: Macmillan Education Ltd, 1977 (rev. edn.).

Roy, Krishna and Chhanda Gupta (eds.), *Essays in Social and Political Philosophy*, New Delhi: Allied Publishers.

Singh, Ranbir and Ghanshyam Singh, *Human Rights Education*, Hyderabad: Law and Society, Nalsar University.

Part IV

Reservation and Reverse Discrimination

CHAPTER 18

Morality and Social Justice

An Analytical Study on Preferential Treatment

Y.V. Satnarayana

THE concept of justice is a complex one. There are three important areas to the function of justice. It is used both for law and for social morality. On the one hand, justice is concerned with the order of society as a whole, and on the other, it is an expression of the rights of individuals in contrast to the claims of general social order. Finally, justice functions as a conservative and reformative principle.

Conservative justice aims to protect the established order of the society, whereas reformative justice calls for revisions of the social order, and redistribution of rights to suit current ideas of fairness. When people speak of "social justice" usually they have in mind the reformative justice. The term "social justice" is generally associated with reformers. Thus reformative justice is intended to produce a more equitable society.[1]

After the advent of democracy, the meaning of justice itself has been expanded to cover almost all spheres of human life. The idea of social justice requires sacrificing certain rights of individuals for the sake of a greater good, or good of society as a whole. Social justice aims at reconciliation of the interests of individuals with the overall interests of the community. Thus the idea of social justice maintains a balance between the rights of individuals and the needs of the society. The ideal of social justice envisages

1. Cf. D.D. Raphael, *Problems of Political Philosophy* (Delhi: The Macmillan Company of India Ltd., 1977), pp. 165-72.

promoting the welfare of the people, especially the poor, needy, and weaker sections of the society.

The formal principle of justice requires that persons who are alike in morally relevant respects ought to be treated alike, and that persons who differ in morally relevant respects ought to be treated differently in proportion to the differences between them. It is called a "formal" principle because it does not specify what characteristics are to be considered as relevant similarities, or differences among persons. Many philosophers have suggested that characteristics for which no person can bear responsibility such as — caste, colour, creed, race, sex and the like — are not to be counted as relevant similarities, or differences when justice is being considered.

The question of justice arises whenever there is concern for apportioning benefits and burdens fairly. If there is no scarcity for desired materials, resources, opportunities, and the like, then the question of justice would not arise. For example, if there were more jobs than applicants, then there would be no question of fairness of procedures for selecting those to get jobs from among applicants.

The socio-economic conditions that exist in contemporary India (also in many countries all over the world) raise certain fundamental moral questions. Some people are very rich, while others are very poor. People belonging to some sections of the society occupy the most privileged positions in the society, and a vast majority of the people belonging to other sections of the society are deprived of them. Some people are so poor that they are dying of starvation. Is this fair? Is the unequal distribution of wealth merely the result of unjust social arrangements that should be changed? What responsibility do the people belonging to affluent sections of the society have towards starving people? Can it be morally right to spend money on luxuries that could be used to save other people from starvation?

The most problematic question of distributive justice is — how to allocate benefits and burdens among the people of a social system? It is a very difficult task to devise universally acceptable criteria for allocation of benefits and burdens. Which characteristics of persons are to be taken as morally relevant in the distribution of benefits and burdens? Is it morally correct to tax the income of those who work, to provide income for those who do not work? To what extent merit, need, effort, or productive contribution ought to be taken into consideration in the distribution of benefits and burdens to the people?

As a response to these questions, philosophers propose various principles of social justice. The wealth or goods of society should be distributed on the basis of certain principles such as need, merit, effort, productive contribution, etc. Joel Feinberg, an American social philosopher, considers the question of distributive justice, and he examines five principles as basic to the just distribution of wealth and goods:[2]

1. The principle of equality, which says that all people should have equal wealth.

2. The principle of need, which states that everyone should have enough to satisfy their basic needs.

3. The principle of merit and achievement, which asserts that wealth and goods should be distributed on the basis of people's merits, or achievements.

4. The principle of contribution, which conveys that people should receive a share of society's wealth and goods on the basis of their contribution to the society.

5. The principle of labour, or effort, which suggests that people should be rewarded according to their labour, or effort.

---

2. Cf. Joel Feinberg, "Justice and Economic Income", in James Rachels (ed.), *Moral Problems* (New York: Harper & Row Publishers, 1979), p. 213.

Feinberg maintains the principle of need to be fundamental to a just distribution of goods. However, the principles of contribution and effort may enter to determine the distribution of left-over goods after everyone's basic needs have been satisfied.

Liberty and equality, as two important moral ideals, play a significant role in the consideration of justice. Philosophers and thinkers disagree on the principles of distributive justice, and on the justifiable limits of government interference with individual liberty.

The Libertarian Concept of Justice

Libertarian, or individualistic conception of justice holds liberty to be the ultimate moral ideal. For the libertarian, individual liberty is more important, and he considers that a society is just which provides maximum liberty to the individual. According to libertarian view, the sole function of the government is to protect the moral rights of people, that is, the right to life, liberty and property against force and fraud. If A has right to X, no one should prevent A from pursuing X, because A is entitled to it.

Providing welfare to those who cannot, or will not, provide for themselves is not a morally justifiable function of government. To make such provisions, the government would have to take from some people against their will in order to give others. Taxing some people to give to others is analogous to robbery. John Hospers, who defends a libertarian position, argues that the laws requiring people to help one another through welfare payments are just like "rob Peter to pay Paul."[3]

The Socialist Conception of Justice

A direct challenge to libertarian viewpoint comes from those who defend socialist conception of justice. While libertarians stress on liberty, or freedom from coercion, the socialists stress on equality, or freedom from want. The libertarians stress negative rights

3. John Hospers, "What Libertarianism Is", in Thomas A. Mappes and James S. Zembaty (eds.), *Social Ethics: Morality and Social Policy* (New York: McGraw-Hill Book Company, 1987), p. 339.

(rights not to interfere with), whereas socialists stress on positive rights — right to food, clothing, shelter, health care, productive work, etc.

Although there are many varieties of socialism, one common element in socialist thought is a commitment to social equality and collective ownership of productive property. Since social equality is the ultimate ideal of socialism, some limitations on individual liberty that are necessary to promote social justice are justified.

The Liberal Conception of Justice

The liberal conception of justice tries to combine both liberty and equality into one ultimate moral ideal. Liberals consider some of the libertarian's negative rights as extremely important. They advocate that social institutions should follow two important functions:

1. To ensure certain basic liberties for all, and
2. To provide basic needs to the disadvantaged members of society.

However, liberals differ from socialists on the communal ownership of the means of production. John Rawls argues that only those social goods are justified that will contribute to raising the position of the least-advantaged groups in the society.

The Marxist Conception of Justice

Marxists, like the socialists, are committed to the ideal of social equality. Marxists oppose the exploitation of workers by the capitalists. They argue that workers under capitalism receive only a part of the value of what they have produced, and the rest, the *surplus value*, goes to capitalists. The capitalists, as owners of the means of production, appropriate this surplus labour of the workers. In a communist society, distribution is to be based on the principle that, "From each according to his abilities, to each according to his needs."

Preferential Treatment and Moral Justification

In recent times, the policies and programmes of preferential treatment, or reverse discrimination have aroused much controversy in many countries all over the world. These policies and programmes gave rise to arguments, law suits, riots and bloodshed in many countries, including India. The significant moral question associated with the problem of preferential treatment is — whether we should set aside the principles of justice for the sake of attaining some larger social good.

The Nature and Content of Preferential Treatment

The practice of favouring, or compensating the victimized groups of the past is described in different phrases such as "preferential discrimination," or "positive discrimination," or "preferential treatment," or "affirmative action," or "reverse discrimination" and so on. This practice is found in many countries all over the world. To mention a few of the many countries where certain social groups receive official government-sanctioned preferences over others are India, USA, Australia, Nigeria, Sri Lanka, Malaysia, Indonesia and Pakistan. The preferential policies and programmes of these countries vary from one another depending on the social, political, economic, and cultural factors existing in those countries.

The practice of discrimination against certain social groups in the past, and its ongoing effects in the present can be addressed in two ways:

1. The first course of action is to stop discrimination against these groups, and treat them on a par with other members of the society. This approach neither involves compensation for the past injustices nor helps to undo the effects of past discrimination.

2. The second course of action is to go further, and give preferential treatment to the victimized groups, temporarily for a fixed period of time, in order to rectify the ongoing effects of the past discrimination.

Many philosophers and thinkers express the view that discontinuation of the practice of discrimination is not simply enough, and the people who have been discriminated in the past must be adequately compensated for the injustices done to them. They maintain that preferential treatment is one of the most favoured ways of compensating past discrimination. The policies and programmes of preferential treatment are intended to neutralize the ongoing effects of past discrimination, and to rectify the social disparities existent in the social system.

The preferential treatment programmes involve fixed quota systems in the field of education, employment, and promotion to the members of the victimized groups. The government identifies some castes, or social groups subjected to injustices in the past, and certain percentage of seats and jobs are reserved for them in education, employment, and promotions. However, the policies and programmes of preferential treatment intended to the victims of the past must be within the scope and limits of the constitution of a territory. The preferential action programmes, to be constitutional, must be based on a compelling state interest. Referring to the preferential treatment programmes, D.H.M. Brooks, a Professor at the University of Capetown, South Africa, argues:

> . . . a mere barring of discriminatory acts . . . may not be enough to cure the evil. Affirmative action is one of the bits of social engineering which has been devised to rectify an entrenched practice of discrimination.[4]

Preferential Treatment and Reverse Discrimination

Discrimination may be defined as making a policy, or a decision, or a judgement on the consideration of irrelevant factors in question such as caste, colour, creed, race, sex, and so on. These factors or characteristics are almost irrelevant to decisions about

4. D.H.M. Brooks, "Why Discrimination is Especially Wrong", in Thomas A. Mappes and James S. Zembaty (eds.), *Social Ethics: Morality and Social Policy*, p. 204.

whom to select to a job, or whom to admit in an institute of higher learning. Hence the policy of discrimination on the basis of irrelevant factors in the matters of education, and employment is considered as unfair and unjust.

However, from a different perspective of neutralizing, or rectifying the effects of past discrimination, and giving an advantage to the victims, the factors such as caste, colour, creed, race, and sex are not considered as irrelevant factors, because the history of discrimination turned them into relevant factors. The most distinctive thing in preferential discrimination is that it takes up the same irrelevant factors used for discrimination in the past, and applies them now in a reverse way to provide special treatment to the victimized groups of the past.

The practice of reverse discrimination can be explained in a different way. Certain social groups or castes have been discriminated against in the past on the basis of certain "morally irrelevant" factors, and subjected to injustices. It is now allowed to use the same factors as "morally relevant" criterion to justify preferential treatment. The use of the same factors in reverse order to provide preferential treatment to the victims of the past is known as reverse discrimination. George Sher, a professor of philosophy at the University of Vermant, argues:

> Past discrimination justifies reverse discrimination insofar as it has adversely affected the competitive position of present group members.[5]

Preferential Treatment and Compensatory Justice

The most plausible approach to the problem of preferential treatment is to claim for compensation to groups whose members have been discriminated in the past. The principle of compensatory justice states that whenever injustice has been done, just compensation, or reparation should be given to the injured persons.

---

5. George Sher, "Justifying Reverse Discrimination in Employment", in John Arthur (ed.), *Morality and Moral Controversies* (New Jersey: Prentice-Hall, Inc. Englewood Cliffs, 1981), p. 330.

It is now a widespread view that the social groups discriminated against in the past should be adequately compensated for the injustices inflicted on them.

The philosophers and thinkers who appeal for compensatory justice argue that preferential treatment programmes are one way of compensating the victimized groups by providing things to these groups which were unjustly denied to them in the past. Even though caste or sex under these conditions are unrelated to education and employment, the principles of compensatory justice appeals to justify the use of caste or sex as relevant criteria to distinguish the equal from the unequal.

Utilitarian Approach

Another approach towards elimination of ongoing effects of past discrimination is grounded on the "Principle of Utility" which states that an action or a practice is morally correct if it produces better consequences. It is not for compensation, or rectification of the past injustices, but for morally good consequences to be produced to the victimized groups of the past.

Richard Wasserstrom, a professor of philosophy at the University of California, argues that preferential programmes can be justified on the basis of utilitarian claim to have good consequences for an integrated and equalitarian society. It becomes relevant to consider the morally desirable consequences that preferential programmes are designed to bring about. The good consequences produced by these programmes will far outweigh the bad consequences, even though those bad consequences include the injustices resulting from reverse discrimination. He argues:

> It is also wrong to think that programmes of preferential treatment in any strong sense is either unjust or unprincipled. . . . Such programmes may reasonably be viewed as potentially valuable and effective means by which to achieve admirable and significant social ideals of equality and integration.[6]

6. Richard Wasserstrom, "A Defence of programmes of Preferential Treatment", in Thomas A. Mappes and James S. Zembaty (eds.), *Social Ethics: Morality and Social Policy*, pp. 218-19.

Thus practices productive of intended results, or good consequences of reverse discrimination, may be morally correct.

Controversies in Preferential Treatment

The proponents of preferential treatment maintain that the individuals who have been discriminated in the past should be given preference for education, jobs and promotion, whereas the opponents argue that preferential treatment puts an unfair burden on innocent people who are not responsible for the past discrimination, and it violates their rights, and establishes a dangerous precedent. Thus there are two equally powerful and opposing standpoints on this issue. Both the proponents and the opponents of preferential treatment have offered convincing arguments to defend their viewpoints.

Arguments in Favour of Preferential Treatment

The proponents of preferential treatment offer the following reasons in support of their argument:

1. The members belonging to certain social groups have been subjected to discrimination in the past, and the consequences of past discrimination put them in a disadvantaged position to compete equally with the members of non-preferred groups.

2. As a result of past discrimination, the members of the victimized groups are under-represented in the institutes of higher learning and desirable occupations. The idea of equality sought for a balanced distribution of benefits and hardships among the members of the social system.

3. Preferential treatment programmes are intended to neutralize the effects of past discrimination as well as to rectify the ongoing social disparities. These programmes are necessary, at least for a fixed period of time, to overcome the competitive handicaps unjustly imposed on the members belonging to victimized groups.

4. Promoting social harmony and social balance is a compelling interest of the state. Hence, it is the duty of the state to design appropriate policies to have a just and equal distribution of positions concerning the affairs of education, employment, and wealth.

5. The doctrine of compensatory justice requires that the people belonging to victimized groups should be adequately compensated for the injustices done to them in the past.

6. The principles of human rights claim for a respectful and dignified life to all the members of a social system. Human dignity and self-respect carry the highest moral values, and they take precedence or outweigh all other considerations.

Arguments against Preferential Treatment

The opponents of preferential discrimination emphasize the following reasons to defend their standpoint:

1. The persons belonging to non-preferred groups of the present are not responsible for the society's past ills, or for the injustices inflicted on certain social groups in the past. Hence it is not morally correct to penalize them for certain historical wrongs.

2. Justice requires the allocation of positions on the basis of merit, intelligence, and ability. It is unfair to ignore persons with merit, and higher qualifications in favour of unmerited, and less qualified persons in the matters of education and employment.

3. To turn down the claims of the persons belonging to non-preferred groups simply on the basis of their caste is morally wrong. Caste is an irrelevant factor, and discrimination on the basis of caste with reference to education and employment is morally unjustifiable.

4. The policy of reverse discrimination violates an individual's right to equal consideration, right to equal opportunity, and right to equal treatment in the affairs of education and employment.

5. Preferential discrimination is a type of reverse discrimination, which is morally wrong. To balance social inequalities, by way of reverse discrimination, would lead to the creation of reverse inequalities. Furthermore, the policy of reverse discrimination involves the continuation of an unjust wrong practice of the past in a reverse way. If the practice of caste-based discrimination in the past is wrong, then preferential discrimination against certain castes at the present is equally wrong.

6. If the criterion for preferential treatment is backwardness, or inequality, or competitive handicap then people belonging to many castes and ethnic groups who are unable to develop adequate competencies due to socio-economic reasons, or geographical disadvantages, must also get the benefits of preferential treatment to overcome these disadvantages. Compensatory benefits should be distributed to the individuals, not as members of a particular caste, but as members of a disadvantaged group. Hence caste-based preferential treatment or caste-based reservation system is irrational and unjustified.

Critical Evaluation

The proponents of preferential treatment programmes have been accused of favouring unjust treatment in reverse, and for undermining the merit. Those who oppose preferential treatment have been blamed for obstructing the fight against injustice, and blocking the legitimate aspirations of the oppressed.

JUSTIFICATION OF PREFERENTIAL TREATMENT

For centuries together, the people belonging to certain social groups were kept away from the most desirable institutes of higher learning and prestigious jobs; deliberately deprived of equal and active participation in the social, political, economic and cultural activities of life; refrained from occupying high, and reputed positions of the society; restrained from getting equal share of wealth and power; prevented from developing competitive abilities and skills on a par with other members of the society. Hence the claim for compensatory benefits or preferential treatment to those people seems to have moral justification.

The persons who have been unjustly discriminated in the past have a prima facie justified claim for compensatory benefits as well as preferential treatment. Therefore, it is the duty of the government to take necessary measures to correct the injustices done to them, and to ensure equal opportunity, or to have equal access to most desirable positions competitively available from the society.

THE CONSEQUENCES OF PAST DISCRIMINATION

Before arriving at the truth, or to make a judgement about the rightness or wrongness of preferential discrimination, one must consider to what extent past privations have adversely affected a person's ability to compete with the members of other groups. The following factors have adversely affected the competitive advantages of the victims of the past, and despite their best efforts, they are unable to reach to the level of their competitors belonging to non-preferred groups:

1. An inaccessible and inadequate education prevented the victims of the past from acquiring certain competitive advantages relative to others.

2. An inadequate income of their parents hampered them from receiving better quality of education comparatively available to others.

3. An inadequate diet, lack of motivation, and poor intellectual stimulation during the early formative period of a person lowers his ability and competence.

4. An inferiority complex and unequal treatment the person gets from the society frustrates, and prevents him to develop his aptitude, competency, and efficiency to compete with other competitors.

5. An unfavourable social environment, which is not conducive, renders the person incapable of putting forth the sustained efforts needed to improve his intelligence, talents, capacities, and capabilities.

The consequences of past discrimination harmed to a great extent the competitive potentialities of the victims, and placed them in a disadvantageous position relative to others. Such an unjustly imposed handicap ought to be neutralized. Towards justification of the reverse discrimination, George Sher argues:

> . . . the key to an adequate justification of reverse discrimination to see that practice, not as the redressing of past privations, but rather a way of neutralizing the present competitive disadvantages caused by those past privations and thus as a way of restoring equal access to those goods which society distributes competitively. When reverse discrimination is justified in this way, many of the difficulties besetting the simpler justification of it disappear.[7]

The claim made by the members of a non-preferred group, to an equal chance for a job, Judith Jarvis Thomson argues, can conflict with society's other legitimate aims and duties. This claim may be overridden by the duty of the state to compensate the injustices done to the victims of the past. If not justice, it is indecent, not to give preferential treatment to them.[8]

Preferential treatment is a form of social justice, and it is intended to compensate people who have been neglected in the past. It is a way of transferring posts and positions, wealth and power, from the groups who have already enjoyed them, to those

7. Sher, p. 330.

8. Cf. Judith Jarvis Thomson, "Preferential Hiring", in John Arthur (ed.) *Morality and Moral Controversies*, pp. 295-300.

who missed them for various reasons. Thus preferential discrimination may be conceived as a mechanism for implementing equality of opportunity, and social justice.

DOES PREFERENTIAL TREATMENT INVOLVE AN UNJUST TREATMENT TO THE MEMBERS OF NON-PREFERRED GROUPS?

Of course, the rejected members belonging to non-preferred groups may complain that they have been treated unjustly for the following reasons:

1. They have been turned down simply on the basis of their caste.
2. It is unfair to penalize, or mistreat them for certain historical wrongs for which they are not responsible.
3. Their merit and qualifications are simply ignored to prefer others.
4. It is unjust to prefer persons with less percentage of marks, lower qualifications, and less competence than persons with higher scores, higher qualifications, and more competence.

Lisa H. Newton, a Professor of Philosophy at Fairfield University, maintains that the use of any criteria other than merit, or qualification for admission, or employment is unjust because these are the only morally relevant characteristics. The bad effects of quota system will far outweigh any social goods produced. She argues:

> The quota system, as employed by the University of California's medical school at Davis or any similar institution, is unjust, for all the same reasons that the discrimination it attempts to reverse is unjust. It diminishes the opportunities of some candidates for a social purpose that has nothing to do with them, to make "reparation" for acts they never committed.[9]

---

9. Lisa H. Newton, "Bakke and Davis: Justice American Style", in Thomas A. Mappes and James S. Zembaty (eds.), *Social Ethics: Morality and Social Policy*, pp. 205-06.

These are very impressive arguments, and to establish the rightness, or justification of preferential programmes, one must properly respond to these arguments in a most convincing manner.

The basic aim of preferential treatment is not to treat unjustly, or unfairly the members of non-preferred groups, but only to neutralize the unfair competitive advantages received by them, or benefitted by them from the historical wrongs. In fact, the benefits they have enjoyed all these years are results of discriminatory practices against certain victimized groups. Therefore, one must understand preferential treatment not as supporting discrimination against members of non-preferred groups, but as a remedial measure to neutralize the consequences of past discrimination.

The difference between the members belonging to non-preferred and preferred groups is that the members of the former group because of their good luck were born in a more advanced social group, whereas the members of the latter group were born in a most disadvantaged social group. As a result of past discrimination, a member born in a disadvantaged group cannot compete fairly, and therefore he is morally entitled for preferential treatment. James Rachels, an American moral philosopher, argues:

> What is important is that, as a result of past discriminatory practices, he has been unfairly handicapped in trying to achieve the sort of academic standing required for admission. If he has a claim to "preferential" treatment now, it is for that reason.[10]

THE DEFICIENCIES INVOLVED IN PREFERENTIAL TREATMENT

The policy of our government identifying "backwardness" of the people with caste, or sub-caste appears to be fundamentally wrong. So far no genuine attempt is made by the government to find out who are really backward, and who really need a helping hand irrespective of whether they belong to this caste, or that caste, or

---

10. James Rachels, "What people Deserve", in John Arthur (ed.), *Morality and Moral Controversies*, p. 348.

other socio-religious groups. The presence of poverty, ignorance, illiteracy, ill-health, etc. is to be found in every community. Our government's assumption that a man must be well off because he belongs to a particular community, or that another must be badly off because he belongs to the government-designated backward community is unrealistic, unscientific and irrational. Indeed, there are well-to-do Harijans, and there are poverty-stricken brāhmaṇas in our society. Thus, there is a profound contradiction between government's objective of a casteless society, and its policy and method of elevating the backward on a caste basis.

The governments, which are in power at the centre as well as in different states of India, should learn certain lessons from the recent violent caste agitations that occurred in a couple of states, namely Rajasthan and Andhra Pradesh.

In Rajasthan, the people belonging to Gujjar caste wanted inclusion of their community in the category of scheduled tribe (ST). The people belonging to Meena caste, who are already in that category opposed Gujjar entry into the ST fold with the fear that their share of reservation benefits would be eroded. Thus Vasundhara Raje government in Rajasthan, is left with the sticky task of striking a balance between Gujjar aspirations, and Meena apprehensions.

Again, in Andhra Pradesh, the agitation launched by the people belonging to Mala and Madiga, the two sub-castes of the scheduled caste (SC) category, on the issue of categorization of sub-castes into four groups created lot of unrest and turmoil in the state. The people belonging to Madiga caste wanted categorization, whereas the people belonging to Mala caste opposed it. The appointment of Justice Usha Mehra Commission by the union government, to enquire and submit a report on the issue of categorization, resulted in a direct fight between people belonging to these two castes.

The experiences of such violent agitations should serve as a lesson on the dangers in the reckless playing of the caste card in order to woo voters. The caste agitations launched, in the recent years, in different parts of India point out to the dangers of encouraging competitive politics. This type of situation in the country suggests an alternative to the caste-based system of reservation or caste-oriented theory of social justice to overcome social disparities.

The preferential treatment programmes which are explicitly and repeatedly defined as "temporary" measures, have not only continued beyond their legally mandated cut-off dates by the subsequent extension for every ten years, but also expanded their scope either accepting more castes into their fold, or spreading to wider realms of the society. This sort of indiscriminate expansion of preferential discrimination leads to an increase in polarization of groups, with non-preferred groups reacting adversely and thereby resulting in group violence and civil war.[11]

This type of situation in the country demands an alternative approach to caste-based system of reservation, or caste-oriented theory of social justice to overcome social disparities. The caste-based reservation system became outdated, and has lost its purpose. It became a tool in the hands of politicians to exploit it for their own selfish interests. The political leaders must desist from making electoral promises on quota system. If we can do away with caste and religion-based reservation, and offer support to every needy person such clamour for inclusion in the reserved category will gradually decline.

The critics of preferential treatment raise their objection to the practice of selecting people on the basis of caste, colour, creed, or sex, which are irrelevant factors to compensate to the injustices done to certain groups in the past. They argue that preferential treatment should be given to all disadvantaged people, irrespective of their caste, colour, creed, or sex. This argument appears to be

---

11. Cf. Thomas Sowell, "Affirmative Action: A worldwide Disaster", in Daniel Bonevac (ed.), *Today's Moral Issues: Classic and Contemporary Perspectives* (California: Mayfield Publishing Company, 1996), p. 567.

very convincing, because disadvantaged and needy people are found in all castes and in all religions.

Thus the purpose and goal of preferential treatment, or quota system to provide compensatory benefits to the people, who are disadvantaged and needy, or to the victimized people of the past, will become ineffective to achieve the intended results, unless government makes an attempt to review the policies and programmes of reservations, and bring about suitable changes necessary in the system.

PREFERENTIAL TREATMENT AND THE PROBLEM OF CREAMY LAYER

Preferential treatment, as it is in practice till now, is not a much controversial issue. People who have been treated unjustly in the past have a prima facie justified claim for preferential treatment to neutralize the consequences of the past discrimination. However, controversy arises with reference to "inclusion or exclusion" of some members of the preferred castes, or groups who are affluent, fortunate, and well developed beyond many other members of those preferred castes. For an ideal and just distribution of compensatory benefits, the criteria earmarked to receive these benefits must be in favour of those members who really deserve them.

The policy of preferential treatment appears to be working on the principle "exploitation of the weak by the strong." The empirical evidences available clearly show that this policy with the passage of time became an instrument in the hands of a few elite members of the preferred group to exploit a large majority of other members of the same group. The benefits resultant from this policy are mostly enjoyed by a few fortunate members who have already advanced well beyond most other undeveloped members of the same group. This pattern of simultaneous progression at the top and retrogression at the bottom within preferred groups is a sort of exploitation of the backward members by the advanced members of the same group. This type of trend needs to be rectified, and the most appropriate method to check this trend is to exclude those members who have already been benefitted, and advanced by the preferential treatment. Moreover, this kind of exploitative nature existent among the members of the same preferred group makes the argument for justification of preferential treatment weaker.

The results of preferential treatment among the members of *ādivāsīs* and *dalits* in India, reveal that most of the seats reserved for them in educational institutions, and most of the prestigious jobs have been received by a select few members of the upper strata of these groups, and a large majority of the members who are at the bottom of those groups received only a marginal per cent of seats and jobs. The same pattern is visible in case of the seats and jobs reserved for "Other Backward Classes (OBCs)" in some Indian states where the OBCs reservation is in practice.

The doctrine of formal justice requires that "similar cases ought to be treated similarly." Accordingly, anyone who has been unjustly injured or disadvantaged must receive similar compensation. For example, all the members of a particular caste, irrespective of their educational and economic progress, or regress belong to that victimized caste. Every disadvantaged member of this caste deserves compensatory benefits as qua victim of that particular caste, but not as qua member of that caste. Membership in a particular caste or group alone cannot be used as a criterion to receive the benefits. Hence, the only kind of justified criteria for compensatory benefits should be in favour of the victims of social justice. What is not rationally justified is extending the provision of compensation indiscriminately to all the members of a victimized caste, or group.

The policies and programmes of preferential treatment must be confined only to the most disadvantaged and deprived members of the preferred castes who really deserve them, but not to every member of that caste, or group. George Sher argues that not all members belonging to a victimized group need preferential treatment, but only those who have suffered the utmost, or whose competitive abilities have been reduced because of past discrimination need relevant privations. She asserts:

> If the point of reverse discrimination is to compensate for competitive disadvantages caused by past discrimination, it will be justified in favour of only those group members whose abilities have actually been reduced; and it would be most implausible to suppose that every black (or even woman) has been affected in this way . . . our account provides no reason to practice reverse discrimination in their favour [who have escaped many of the competitive handicaps].[12]

It would be most implausible to suppose that every member of a backward caste has been affected due to discrimination in the past. At least some members of those castes with affluent and advantaged background surely have escaped many disadvantages, if not all, of competitive handicaps. Therefore, there is no legitimate reason to extend the benefits of preferential treatment to them at the expense of disadvantaged members of those castes, who really deserve the benefits.

A five-judge Constitution Bench of the Supreme Court of India, in its judgement delivered on 19 October 2006, held that the "creamy layer" among the SCs and STs must necessarily be excluded from the purview of reservation in public employment and promotions. The Bench also made it clear that even if the state has compelling reasons, the state will have to see that its reservation provision for recruitment "does not lead to excessiveness so as to breach the ceiling limit of 50 per cent or obliterate the creamy layer or extend the reservation indefinitely."[13] In order to maintain the formal equality within the members of a preferred group, the Bench says that the concept of "creamy layer" which is a qualitative exclusion has to be retained as a constitutional requirement.

---

12. Sher, p. 225.
13. *The Hindu*, Newspaper 20 October 2006, p. 1.

For obvious reasons of vote bank politics, no political leader, or no political party in India, would have dared to address the issue of creamy layer for all these years. The Supreme Court has shown them the right direction to contemplate on this issue, and come to a right decision. After more than five decades of the implementation of reservation policy, at least now, the government should come out to assess the costs and benefits resultant from this policy, and take necessary measures to rectify the deficiencies, if any, involved in the quota system.

Once the beneficiaries of the reservation are advanced and developed to a higher level in the society, there is no logic in getting the benefits endlessly. If the upper strata in each preferred caste are not excluded from competing with less privileged, and more oppressed among them, the objectives of social justice would not be achieved. Unless and until the people, who have been deprived of getting the benefits of quota system within the preferred groups, realize the fact, and start a movement to fight for their rights, and make a demand for equal share there is no possibility to receive most desirable benefits intended for them.

The hue and cry made by the persons belonging to the creamy layer, obviously, is not for the benefit of the deprived members of their own caste, but to cling on to the benefits that they are enjoying as members of that caste.

Concluding Remarks

The critics of preferential treatment programmes very often claim that such programmes, even effective, are unjustifiable in some important sense that they contradict an individual's right to equal consideration, equal opportunity, and equal treatment concerning education and employment. It is true that the policies and programmes of preferential treatment are unfair, or unjust in some sense, but in the overall interest of maintaining social stability and social harmony, and towards achieving the goal of social justice to certain groups of people who have been neglected in the past, the state is compelled to offer such programmes. Moreover, these programmes become necessitated as a result of certain institutions, which systematically and unjustifiably concentrated power, authority, wealth and goods in the hands of some sections of the society, and relegated some other sections to a subordinate position in the society.

In the matters of education and employment, no doubt, merit and qualifications are very much relevant, but they are not the decisive factors. One must also take into consideration certain factors resultant from discrimination, against certain castes in the past, disadvantages resultant from socio-economic inequalities, differences between the rural and the urban, the rich and the poor and geographical disadvantages.

The distress and the discomfort, the hardships and the handicaps, the injuries and the injustices, the impediments and the inconveniences, the prejudices and the privations, and the torment and the torture resultant from the past discrimination, or imperfect social arrangements must also be taken into consideration in the distribution of society's most desirable positions at the time of selections, provided the candidates competing to these positions are qualified, admissible, and desirable.

The vote bank politics of political parties, and the irrational and impracticable statements of the political leaders, create wrong impressions in the minds of the members of preferred groups that the quota system of reservations will continue in the same nature and form forever. In the light of the recent Supreme Court ruling, it is very clear that the practice of reservation system is only a temporary measure, and it cannot be continued indefinitely. At least now, it is the responsibility of the government as well as political leaders to educate the members of the preferred groups so that the practice of reservation system is not a permanent panacea for them to overcome their competitive disadvantages resultant from the past discrimination.

Most of the political leaders, if not all, to whatever political party they may belong, became habituated to consider every social issue from the viewpoint of attracting more votes, or more people into their fold to capture political power and positions, ignoring their overall social and constitutional responsibilities. They make unrealistic and unjustifiable promises to the people belonging to different regions, different castes, different religions, ignoring the consequences of these promises on social harmony, and social integrity.

The people of India, more or less, lost their faith in the political leaders of this country. Under these circumstances, the people of India are looking, hopefully and faithfully, towards the sensitive and vigilant judicial system of the country to bring about a change in the attitude and thinking of our political leaders, and show to them the right direction and procedure to be followed.

In recent years, the Supreme Court and the High Courts in India have redefined their role, and perceived a need for correcting aberrations and shortcomings in all walks of social life. The judiciary justifiably takes credit for imposing restrictions to power and authority of the political leaders. The uncaring and irresponsible attitude of the politicians and bureaucrats compelled the judiciary to take matters of good governance and public policy in their hands. A concerned and sensitive judiciary, indeed, is the most valuable asset of a democratic system.

CHAPTER 19

Reservation and Social Disintegration

Mahesh Singh

THE policy of reservation, in the affairs of governance applicable to the downtrodden, is considered to be a political device to bring out freedom, equality, justice and fraternity in the modern Indian society. It is believed that it will prove itself to be a strong string to integrate the Indian society divided into different castes and classes; rich and poor since long. But the result that we come across in the implementation of reservation policy is not much heartening, rather going in reverse direction. It has become a permanent source of dividing Indians into reservationists and anti-reservationists. It brings forth despondency, dejection, depression and, finally, a sense of unfavourableness in the minds of those who are deprived of their rights due to reservation policy. On the other side, it causes the feelings of separation, alienation and hatred in the minds of reservationists who take anti-reservationists as the class of the oppressors who have been suppressing their causes since thousand of years till date. The policy of reservation, thus, has become an issue of confrontation and fight. Reservation-based agitations, which began in the year 1978, continued till yester years. There is no guarantee of its non-recurrence in future. India suffered great loss of national property due to agitations on the issue of reservation.

From the perusal of the arguments advanced by both pro- and anti-reservationists, it becomes clear that the policy of reservation is an important constituent of justice to which our Constitution is committed. But, in fact, the policy of reservation has become a suitable tool in the hands of politicians for reserving vote bank and coming to power. No political party is seen eagerly interested in solving the issue; rather they are keen to make it afresh. During the 60 years of Independence, we see that the politicians have no adequate plan to bring the downtrodden at par with general category Indians. Had there been any such commitment in the minds of the politicians for the economic development of the poor, the policy of reservation must have got a shape quite different from the present one and, consequently, it would not have been a source of disintegration of the Indian society.

If we look at the historical background of the present scheme of reservation, as a principle, it was accepted in the Poona Pact much before the Independence of India. In the said pact, Mahatma Gandhi agreed with Dr. B.R. Ambedkar to reserve seats for the scheduled castes (SCs) and scheduled tribes (STs) in the parliament and state assemblies; and it was implemented with effect from 26 January 1950 along with the implementation of the Indian Constitution. As the percentage of SCs and STs was 23 per cent of the total population of India, 22.5 per cent reservation was also allotted to them in the admission to educational institutions, including the technical ones. As the reservation of SCs and STs was the demand of social justice, no opposition was staged from any section of the society. But it can be mentioned here that even the reservation to SCs and STs was not cent per cent conducive to the health of integration of Indian society. Food is the first and foremost requirement for life. Those who are not able to make both ends meet are naturally socially and educationally backward. Poverty is the root cause of every kind of humiliation. Reversibly, a wealthy person of any caste is supposed to belong to the higher class; he is supposed to be educated, at home in scriptures, virtuous and adorable and, in short, wealth entails all the virtues. The poor are found in every caste and class. So poverty based reservation would have been applicable to every section of society. The poor themselves form a class and the rich another. This dichotomy of the poor and the rich is a reality of social philosophy.

So the reservation initiated by Ambedkar is not a need-based reservation; it is rather based on the deep-rooted societal divides.

In support of the thesis that reservation should be based on poverty, the example of West Bengal government can be cited. The state of West Bengal promulgated the scheme of reservation on the basis of economic backwardness. Karpoori Thakur, in his scheme of reservation for forward classes, considered poverty as the sole criterion. Even the present Chief Minister of Uttar Pradesh, Mayawati, has recently announced 10 per cent reservation for poor in forward class. The Supreme Court of India, time and again, suggested that poverty is the most suitable criterion of reservation. All this proves that the present policy of India having reservation on the ground of social and educational backwardness is not in the interest of all eligible for reservation. It is not comprehensive and all-inclusive, and, reversibly, creates a situation of social disintegration.

The second phase of promulgating reservation policy for socially and educationally backward castes invited a long debate on its justification and witnessed strong protests and bloody scenes. Under the Article 340 of the Indian Constitution, Morarji Desai, the then Prime Minister of India, formed a committee chaired by B.P. Mandal to report on the social and educational position of backward classes, so that the government may stand by their side in making their condition better. Prior to the Mandal Commission, in 1953 a committee for the same was set up under the chairmanship of Kaka Kalelkar. The committee submitted its report on 30 March 1955, to the then President Dr Rajendra Prasad. The then government did not act upon this report. Kalelkar, while submitting his report to the President of India, remarked that the criterion for backwardness should not be caste, but something other than that. When our Constitution is committed to a casteless and a classless society, we should not attach any importance to it in any way. Individual and family should be taken to make the point of reference in considering backwardness.[1] But our political

---

1. *Dainik Jagaran*, Patna edn., 2 November 2006.

leaders did not pay attention to the suggestions of Kalelkar. However, later on, in the Mandal Commission castes were taken into consideration. B.P. Mandal inferred that the numerical strength of the backward castes was 52 per cent of the total population of India, and suggested reservation accordingly. The Supreme Court of India has already given its verdict of not more than 50 per cent reservation of seats. And before the report of Mandal Commission, 22 per cent of reservation was allotted to SCs and STs. So only 27 per cent seats were reserved for socially and educationally backward castes. Mandal submitted his report on 19 May 1980 when Indra Gandhi was the Prime Minister of India. Mrs. Gandhi did not find it proper to enact it, and resultantly, it was kept in abeyance. When V.P. Singh became the Prime Minister of India in 1990, he, without taking it to the parliament for a healthy debate on the whole issue, implemented Mandal Commission report in haste. The entire report of the Mandal Commission was not implemented then. Only reservation in government services was implemented. When reservation in admission to the technical institutes was introduced last year, students of general category made a hue and cry. Resultantly, the issue of reservation again came to light. Lately, leaders of political parties have started advocating for reservation of jobs even in the private companies of India for the reservationists, but management of the private companies is declining the proposal of the government. Some of the big companies were ready to provide quality education to the students of the reserve category and are ready to provide them jobs, as well. Such proposal from the private companies should be an eye-opener to the government agencies.

A number of questions have been raised against the provision of reservation to the backward castes. Some lawyers hold the view that Article 340 of the Indian Constitution does not stand for the reservation of backward classes in the true sense of the term. Some are of the opinion that the actual number of socially and educationally backward castes does not constitute 52 per cent of the total population of the country at present. A number of backward castes are now in a better position. They are not backward from any point of view. It is a well-known fact that, in the present position of things, the benefits of reservation go to the affluent castes among the backwards. Most of the backward castes do not qualify for availing the opportunity of reservation. As per direction laid down in the Constitution, there should be a review of reservation every 10 years. No family should be allowed to get the privilege of reservation for more than two terms; otherwise the benefits of reservation will not reach the lowest strata in the next thousand years. Moreover, there should not be reservation in case of promotion. Social justice never demands that a senior and competent incumbent is compulsorily made junior on the ground of his belonging to a forward class. This type of injustice in the name of social justice cannot help integrate the society. Again, it is not a reality that 50 per cent of jobs in the state and central service are meant for general category of candidates. The fact is that the meritorious candidates coming from reservationist class fill almost half of the seats of general quota, and the rest of the seats go to the general quota. So, altogether 75 to 80 per cent of the seats in the government services go to reservationists, and the candidates in the general category, in spite of their excellence and brilliance, are deprived of the opportunity. Any kind of differentiation on the ground of caste, creed, religion, etc. goes against the spirit of Indian Constitution and leads to reverse discrimination in the present scheme of reservation. In other words, candidates of the forward class are considered to be second-rate citizens of the motherland.

There are, no doubt, a number of discrepancies involved in the present form of reservation that cannot be discussed in this article. But the crux of the problem is: how the big gap existing in the present Indian society will be bridged? Our attention should be drawn towards the solution of the problem. There are grievances on both sides. But the rationalist of the society should think that the reservationists of the present time have suffered a lot for the noble cause of maintaining the societal order. They must be given their rewards. The forward is the one who comes forward for the upliftment of the downtrodden. Social justice stands for the flow from the upper to the lower, from haves to have-nots. But this kind of ethical attitude can be helpful to the deprived class of the society only when the government comes forward with an open heart for the upliftment of the lower strata of the society. The fate of the poor of India cannot change with mere sympathy shown to them and with a little help from private agencies. The government should come with a strong determination and time bound programmes to remove the stigma of reservation.

To my mind, the remedy of the problem of reservation and, thereby, social disintegration lies in education. For making young generation of SC and ST educated, the government should encourage them by giving them financial package. I have my personal experience of working among *dalit*s. I tried to motivate them to send their wards to schools. But they showed their inability, as the young boys are the bread earners of their families. If they send their wards to school the family would face starvation. So I feel that for making the *dalit*s educated, we have to make first their families economically sound. Various small-scale industries, cottage industries, etc. should be given to them by the government so that they may spare their children for education.

By education I do not mean only literacy; by education I mean the education that can bring a job. So, technically, education should be given to the reservationist class. For this type of education, they should be provided suitable conditions. It is the duty of the government and industrialists of the Indian society to come forward to help the needy sections. Education — and not the benefit of reservation — will elevate the social and cultural position of the *dalit*s. The society, which is formed by the qualified, educated, men of character and determination, is the civilized society. It is education which will generate scientific outlook of the people and will eradicate all ill feeling of higher and lower castes, the problem like untouchability and dichotomy of oppressed and oppressors. Our former President Dr A.P.J. Abdul Kalam emphasizes the importance of quality education for all sections of the Indian society. Leaders like Lalu Prasad Yadav, on the eve of the birth anniversary of Karpoori Thakur, exhorted the reservationists to go to educational institutes. He said to them that Mandal commission would not pay any longer. A civilized and organized society is known not by the number of its members, but by their quality and wisdom. We should, therefore, create an atmosphere in which knowledge and wisdom may prevail in society.

The mushroom growth of population is a big danger in every respect for the modern Indian society. Our leaders have become silent on this burning issue. But it is for us to highlight the bad implications of growing birth rate of India. Any government is not capable of providing work to every hand. Hence, people should be educated to check population growth immediately in the interest of the nation. Birth control should be a national policy and it should be strictly implemented in every community of Indian society. Though it would be a hard work, in my opinion, it should be a law for reservationists. How would a government be able to provide jobs for such a huge number of people? The government should, therefore, come forward with a policy that the family having two children would be entitled for receiving the benefit of reservation. To check the birth rate is in the interest of happiness and development of every family and every society.

Last but not the least; my submission would be to criticize our ancient pattern of social organization known as "Manuvadi arrangement." First of all, we should know that Manu was not a brāhmaṇa; he was a kṣatriya king. He gave a system for the welfare of the society of his time. The system established by Manu is not beneficial to the present-day society. So it should be given up. No arrangement or system concerning governance is true and tenable forever. A time would come when the present system of governance will be outdated and a new system will be introduced. Mahatma Gandhi, who is generally known as the forerunner to champion the cause of the *harijans*, has been disowned by *harijans* themselves. *Dalit* society condemns the Mahatma, and the term *harijan* is taken to be an abusive one. Dr Ambedkar, who burnt *Manu-Smṛti*, is called the Manu of independent India, and the Indian Constitution drafted by him is called "Modern *Manu-Smṛti*." We all elevate this elevating tendency. There should be feeling of upgradation, elevation for a composite and coherent society.

We should bear in mind that the mundane law is never exclusive. Our attempts should be to avoid the bad and adopt the good. We should take what was good in our ancient way of life and leave what is not good for the health of the modern society. We should do what we can to the needy persons of present and leave aside what harm we did in the past. Nothing but our rational thinking will bring forth good to the present modern Indian society.

CHAPTER 20

Reverse Discrimination
Its Meaning and Justification

Prabhu Narayan Mandal

REVERSE discrimination, as the name suggests, refers to discrimination itself, but it is discrimination of a kind that works in reverse order. It is discrimination in favour of the members of the disadvantaged groups, groups which have been discriminated against in the past and have, thus, suffered privation and consequent injustices. Reverse discrimination is also known as "affirmative action,"[1] which precisely is nothing but giving preferential treatment to the members of the disadvantaged groups by providing them greater and special opportunities. As the privations born of past discrimination lead to inequality in the society, social justice fails to be realized. Therefore, in order to ensure social justice inequality needs to be removed. Affirmative action or reverse discrimination has been thought of to be one of the potent and most effective ways of ensuring social justice.

Different sorts of justifications have been offered for reverse discrimination and programmes that use preferential policies. We shall discuss here some very important justifications and examine them to see if these justifications can be accepted without qualification. These justifications are as follows:

Justification in Terms of Compensatory Justice

The programmes which use preferential policies to provide greater opportunities to members of disadvantaged groups are justifiable,

---

1. Peter Singer, *Practical Ethics* (Cambridge: Cambridge University Press, First Indian Edition, 2000), p. 45.

in the first place, on grounds of compensatory justice. The proponents of this justification argue that the actual recipients of these opportunities deserve compensation for wrongs they have suffered. It is believed that the benefits provided to those individuals for wrongs they suffered will serve to bring them up to the level of wealth and welfare that they would now have, if they had not been disadvantaged.

There is, however, a controversy with regard to the question whether compensatory benefits should be provided to those particular individuals who have been harmed substantially by discrimination or to all members of groups that have frequently been subjected to discrimination. Paul W. Taylor is of the view that compensatory benefits should be provided to all members of the disadvantaged groups. He says,

> When an injustice has been committed to a group of persons, some form of compensation or reparation must be made to that group.[2]

He further argues that group rights to compensation are not rights against particular wrong-doers, but are against society as a whole. As he puts it:

> The obligation to offer such benefits to the group as a whole is an obligation that falls on society in general, not on any particular person. For it is society in general that through its established social practice brought upon itself the obligation.[3]

James W. Nickel, on the other hand, does not agree with Taylor's view. Nickel argues that if compensation benefits are allowed to the whole group, then these benefits will go even to those persons who personally have not sustained any injury. Group rights to

---

2. Paul W. Taylor, cited in James W. Nickel, "Preferential Policies in Hiring and Admissions: A Jurisprudential Approach", in *Ethics: Theory and Practice*, ed. Manuel Velasquez and Cynthica Rostankowki (New Jersey: Prentice Hall, Englewood Chiffs, 1985), p. 403.
3. Ibid., p. 403.

compensation, if at all they are to be justified, can be justified on considerations other than compensatory justice. These other considerations include consideration of redistribution, utility or administrative convenience.[4]

Justification in Terms of Distributive Justice

Distributive justice consists in the fair distribution of benefits and burdens. It is concerned not with providing compensation for past discrimination or privation but with eliminating present inequities. Distributive justice does not require that all people should have the same income or equally good jobs. It only requires that benefits and burdens should be distributed fairly in accordance with relevant considerations such as rights, deserts, merits, contributions and needs of beneficiaries. It is a well-known fact that good education leads to good jobs; good jobs provide income, security and status. Distributive justice requires that education and jobs should be distributed in such a way that previously deprived gets a bigger share. This certainly helps in reducing distributive inequities considerably. Preferential treatment in terms of providing bigger share to the previously deprived thus finds more strengthened justification in distributive justice.

Justification in Terms of Utility

Preferential treatment seems to be justified also on grounds of utility. The opponents of this justification argue that preferential treatment is justified because it leads to greater public welfare. They believe that public welfare can be promoted by eliminating poverty as well as economic inequality. Extreme poverty is highly objectionable to them because it involves unmet needs and suffering, and also because it leads to crime, strife and lack of self-respect. It requires, therefore, to be eradicated first and thereafter income needs to be distributed in such a way that economic inequality is removed. Unless economic inequality is

---

4. Taylor, p. 404.

removed, public good cannot go to the large number of people. Preferential policy comes here as a very effective measure to facilitate the distribution of public good among the greater number of people.

The use of preferential policies although is justified on the grounds mentioned above, but it is at the same time objected to on several counts. The grounds of objection are as follows:

PROBLEM OF INCOMPETENCE

The critics of preferential policy allege that significant reduction in the efficiency and productivity of companies and institutions is likely to follow if unqualified persons are hired on preferential basis.

This defect, however, can be rectified easily if preferential policies are restricted to those only who are adequately qualified and are not allowed to extend to the unqualified.

PROBLEM OF UNFAIR BURDENS

The problem of unfair burden, perhaps, is the most serious problem before the advocates of preferential policies. Use of preferential policies is objected to on the ground that it unfairly places the burden of helping those who are preferred on those who are, thereby, excluded. The critics argue that the individuals whose superior qualifications will have to be bypassed in the reverse discriminatory process are not solely responsible for the privations to be compensated for. If, at all, they are responsible, others like him are also responsible. But reverse discrimination seeks to compensate for the privations in question at the expense of those individuals alone whose superior qualifications will have to be bypassed. This is obviously highly unfair.

But this objection, if probed deeply, proves untenable. Let us consider here the sorts of privations that people who are forced to do menial and low-paying jobs suffer. The privations that they suffer pertain mainly to housing, food and education. The persons who are forced to do menial and low-paying jobs have to live in substandard homes, subsist on improper and imbalanced diets and provide inadequate education to their children. Adequate housing, food and education are, no doubt, goods in and of themselves, but they are also goods in a different sense entirely. It is a well-known fact that the sorts of nourishment and education a person receives as a child usually affect the kind of skills and capacities he requires as an adult — including, of course, the very skills which are needed if he is to compete on equal terms for jobs and other goods. A child who is deprived of adequate food and education may, therefore, lose not only the immediate enjoyments which a better and comfortable environment brings, but, also, the subsequent ability to compete equally for other things. But to lose this ability to compete is, in essence, to lose one's access to the goods that are being competed for, and this, surely, is itself a privation, which ought to be compensated for. But the question is: How can it be compensated for? The reply obviously would be: if the lost good is just the ability to compete on equal terms for things like desirable jobs, then surely the most appropriate way of compensating for what has been lost is just to do away with the necessity of competing on equal terms for those goods. Reverse discrimination may, therefore, be viewed not as the redressing of past privations, but rather as a way of neutralizing the present competitive disadvantage caused by those past privations. Reverse discrimination, thus, enables the members of the disadvantaged groups to have equal access to those goods that are distributed competitively. Reverse discrimination viewed, thus, does not seem to place entire burden of redress upon those individuals whose superior qualifications are bypassed. Since reverse discrimination helps in reducing the gap between the privileged and the disadvantaged, and, thereby, in removing social inequities, it cannot be called unfair keeping in view the greater public welfare it leads to ultimately.

To sum up, reverse discrimination, with all its fairness, is justified in so far as it neutralizes competitive disadvantage caused by past privation.

CHAPTER 21

Reservation and Reverse Discrimination

M.P. Chaurasia

DISCRIMINATION among human beings is an age-old problem. Since the very dawn of the civilization, discriminations between man and woman, ethnic and civilized people, caste and class, and lastly among same race exist in our society.[1]All these discriminations can be divided into four categories: caste discrimination, race discrimination, religious discrimination and sex discrimination. In other words, our civilizations are nourished and developed on the basis of human discrimination. J.P. Thiroux has rightly mentioned that anybody who has been to school or has read any history knows that prejudice and unfair discrimination against blacks, women, *harijans*, Muslims and tribal groups have been going on from time immemorial, and for this reason, I don't think it is necessary to discuss the problems in detail.[2]

In 1969, the renowned educationist Arther Jenson in an article published in the *Harward Educational Review* supported the view of race discrimination. But the students of the same university protested against him and he was dismissed from the university.[3] The ground for such a view made by him was the rational superiority of the white people in comparison with the black. Here, my chief purpose is to deal with the methods which have been

---

1. Peter Singer, *Practical Ethics* (Cambridge: Cambridge University Press, First Indian Edition, 2000), p. 21.
2. J.P. Thiroux, *Ethics: Theory and Practice*, p. 300.
3. Barry R. Gross (ed.), *Reverse Discrimination*, p. 117.

used to solve these problems and also some of the negative consequences caused by these methods.

Here, the term "discrimination" is used in the sense to differentiate among people in a prejudiced way in social behaviour or in hiring, promoting or firing. The term "prejudice" is based not upon any logical or scientific ground, rather it is based on opinions one has been taught, has heard or has wrongly read. Recently Nobel prize winner scientist Robert Watson has supported such racial discrimination and he has mentioned that American whites are more intelligent than African blacks. But another genome scientist Roser Cornberg has refuted such a view. According to him, on the basis of gene construction no race is inferior to any other race.[4] Today human equality becomes the fundamental principle of the world politics, and ethics, as Peter Singer holds, "Human equality is a fundamental principle and not a factual statement."[5]

The term "discrimination" does not denote a wrong thing, as in the case of choosing one's friend or wife one is quite right in discriminating among people — even in preferring one candidate between two well qualified applicants in an attempt to choose the best person for the job. But problems are there when the discrimination is based on people's race, religion, sex, sexual preference, caste, creed and culture rather than on the basis of their qualifications for a job or in social dealings.

Affirmative action is here used in a peculiar sense which means the process of trying to avoid future discrimination in employment practices and social dealings. An effective effort should be made to revise the problems arising since a very long time. In other words, it is a kind of compensation for the past discrimination which was done by our forefathers. In the form of reservation for scheduled castes/scheduled tribes, backward class and women affirmative actions have been taken in India. In the same way

4. *Hindustan* (Hindi), Patna edn., 07 January 2008.

5. Singer, p. 21.

"reverse discrimination" is a term which describes the plight of some previously privileged people who have, in turn, been discriminated against when affirmative action programmes have been instituted. Reverse discrimination would occur, for example, if a company or government agency hired a *harijan*, tribe male or female who possessed less qualification than a *savarṇa* person mainly because of their race, caste or sex. In this way it can be regarded as a negative step. In the same way, if an individual belongs to a lower caste and he has been badly treated by a civilized people, it is also immoral and negative conduct.

But this reverse discrimination opens other problematic areas which involve extreme points of view. In India, as we have seen above, reservation policy may be considered as affirmative action. Now it is the Herculean task of applied ethics to examine the pro and con effects of this reverse discrimination. Straightforwardly speaking, I have nothing to say either for or against this affirmative action in the government sector, because there everything is defined in terms of vote-bank. So far as the private sector is concerned, affirmative action is a kind of interference in one's individual freedom. It is possible that one's forefather had been committing discrimination among people in the past, but how can it be the mistake of the present owner/generation? And if fault is not committed from his side, how can he be corrected for the misdeeds of his ancestors? It is also possible that the present owner/generations themselves were guilty of recent past discrimination, they should not be forced to hire those discriminated against to help the less qualified people just to consolidate their business, nor should they be responsible for giving additional training to people who are unqualified because of past discrimination. Ethically, no one has the right to compel any *savarna* or corporate to pay for a problem they never participated in.

In modern India, hardly any person can support discrimination on the basis of caste, religion and race. Here I do not like to touch upon the problem of sex discrimination. We all know that sex discrimination either in social dealing or in employment practices is one of the most heinous kinds of negative action, because such act goes against the survival and better advancement of human beings. Undoubtedly, we have not committed such discrimination — although it is highly questionable that we have not — but our forefathers did, therefore, we, as fellow human beings and good citizens, owe the victims of discrimination some sort of recompense for the immoral actions committed against them. Every effort must be made immediately to put affirmative action into effect. In this way reverse discrimination means adversity of privileged class. Is it so? No, because discrimination in either form is an unethical act as it goes against the Value of Life Principle, the Principle of Goodness and, lastly, the Principle of Justice. We should not commit unjust conduct with fellow beings and should not ignore the importance of goodness in human life.

In India, since Independence several attempts have been made by the union and state governments for the sake of reverse discrimination or affirmative action. We have seen the pro and con sides of the affirmative action and we have also supported the reverse discrimination on humanitarian ground. So far as the livelihood, survival, and betterment of the discriminated people are concerned, nobody should have objection and every effort should be made by the government and our society too. So far as social sector is concerned, if some people even today commit such discrimination, government, as a representative of all members of society, certainly has an obligation to mandate affirmative action and to attempt to enforce it. If possible government should take some coercive steps to stop social discrimination. J.P. Thiroux has recommended even fines and imprisonment for such heinous acts.[6]

However, there are several crucial fields where talent and qualification should never be ignored for the sake of compensation because it would lastly hamper all human beings. In the field of atomic research, I would like to put an example from the Jean

---

6. Thiroux, p. 367.

Paul Sartre's book *Being and Nothingness*. Sartre has discussed the situation in a battlefield where the commanding officer has received an S.O.S. and he has to interpret the order within five minutes. We civilians are unable to realize the anguish of the commanding officer. His single wrong decision may lead to the end of thousands of human life. In this crucial time the person concerned does not have more time to think. Only his foresightedness and intelligence are the means to take right decision, thereby the life of thousands of people and the fate of the nation could be saved. And foresightedness and intelligence come after proper education and training. This is why I have advised to relax reservation in crucial affairs. It is the task of the government to educate people properly and so train them that they can compete with anyone in any situation.

CHAPTER 22

Gandhi and Ambedkar

Self-Purification versus Self-Respect

Alok Tandon

WHEN we talk about social justice in Indian context, issue of liberation of *dalits* is of paramount importance. However, we cannot understand the *dalit* discourse of today without knowing about its historical origin in two divergent yet complementary thought processes of Gandhi and Ambedkar, the two key figures of debate before and after Independence. Their debate is not only of academic interest, for it touches upon some fundamental questions about the structure of Indian society which concern not only its past but also its future. One may ask, why, in spite of Gandhi's movement against untouchability and establishment of Harijan Sewak Sangh, *dalits* today are attracted more towards Ambedkar. Actually, they are mostly opposed to Gandhi. Does this signify failure of Gandhi, his followers and his ideology? To answer this question, we need to make a reappraisal of the historical Gandhi–Ambedkar debate. The present paper is a modest attempt in that direction.

I

Prior to comparing the views of Gandhi and Ambedkar, we should get rid of some baseless assumptions about their thought patterns. To label Gandhi as a Sanātanī and Brāhmanical Hindu is as untrue as to consider Ambedkar only a *dalit* leader instead of a nationalist leader. For Gandhi, no religious text, whether it be *Manu–Smṛti*, Vedas or Upaniṣads, was sacrosanct. And, if Ambedkar had been only a *dalit* leader, Gandhi would have never suggested his name for the presidentship of constituent assembly.

Now, let us understand the clear-cut differences between Gandhi and Ambedkar. First one is that of perspectives. Whereas Gandhi's primary aim was the struggle against British domination for which he tried to establish unity among different communities, for Ambedkar, struggle against dehumanization of *dalit*s in Indian society was more important than ending of British rule. That's why Gandhi tried to reduce the gap between upper and lower castes, but Ambedkar considered them as enemies.

Varṇa-vyavasthā is another case in point on which Gandhi and Ambedkar had fundamental differences. Except in his last few years, Gandhi, throughout his life, supported it. For him, there is no relation between *varṇāśrama dharma* and untouchability. Therefore, instead of asking untouchables to fight for their social and political rights, he tried to change Hindu society through change of heart of upper caste people by their self-purification. He was not agreeable to the separation of untouchables from Hindu society and thus, though he accepted the special rights of the Muslims and Sikhs due to their minority status, he not only rejected separate electorate zone for *harijan*s but also started fast unto death against it. In contrast, Ambedkar strongly opposed Hindu *dharma* and Hindu society embedded with caste structure. His primary concern was to destroy this unjust and inhuman structure and for this purpose, he was not averse to taking help from the British government. He alleged that neither Gandhians nor liberal Hindus nor Marxists ever took caste injustice seriously. That is the reason why he chose Buddhism as an external alternative for scheduled castes (SCs). Whereas Gandhi treated relationship between hereditary caste and profession as permanent and wished to enhance its dignity, Ambedkar wanted to break it completely.

Both, Gandhi and Ambedkar, differed significantly about the role of government in fighting caste injustice. Ambedkar was more influenced by modern, scientific and Western social and political ideas which inspired him to use state power under democratic framework for resolving the *dalit* problems. For Gandhi, the solution could be found without the use of state power.

Gandhi developed a critique of modernity whereas Ambedkar endorsed it. The model of development Gandhi suggested was based on a conception of independent villages. But Ambedkar believed in modern democratic state based on equal citizenship. On this issue, he was closer to Nehru than Gandhi. He was afraid that if the established system and structure of Indian villages was continued, *dalit*s would never be liberated from inhuman treatment meted out to them. Therefore, one can say that the place occupied by truth and non-violence in Gandhi's thinking can be compared to similar status granted to liberty, equality and fraternity in Ambedkar's thought.

Both had deep differences regarding means to adopt leadership issues in *dalit* liberation. For Gandhi, this was a movement of ethical reform, but for Ambedkar, this was not sufficient. Instead of symbolic change, he wanted permanent structural change. Therefore, he concentrated on education, jobs and political rights. Similarly, Ambedkar wished for emergence of leadership from within the SCs which should be knowledgeable, honest and self-respecting, unlike that of Congress leadership which was flattering and corrupt. Certainly, his political and cultural philosophy was different from that of Gandhi and he was willing to adopt alternative cultural values and symbols to define, not only a single member of SC but the whole movement.

When we think a little deeper, we become aware that for Gandhi, the problem of untouchability is the problem of "self," the whole "Hindu self." Since untouchable is a part of larger self, self-purification is the sacred duty and the solution to the problem. He himself wrote in the *Harijan* on 15 April 1933: "The movement for removal of untouchability is a movement of self-purification." For Gandhi, this was mainly a religious issue and that too, an inner problem of Hindu religion. But Ambedkar saw socio-economic and political structure of power behind it and focused on developing an independent political identity for *dalit*s. For him, this was not a religious but an issue of rights of citizens. The question was not of self-purification of upper castes but of self-respect of *dalit*s.

II

Before we critically evaluate the debate between Gandhi and Ambedkar, we must understand the difference between their social backgrounds, life situations, fields of activity and political styles. Ambedkar was born in a *dalit* family. For him, the exploitation and inhuman treatment due to unequal caste structure was a truth of self-experience. Whereas Gandhi could never experience the same as he was born and brought up in an upper caste family. Though, due to his Jaina–Vaiṣṇava background, sensitive mind and experience of racial hatred in South Africa, Gandhi was radically transformed and thus, the suffering of untouchables was not unfelt for him, but we must keep in mind the distinction between self-experience, empathy and sympathy to understand their differences. We have already discussed their different priorities, due to which their field of action, styles of working and communication differed considerably. But, as a result of critical debate between the two, both influenced each other in updating their views.

It is true that the question of *dalit* liberation was not the number one issue for Gandhi. He could wait to solve the issue of *dalits* till the success of liberation struggle against colonial domination. Ambedkar's disagreement was natural as *dalit* issue was the most important issue for him. But, the question is, did Gandhi commit a mistake in not treating the issue of *dalit*s as number one issue? Perhaps not. Historically speaking, the agenda of anti-colonial liberation struggle was the main issue of that period. Without assigning it top priority Gandhi could never become the man of the century. But this does not mean that Gandhi ignored the *dalit*s. He did whatever was possible for him, doing even the work of a *bhaṅgī*. But, for him, the problem of injustice to *dalit*s was a part of larger social reconstruction, not a matter of sole commitment as in the case of Ambedkar. Ambedkar did not participate much in the freedom struggle, but we can say for Gandhi that untouchability was one of his central concerns. Gandhi was the first to raise the issue of untouchability as a prominent issue in Indian politics. But, even then, he did not make it a matter of life and death because he was equally concerned with the liberation of woman, Muslims, Sikhs along with *dalit*s. This was not possible in a day but required creation of a new civilization.

Even with his priority to nationalist struggle, Gandhi did not undermine the struggle against untouchability. But his perspective was mainly spiritual in which solution lies with spiritual transformation of self. This was the pre-Ambedkar understanding till 1930.

But injustice to *dalit*s is not restricted to untouchability alone. Ambedkar's firm conviction was that until caste system was destroyed, untouchability could not be removed. After the debate with Ambedkar, Gandhi shifted his stand on the caste system and announced in 1935 that it must be destroyed. Though he gave his blessings to inter-caste marriages and parties, yet he kept silence on *varṇa-vyavasthā*. He also did not use such strong words against Hindu caste system as he used against British rule as well as against untouchability. This should be called a lack on his part. Actually, caste system in India is not only a structure of cultural values. Parallel to caste hierarchy, it is also a structure of unequal distribution of power and wealth. Thus, struggle against caste system cannot remain on spiritual plane; it has to recognize material demands of the *dalit*s too. Gandhi failed to recognize this. Such a divided reaction is still prevalent among the liberal supporters of *dalit* movement. Attention is drawn to positive dimensions of caste system to argue that castes do provide its members with an identity. One can further argue that it acts as a check to the uniformity being created by the globalization process. But from the *dalit* perspective, this picture is totally opposite. Instead of giving them security and identity, caste system continuously insults them. Identity of a *dalit* is a source of life-long suffering for him which cannot be easily erased. Thus, all efforts to defend caste system or to see it in positive terms become doubtful from *dalit* angle. Gandhi, perhaps due to his opposition to inhuman tendencies of modern civilization, became soft towards the dangerous structures inherent in a society organized on the basis of caste system. He did not see any fault with the organizing principle of caste system. The problem, according to him, lies with its application which can be reformed by a powerful social movement. But, the difference between the organizing principle and its application cannot be justified on the basis of any rational argument. Ambedkar rejected Gandhi's viewpoint totally but organized his *dalit* movement on the basis of Gandhian *satyāgraha*.

Gandhi's model of removal of untouchability had some fundamental weaknesses. Self-purification was seen as a sacred ritual which imposed a moral responsibility on the shoulders of an upper caste Hindu. This created a moral halo around him which further alienated *harijan*s. Guilt-ridden Hindu-self needed untouchables for atonement. Such heroism on the part of upper caste Hindu reformer made dwarfs out of *harijan*s. Relationship between the Hindu reformer and *harijan* became that of guardian and his ward. Gandhian movement among *harijan*s did produce an obliged leadership which was very soft, flattering and weak, lacking in self-respect for launching struggle. Such leadership was unfit for challenging socio-cultural structure of Hindu society. Therefore, Ambedkar's criticism that the ritual of self-purification converted *harijan*s into mere objects seems correct. Playing such script, they could never become heroes on the platform of history. They were condemned to reflect, like a mirror, disappointment and glory of their masters.

Gandhi himself admitted that entry of *harijan*s into temples was not as important as was the change of heart of narrow minded members of upper castes so that they realize that it was wrong to stop *harijan*s. But one cannot deny the truth in radical critics' observation that though Gandhi asked to repent for the sin of untouchability yet he failed to pinpoint underlying socio-economic roots of it. The possibility of change of heart was also historically not fulfilled for the majority of *harijans*. Had it not been so, there would have been no need for passing laws and going to courts. Rigidity of mental attitudes born out of thousands of years of conditioning cannot be changed overnight by preaching morality. Laws also have their limitation. Those who are going to be benefitted by those laws should be conscious and politically powerful to get them implemented. Therefore, Ambedkar's effort to organize *dalit*s to make them politically powerful appears as a step in right direction.

Should we say in the end that Ambedkar comes out victorious in this debate? There is sufficient evidence to prove that both, Gandhi and Ambedkar, influenced each other. For Gandhi, the question of upliftment of *harijan*s was no longer restricted to removal of untouchability alone. It was a broader economic issue as suggested by Ambedkar; whereas Ambedkar accepted the importance of religion in this struggle. The debate transformed both of them.

We can draw some important conclusions from the above discussion of historical debate between the two thinker-leaders. Both were addressing separately to different caste groups. Gandhi tried to stir the souls of upper caste persons whereas Ambedkar raised the consciousness of *dalit*s. Keeping in mind the weak socio-economic conditions and low level of political awareness among *dalit*s of that period, Gandhi's effort to kindle an urge for repentance and justice in upper castes appears justified. In such difficult circumstances, any movement of *dalit*s, to succeed required active co-operation of open-minded and active members of the higher castes. Thus, Gandhi prepared the ground for early stages of *dalit* movement. Ambedkar's contribution lies in converting *dalit*s into an independent political force. His other major contributions are: reservation, law against untouchability, religious reform and help in drafting the Constitution of India. Reservation is not Ambedkar's original contribution. What he did was to use reservation as a successful weapon for *dalit* upliftment. Transformation of the son of a village labourer of *dalit* community into a bureaucrat is really an earth shaking incident with wide repercussions for Indian society. But Ambedkar's aim was to destroy caste system. History has proved otherwise. Untouchability may no longer be the basis of caste identity today, yet a new political *avtāra* of caste has emerged in Indian political scene after Independence. Actually, the new *dalit* identity is separatist to the core and lacks a clear-cut vision for social revolution. Therefore, the followers of this ideology have failed to perform any positive role in the society, going beyond their caste hatred. Benefits of reservation have been cornered by the elite among *dalit*s, making such strategy for *dalit* liberation questionable in the eyes of many.

Now, we can understand the relevance of Gandhi today. Complete solution to *dalit* problem is not possible till there is radical transformation of non-*dalit* community. Thus, Gandhi is more relevant for higher castes than he is for *dalit*s. Without the purification of their hearts, as suggested by Gandhi, upper caste men cannot expect respect from *dalit*s. Similarly, conversion of self-respect into castiest pride among *dalit* will only lead to further caste conflicts. Therefore, we can conclude that despite differences, both Gandhi and Ambedkar may complement each other in *dalit* liberation. But we should not look for answers to all contemporary problems in their thoughts.

Part V
Socio-Centric Morality

CHAPTER 23

Hindu View of Social Justice

S.P. Dubey

THE theme of this volume is *Morality and Social Justice*. Hence it is obligatory to reflect upon both the concepts, namely morality and social justice. We know that morality and social justice form a major part of ethics. Ethics is the philosophical study of morality. Moral philosophy is concerned with individual and social morality. Moral philosophy insists on the individual responsibility for moral acts. Whether an individual acts on rational grounds or non-rational grounds is an important issue. On one side of the issue are philosophers like Kant who hold that reason alone accounts for right or wrong acts. Reason for them is both the pilot and the engine of moral agency. It guides our moral duty and also produces the desire to do one's duty. On the other side are philosophers like Hume and Mill who take reason to be one of the several capacities that constitute moral agency. According to them reason works strictly in the service of natural and sublimated desires. The desire to act rightly or the aversions to acting wrongly are not products or reason. They are acquired through socialization. These views are tested by questions about freedom. One cannot be responsible for one's action if one is incapable of acting freely. The capacity for free action is essential to moral agency. Whether this capacity fits within a deterministic universe or it should be jettisoned are questions to which a student of moral philosophy must furnish answers. At this point ethics descends into metaphysics. In Indian ethics we always find a blending of rational (in the present context empirical) and the metaphysical. While dealing with *dharma* shortly, we shall make this point more clear. The ideal of Indian ethics is *sarve bhavantu sukhinaḥ*. The *Chāndogya*

Upaniṣad[1] treats all existence as *Brahman* (*sarvaṁ khalu idaṁ brahma*). The *Ṛgveda*[2] tell us that all that is and shall be is nothing but *Puruṣa: puruṣa evedaṁ sarvaṁ*. . . . If such is the case, there is hardly any scope for real inequality or injustice in the society.

Now coming to the second part of the theme of this book, we find that social justice is a concept of universal concern from time immemorial. In Greek tradition, the key concept for social justice was *arête* (virtue). In Chinese tradition *li* (propriety) and *yi* (ought and righteousness) played important role in the realm of social justice. In India the Vedic concept of *ṛta* signified cosmic order. Varuṇa was the king who ordained justice to everyone. But if we try to have an overview of Vedic tradition, we find that in the traditional Hindu (Vedic/ Sanātana) philosophy the concept of *dharma* is the key term for understanding social justice. The idea of *dharma* as a *puruṣārtha* stands for the ideas of individual perfection and personal development. The idea of *dharma* and that of social justice are significant at human level and may be treated as ethical values. Since ethical values point not merely to the individual but to the situation where the individual enters into enduring relationships with others, the intimate relationship between the individual and the society cannot be denied. The individual is endowed with an outgoing as well as inward looking tendency. The real significance of the ideal of justice can be gathered only by reflecting about its relevance for the growing individual. Social justice gets significance only as an ethico-social value for the individual.

The ethical philosophy of *dharma* clearly indicates that the basic idea that social justice is a value inspires the individual on to developing concern for principles of objectivity while dealing with his fellowmen. The concern for justice originates as an ethical value worthy of pursuit by the individual. We find expansiveness of the individual's concern for others. The social stage of justice

---

1. *Chāndogya Upaniṣad*, III.14.i.
2. *Ṛgveda*, X.90.2.

connotes the idea that the frame of reference gradually shifts from the individual to the growing individual. Humanity is the ultimate reference-point and the comprehensiveness of concern developed by the individual is made possible by the inwardization and reflectiveness that the individual brings to bear on the ideals that society itself possesses.

The metaphysical dimension of *dharma* has been mostly misunderstood. The idea of *mokṣa* and the idealization of human life in its institutional and day-to-day spheres are intimately related. The ultimate and empirical concerns are not opposed. The Hindu theory of social justice, as suggested by the philosophy of *dharma*, lays emphasis on the process of transforming one's life in the light of the ideals envisaged and aimed at. The effect of the transformation of personality of the individual by leading a dhārmic life is obvious and offers us an insight into the Hindu theory of social justice which takes due note of both the metaphysical and the social dimensions of human life. They are not two realms but two aspects of the same process. But overemphasizing either the social or the metaphysical has to be avoided. The overenthusiasm for either of the approaches to the total understanding of man ought to be carefully guarded against. A perspective which does justice to the social as well as metaphysical aspects of human life should be more acceptable. This holds the key to unraveling many elusive problems concerning human life.

Various treatises of Hinduism express great concern for social values. But, while doing so, they focus their attention on the individual who has to have a scheme of values and the ultimate ideal to be realized. Of course, we do find a dominant current in Dharmaśāstra texts for this worldly concern (*pravṛtti* aspect) but the metaphysical roots of social life are also indicated by them. All the same, we must concede that the normative rather than the empirical approach to man and society find favour with the Hindu ethical philosophers.

In a well-known text, the *Bṛhadāraṇyaka Upaniṣad*[3] summarizes a whole philosophy of Indian ethics in the three commands: Cultivate self-control (*damayata*), be generous (*datta*) and have compassion (*dayadhvam*).

Dharma is the moral principle which governs the universe. The strength of a man who exemplifies in his life the principle of *dharma* is enormous. Even if a person is physically weak, he should not feel the want of physical strength if he is morally strong. The supremacy of the moral ideal is described in a poetic form in the *Bṛhadāraṇyaka Upaniṣad.*[4] It says that even after creating the four *varṇas*, Prajāpati felt incompleteness of his work. So he created *dharma*, the supreme ideal of happiness and welfare:

> He created further an excellent form, justice. This is the power of the kṣatriya class, viz. justice. Therefore, there is nothing higher than justice. So a weak man hopes to defeat strong men by means of justice as one does through a king. Verily, that which is justice is true.

The Upaniṣad identifies truth with *dharma*. Truth in action is *dharma*. Śaṅkara, in his commentary on the text, clarifies the relationship between the three significant terms, *ṛta, satya* and *dharma*. *Ṛta* denotes the mental perception of truth, *satya* suggests its expression in words, and *dharma* is the observance of truth in the conduct of life.

The *Mahābhārata*[5] holds that "one is said to know what morality or righteousness is, who is always the friend of all creatures and who is always engaged in the good of all, in thought, word and deed." The attitude of considering entire being (not only humanity) as an end-in-itself is the projection of the deepest humanity that man is capable of.

---

3. *Bṛhadāraṇyaka Upaniṣad*, V.2.3.
4. Ibid., XIV.I.4.
5. Vedavyāsa, *Mahābhārata*, XII.254.9.

The dhārmic life for a Hindu is built upon certain rules and regulations to be followed by everyone. The *Taittirīya Upaniṣad*[6] exhorts the outgoing graduate:

> Speak the truth. Do your duty. Do not neglect the study of the scripture. Do not cut the thread of progeny. Swerve not from truth. Deviate not from the path of Good. Revere greatness. Let your mother be a god to you; let your father be a god to you; let your teacher be a god to you; let your guest be a god to you . . ..

The *Mahābhārata*[7] says that the teacher who keeps waiting a student for more than a year accrues all the sins of the latter. This might also be applicable to today's supervisors for doctoral research. The case of Raikava in the *Chāndogya Upaniṣad*[8] is also an exemplary one so far as the worth of spiritual knowledge is concerned. The flying swan Bhāllakṣa tells his friend that the fame of king Jñānaśruti stands nowhere as compared to that of Raikva, a cartman (obviously, of humble origin). Overhearing the talk, the king finds out the cartman and learns from him the secrets of that god whom Raikva adores.

As the emphasis in the dhārmic life is on duties rather than on rights, the feeling of individuality is slowly got over. The Hindu concept of *dharma* is one of discharging one's duties to oneself, to one's kith and kin and society, to the state and country and to the past cultural inheritance and the future. The statement of Vidura in the *Mahābhārata*[9] is noteworthy here. "We should abandon the individual for the family, the family for the village, and the village for the district: *tyajedekam kulāsyarthe. . . .*"

An ideal like social justice which may have humanity at large as the ultimate point of reference cannot be considered merely in

---

6. *Taittirīya Upaniṣad*, I.11.i.
7. *Mahābhārata*, "Droṇa Parva", 50.21.
8. *Chāndogya Upaniṣad*, IV.1.i-v.
9. *Mahābhārata*, "Ādi Parva", 107.32.

terms of social institutions but gets its meaning and significance in the idealized conception of life that the individuals who man the institutions bring to bear on them. The Hindu conception of *dharma* as a principle of individual and institutional life makes for an idealized conception of personal and social life. It is because of this that in the Hindu tradition the concept of Good and the good life holds the key for the theory of social justice.

The idealization of morality in the philosophy of *dharma* leads us to its being applied to specific spheres of human life. For instance, the idealization in regard to the economic institution of property is responsible for the Hindu view that property is not to be considered except in terms of its social utility. The ethical means of acquisition is also insisted upon. Hoarding is an anti-social act.

In the idealization of the state the functions of the office of kingship is indicated. The Dharmaśāstras (and even the *Arthaśāstra*) maintain that the king is expected to have no consideration other than justice while dealing with his subjects. In the words of Kauṭilya,[10] the kṣatriya has to use punishment (*daṇḍa)* in order to establish justice (*nīti*). Kāmandakī[11] affirms that in the absence of punishment the world will revert to the state of the strong devouring the weak (*matsya-nyāya*). The *Mahābhārata*[12] points out that the chastisement was ordained by the creator himself for protecting *dharma* and *artha,* for happiness of all and making people righteous and modest. The state, in order to enable the individuals to follow their *svadharma* and *sādhāraṇa dharmas*, is justified in resorting to the use of force. But force is only a means to prevent disorder. The power of punishment is not the wielding of naked power according to whims.

The idea of freedom from debt (*anaṛṇya*) is another concept which gives the Hindu society a clue to social justice. Although

---

10. Kauṭilya, *Arthaśāstra*, vol. I, p. 4.
11. Kāmandakī, *Nītiśāstra,* vol. II, pp. 40, 42-43.
12. *Mahābhārata,* XII.15.35.

we remain indebted to a couple of institutions throughout our life, we should try to pay back the obligations or debts (moral as well as physical). We are indebted to our parents (*pitṛ-ṛṇa*), to our teachers (*guru ṛna*) and so on. We should perform such actions that fulfil our obligations to them. Physically (or more correctly, economically) also we must be free from debt. In the context of Yakṣa-Yudhiṣṭhira dialogue the *Mahābhārata* tells us that one who is free from debts is the happy person: *aṛṇī capravāsī ca sa vaicāra modate*.

In today's India, when we have a pluralistic society, the norms presented by traditional Hinduism may not be applicable to all. Therefore, we look towards international institutions for understanding problems and their solutions. Now we have Human Rights declaration, commissions for women, laws against dowry, child labour, protection of old parents and so on. But violence at domestic and social level, discrimination of gender and caste and many problems like these are not getting lasting solutions. We have to struggle constantly for this. Proper education of our mind is the only answer to social inequalities and injustice. Philosophy, as a discipline, is inclusive of moral sciences and has a special role to play in the context.

CHAPTER 24

Socio-Ethical Dimension of Mahābhārata Morality

Rajjan Kumar

The approach of Indian philosophy to truth and reality is essentially moral and practical and this fact is very well explained by the *Mahābhārata*, a very comprehensive work known as a virtual encyclopaedia in which all kinds of major problems of life have been considered. Morality constitutes the keynote of a man's empirical and social life. The world is to be looked upon as positive and essential as it is based on truth. It is our duty to respect the world, to respect the society to which we belong and also to respect all relations, which exist between man and man. The harmony between moral and social life has been depicted in a rational and convincing manner in the *Mahābhārata*.

Metaphysics, Ethics and Society

In India we find an intimate relationship between philosophy and life. Philosophy has never been only an intellectual exercise in India; rather it has the practical importance insofar as it influences the formation of the views towards the life and the world. Every major system of Indian philosophy is concerned with the practical and tragic problems of human life and tries to grasp the reality in order to solve the problems of human life in the light and context of the truths so grasped. In India, thus, philosophy is for life, it is to be lived.

The social thoughts depend in the final analysis upon the philosophical and spiritual thought and ideals. In India the social thoughts were integrally related to general philosophy and metaphysics; there was no separation of social, political, moral and religious affairs. The social theories proceeded from a conscious thinking in terms of metaphysical and ethical principles. It derives from rational contemplation to discover the place of man and his social organization in the cosmic scheme. And it is tried to find out the purpose of man and the nature of social organization necessary to allow him to fulfil that purpose.

Indian social thoughts, as a whole, cannot be isolated from the main body of Indian philosophy acclaimed as Hindu philosophy.[1] Some of the dominant concepts of Hinduism like the theory of reality, the concept of the dualism of body and soul, the theory of transmigration and *karma*, and of the *mokṣa*, etc. coloured its social thought or even political thought too.[2] These theological, religious and philosophical concepts have direct bearing on the ethical, social and political thought of the *Mahābhārata*. The latter is based upon an understanding of the meaning and purpose of human existence, its real needs and interests and its final goal.

The *Mahābhārata*, consequently, draws a scheme for conducting human life in accordance with that meaning and purpose so that the ultimate goal of human life, its aspirations and its mission may be achieved. Hence, in order to understand the significance of the social and political thought of the *Mahābhārata*, its philosophical background must be understood. The ultimate purpose of the teachings of the *Mahābhārata* is thoroughly and essentially an ethical one. "To preach morality is easy, to give it a foundation is hard," says Schopenhauer. And it is the problem of giving morality a foundation with which the author of the *Mahābhārata* is engrossed. He tries to search for a basic principle of morality and make it rationally acceptable.

The real problem of ethics lies in the apparent conflict between individual pleasure and social good. Impelled by the self-interest

---

1. For recent valuable study on Indian philosophy, see D. Mackenzie Brown, *The White Umbrella* (Bombay: Jaico Publishing House, 1964).
2. A.S. Altekar, *The State and Government in Ancient India* (New Delhi: Motilal Banarsidass, 1962), pp. 55-57.

and the desire for sensual pleasures, man takes resort to such activities, which go against social good. Ethics, therefore, tries to bring about a harmony between individual and social good by assimilating individual good into the social good.

Knowledge of the perfect life under ideal conditions is the aim of Indian thinkers and they try to find out how such a life can be attained. They not only try to understand the mutual relationship of men in their social and political communities but also visualize an ideal scheme of life in which the ultimate end of men can be fulfilled. This visualization of the ultimate end of men and its fulfilment through an ideal organization of the socio-political life is the purpose of their philosophical enquiry.

Dharma, the most important concept of Indian thought is well accepted by *Mahābhārata* to draw a sketch for an ideal social life or society. It tries to reconcile the opposition between the individual good and social good. It lays down a way of life, which aims at securing the material well-being, spiritual development and moral perfection, and the unhampered growth of both the individual and society. It is well said: "it is *dharma* which conduces to the stability of society and the maintenance of social-order and well-being."

There is not much unity in the metaphysical thought of the *Mahābhārata*. It lacks a unified philosophical system and hardly contains in its jumble of conflicting ideas a system of consistency.[3] It is a conglomeration of very diverse views, and what appears as very peculiar is the fact that these diverse views are presented in "immediate proximity to one another without any sense of incongruity."[4] This is due to the fact that, although ascribed to one another, the *Mahābhārata* is a vast composite work, a veritable encyclopaedia of Hindu philosophy, ethics, religion, legends, law,

---

3. S.K. Dey, *History of Philosophy: Eastern and Western* (George Allen & Unwin, 1957), p. 85.
4. A.B. Keith, *The Sāṁkhya System* (Kolkata: Calcutta University, 1924), p. 36.

political science, sociology, etc. — a whole literature spreading over many centuries, resulting in a mixture of many elements of thought, even contradictory ones.[5]

Another important feature of the epic thought is the intermingling of the religious and philosophical ideas. The *Mahābhārata* aims at providing a religious thought which may satisfy all; and for this it tries to harmonize the conflicting philosophies which were current at the time around the *Kṛṣṇaite* theism. Hence, we find in the *Mahābhārata* a "theistic tinge which constantly intrudes."[6]

There are, in this great epic, an attempt to synthesize and integrate the four systems of thought — the Vedic ritualism, the Sāṁkhya and Yoga dualism, the Upaniṣadic idealistic monism and the Vaiṣṇava theism. The great virtue of the *Mahābhārata* is that instead of dilating the points of difference among the various systems of thought and practice, it lays stress upon the points of agreement among them, and thereby brings about a philosophical and religious synthesis and a workable system of ethics and morality.

Dharma, Morality and Society

The concept of *dharma* is the most important concept of Indian thought. It is the key to the Hindu ethics, both individual and social, and also the basis of individual progress and social welfare. Right through the ages it has permeated Indian thinking and life and has formulated a norm of thought and behaviour for the large majority of people in India. It embraced the whole life of man and "was not a creed or religion but a mode of life or a code of conduct which regulated man's work and activities as a member of society and as an individual and was intended to bring about the gradual development of a man and to enable him to reach what was deemed to be the goal of human existence."[7]

---

5. Dey, p. 85.
6. Keith, p. 36.
7. P.V. Kane, *History of Dharmaśāstra*, vol. II, p. 2.

Dharma seeks to resolve conflicts of human life.[8] It tries to reconcile the opposition between the individual good and social good. It lays down a way of life, which aims at securing the material well-being, spiritual development and moral perfection, and unhampered growth of both the individual and society. To the extent society and the individual respect the *dharma*, they are protected, and to the extent they make inroads into it, they are undermined.[9]

The full implication of *dharma* cannot be conveyed by the English word "religion" into which it is generally translated. It is a term of wide implications and conveys many ideas. The term *dharma* is derived from the root *dhṛ* which means to sustain, uphold or to hold together and nourish, i.e. it is the principle which sustains — the moral law, which sustains the world, human society and the individual.[10] It is the principle which holds together signifying thereby the principle of order, social or moral. The world order is *dharma*.

Dharma holds and sustains a thing and saves it from disintegration. It is the principle which is responsible for a thing or phenomenon functioning as it does and not in a different way. It is the nature of things that makes them what they are. The *dharma* of a thing is its intrinsic property, its real nature and its true being, by virtue of which it is what it is and ought to behave in a way it should. If it does otherwise, it is *adharma*, which will lead it to ultimate disintegration.[11] *Dharma*, therefore, sustains society. It permeates all.

Though the term *dharma* is generally used to the religiously ordained duty, it signifies morality, justice, right conduct, duty and the intrinsic nature of a thing. Besides, it also stands for a

---

8. S. Radhakrishnan, *Religion and Society*, pp. 105-06.
9. *Manu-Smṛti*, 8:15.
10. *Ṛgveda*, I.187; *Atharvaveda*, XII.7; *Vajasaneyī-Saṁhitā*, XXXVIII.17.
11. Woodroffe, *Sakti and Sakta*, (Madras: Ganesh & Co, 1965), p. 3.

principle of reason, the law of causality, which is the law of reason that runs through the world. It is, moreover, "a mystic force capable of rewarding and punishing human being." And over and above these, it means one's duty in the station he is placed.[12]

Varṇa-Vyvasthā, Dharma and Society

The epic *Mahābhārata* always reminds us that *dharma* is subtle. It is not simple and unitary but many-sided and complex. *Dharma*, in the sphere of an individual member of society, is the integration of his personality, which requires the control of his passions by reason and his moral obligation to society. It lies in the performance of his *svadharma* without attachment. *Dharma* in the sphere of society is the social solidarity, which is brought by *varṇāśrama vyavaśthā*, which establishes an organic unity amongst the various classes of society and balances *pravr̥tti* and *nivr̥tti*.

The *Mahābhārata* accepts the divine origin of the *varṇa-vyavasthā* and its heretical stratification[13]; but at the same time it is also conscious of the injustice involved in such a social gradation based merely on birth and, therefore, it tries to justify it on metaphysical and ethical considerations. We have already seen how the four *varṇa*s were created from different organs of the Great *Puruṣa*. An allegorical meaning and significance is attached to the whole of the Puruṣa-Sūkta,[14] and it is suggested that the whole universe as well as the body social is the Great *Puruṣa*. The *Puruṣa* is described as being himself "whole universe," whatever has been and whatever shall be.[15]

The moon came out of his mind, the sun from his eyes, Indra and Agni were created from his mouth, air or wind from his breath,

---

12. B.G. Gokhale, *Indian Thought through the Ages* (Bombay: Asia Publishing House, 1961), p. 24.
13. Vedavyāsa, *Mahābhārata*, XII.46.68; XII.72.4-5; XII.188.4-5; XIII.48.3.
14. Prabhu, *Hindu Social Organisation* (Bombay: Popular Prakashan, 1963), p. 286.
15. *R̥gveda*, X.90.2.

and further from his navel arose atmosphere (*antarikṣa*), from his head the sky, from his feet the earth, and from his ears the four quarters (*diśāyeṅ*). In this manner the world was created.[16] Thus, symbolically the microcosmic elements have been traced to, and identified with, the macrocosmic ones. Not only the universe but "the whole social organization is here conceived of symbolically as one human being, the 'Body Social,' we may say — with its limbs representing the social classes based on the principle of division of labour."[17]

Mahābhārata too, like the *R̥gveda*, symbolically identifies different classes with the different limbs of the human body performing different functions suited to them. Thus the whole society is an organism, and every class is designed to perform a particular function in society so as to fulfil its obligation to the body-social, as the different organs of the body do and thereby jointly share the constructive contribution to the social well-being; and the privileges to certain *varṇa*s are nothing but certain facilities to them to fulfil their obligations in an efficient way. Each class is an integral part of the whole fabric of society.

The classes of the society are supposed to stand in relation to the social organization in the same relationship as the different organs of the Primeval Man to his body. *Varṇa-vyavasthā* stands for an organic as against atomistic conception of society. The four classes[18] as described in the Puruṣa-Sūkta, constituting the body-social as divinely ordained, may be said to be natural. It appears that *R̥gveda* wants to convey the idea that the division of society into classes is natural. In Anuśāsana-Parva of the *Mahābhārata* also, the natural character of *varṇa-vyavasthā* based on natural disposition and qualities of man is emphasized.[19]

---

16. Ibid., X.90.13-14; *Mahābhārata*, XIII.46.49.
17. Prabhu, op. cit., p. 286.
18. *Vedic Index*, vol. II, p. 247. Also see Kane, vol. II, part I, p. 27.
19. *Mahābhārata*, XIII.143.6.

The Puruṣa-Sūkta does not directly refer to the gradation of the four classes, which, however, can be imputed to it by implication. It is the *Taittirīya Saṁhitā* which, ascribing the origin of the four classes to the different limbs of the creator, adds an explanation of the gradation of the social status and says that brāhmaṇas are declared to be the foremost, because they were created from the face; the rājanyas were vigorous, because they were created from the hand; the vaiśyas were meant to eat (referring to their liability to excessive taxation), because they were created from the stomach; and as the śūdras were created from the feet they were the "footmen," the servants of the other *varṇa*s.[20]

The *Mahābhārata* accepts this basic gradation at several places.[21] It is maintained that the creator ordains the functions of the four orders just at the time of birth.[22] Thus the work, the pattern of behaviour and its hierarchy of gradation are pre-oriented by God in which the brāhmaṇas are at the head and the śūdras at the bottom. This appears to be the general acceptance in the *Mahābhārata.*[23]

But at many occasions it has been pointed out that the epic itself is quite conscious of the injustice involved in this traditional theory.[24] At some places, therefore, the *Mahābhārata* explains and justifies the *varṇa* system and its gradation on the basis of colour. In the dialogue between Bhṛgu and Bharadvāja, the former says that originally there was no differentiation of *varṇa*s. Being born from the same *Brahman*, the whole of the world consisted of brāhmaṇas. Later on, however, due to differences in work the *varṇa*s evolved.[25]

---

20. *Taittirīya Saṁhitā*, VII.1.1.4-6.
21. *Mahābhārata*, XII.72.4-5; VIII.23.32; X.3.18-20; XIII.48.3.
22. Ibid., XII.72.5-8.
23. Dhairyabala P. Vora, *Evolution of Morals in the Epics* (Bombay: 1959), p. 126.
24. *Mahābhārata*, XII.188.6-9.
25. Ibid., XII.188.10.

All were originally brāhmaṇas and were white in colour, but later on those brāhmaṇas who left their own *dharma,* indulged in enjoyments, became subject to anger and hardness and performed courageous deeds became "red" and assumed kṣatriyahood. Those who adopted agriculture became "yellow" and were called vaiśyas. Those who resorted to untruth, violence, and impiety became black and came to be called śūdras.[26] Thus, the four divisions of mankind — brāhmaṇas, kṣatriyas, vaiśyas and śūdras — assumed white, red, yellow and black complexions respectively.[27] Thus, falling out from their duties, some of the original brāhmaṇas turned into the three lower *varṇa*s.

Varṇa, Karma and Society

Another explanation of the *varṇa* is given on the basis of the theory of *karma*. The *Chāndogya Upaniṣad*[28] has already given an explanation of it on the basis of this theory. In the *Mahābhārata*[29] it is said that the *dvija*s who do not regard this world to be a manifestation of *Brahman* and avoid *dharma* and follow different conceptions, are born in different *varṇa*s as well as in different *yoni*s.

The reason of one's being born in a low *varṇa* is his previous *karma*. It is difficult to overcome the consequences of one's past deeds. The birth in a lower class is caused by sins committed in one's former life.[30] In the Anuśāsana-Parva it is said that a person of lower origin may attain the status of a higher *varṇa* in the next birth by following his own *dharma* in this life, and conversely, the person who does not follow his own *dharma* will be born in a lower *varṇa*.[31] The *Mahābhārata* wants to show that the status of every individual in life is determined by his *karma* or action of his previous lives, and that his salvation depends on due observance

26. Ibid., XII.188.11-13.
27. Ibid., XII.5.
28. *Chāndogya Upanisad*, V.10.7.
29. *Mahābhārata*, XII.188.16-17.
30. Ibid., III.208.2, 11.
31. Ibid., XIII.143.7-14.

of his *dharma*, i.e. the practice of virtues and the performance of duty in the station of life in which he is placed.

The *Gītā* too upholds the theory that the traits of individuals are inherent right from the beginning, based on their past deeds.[32] Even though a man does not want to do a particular type of work he is driven to do it by the compulsive power of his nature.[33] Thus the *Gītā* tries to justify the division of society into classes on the principle of *karma* and *svabhāva* even though this theory fails to explain "how individuals at the very beginning of the creation came to be possessed of particular qualities and capacities."[34]

Moral Behaviour, Duty and Society

The word *dharma* generally means the pattern or ideal of moral behaviour. But it also means "property" and "function" of a thing in that sense in which these terms are used in physics or chemistry. The function of a thing derives directly from the intrinsic quality or property of the thing concerned. This is why the *Gītā* defines *dharma* as the innate law of an entity and the behaviour and action proceeding from and determined by that *svabhāva* or inner nature (*svabhāva nityam karma*).[35]

But so far as inanimate things are concerned, the relationship between nature and function is direct and automatic, but in the case of human beings, the relationship between *svabhāva* and *karma* is not automatic. The *karma* amongst human beings does not follow automatically from *svabhāva* but has to be adjusted and deliberately made to conform to it. Herein lies the necessity of *dharma* in the human world.[36]

Human society is a graded organization, because men have

---

32. *Gītā*, VI.41-46.
33. Ibid., XVIII.60.
34. Ghurye, *Caste, Class and Occupation* (Bombay: 1961), p. 64.
35. *Gītā*, XVIII.47.
36. Krishna Chaitnya, *Sanskrit Poetics* (Bombay: Asia Publishing House, 1965), p. 346.

different mental constitutions, different psychological make-up, different temperaments, different aptitudes, different capacities and different vocations. There must be, as a result of it, gradation of duty. The duty in one state of life, in one set of circumstances will not and cannot be that of another. Potentialities and limitations differ from man to man according to the different permutation and combination of the three *guṇa*s (*sattva, rajas* and *tamas*) in him.

Hence, it is but natural that society is divided into different classes, which can be grouped into four orders. Ideally the *varṇa* organization of the Hindu society gives little basis for exclusiveness or for distinction of superiority and inferiority. It only emphasizes that society is a partnership with a division of functions. This fact was accepted in Indian social organization and was stressed by morality and religion from the earliest times. Different rules of conduct and different duties for different types of men have always been prescribed.

The *Gītā* stressed that man should realize this fact and shape his ideals according to the status to which he belongs, and follow his *svadharma*, that is, do his duty according to his temperament and the requirement of the society. The activities of the four *varṇa*s are distinguished in accordance with the qualities of their nature.[37] Thus the *Gītā* shifts the emphasis from birth to the nature of individual man. It is nature and quality that determines one's station in life. The *varṇa* system recognizes that different men should contribute to the general good in different ways.

Society is a functional organization, and all functions, which are essential for the well-being of society, are to be regarded as socially equal. Since all are equally necessary for society, there is nothing degrading or elevating so far as the different functions required for society are concerned. What matters is the right performance of duties. "Devoted each to his own duty man attains perfection."[38]

37. *Gītā*, XVIII.41.

38. *Gītā*, XVIII.45.

Within the power of our own nature and being, true to our feelings and impulses we must fulfil our duties. Better is one's own *dharma*, though imperfectly carried out, than the *dharma* of another carried out perfectly. One does not incur sin, when one does the duties ordained by one's own nature.[39] One should not give up the work suited to one's nature, though it may be defective, for all enterprises are clouded by defects as fire by smoke.[40]

The fourfold category of individual natures is not artificial. They are inherent in men. It is on this natural division that the *Gītā* builds the firm foundation of the fourfold order of society, the *caturvarṇa.* Lord Kr̥ṣṇa says, "The fourfold order was created by Me according to the division of quality and work."[41] Thus in explaining the basis of the fourfold order of society the *Gītā* lays stress on *guṇa* and *karma* and not on birth. "The class determined by temperament and vocation is not a caste determined by birth and heredity."[42] The works of the brāhmaṇas, kṣatriyas, vaiśyas and śūdras, are divided according to the qualities (*guṇa*s) born of their own inner nature, spiritual temperament and essential character (*svabhāva*).

It is very much cwlear that though the central concept of *Mahābhārata* is *dharma,* around which all other ideas revolve, it is *dharma* or justice, which has been again and again emphasized throughout its pages. The epic itself is not to be regarded as a mere story of intrigues and battles, but as an allegory of the struggle between good and evil, *dharma* and *adharma,* justice and injustice, and the ultimate triumph of the good over evil. All these are considered the different ideals of socio-spiritual morality of the *Mahābhārata*.

---

39. Ibid., XVIII.47.
40. Ibid., XVIII.48.
41. Ibid., IV.13.
42. Radhakrishanan, *Bhagavad Gītā* (George Allen & Unwin, 1948), p. 161.

CHAPTER 25

Morality and Social Justice in Islam

Sajida Adeeb

MORALITY and justice are central to all religions, and so is the case with Islam which regards these two interrelated features as complementary to each other. There can be no justice without morality and no morality without justice. What is just is moral and what is moral is just. Justice is an integral part of divine activity. Only a just and healthy society has the highest regard for peace and hatred for obliteration. An unjust social system cannot sustain humanity, therefore, a morally just system is absolutely essential. After briefly defining the concept of morality and social justice in general and Islamic concept in particular, I intend to discuss about the way Islam deals with issues such as these.

Morality (from the Latin *moralitas* "manner, character, proper behaviour") has three principal meanings. In its first descriptive usage, morality means a code of conduct held to be authoritative in matters of right and wrong, whether by society, philosophy, religion, or individual conscience. In its second, normative, and universal sense, morality refers to an ideal code of conduct, one which would be espoused in preference to alternatives by all rational people, under specified conditions. To deny "morality" in this sense is a position known as moral scepticism. In its third usage "morality" is synonymous with ethics, the systematic philosophical study of the moral domain. Further the *Stanford Encyclopaedia of Philosophy*, states that morality is an informal public system applying to all rational persons, governing behaviour that affects others, and has the lessening of evil or harm as its goal.

Man's moral sense enables him to differentiate between right and wrong. Without subjecting behaviour to a common standard of vice and virtue, social evolution is not possible. This is the reason why even the primitive societies had words which denoted difference between good and bad. We are aware of the fact that man has been blessed with an innate sense of morality, which has served to guide him through the age, enabling him to distinguish between right and wrong or good and evil. Although the degree to which a certain quality is interpreted as being either good or evil may vary from person to person, there is more or less a universal consensus regarding the classification of what constitutes a moral deed or attribute and what does not.

> In the beginning of recorded ethical and legal thought the term justice was used as equivalent to righteousness in general. Justice comprised the whole of virtue and complete conformity with the approved pattern of moral conduct.[1]

Social Justice

Justice concerns the proper ordering of things and persons within a society. As a concept it has been subject to philosophical, legal, and theological reflection and debate throughout history. According to most theories of justice, it is overwhelmingly important. John Rawls, for instance, claims that "Justice is the first virtue of social institutions, as truth is of systems of thought." Justice has always been an extremely important issue in the realm of philosophy. Although "justice is sometimes used as a synonym for law or lawfulness; it has a broader sense, closer to fairness."[2]

Social justice refers to the concept of a society in which justice is achieved in all respects, rather than merely the administration of law. It is generally thought of as a society which affords individuals and groups fair treatment and a just share of the

1. Humo Tolang, *International Encyclopaedia of the Social Sciences*, (New York: Macmillan and Free Press, 1968), vol. IV, p. 341.
2. Paul Edwards, *Encyclopaedia of Philosophy* (New York and London: Macmillan Company and Free Press, 1967), vol. 4, p. 298.

benefits of society. It can also refer to the distribution of advantages and disadvantages within a society. Plato sees a just society as one that fulfils the needs of the individuals.

Social justice is both a philosophical problem and an important issue in politics, religion, and civil society. Most individuals wish to live in a just society, but different political ideologies have different conceptions of what a "just society" actually is. The term "social justice" is often employed by the political Left to describe a society with a greater degree of economic egalitarianism; social justice is also a concept that is used to describe the movement towards a socially just world.

Social Justice in Islam

Justice has been a very important issue in the history of Muslim intellectual thought and played an important role in the areas of theology, law, and politics. The Arabic word for justice is *adl*. In his dictionary *Lughat al-Qur'an*, Abdul-Rasheed describes its various meanings. The word *adl* has been used to mean balance, equity, proportion, symmetry, compensation, etc.[3] Islam attaches the highest importance to justice. In fact, Divine Justice is the backbone of the whole act of creation. The balance and the due proportion evident in the world are a manifestation of God's Justice. Justice is fundamental to Islam which is absolutely essential to maintain a peaceful and harmonious society, as Islam itself means peace which is indispensable for a society to flourish. There cannot be peace in a society where there is no justice. Therefore, it is necessary to have justice for the establishment of peace.

Islam avoids extremes so as to maintain balance and orderliness in society. Justice to all is Islam's essence as it enables man to lead a good and happy life and at the same time strengthens bonds of human brotherhood and fortifies the social fabric. Whenever the Holy Qur'an speaks of fellow human beings (*An-nās*) and the importance of dealing with them justly and kindly, it

3. *Lughat al-Qur'an,* Numani Abkal Rasheed (Delhi), vol. IV, pp. 247-49.

does not enunciate the principle with reference to Muslims only but to all mankind. Justice in Islam is termed *adl* which means to divide two things equally or to keep the balance. This term is used in the Holy Qur'an for justice in all matters. Islam teaches the believers to be fair in their dealings. The Holy Qur'an says that:

> *And when ye judge between man and man, that ye judge with justice.*[4]

Islam not only ordains the believers to do justice among themselves but also exhorts them to do full justice even in the case of their enemies. The Holy Qur'an says:

> *And let not the hatred of others to you make you swerve to wrong and depart from justice.*[5]

Justice and righteousness are the cornerstones of the Islamic way of life. Socially just acts are moral acts according to Islam which does not stand for any social disparity.

Islam through its concept of justice promotes individual and social welfare. In addition to this, it looks after the development of the individual and society. Social justice can be dispensed with by maintaining a balance between the individual's rights and the social obligations. It can be achieved by allowing the individual to have his share in all the socio-economic spheres not only as a matter of right but also as a responsibility. The term *mizaan* or balance has a special reference to this matter. It is also important to note that Islam does not only correct the individual moral behaviour and attitude but also presents moral norms for the society. Justice in Islam is not merely a normative concept but also a positive one. It has practical implications affecting the social and individual life. It is a virtue as well as a concept having metaphysical bearing.

Justice also means power which is exercised by individuals. It

---

4. *Al-Qur'an*, IV:58.
5. Ibid., V:8.

is a power to judge individual actions as right or wrong. The power is sometimes institutionalized: in the case of a monarch, a dictator, a head of the family or a judge of a court. His decision, as the case may be, is final. He is given the power to judge. It is sometimes delegated, sometimes assumed. In the case of religions including Islam the power of justice rests with the necessary Being, the God. He is the source from where it originates and terminates. Justice in Islam is dispensed with the guiding principles laid down in the Holy Qur'an and the *sharia*. The power of justice is exercised by the individual in a hierarchical manner whereas in religions there is only one authority of justice which is absolute in nature, form, and content.

The world is not without a purpose or a goal; it is throughout teleological and to this universal teleology human beings are no exceptions. To every one of them there is a goal and that goal is God Himself.[6] The real goal of man according to the Holy Qur'an is the assimilation of Divine attributes. These attributes can be summarized as life, eternity, unity, power, truth, beauty, justice, love, and goodness. Justice is a divine attribute and the Holy Qur'an emphasizes that we should adopt it as a moral ideal. God commands people to be just towards one another and in judging between man and man, to judge justly, for He loves those who judge equitably.[7] All believers stand firmly for justice even if it goes against themselves, their parents, their kith and kin, without any distinction of rich and poor. God's Revelation itself is an embodiment of truth and justice; it is revealed with the balance (of right and wrong) so that people may stand forth for justice. The value of justice is absolute and morally binding and the believers are, therefore, warned that they should not let the hatred of some people lead them to transgress the limits of justice or make them depart from the ideal of justice, for justice is very near to piety and righteousness.

---

6. *Al-Qur'an*, LIII:42.
7. Ibid., V:45.

Justice demands that people should be true in word and deed, faithfully observe the contracts which they have made and fulfil all obligations. When Muslims enter into treaties with people of other faiths, they must fulfil their engagements to the end and be true to them, for that is the demand of righteousness. They are also advised to establish the system of weights with justice and not to skimp in the balance and cause thereby a loss to others by fraud, and unjustly withhold from others what is due to them, for that would lead to the spread of mischief in the world.

In ancient times the concept of human inequality, which was prevalent everywhere, gave rise to social injustice in every society. For example, the Greek philosopher, Aristotle, regarded certain classes of individuals as natural slaves. In modern times, this idea has been further strengthened. The white races considered themselves invested with the natural right to subjugate the rest of the world in order to civilize it. The world of today can be broadly divided into two parts — the traditional and the scientific.

Believers in *karma*, the theory that anyone born today necessarily shoulders the burden of his past deeds, influence the traditional world to a large extent. As they see it, it is the law of nature and as such, has to be submitted to unquestioningly. A belief of this nature obviously stifles any possible motivation for social justice. In the light of such a belief "injustice" simply becomes "nature's verdict." The human beings have to suffer in this world for their misdeeds in their previous life cycle. Given this state of affairs, it is just not possible for anyone to alleviate human suffering in which case there can be no motivation to act out of a sense of justice. The theory has been advanced that if people suffer a variety of afflictions it is "their own fault." That is to say that those who are made to feel inferior in the treatment they receive from others are, in fact, suffering the consequences of their own shortcomings. It is as if they were fated to be the victims of injustice and the perpetrators are not, therefore, to be blamed.

The scientific world is likewise under the influence of the concept of human inequality, but for another reason — the general acceptance gained by the theory of evolution. The concept of the biological evolution of life seeks to explain the differences in the existing species, advancing the theory that in the process of evolution some have gone forward while others have been left behind. Modern psychological and biological research on race has clearly upheld the teachings of Islam, so that from the academic point of view, other theories stand refuted. All modern research points to human beings as members of one Great Family, all bound together by the same biological brotherhood.[8]

With the advent of Islam, all ideas based on an inherent inequality lost ground. With great persistence Islam presented to the world the concept that, in spite of outward differences, all human beings are equal. All are entitled to equal social status and equal rights. No one is inferior or superior. Islam's great contribution to social justice is to give equal honour and respect to all human beings, weak or strong, kings or commoners. Here is a reference from the Holy Qur'an supporting the said issue:

> Men, we have created you from a male and a female, and made you into nations and tribes that you might get to know one another. The noblest of you in Allah's sight is the most righteous of you. Allah is wise and all knowing.[9]

According to this verse of the Holy Qur'an, the differences of colour and race found among human beings are for the purpose, not of discrimination, but of identification. Men in essence are equal. What really distinguishes one man from another is character. His superiority can, therefore, be spoken of only in terms of the degree to which a man is pious and honourable. The truly honourable man is one who is God-fearing and who recognizes and fulfils his duties with regard to God and his fellow men.

On the occasion of the final pilgrimage, the Prophet delivered his last sermon. One of the things he said is recorded in these words:

---

8. *Newsweek*, 11 January 1988.

9. Al-Qur'an, 49:13.

> *O people listen carefully, your Lord is one Lord, and there is no doubt about it. Your ancestor is one ancestor, there is no doubt about it. Listen well to my words: no Arab has any superiority over a non-Arab, and no non-Arab is superior to an Arab. No black is superior to a brown or red, and no red superior to any black. If there is any superiority in anyone it is due to his God-fearing qualities. Have I conveyed the message?*

the Prophet asked the people. The people answered from all corners, "Indeed, so God be witness." Then the Prophet said:

> *Let him that is present tell it unto him that is absent.*[10]

The Prophet made this declaration in the final year of his life at a time when the whole of Arabia had been conquered. As such, it was not the declaration of a reformer, but of a ruler of the time. His definition of human equality and justice amongst people was not only listened to as a theory, but was immediately put into practice. In his declaration, the Prophet told the people that there is only one Creator of this world and all the human beings are created by him. All human beings are equal, being each other's brothers and sisters. They might differ in respect of appearance, but as to honour, status and the right to justice, there is no difference between them.

Abu Hamid Muhammad Al-Ghazzali (CE 1058–1111) is generally regarded as the Islamic equivalent of Kant. He was a prolific and influential scholar. The central objective of Ghazzali in all his writings was the unity of knowledge, rooted in the Oneness of God, and reason (i.e. intellect plus free will) as the path for all moral concepts ultimately leading to the belief in God. Ghazzali's ideas of good governance are totally based on Islamic social justice. The concept of *adl* is refreshing and relevant even today, for, as humanity approaches a new trend termed as globalization, and is integrating people and cultures of the world, demands for global equity and good governance are at the top of the international reform agenda. Ghazzali's ideas are especially relevant for a critical

10. *Al-Jamili Ahkam al-Qur'an*, XVI:342.

analysis of a discipline, i.e. socio-economic development based on social justice.

Fundamentally, along with Immanuel Kant and T.H. Green, Muslims are on common ground insofar as they feel that they "are entitled to postulate the moral freedom of man and the existence of God as primary truths on which we can base our existence as spiritual beings."[11] Thus in Islam, balance and justice are central to the design and order underlying God's approval or endorsement in the ultimate Reckoning on the Day of Judgement. It is the consequence of Divine Justice that man has free will because, without free will, man does not merit either reward or punishment for his deeds. For this reason, the great scholars of Islam have called free will as the Principle of Justice. Social justice is an important prerequisite for peace in the world since an unjust social system is a temporarily dormant volcano whose eruption can be expected any moment.

Social Justice in Islam is perhaps the best-known work of Sayyad Qutub, a leading figure in the Muslim Brethren of Egypt. *Social Justice in Islam* confounds many prevalent prejudices about both Sayyad Qutub and Islam. The book explores the political implications of the Muslim practice of *ẓakāt* which is ordinarily viewed as a form of charity, a type of alms for the poor. Qutub argues that *ẓakāt*, properly understood, provides a means for rectifying the imbalances and momentary instabilities of the society and economy while preserving private property and commerce; enables the protection and just distribution of common goods; and provides both principles and practices that secure social welfare without breeding dependency or diminishing human dignity. The most illuminating aspect of the book is the recognition of the importance of human dignity to economic justice and political order. Qutub is of interest not only to Muslims but to anyone interested in political economy.

---

11. A.C. Bradley, *Introduction to T.H. Green's Prolegomena to Ethics*, 5th edn., p. iv.

According to Islam, in conformity with all the other religions, only just actions are considered as moral actions which include socially just actions as well. Taken in its broader sense, justice is action in accordance with the requirements of some law. This sort of justice is often thought of as something higher than a society's legal system. It is in those cases where an action seems to violate some universal rule of conduct that we are likely to call it "unjust." In its narrower sense, justice is fairness. It is action that pays due regard to the proper interests, property, and safety of one's fellows. Parties concerned with fairness typically strive to work out something comfortable and adopt procedures that resemble rules of a game. They work to ensure that people receive their "fair share" of benefits and burdens and adhere to a system of "fair play." Immoral social justice system is not a part of Islamic ethos.

Justice in Islam is not only an ethical value but also included in its faith. Muslims believe in its being one of the attributes of God. Islam enjoins upon man a way of life that promotes goodness and saves society from evil. Muslims are invoked not only to practise virtue but to actively establish it in their immediate environment and to eradicate vice and corruption. The nature of Islamic belief about human life makes social justice essentially an all-embracing justice which does not take into account merely material and economic factors; for Islam does not divide the individual into body and soul, into differing intellectual and spiritual sides. But Islam believes in the unity of body and soul in the individual, and in an identity of aim in the individual and in the society. So, Islam sets the principle of individual responsibility over that of individual freedom; and beside them both it sets the principle of social responsibility, which makes demands alike on the individual and on society. According to Sayyad Qutub, on the following three foundations, Islam establishes social justice: firstly an absolute freedom of conscience, secondly a complete equality of all mankind, and thirdly a permanent mutual responsibility in society.[12]

Thus complete social justice cannot be assured, nor can its efficiency and permanence be guaranteed, unless it arises from an inner conviction of the spirit; it must be claimed by the individual; it must be needed by society; and there must be a belief that it will serve the highest purposes of mankind. Therefore, Islam emphasizes all sides of life and all aspects of freedom. Islam looks at man as forming a unity whose spiritual desires cannot be separated from his bodily appetites, and whose moral needs cannot be divorced from his material and social needs. Islam insists strongly that glory and honour are the rights of man, and insists on the guarantee of an absolute social justice, under which man shall not suffer from neglect. In conclusion, we can say that morality and justice are amongst the most significant aspects of Islam in guiding human life to greater richness and integrity.

---

12. Sayyad Qutub, *Social Justice in Islam*, Eng. tr. John. B. Hardie, p. 68.

CHAPTER 26

Islamic Morality with Special Reference to Justice

An Ethical Justification

Md. Sirajul Islam

THE tradition of morality is very primitive. In spite of its various changes and variegated forms it is still a worthy discipline of the annals of mankind. J.S. Mill, H. Sidgwick and G.E. Moore are the most ardent representatives of Western morality and their moral disciplines are familiar as normative ethics. In the course of time the normative ethics has been distinguished from meta-ethics, which generally discussed the nature of ethical concepts. Indeed, as a result of the emergence of non-cognitive theories of meta-ethics the normative ethical importance becomes in question. Non-cognitive theories of ethics imply that our ultimate ethical principles depend on our ultimate attitudes and preferences, and ultimate ethical principles become fruitless within the fields of personal decision, persuasion, and advice. There are endless controversies related to this debate.

Morality is common to all religions; therefore, its history is very primitive. It is a binding force to all by which man's actions and conducts may be checked and lead him in the right direction. Hence, in broader outlook, morality is a regulating force/principle in the society that helps to judge human action to maintain social integrity and welfare of all beings. Morality can be understood in two ways, i.e. broad and narrow. In broader outlook it consists as the part and parcel of the whole field of human endeavour and striving. It poses enquiry for man's good conduct that plays an organizing role in the whole field to establish value in the society. Here it expects that accounts of virtues, obligations, sanctions, feelings, etc. will be geared in the long run to describe human values and modes of achieving or realizing them. But in the narrow sense it limits the enquiry into the moral phenomenon only and motivates the people to understand the idea of obligation or duty. It only says that *ought to be* or *ought to be realized* comes into the fold of morality.[1] Islamic morality is not akin to this type of morality. In encompassing these above two points Islam goes forward to understand its *divine nature,* as well as *the interests, and needs of the society and human beings* without any discrimination of caste and creed. In Islam, the conduct of human beings is found in their ideals of character and in their concept of virtue and vice. In Islam, all offensive deeds and malicious character are abominable to Allah (God); these are considered as bad actions, and for these a performer will be punished, because, here Allah (God) is for maintaining justice (*adl*), peace (*salām*) and tranquillity of mind. In this present time people are much more inclined towards barbaric deeds that are really a disgrace to human personality. The notable historian Shahristani maintains that basically there were four fundamental problems that drew the interest of the then Muslims. They were: (a) the problem of the freedom of will, (b) the problem of God and His attributes, (c) the problem of the distinction between belief and action, and (d) the dispute between reason and revelation. The controversies were elevated to the maximum during the period of Jabrites and Qadrites, and similarly between Mutazilaites and Ashrites. They elevated Islam and its moral discipline in the logical manner.[2]

Islamic morality is not similar to Marxist morality, which is basically materialistic and dialectical in nature. It demystifies morality and uses it in a much more restricted sense. Marxism

1. May Edel and Abraham Edel, "The Range of Moral Differences", in *The Range of Ethics* (New Delhi: Affiliated East-West Press Pvt. Ltd., 1966), pp. 18-19.
2. A.K. Sliahrislanij, "Kitab al-Milal wan-Nahal", cited in M. Rafique, *Indian and Islamic Philosophy* (New Delhi: Ashish Publishing House), p. 3.

believes that all ethical notions and disciplines have a specific socio-historical origin and they are relative to particular form of life or the society as well. Therefore, it states that the source of morality is to be derived from the society and the life of human being. In Marxist's words it can be defined as "circumstances make men, just as men make circumstances." There are diversified forms of morality in the world and every moral discipline claims to be true and correct. It is worthy to mention that Islamic morality is something different from the pure philosophical morality. Philosophical morality mainly starts with the psychological constitution of man's nature and the obligation laid on him as a social being, but in Islamic morality the basic assumption is faith (*imān*) on God, and here moral prescriptions are given by Him, which is not mere human speculation but Divine command. Islamic morality was set forth in the dark ages of human civilization (*aiyam-e Jaheliyat*) where political upheaval and bloodshed was a usual incident (in the Arabian society). It was laid down to develop the quality of man (*'awsaf*) to elevate him as complete *al-tam* in his dispositions or to lead a virtuous life in eschewing evils in the life. *Al-insan-ul-tam* or *Al-insan-ul-kamil* means a person who is not weak in virtue and, at the same time, fit to completely dissociate himself from performing any vice. This person is to be equivalent to angels (*farištā*) who are entirely free from all evil desires and phenomenal hankerings.[3] Hence, Islamic morality is centred on *Divine norms and wills* by which a man can behave, but at the same time Islam accepts the freedom of man and tells that he is free to choose (*ithar*) and also free to perform his deed according to his own intention (*khayāl*). In Islam, there is a perfect equilibrium between Divine will and human freedom where morality is called *al 'ilm al-akhlāq* [the science of (human) behaviour], where *equality and justice* are interwoven and Islamic morality lays stress on equality and justice because it believes in justice for establishing equality or that for establishing equality justice is essentially

3. S.R. Sharma, *Philosophy and Ethics in Islam* (New Delhi: Omsons Publications, 2001), p. 236.

needed. The Holy Qur'an has prescribed numerous virtuous ideals to maintain a disciplined life or perform good dispositions and deeds *(akhlāq wa husni mu' amalat)* which are generally familiar as *Tahdhi al akhlāq*. These moral prescriptions are not only enunciated for common men but also to the Prophet Hadrat Muhammad (s) himself. The lives of the four pious *Khulafah*/Caliphs (*Khulafah-e Reshedin*) are vivid instances to establish moral discipline in Islam. The appellation *Amir-ul-Mumenin* or *Shaykh-ul-Mumenin* was applied to them in the then Muslim society. Here, society is a nexus of connections among human beings.[4] One basic question may emerge here: "What is man? Is he merely a social animal? Can he be happy if his animal urges and needs are fulfilled?" We can unequivocally reply "No," because, man is a *multidimensional being*. The aim of Islamic society is to establish sane and healthy society that needs pious character, personal responsibility, individual liberty and dignity, social as well as individual justice, fellow-feeling, collective good, etc. According to Islam, pious self is free from egotism, petty egoism, pride and prejudice and at the same time it will be characterized by love and compassion. Thus, Islam is conscious to promote the inner abilities of human being. There are numerous lines in the Holy Qur'an and *Hadith* concerning the development of moral urge of human being. It is almost impossible to indicate all these moral impulses/ordains here in a single article. However, some are noted down to understand Islamic moral outlook as: *al-wudd* (love), *al-'iffa* (continence), *al-tasawwuun* (self-control), *al-waqara* (dignity), *al-rahma* (mercy), *ida'al imana* (trustworthiness), *al-tawadhu* (humility), *al-sidq al lahja* (truth of speech), *al sakha* (generosity), *al sabr* (steadfastness), *al hilm* (tranquillity), *al wafa wafa* (fulfilment of promise), *salamat al niha* (good intention) and many others. The vicious dispositions are generally considered as: al *kidhb* (falsehood), *al khubth* (deceit), *at bukhl* (avarice), *al jawr* (injustice) and so on. Not only the Holy Qur'an but also the *Hadith* (Bukhari) states about morality as

4. Sharma, p. 235.

innamal amala wa binniyat, i.e. your deed will be counted in accordance to your intention, which seems highly moral prescription.[5]

Islam is not merely a religion, it is *din,* which means complete code of life that is mainly based upon rights, duties, freedoms and responsibilities of a matured human being irrespective of whether he/she acts as a member of the society. Since Islam is a complete code of life, generally it codifies laws and principles that touch upon morality. In Islam, these laws and principles are divine commands which are purely unconditional prescriptions to mankind and not for a particular community. In this respect the Holy Qur'an says: *innaka la'ala khuluqun azim,* i.e. "verily thou art of excellent morals."[6] It is a Divine attestation regarding the duties and responsibilities of all human beings and in broader aspect it speaks that you should act in such a way as to will thy law as universal and at the same time treat humanity as your own. In Islam the entire universe is divided into various worlds and all are devoid of morality except one. These worlds are roughly to be classified as *Alam-al-Haq* (the world of Truth), *Alam-i Ruh* (the world of spirit) *Alam-i Malaqut* (the Angelic world), *al Burzakh* (intermediary world), and *Alam-i Khalq* (mundane world). Morality is not applicable to the above worlds except *Alam-i Khalq*. *Alam-i Khalq* is again subdivided into two as animate and inanimate. Inanimate world is completely free from moral duties and responsibilities, but the entire animate world is also not in the fold of morality in Islam. It believes, only few portion of animate world is associated with morality. More particularly we can say that the Islamic moral ideals are mainly based on the human being and only the matured normal human being is in the fold of morality, since he/she is responsible for his/her deeds. In Islam baby, imbecile, moron and immature people are fully outside of its moral range, thus they are not responsible for their deeds.

---

5. Imam Bukhari, *Hadith,* no. 1.
6. *Al-Qur'an,* LXVIII:5.

Islam believes that human being is the combination of *animal* and *spiritual* potentiality, so *good* and *bad* possibilities are inherent in him. It does not renounce the psychological, emotional, physical and social nature of man and that are in the state of flux as well. There are many evidences of changes in his/her life and community living. Modern man has changed nature, he has transformed atoms into the source of violent energy, he explored the techniques to float in the water, he transformed barren desert into fertile land; however, he has almost failed to change human nature. Do we believe that we cannot change human nature at all? What Islam thinks on this point? It is generally believed that Islam is dead against any change, but it is not true. The Holy Qur'an clearly states that "Verily never will Allah change the condition of a people until they change what is in themselves" (13:11).[7] So, the authentic change is permissible in Islam but that must be wholesome for humanity at large. The act that man can change from the state of the carnal self (*al nafs al ammarah*) to the state of the self at peace (*al-naf-al-mutma 'innah*) through a good deal of conscious struggle (*jihad*) and deliberate effort necessarily suggests that man is free in performance of his deeds that presupposes the freedom of his choice (*ikhtiycir-al-azad*).[8] It is obvious that the society is not static, rather it is in the process of continuous change. Similarly, moral principles are in, a state of change and the traditional morality becomes obsolete in the new millennium. Legitimately the fates of Islamic moral prescriptions are in doubt. History attests that moral disciplines and principles are imposed upon the society to regulate human conduct and moral character. Islam claims that its moral prescriptions are not phenomenal in outlook rather Divine in nature, as we have stated earlier.

As we have already maintained that in Islamic morality the *faith* itself is the first and foremost of all duties. Most of the moral prescriptions are considered as of higher category than mere doctrines; and they are efficacious even today. All Muslims are

---

7. *Al-Qur'an*, XIII:2.

8. *Al-Qur'an*, XV: 29; XII: 53; lXXXIX: 27.

more or less aware concerning Islamic moral prescriptions and they are seeing it as the part of a good religious upbringing. Islamic *Shariah* (the canon of law) clearly states that the real goal of man is to attain Divine attributes, as the Qur'an says, *takhallaqu bekuluqillah,* i.e. you should dye yourself in the attributes of Allah. Its basic attributes are *life, eternity, unity, power, truth, beauty, justice, love* and *goodness.* Hence, Islamic moral prescriptions are eternal attributes of Allah that are eternally inhering to Him. The notable theologian al-Ghazzali has laid emphasis on maintaining moral life and said morality can help the people as a medicine for the sick.[9]

Moral acts are roughly classified in Islam as follows:[10]

1. *Amal-e Farz* — Compulsory acts, the practice of which is an absolute duty and therefore rewarded and the omission of which is punished severely.
2. *Amal-e Wajib-* — Semi-compulsory acts, the practice of which is an absolute duty and therefore rewarded and the omission of which is punished. This action is almost similar to the first one but a little softer than *farz* action.
3. *Amal-e Sunnah* — Tradition-based acts, which are recommended by the law, and are the subject of reward, but the neglect of which does not call for strict punishment.
4. *Amal-e Muba* — Beneficial acts, which are permitted by the *Shariah,* but in the eyes of the Islamic law it is almost a matter of indifference.
5. *Amal-e Maqruh* — Near to forbidden acts but softer than *haram* (non-permissible actions).
6. *Amal-e-Nafl* — Optional acts, performance of which are rewardable but violation of that cannot be treated as punishable.

---

9. S.R. Sharma, op. cit., p. 27.
10. Ibid., p. 28.

7. *Amal-e Khilaf* — Acts which are disapproved by the canon of law but are not held as strictly punishable.

8. *Amal-e Haram* — Non-permissible acts which are forbidden by the law and which demand unconditional punishment.

In developing Islamic morality as a separate philosophical discipline the role of *ulemas* and philosophers are very important. Before their emergence, Prophet's life, deeds and his various moods were simply accepted by the believers as moral discipline. They stressed upon it on the ground that Prophet Hazrat Muhammad himself was a vivid instance of moral discipline; he devoted his entire life in practising morality of the Holy Qur'an. Muslim scholars were vehemently inspired by the Greek morality to appear as a separate discipline; however, they established their morality as an independent discipline. Al-Ghazzali, a notable Islamic theologian invariably quoted from the Holy Qur'an and the traditions (*hadith*) in support of his moral views. He laid stress upon the spiritual values rather than the phenomenal values of human action, such as *shukr* (gratitude), *taubah* (repentance), *tawakkul* (reliance), etc. He apprehends that *al-insan-al-kamil* means a man who followed strictly all moral laws and ordains of *Shariah*. Thus, asceticism is the spirit that pervades throughout his morality which was not common to Greek morality. Hence, Islamic morality is basically a prefect representation the moral ideals which Prophet Muhammad followed himself. Islam does not tell about heroic virtue, like *courage*, etc. It tells about *simplicity in life* which is very rare in the present world.

Islam counteracts to the tendencies of vices, like luxury, pride, envy and indulged people to act in the just way. Islam says *ku anfusekum wa ahlekum nara,* i.e. live and let the others live. It emphasizes on the duties and responsibilities of a person to other individuals and the society as a whole.[11] It touched upon the *self-*

11. M.M. Sharif, *A History of Muslim Philosophy* (Wiesbaden: Otto Harrasowitz, 1963), vol. I, p. 625.

respect and *the dignity of man* that presuppose a social set-up. In Islam, life of human being is worthy and superior to the life of other animate beings of the world. The Holy Qur'an says "people are to partake of the good things of the world,"[12] "wear modestly, eat and drink as per Islamic law without going to excess."[13] "Man is advised not to forget his real position in the world."[14] "Wealth and property are good things to be enjoyed and appreciated and are the blessings of God,"[15] "which make life smooth and comfortable."[16] "The present world is a place of sojourn and a place of departure."[17] "Its enjoyments are short[18] and comforts are few."[19] "The good acts that we will perform in this world will run before us to illumine our path in the next world, it will help you to obtain greater perfection."[20] "Indeed we sent our Messengers with clear evidence and we revealed to them the scriptures and the standard to show what was right and what was wrong, so the people might conduct themselves with fairness."[21] "You will indeed be questioned about what you used to do."[22] "Worship Allah, and do good so that you may prosper."[23] "They call to virtue, effort to what is good and restrain from evil. It is such people who shall prosper."[24] "This is paradise which you have

---

12. *Al-Qur'an*, VII:32.
13. Ibid., VII:31.
14. Ibid., XXVII:77.
15. Ibid., XVII:6.
16. Ibid., LXXXIV:14.
17. Ibid., VI:98.
18. Ibid., IV:77.
19. Ibid., IX:38.
20. Ibid., LXVII:2;VII:12; LXIV:8.
21. Ibid., LVII:25.
22. Ibid., XVI:93.
23. Ibid., XXII:77.
24. Ibid., CXI:104.

inherited by your righteous deeds."[25] "As for who reports, believes and does what is right, it is hoped that he will prosper."[26] "Allah will tell them of what they did. He has kept an account of it while they have forgotten."[27] "On that day everyone will find himself confronted with whatever good and evil he has done."[28] "They have the reward of their deeds."[29] "Every soul shall bear the good and the evil for which it has laboured."[30] "They are the blessed who longing for it themselves bestowed their food on the poor and the orphan and the captive."[31] "Be of those who enjoin steadfastness and compassion on others."[32]

In Islam, moral order works without any favour of *individual;* rather it lays emphasis upon the *collective benefit* of the society.[33] God has entered into covenant with men within the limit of this moral order — with man as such and not with particular nations or races.[34] Some of its collective benefits are narrated here in a nutshell.

UNITY

Islam gives the greatest emphasis on unity. It is a unity of God as well as the unity of internal and external life. In Islam, it is an essential prerequisite of moral life but it should not be mere verbal utterance, it must be accompanied by good deeds and good minds. The Holy Qur'an in this context says: "those who patiently persevere in the path of righteousness will be in possession of a

25. *Al-Qur'an*, XXXIII:72.
26. Ibid., XXVII:67.
27. Ibid., LVII:6.
28. Ibid., III:30.
29. Ibid., II:228.
30. Ibid., XCII:18-20.
31. Ibid., LXXXI:8, 90.
32. Ibid., XC:12.
33. Ibid., V:20.
34. Ibid., III:81, 187; V:8, 13.

determining factor in all the affairs in the life."[35] Externally, the ideal of unity demands that man should develop a healthy society which traverses the middle path of rectitude avoiding all forms of extreme. Islam advised the righteous to live together and strive for it, so that tumult, oppression and mischief are removed from the society, it will help to entail peace and harmony in the society as well.

TRUTH AND KNOWLEDGE

Truth is one of the important moral ideals in Islam. For truth people will have to develop knowledge and the adequate knowledge will help the people to distinguish between right and wrong. Islam believes that both right and wrong are never equal and true in the same time, they are antagonistic to each other. The Holy Qur'an advises to pray to the Prophet Hazrat Muhammad for the advancement of knowledge (*Rabby zidny 'ilman*).[36] "It will help to distinguish right from wrong. It is through knowledge and reflection on the phenomena of nature, the heaven and the earth that Abraham and Joseph were able to arrive at the ultimate Truth."[37]

FREEDOM

The problem of the freedom of will has been discussed in Islam in very systematic order. According to Islam, man can-not create anything. God is the only creator (*khaliq*), man only possesses the power (*qudrah*) and choice (*ikhtiyar*). Hence, the action of man and all creatures are created by God like the *pre-established harmony* of Leibnitz. Man or creature can only acquire (*kasb*) it. It, thus, gives man the power of consciousness about freedom and not absolute freedom in the real sense. God, in Islam, is an unmoved mover of the material world and only the efficient cause of all creation. Whatever happens in the world happens according to the necessary

35. *Al-Qur'an*, III:186.
36. Ibid., XX:114.
37. Ibid., VI:75,79; XII:37, 39.

system and a pre-determined plan. There is nothing accidental in the world. However, man is responsible for his actions because God bestowed freedom of choice (*ikhtiyar*) and conviction (*I'tqad*) to him for performance of activities with strong impulse (*raghbah*). That is why Islamic morality (*taufiq*)[38] can be identified in various ways as under[39] —

1. *Hidayah* (guidance from God) which is the very condition of all virtues. It stands for the telling of the moral from the immoral, the good from the bad and the right from the wrong. It helps to identify good and evil.

2. *Rushd* (direction): Mere knowledge of good actions might be necessary but is not sufficient for their performance. It needs strong will to direct.

3. *Tasdiq* (setting aright): It is the power from God which makes the body to obey, the will to apprehend the end.

4. *Ta'id* (confirmation): It makes circumstances congenial for the actualization of the will.

VALUE

To lead pious life is an inevitable act in Islam and is considered as an unavoidable value of morality. Pious life in Islam signifies the purified self that is free from evil deeds. In this regard the Holy Qur'an says: "he will indeed be successful who purifies soul and he will fail who corrupts it."[40] The moral agent who is sincerely set upon his acts must also form the habit of meditation and reflection that beautify man and the world as well. Generally the notion of beauty is universally recognized as an *intrinsic value.* Whatever is beautiful is loveable by the human being due to *its intrinsic value* and that value is *end in itself,* thus beautiful and loveable are interwoven here.

---

38. Sharif, pp. 226-27.

39. Ibid., 628.

40. *Al-Qur'an*, XC:9-10.

LOVE

Islam demands discharging loving attitude towards all. Here love is a moral ideal, so the Holy Qur'an tells us, it is one of the major characteristics of Islamic morality that the believers should be compassionate and loving to one another.[41] They should walk on the earth in humility and hold to forgiveness;[42] they are friendly to one another.[43] At present, the loving attitude and behaviour are in the diminishing order. Its crisis is evident everywhere, but Islam preseribes it as an essential duty of human beings.

GOODNESS

In the eyes of Islam, goodness is an important attribute of Allah (God). Therefore, it is a necessary duty of all human beings to discharge well and good towards all and love those who perform well.[44] So, people should strive together and do all that is good,[45] it is the foremost duty of all human beings.[46] In establishing good he must eschew evil. In the eyes of Islam, good and evil are never treated as same, rather they are antagonistic to each other just as light and darkness.

BEAUTY

God created everything as his excellence of beauty and he is an embodiment of beauty (*husn*). Man is created in the best of moulds and is given a most beautiful shape,[47] that is why he is different from other species in the universe. Those who will perform beautiful deeds shall have the highest reward in this world and the life hereafter.[48]

---

41. *Al-Qur'an*, XLVII:29.
42. Ibid., VII: 199.
43. Ibid., II: 109; XLII:37.
44. Ibid., XXVII: LXXVII; II; 114, 195; XXI:90. Also see Syed Amir Ali, *The Spirit of Islam* (London: Christopher's , 1961), pp. 15, 1-157.
45. *Al-Qur'an*, II:41.
46. Ibid., XXXV:32.
47. Ibid., IXIV:3; XCV:4.
48. Ibid., III:172.48.

JUSTICE

In Islam the concept of justice has very specific importance. As far as justice is concerned Islam is the first religion which recognized the necessity of justice as an inevitable part of religion. The development of balanced society is highly necessary to protect humanity. If all-round justice is established in the society then the various conditions will be favourable for its growth and development. On the other hand, any kind of injustice will generate disturbance, retrogression and decay of the society. Hence, it is one of the important features of Islamic morality to establish justice in all levels of the society. In this context the Holy Qur'an stresses upon it as:

1. "Use indulgence and command what is just and turn away from the ignorant."[49]

2. "O ye who believe, stand out firmly for justice, as witness to Allah, even as against yourselves or your parents or your kin or whether it will go against rich, or poor."[50]

3. ". . . men may steadfast injustice."[51]

4. "Judge rightly between the people and do not follow your own caprices, which will deviate you from the path of Allah."[52]

5. "The patient and the truthful, the lowly and charitable, they seek pardon at each daybreak."[53]

6. "Be good to parents and to kindred and to orphans and to the poor and to the neighbour whether kinsman or newcomer and to a fellow traveller and to the way-farer

---

49. *Al-Qur'an*, VII:198.
50. Ibid., IV:58, 65, 105,135.
51. Ibid., VII:29; XVI: 90.
52. Ibid., XXXVIII:25&26
53. Ibid., III:16.

> and to the slaves whom your light hands hold; verily god loveth not the proud, the vain boaster."[54]

In Islam, justice (*adl*) is Allah's attribute, Muslims accept it in a broader outlook, and it is more penetrative than the subtler justice in speculations of the Greek philosophers. It searches out the innermost motives of all actions in strengthening God's omniscient attitude. In establishing justice, Islam encourages man for maintaining *moral duties and responsibilities* that are most essential to moral justifications. We have already stated that not only the Holy Qur'an but also the *Hadith* (Bukhari) states about morality as *innamal amala wa binniyat,* i.e. your deed will be counted in accordance with your intention, which seems a highly moral prescription.

EQUALITY AND JUSTICE

In maintaining a balanced society, Islamic morality envisages upon equality, which it asserts a necessary pre-condition of just society. It declares that all human beings are the descendants of one Adam (*kullukum ibn Adama*) and all men are basically equal, similarly it negates any special position to anybody. All men possess a common nature and in this regard they have no basic difference between one another. The difference in rights on the basis of race, class, and tribe which existed among the various groups of the society of those days is denied completely by Islam. So, it states that "All men are equal like the teeth of the same comb."

Before the advent of Islam there was no legal and moral system in the Arabian society. They only thought that a human being as a living entity has certain physiological and biological characteristics culminating in a developed nervous system and brain. Islam has given them legal and moral rights and says humanity can never be counted on the basis of the colour of skin, power of muscle, shape of limbs, height, race and beauty of the face. It recognized the self-conscious ability of a human being

---

54. *Al-Qur'an*, IV:36.

that integrated him without providing any special privilege and position in the legal rights of the society.

ISLAMIC JUSTICE

Islamic justice may be classified as follows:

Economic Justice

In a particular society, economy has a pivotal role, but its arbitrary use entails chaos in the society among the different groups/people. Hence, economic justice is obviously essential. The economic justice means the equal distribution of the wealth without its accumulation in the hands of particular group/people. To forbid the accumulation of economic wealth in the hands of a few people it emphasizes on the banning of interest-based loans and prohibits bequest to the detriment of the near relatives.[55] Islam believes the difference between the rich and poor is normal, and accepts that all men can never be rich or poor at the same time. Thus we can only minimize difference so that a balanced society may evolve. It reminds the rich men concerning their moral responsibility to take care of the poor Muslim people. In this regard *ẓakāt* system is prevalent in Islam, which is nothing but a compulsory charity of the rich people (*sahib-e-nisab*) to the poor. The believers of Islam are expected to distribute a certain portion (2.5 per cent) of their income to the poor and needy. It is not an alms giving but a right (*haq*) of the poor Muslim and destitute people so that economic justice may prevail in the society.

Political justice

Islam says that politics has an important role in the society. To maintain political justice, Islam utilized the democratic form of government in order to stop the formation of hereditary rule. Islam banned monarchy and autocratic whims from the society.

---

55. Muhammad Ilamidullah, *Introduction to Islam* (New Delhi: Kitab Bhavan, 1992), p. 5.

Islamic justice prevails in its religious duties and requisites where the Muslims of all corners may take equal share in disparaging all differences of castes, colours and groups. Poor and rich, king and beggar, black and white people may take part in their religious duties equally without any discrimination. Its five pillars and religious holy book are equally open for all. Here piety is the moral criterion of the greatness of the individual.

Social Justice

Islamic social justice is well recognized by all. In its eyes all human beings are related to one another in brotherly relationship because they are the part of one another. It instigates the Muslims to enjoy equal share in the well-being of all. Though Muslims are belonging to a separate community, however, its ideals are not for them only, rather they are applicable to all mankind for their uplift and progress.

Today, man and society are passing through a very crucial stage. We can purchase embryos, human sperm from the market. Surrogate mother and cloning organism are becoming popular day by day. Generally the necessities of Islamic moral ideals are in question. People are raising their fingers against the traditional moral ideals of Islam. Besides one question which emerges naturally is, "What are the bonds which may unite people of different nationalities and races together?" I think it is morality; the true practice of moral ideals can only do this. It is quite vivid to us that, in spite of our claims, we will have to develop moral sense. Even in this twentyfirst century we have witnessed various barbaric attacks, blood shedding and brutalities that are undoubtedly a disgrace to our present civilization. The faster progress of scientific and technological devices and super-industrialization are shifting people from sacrificial notion towards selfish endeavours and this alienation is putting adverse effect on morality. Islam cannot remain aloof from these effects. Good neighbouring and good citizenship are becoming almost fancy. As a result, society is moving towards the state of moral degradation and we perceive the decline in respect to the senior, noble personalities, etc.[56] Hence the success of Islamic morality is to be considered as an eternal principle in preserving all these sides. Thus the success of Islamic morality lies behind all these. I think it is still necessary and similarly efficacious after its innumerable changes, because, it is not for Muslims alone but for all human beings. It is our duty to practise its moral teachings dispassionately to lead a peaceful life in this world and the life hereafter.

56. Basir A. Dar, *Qur'anic Ethics* (Delhi: Adam Publishers and Distributors, 2000), pp. 28-31.

CHAPTER 27

Morality in Islam
An Appraisal

Md. Imteyazul Haque Khan

ISLAM lays great stress on cultivating good manners, ethical values and performance of pious deeds. After declaration of faith that there is no God but Allah and Muhammad is the messenger of Allah, Islam attaches far greater importance to righteous acts. Righteous acts have been described in the Holy Qur'an at several places. Prophet Mohammad taught and practised good manners and ethical values throughout his life, because he considered that only the good manners and morality would set-up an atmosphere of peace and amity throughout the world. He himself said "I have been sent down by God to teach moral virtues and to evolve them to highest perfection."[1]

Before discussing the issue of morality in Islam, it would be pertinent to first know and understand the meaning of "morality" itself. As per *Advanced Learner's Dictionary*, "morality" means "Standard principles of good behaviour, teaching good behaviour or the chief characters being personification of virtues and vices." As its meaning indicates, morality is basically possession of all good behaviour and virtues.

Similarly, we must know the meaning of "Islam" also. "Islam" is an Arabic word which connotes submission, surrender and obedience. Its another literal meaning is "peace" and it signifies that one can attain real peace of body as well as mind only through submission and obedience to Allah. So, Islam is not only a religion, but a complete code of conduct. Prophet Muhammad himself was

1. Muatta Imam Malik, *Hadith*, p. 8.

the embodiment of the Qur'anic teachings. The message of the Holy Qur'an can easily be understood by all the actions and deeds of Prophet Muhammad, who lived his whole life as wished by Allah, practising all the essentials of perfect morality. As a matter of fact the message of the Holy Qur'an is the morality of the Prophet, which is relevant for every period and time even in the twenty-first century.

"Moral" means principles of right and wrong and "morality" implies "a particular system of moral principles." The Holy Qur'an at several places stresses on good moral character and virtues and ask the people to follow the path of morality. The Holy Qur'an says:

> O mankind! We have created you from a single pair of male and female, constituted into diverse peoples and nations that you know and co-operate with one another. The best among you in the sight of God is the most pious, the most virtuous.[2]

So, what Prophet Muhammad practised is the prophetic morality denoting a particular system of prophetic moral principles, which is absolutely based on the Holy Qur'an. It is divine and religion-based. It is not the result of experience, observation and research. It is purely God-gifted and God-oriented, which prepares man for leading a God-centred life. It completely harmonizes with human nature. The creator of man and the giver of morality is God.

Before going in detail about the issue of morality in Islam, we must have some knowledge of the world and especially that of Arabia where Prophet Muhammad was born in Mecca in 570. Arabia is a peninsula connected with both Africa and Asia but geographically somewhat isolated. Much of its territory is high rocky and barren with only a few fertile regions dotted here and there. Before the advent of Islam people of Arabia were tribal in nature and loved warfare. Inter-tribal rivalries led to bloody wars for centuries and from generation to generation. They plundered

2. *Al-Qur'an* Surah-al-Hujrat 49:13.

the borders, robbed caravans and indulged in all the evils. Womenfolk were highly neglected and they even preferred to bury a female child after her birth. Thus, they were all groping in the pool of darkness.

Prophet Muhammad came with a light to end the darkness. He taught them the lessons of love and affection. He preached that God is one and is creator of the universe. He taught the people to honour their fellowmen, their parents, the poor, and orphans, to be honest and to be temperate and just to everyone. Prophet Muhammad possessed, practised and demonstrated all the good virtues of good behaviour — tolerance, forbearance, endurance, patience, large-heartedness, magnanimity and generosity. Hundreds of examples are there in the biography of the Holy Prophet to prove his utmost degree of sympathy for people in general, his kindness to everyone, his mercy for the whole world, and for love, affection, forgiveness and peace all around.

All the above elements are reflected in his teachings, treatments and behaviour with his companions and the people in general. These elements were never confined to the Muslims alone, but all mankind as well. In fact, the Holy Prophet guided the people to bring them from darkness of ignorance to the light of knowledge. In the light of the Holy Qur'an and the *Sunnah*, morality is the perfect religion and also the perfect world. Islam believes that if any nation loses its honour in the eyes of Allah or commands no respect among the people, it so happens because of its losing good moral character and honourable traits. Islam strictly directs its followers to behave with their parents with utmost respect and affection, behave properly with their relatives, poor, orphans, neighbours, and even with unknown persons and their slaves.[3]

Prophet Muhammad said "He is no true Muslim who eateth his fill and leaveth his neighbours hungry."[4] Islamic morality

---

3. *Al-Qur'an*, Al Nisa 4:35.

4. Jamuaul Fawaid, *Hadith*, no. 8283; Tabrani, vol. I, *Hadith*, no. 751.

strictly adheres to the principle of excellent treatment to one's neighbours. Prophet said "Nobody can be a Muslim unless his heart and tongue have also submitted and he cannot be a believer unless his neighbour is not secured from his misdemeanour."[5] Once a companion asked the Prophet "What is meant by misdemeanour?" Prophet replied "Excess and oppression."[6]

Man's life is engulfed in good and evil, and he is often driven to one of them by inner motivatives or outside factors. Islam protects a man against the temptation of evil by revealing its harm, warning against it and calling on its victims to run to righteousness as God has instructed mankind. This is because righteousness leads to moral promotions and brings well-being and peace (*kamil*) to people. If a man is not armed with righteousness, his embarkment upon good becomes weaker and he gets easily exposed to involvement in vice. Islam gives special care to righteousness, offering God's promises of good reward in both the present world and in the world hereafter.

Morality in Islam acquires the topmost importance. Only a man of good moral character can be a good Muslim. It is also no secret for anyone that good moral character does not develop suddenly. It takes time. Moral values do not become firm or strong in the beginning. It requires consistency and is acquired gradually. One may have to cross many stages for strengthening of the virtues of good moral character. In the process, Islam lays stress on some factors, viz. peace, co-operation, building of a good character, company of good people, shedding of arrogance and some prohibitions.

Making peace among people is one of the basic aims of Islam. In Islam, real good means that a man should seek to make peace amongst the people in general and love for all. Similarly, Islam

---

5. Sahih-Al-Muslim, *Hadith*, pp. 50, 137; Sahih Al-Bukhari, *Hadith*, pp. 349-50.
6. Sahih-Al-Muslim, *Hadith*, pp. 50, 137; Sahih Al-Bukhari, *Hadith*, pp. 349-50; Jama Tirmidhi, *Hadith*, p. 220.

instructs its believers to develop a feeling of co-operation for welfare of the community. But Islam calls for co-operation only when co-operation means the happiness of all, so that when people turn to it they may attain the prosperity and peace they yearn for. At the same time it warns the people against co-operation in forbidden deeds that leads to the corruption of individual and society as well.

Similarly, Islam advocates building a good character, and, in the process, lays great stress on forbearance, forgiveness, honesty, trust, keeping promises, altruism, kind speech and to stay in the company of good people. The company of good people brings grace to one's moral. At the same time, the company of wicked ones leads to degraded moral character and encourages a person to commit evil. Indeed, a good friend is a precious favour one might enjoy having in his life. A good friend provides all help in time of distress. He may become an honest guide to happiness and success.

Islam is strictly against arrogance because it is a social vice that sows the seeds of separation and hostility among individuals. Arrogance also puts an end to co-operation and amity among the people. It forbids a person from showing love and affection to others. An arrogant person blinds himself to his personal faults and defects, and gives himself more esteem than he deserves. Those who take pride in themselves refuse to listen to others' advice. Such people cannot benefit from the knowledge of experienced men or from the goodness of good people, and thus they fall into ignorance and delusion, and for them more promotion becomes almost impossible.

Prohibited deeds include the use of wine and gambling. Wine and similar alcoholic beverages lead to countless harmful consequences. They stimulate the drinker to abandon the established morality and commit all ugly and wicked deeds. Many acts of discord and disturbances of peace as well as the crimes owe to the consumption of alcohol and to the gambling places. Similarly, lying is regarded the origin of all vices. Likewise disloyalty, braking of promises, false accusations, adultery, anger, etc. are the great vices and a true Muslim keeps himself far away from all these vices.

Islam clearly believes that morality cannot be generated in a person by dint of coercion or force. Islam truly believes that no faith can be developed in any person by means of force or by adopting methods of terrorism. It believes that only personal and intellectual freedom is the sole basis of responsibility and accountability. Islam understands this reality and respects it. It builds-up its edifice on the foundation of the excellent moral character.

Morals of Islam act on human nature similar to that of fire which purifies iron and melts it so that it can be moulded into an effective instrument. The credit of it must go to Prophet Muhammad who came on earth to guide people from darkness into light and lead them to path of salvation, progress and prosperity. Islam believes that all human beings regardless of caste, creed, colour, language, culture and origin form one community.

Islam is not a mere creed. It is a life to be lived in the present. It is a religion of right doing, right thinking and right speaking founded on divine love, universal charity and equality of man in the sight of the Lord and enshrines righteousness and justification by work. Islam teaches sobriety, temperance, charity, justice and equality as the commandments of God. It declares that individual perfection is possible in our earthly existence and believes that man's original nature is essentially good.

However, morality for the sake of morality is not the real type of morality. In Islam real morality is the prophetic morality. The Holy Prophet, in fact, pursued the morality based on religion (Islam). It keeps expectation only from God and not from man. As a result, the frustration in case of not getting the reward of good deeds cannot make man its victim, because the return is confirmed from God Almighty. The follower of prophetic morality never loses his heart.

The morality in Islam adopts a holistic approach to life. It declares that everything is related with each other. The moral aspect; of life affect the social aspect; social aspect influences economic aspect; economic aspect; changes psychological aspects of life; so on and so forth. Man is treated as a single unit and every part of man's life is interrelated and intermingled.

The morality in Islam is truly universal morality. It conveys the concept of universal brotherhood on the basis of blood. Adam was the father of all mankind. So, no difference is found on the basis of colour, caste or creed. The only difference between the different people is *taqwa* (piety). A pious person is more superior to a non-pious in the eyes of God. No other criterion is considered valuable by God.[7]

The claim of tongue is worthless without the deed. If there is a contradiction between sayings and deed, it is called hypocrisy. The Holy Prophet's teachings point out that *imān* is the combination of acceptance by the heart and action by the body. Prophet Muhammad taught that morality in Islam is a single-track morality. What others do is not the behaviour moulder of a man. A person should do good if others do good to him, but he should not do injustice if others don't do justice to him.[8] To repel the evil with good is the formula of Islamic morality.

When a person follows the system, mentioned above, the self-corrective mechanism starts automatically, because it wants to bring reform in man from inner self to outer self. The mental canvas of the man enlarges as a result of the large-heartedness; and broad-mindedness appears in the behaviour of the followers.

The morality in Islam not only discusses the rights and duties of a person but also highlights the fundamental prohibitions. A clear concept of permissible and prohibitted acts is given in it. The prohibited list is not very large. It is very easy to escape from

---

7. *Al-Qur'an*, Surah Al Hujrat: 49:13.
8. Jamaul Fawaid, *Hadith*, no. 9692.

it. Obedience can be conditional or unconditional. The unconditional obedience is the only and exclusive right of God. All other types of obedience must be conditional. There is no obedience to evil. Only good act will be obeyed.

In Islam there is no difference between worldly and religious life. Even if you are drinking a glass of water, as suggested by the Holy Prophet, it is religious. So we can say that proper utilization of worldly life is *deen* (religion). The prophetic morality favours material prosperity in comparison with materialism. Moreover, spiritual life is also a part of social life. Full socialization develops spirituality in man, but the condition is, it must be God-oriented.

The morality in Islam fulfils all necessities and trains man to control his desires. The control over the body parts is stressed in this system. The body is considered a precious gift of God and the life is an examination. With the help of the body and its faculties man has to clear this worldly test and trial. The anti body attitude of man corrupts all the aims. That is why suicide is absolutely prohibited.

Material prosperity is desirable, though not a goal in itself. The goal of all our practical activities always ought to be the creation and the maintenance of such personal and social conditions as might be helpful for the development of moral stamina in men. In accordance with this principle, Islam leads towards a consciousness of moral responsibility in everything he does, howsoever great or small.

Islam does not admit the existence of a conflict between the moral and the socio-economic requirements of our existence. In everything there can be only one choice: the choice between right and wrong, and nothing in between. Hence, the intense insistence on action is an indispensable element of morality.

According to this morality, the combination of moral power and material power brings justice in the society. However, the balance of the world is disturbed today. One who has moral power does not own material power and whoever has material power does not have moral power. So some are weak and honest, and others are strong and corrupt.

Morality in Islam adopts a universal approach. Each good thing (wisdom) is everyone's property. Only the Holy Prophet is the recommended model of God, all others are teachers. Man can learn good things from everyone. The morality that the Holy Prophet taught us is the solution of all contemporary problems. Today we have sunk into deep sins, vices, crimes, corruption, and anti-social activities. Humanity has reached its lowest ebb. Materialism has overshadowed the finer aspects of life. Lessons of morality from the life of Prophet Muhammad can provide us a brighter path. Prophet Muhammad had said, "A man with bad manners and a bad moral conduct shall not enter paradise. No sin is more detestable to God than bad manner."[9] He also said, "The best of you are those who possess the best of manners."[10]

As regards Prophet Muhammad, his advent was to disseminate good manners and ethical values in order to set up an atmosphere of peace and amity throughout the world. As he himself said, "I have been sent down by God to teach moral virtues and to evolve them to highest perfection."[11] As a matter of fact four of the five articles of faith of Islam — observe prayer, fast, *ẓakāt* and *hajj* — lay great emphasis on cultivating ethical values and sublime norms. While exhorting Muslims to observe prayer it has been said that "It forbids indecency and repugnant things."[12] Similarly, fast teach us piety and self-control. In a simiar tone, *ẓakāt* inculcates in us the sentiments of sympathy, co-operation with our brothers who are in need and difficulty. *Hajj* is also a means of co-operation and help in building up our character by enforcing discipline in us. Actually, the main aim behind these fundamental articles is to reform the morals in the believers and foster the sentiments of

---

9. Sahih Al-Bukhari, *Hadith*, no. 6056; Sahih-Al-Muslim, *Hadith*, p.105.
10. Abu-Daud, *Hadith*, no. 2612; Sahih Al-Bukhari, *Hadith*, pp. 353, 355.
11. Muatta Imam Malik, *Hadith*, p. 8.
12. *Al-Qur'an*, Surah-Al-Ankabut 29:45.

mutual love and co-operation and sense of realization for each other's help in need.[13]

Islam respects the human nature and considers its teachings as the voice of the nature.[14] It warns the rebellious natures and reforms their point-of-view. It turns the wind of desire to the right direction and tries to build excellent moral character and the tendency to exemplary treatment of others.[15]

Islam fights against moral crimes. At first it imagines that every man wants to lead a decent life and wants to live by the sweat of his brow and enjoy luxuries on what he earns from his own labours, that is he does not depend on thefts and looting. Then why do they do so? To meet the necessities of life. That is why Islam says that the necessities and the means should be in abundant quantities. This is the responsibility of the society. If the society is deficient and compels the individual to steal, then the responsibility of the crime falls on the deficient society and not on the head of the individual. But if society provides all that and even then an individual commits crime, he should be punished. But Islam desires delay in inflicting punishment. Prophet said, "It is better if the Imam pardons somebody by error than he penalizes him by error."[16]

Islam also says that progress and survival of the nations, the nourishment and development of their civilization and culture, and the consolidation of their power and strength depend on morality. If the people have excellent moral character, then all the qualities will be found in them, but if their moral character is at a lower level, then kingdom and rule will soon end.

It is a justified fact that nations live till their morality lives. When their moral character declines, they also decline. In this

13. S. Sulaiman Nadvi, *Siratun Nabi*, vol. V, p. 185.
14. Sahih Al-Bukhari, *Hadith*, no. 1933.
15. *Al-Qur'an*, Al-Ma'arij 19:29.
16. Jamuaul Fawaid, *Hadith*, no. 5183; Al Tirmidhi, *Hadith*, no. 1438.

backdrop, the Holy Qur'an and the *Sunnah* have emphasized, quite rightly, that morality is the perfect religion and also the perfect world. Hence, it is imperative that we must amend our loose morality and lifestyle and shun such acts that tend to create divergences amongst people. Every individual Muslim has to regard himself as personally responsible for all happenings around him and to strive for the establishment of right and the abolition of wrong at every time and in every direction.

> You are the best community that has been sent forth to mankind. You enjoin the right and forbid the wrong, and you have faith in God.[17]

This is the moral justification of the healthy activism of Islam, a justification of the early Islamic conquests. It has meant, and it means even today, the construction of a worldly frame for the best possible spiritual development of man. For, according to the teachings of Islam moral knowledge automatically forces moral responsibility upon man. A mere platonic discernment between right and the wrong, without the urge to promote right and to destroy wrong, is a gross immorality in itself. In Islam morality lives and dies with the human endeavour to establish its victory upon earth.

We must keep in mind that *imān* is the integral part of Islam, but it can be perfected only with the best conduct. Islam believes that those who have achieved moral excellence are the most perfect believers. Thus to be a true Islamic (wo)man it is very important to adopt the path of perfect morality; and all such acts that create divergences amongst people must be shunned. Believers in Islam call people towards mannerism and morality. They believe in conquering people with all good manners and highly valuable morality as well as with their power of piety and righteousness, and bring into existence a peaceful society in which people respect one another, feed the poor and the guest, and they remain hungry all the night.

---

17. *Al-Qur'an*, Surah-Al-Imaran 3:110.

Suggested Reading

Al-Maghrabi, Maulana Md. *Jamaul Fawaid*, Arabic text, Maktaba Al-Rushd, Reyadh, K.S.A., 2005 (copy available at Emarat Sharia, Phulwari Sharif, Patna). It may be noted the text contains over 11,000 *Hadith*.

Ali, Shyed Amer, *The Spirit of Islam*, New Delhi: Delhi Kutubkhana Ishayatul Islam.

Bukhari, Imam, *Sahih Al-Bukhari*, Urdu tr. Maulana Abdul Hakim Khan Akhtar, Delhi: Aitaqad Publishing House, 1986.

Hussain, Ashfaque, *The Spirit of Islam*, Bombay: Asia Publishing House, Bombay, 1958.

Hussain, Athar, *Prophet Mohammad and His Mission*, Mumbai: Asia Publishing House, 1967.

Hussaini, S.A.Q., *Mohammad and His Early Caliphs*, Kolkata, 1965.

Ishaque, Ibn, *Kitab Sirat Rasul Allah* (*The Life of Mohammad*), Eng. tr. A. Dilloump, New Delhi: Oxford University Press, 1955.

Khuda Bakhsh, *Essays: Indian and Islamuc*, Idara Adbiyat, Delhi, 1977.

Khwaja, Ahmad Jamal, *Quest for Islam*, New Delhi: Allied Publishing House, 1967.

Muslim, Imam, *Sahih-Al-Muslim*, Urdu tr. Maulana Wahiduzzaman, Delhi: Aitaqad Publishing House, 1986.

Tabbarah, Afif A., *The Spirit of Islam: Doctrine and Teachings*, Eng. tr Hasan T. Shoucair, New Delhi: Islamic Book Service.

Tirmidhi, Imam, *Jama Tirmidhi*, Urdu tr. Maulana Md. Siddique Sayeedi Hazarvi, Lahore: Farid Book Stall, 1984.

Watt, W.N., *Mohammad at Mecca*, New Delhi: Oxford University Press, 1953.

Watt, W.N., *Mohhamad at Medina*, New Delhi: Oxford University Press, 1954.

CHAPTER 28

Social Justice
One of the Greatest Gifts of Buddhism to the World

Abha Singh

THE concept of social justice, which was central to the political thought generating and sustaining the French Revolution of 1789, as conceived by modern theorists, is barely two hundred years old. In the Western tradition when we turn to earlier periods, we find that whenever and wherever social institutions like family, clan, occupations, etc. arose, justice was sought in thought and beliefs of mankind, and social justice had no role in it. However, the idea of human dignity and the importance of human existence has been the basis of all cultures. Still, almost all of the ancient philosophies and religions paid scant attention to issues of social justice in the modern sense. Walking down the memory lane to Protestantism and the Renaissance, and ultimately back to the Biblical concept of human being, we see that social issues have been addressed from early times. However, it did not concern itself with the basic questions of social justice. It was only from the eighteenth century that social justice emerged as an important issue in political thought and social philosophy in the West; and the use of the term "social justice" in official documents started from the latter part of the nineteenth century.

Normally, social justice means justice sought by the individual in all spheres of social life. It involves certain rights that are held to be exercisable by the individual against those who possess political and economic power and against harmful social customs as well. Nevertheless, society has also some rights *vis-à-vis* the individuals, who compose it. The rights of the society, however, take the shape of duties and obligations of individuals. Rights of individuals may be designated as freedom and equality, while social rights may be designated as the moral and legal obligations of individuals. As an individual can experience freedom only in a society, which is necessarily moral, the rights and duties of the individual may be held as inter-connected. Hence a healthy society would comprise a couple of essential components — freedom and morality. Moreover, in the development of an individual, i.e. his talents and capabilities, the role of society is crucial. In other words, progress of the individual is impossible in the absence of a progressive society, a society which contributes to the progress of the individual. Thus, the most important issue of social justice is how to save morality without undermining individual freedom and moral sense.

In the backdrop of the above discussion it can be safely held that the concept of social justice is quite close to the concept of humanism. Humanism may be defined as a philosophy and an attitude of mind which gives primacy to human individual and recognizes his/her right to live as a free individual with dignity. Such recognition is the basic principle of social justice. Thus, humanism provides philosophical background to the concept of social justice.

Buddha realized the deeper significance of human existence. He concentrated upon the primacy of human interests and felt that no super human or divine entity, other than his deeds, would be able to change man's destiny. Hence, the Buddhist philosophy may be characterized as Humanism. Humanism is not merely a theory but it is predominantly practical in outlook. Basically, it is concerned with the ways that would be helpful in the elimination of human suffering. Buddha fully realized the voidness of mere theoretical solution of suffering. It is due to this reason that his doctrine of "Four Noble Truths" is not only able to explain clearly the human suffering, but also the way to its elimination in the form of "Eightfold Path." Through the recognition of theory and practice Buddha discovered the way to the humanization of man and the regeneration of man as a strictly human being. All this projects Buddha as an ardent supporter of social justice and, thereupon, a champion of human rights.

Interestingly, more than two thousand years back Gautama Buddha raised the issue of liberty, equality and fraternity as a revolt against the tyrannical, hierarchical social system in India. Although Buddhist thought seldom addresses the issue of social justice in the modern sense, that is, in terms of such things as human rights, the fair distribution of resources, the impartial rule of law, and political freedom, still it takes up social issues sincerely and upholds that communal good can be realized through the promotion of individual morality. Search for enlightenment holds primacy in Buddhism. Having taught his disciples and helped them become enlightened, he then urged them to preach to others. Buddha asked his disciples to work for others, but asserted that in order to help others one must first become enlightened and, thereupon, be healed. It has been clarified through one of Buddhist dictums: "One who is sick cannot cure others." Hence, it would not be proper to claim that Buddhism is oblivious to the interpersonal dimension of human experience. The original belief that one who is sick cannot cure others came to be radically transformed by the *bodhisattva* ideal which appeared in the later phase of Buddhism known as Mahāyāna Buddhism.

Although Buddhism is mainly concerned with ethical problem, viz. that of suffering, it presupposed the metaphysical problem that everything is impermanent. Buddha felt that the two problems are correlated. Therefore, in order to discuss social justice in Buddhist perspective it is apparently proper to discuss it in the light of the two basic tendencies in Buddhist thinking — metaphysical and ethical.

Metaphysical Point of View

The crux of metaphysical viewpoint in Buddhism is that all things are subject to change and decay (*sarvam anityam*). It is based on the Buddhist cardinal doctrine of "everything is suffering" (*sarvam duḥkham*). Buddha was absolutely convinced through his own observation that the whole world is full of misery. Long and arduous years of penance made him realize that misery is due to the transient character of reality. Explaining this aspect of Buddhism, Rhys Davids says:

> According to Buddhist, there is no being, there is only a becoming, the state of every individual being unstable, temporary and sure to pass away. Everything, be it person, a thing or a god, is, therefore merely a putting together, of component elements. Further, in each individual without exception, the relation of its component parts is eternally changing and never the same for two consecutive moments. Putting together implies becoming; becoming means becoming different, and becoming different cannot arise without dissolution, a passing away, which must inevitably at some time or other be complete. [1]

Apropos to the thesis of impermanence, it appears that the concept of "social justice" would be alien in relation to Buddhist philosophy. This is for the simple reason that the basic precept of social justice involves an autonomous and free individual, which appears to be contradictory to the principle of impermanence. Moreover, justice presupposes others as well; and it is the other which makes the concept of justice meaningful.

Undoubtedly, Buddhism is a man-centred religion, but the centrality of man does not in any way go against the theory of impermanence. However, Buddhist's concept of man is somewhat different from the common view that there is an abiding substance in man. The general belief is that while body goes through changes, *ātma* does not change. However, according to Buddha, there is no such soul, as there is no continuity of an identical substance in man. But he does not deny the continuity of the stream of successive states that compose one's life. In his view, life is an unbroken series of states in which each of the state depends on

1. Rhys Davids, *Early Buddhism*, as quoted in S.S. Barlingay, *Re-understanding Indian Philosphy* (New Delhi: D.K. Printworld (P) Ltd., 1998), p. 135.

the condition just preceding and gives rise to one just succeeding it. Thus, Buddha explained continuity of life series on the basis of causal connection running through different series. Hence, in order to focus Buddhist view on social justice, it is seemingly plausible to project it in the light of their concept of man.

Concept of Man in Buddhism

By denying the existence of any supernatural controlling power, Buddhists reject ritualism and emphasize upon human will and action. They posit man as the maker of his destiny.

The importance of human action and will may be derived from the last sermon of Buddha to his disciples whom he preached to take only themselves as their guide and light. Buddha says,

> You should be carried away in favour of a doctrine . . . neither by hearsay, nor by tradition, nor by scriptural authority nor by mere logic or argumentation, nor even by teacher's personal charm, and such other things. You should accept a doctrine only after employing your own reason and discretion, after having known it to your utter satisfaction and conviction.[2]

Such views of Buddha led early Buddhists to adopt a consistently dynamic and analytic approach to personal identity. But Buddhists were not interested in understanding man's nature for its own sake. Their highest goal was *nirvāṇa,* which they characterized as the cessation of all suffering. Being a thorough realist and empiricist, Buddha not only accepted the reality of man, he also did not rest content with the realization of the plight of man.

However, Buddhists' view of man is an implication of their doctrine of "self." They used the word 'self' to denote two separate entities, one is metaphysical and another is psychological. The latter sense of self is identified with that of "man." Hence, the denial of self, in the former sense, does not mean the denial of man. The denial is restricted to a unitary, homogeneous, non-

---

2. *Kindred Sayings,* cited in G.S.P. Misra, *Development of Buddhist Ethics* (New Delhi: Munshiram Manoharlal Pub., 1995), p. 73.

empirical substance called *atta*, "self." Either such a substance itself has been held illusory or the identification of empirical self with it has been questioned. This is signified by the *anatta* (no-self) doctrine. But denial of unitary self is not denial of soul.[3]

Additionally, in the Pali texts[4] man is viewed as a union of body (form, i.e. *nāma*) and consciousness (*rūpa*). While consciousness denotes the mental aspect of man, body denotes the physical. Hence, personhood is ascribed as a composition of body, feelings, cognition, activities and consciousness. These five factors are supposed to be the base of the cosmos as well. Hence, man is a microcosm of the macrocosm. Birth is explained as the unification of the said factors, and death as their breaking up which leads consciousness to move on to start a new person. The stream flows on a continual flux that still retains a distinct identity. Every link of the series influences the following links and the links that come later. All links belonging to the same chain automatically accept the responsibility for the deeds by the preceding link. The series or link of lives reaches a final end only when one succeeds in overpowering one's ignorance (inability to see the truth) and attachments which requires arduous mental and physical training and a special kind of intellectual ability. Realizing the peculiarity of human existence, Buddhists assert that man recognizes the distinction between what he is and what he is destined to be. Hence, what man is destined to be is not unconcerned with what man is. In other words, the goal is enlightenment which is concerned with the spiritual aspect of life; it cannot be separated from the other aspects of life, such as social, political, psychological, cultural, etc. Since all these are concerned with the ethical life of man, it is now appropriate to discuss Buddhist's ethical viewpoint.

---

3. Pratap Chandra, "The Buddhist Concept of Man", in *Concept of Man in Philosophy*, ed. R.A. Sinari (Shimla: Indian Institute of Advanced Study, 1991), p. 151.

4. Cf. "*Payasi-sutta*" in *Dīgha-nikāya*, eds. T.W. Rhys Davids and J.E. Carpenter (P.T.S edition, 1890-1941), vol. II, p. 333.

Ethical Point of View

Emphasizing on human will and action, Buddhists assert that man is the ultimate architect of his own destiny. Besides, they put equal stress on wisdom and on the development of character towards moral excellence for the benefit of both individual and society. Buddha ascribes man with profound freedom. Buddhists purport that towards the attainment of a higher state of existence this freedom should be exercised by everybody. Buddhism, however, is humanism in the sense that it rejoices in the possibility of a true freedom as something inherent in human nature. For Buddhism, the ultimate freedom is to achieve full release from the root causes of all suffering: greed, hatred and delusion, which clearly are also the root causes of all social evils.

It will not be an exaggeration to state that the Buddhist ethics fully rests on a rational basis rather than on theological basis as is found in early Vedic ethics. Hence, Buddhists enjoined a short list of responsibilities to individuals through the five precepts which were taught in the Buddhist world from the time of Buddha. The precepts are as follows:[5]

I undertake the precept:

(i) to abstain from the taking of life;
(ii) not to take that which is not given;
(iii) to abstain from misconduct in sensual actions;
(iv) to abstain from false speech; and
(v) to abstain from liquor that causes intoxication and indolence.

These precepts were applicable to each individual and, thereupon, to all sections of society. To weaken, and finally get rid of them in oneself, and, in society, is the basis of Buddhist ethics. And here Buddhist social action plays a predominant role.

In Buddhist social philosophy we find that the society was

---

5. Sallie B. King, "A Buddhist Perspective on a Global Ethics and Human Rights", *Journal of Dharma*, vol. XX, no.1, Jan.-March 1995, p. 129.

supposed to involve three divisions. These divisions were the *Saṁgha*, i.e. the spiritual community, the society of the common people or householders, and the state which was supposed to take care of the former. The three were conceived as interlinked and interdependent, as the well-being of one depended upon the well-being of the other two.

As I have discussed elsewhere,[6] society is a world comprising individual persons, each intrinsically valuable. Every rational society tries to foster and encourage the highest possible development of all the capacities of personality in all of its members. The end is justice or right ordering of a society and is called social justice. It is a balance between individual rights and social control. It ensures the fulfilment of the legitimate expectations of the individual under the existing laws. It is also an assurance to provide him benefits and protection in case of any violation or encroachment of one's rights. In other words, social justice is an integrative concept. Therefore, in order to ascertain social justice in Buddhist's perspective, it appears plausible to discuss it with equal stress on all the three aspects of it, viz. legal justice, political justice and economic justice, as the *Tripiṭaka*s do contain social, political and economic teachings.

LEGAL JUSTICE

Legal justice is equality in the eyes of law. Every strata of people are subject to the same legal system. Although at the time of Buddha there was no full-fledged system of law as today, still the spirit of legal justice was, undoubtedly, inherent in the idea of equality, as Buddha was in favour of providing equal platform to each and every individual irrespective of caste, creed and sex.

Buddhists viewed all human beings as equal; therefore Buddhism was committed to the principle of human equality. Buddha attacked the caste system which divided the society in

6. Abha Singh, "Varnadharma Through the Prism of Social Justice", *Indian Philosophical Quarterly*, vol. XXVIII, no. 2, April 2001, p. 169.

upper and lower castes, thereby depriving the lower castes of certain rights such as the study of Vedas. Repudiating the superiority by birth, he declared that:

> No brāhmaṇa is such by birth
> No outcaste is such by birth
> An outcaste is such by his deeds
> A brāhmaṇa is such by his deeds.[7]

Buddha has been considered as a democratic crusader against the inequalities of the caste system and the empty pretensions of the Brāhmanical theology. He is regarded as having weakened the foundations of the prevalent religious and social structure by repudiating the revelatory character of the Vedas and by challenging the arrogant claims to dignity, importance and merit to brāhmaṇa priests. The following lines clearly depict the rejection of ascriptive superiority based on the physical fact of birth in a particular *gotra* and family:

> Ask not of race, but ask of conduct,
> From the stick is born the sacred fire;
> The wise ascetic though lowly born
> Is noble in his modest self control.[8]

Again, in the Brāhmaṇavagga of the *Dhammapada* we find some of the classic verses eulogizing the moral attributes of a brāhmaṇa:

> I do not call a man a brāhmaṇa because of his origin or of his mother; he is indeed arrogant, and he is wealthy. But the poor who is free from all attachments, him I call indeed a brāhmaṇa.
>
> Him I call a brāhmaṇa who does not cling to sensual pleasures, like water on a lotus leaf, like a mustard seed on the point of a needle.[9]

Another prime feature of social justice at the age of Buddha

---

7. *Sutta Nipata*, cited in G.S.P. Misra, *Development of Buddhist Ethics*, p. 110.
8. Cf. *Saṁyutta*, vol. VII, pp. 1, 9.
9. *Dhammapada* (Nalanda edition of the Tripiṭakas), Eng. tr. Max Müller, nos. 396-401.

featured in the treatment of slaves. Buddha condemned slavery in every form. Buddha may be declared as the pioneer of abolition of slavery. He avers five ways in which a master should serve his employees.[10] These are:

(a) Work should be assigned in proportion to the employee's health,

(b) Due food and wages be given to them,

(c) Proper care should be taken in his sickness,

(d) Specially tasty luxuries should be shared with him, and

(e) Holidays should be given to them at due intervals.

Buddha was so much compassionate for the working class that he stressed that they be treated with as much consideration as a member of one's own family.

Again, at the time of Buddha the status of women had considerably gone down. Buddha tried to give a place of honour to women. He did not accept the prevailing Brāhmanic view that a son was indispensable for a man's salvation. Although in the early years Buddha refused to admit women to the *Saṁgha* or community of celibates, later on he allowed the order of the nuns to be founded. Nevertheless, "he enjoined on a young girl of marriageable age the universal virtue of loyalty, respect and obedience to elders, efficiency in house-keeping, love of peace, etc. But nowhere in *pativratyam* (loyalty and devotion to husband) the later Brāhmanic ideal of surrender and all-absorbing devotion to husband was preached.[11] Buddhism recognized the individuality and independence of women, and their parity with men. Hence, a girl could remain unmarried by becoming a *bhikkhuṇī*. Even a

---

10. Prabha Chopra, "Contribution of Buddhism to Human Rights and Status of Women", in *Contribution of Buddhism to World Civilization and Culture,* ed. P.N. Chopra (New Delhi: S. Chand & Company Ltd., 1983), p. 127.

11. Ibid., p. 129.

widow could find respite in renunciation. Buddhism also checked the spread of *purdah* (veil) system that was prevalent in some royal households.

From the evidence of the Buddha's discourses or *sutta*s in the *Dīgha Nikāya*, it is clear that early Buddhists were very much concerned with the creation of social conditions favourable to the individual cultivation of Buddhist values. An outstanding example of this, in later times, is the remarkable "welfare state" created by the Buddhist emperor, Aśoka (274-236 BCE). Walpola Rahula stated the situation — perhaps at its strongest — when he wrote that

> Buddhism arose in India as a spiritual force against social injustices, against degrading superstitious rites, ceremonies and sacrifices; it denounced the tyranny of the caste system and advocated the equality of all men; it emancipated woman and gave her complete spiritual freedom.[12]

It is clear from the facts, stated above, that we cannot characterize Buddha as having begun with the explicit intention of challenging the brāhmaṇa priesthood, and raising the economic and social status of the downtrodden, the slaves and the outcasts. But he stressed the cultivation of those elevated sentiments such as a sense of universal compassion (*metta*) and creative altruism, the fostering of which was bound to reduce social exploitation and social tension.

Through the cultivation of compassion it is possible to rise above the drives of physical nature and also above the socially antipathetic forces of opposition, conflict and antagonistic competition. Social accommodation and adaptation are bound to follow as the consequences of the practice of *metta*. With its notions of *maitrī* and *karuṇā*, Buddhism teaches man to cultivate that softness of feelings which shudders to commit the least injury to the creatures.

---

12. Walpola Rahula, *Zen and the Taming of the Bull: Essays* (Gordon Fraser, 1978).

In the language of modern social sciences, the message of Buddha conveys that merit has to replace all kinds of subjective considerations like bias, caste preference, prejudice etc. The Madhurīya Sutta of the *Majjhima Nikāya* propounds absolute equality of all the four orders so far as the punishment for evil deeds and reward for meritorious actions, both in this secular world and beyond, are concerned. It ridicules the claims of Brāhmanical superiority as unfounded and illogical.

In short, Buddhist social action is justified ultimately and, above all, by the existence of social as well as individual *karma*. It is concerned with relieving suffering immediately, and ultimately believes in creating social conditions which will favour the end of suffering through the individual achievement of transcendent wisdom.

POLITICAL JUSTICE

The basis of political justice is that politically or economically stronger people must not be empowered to violate legal system.

Verily in Buddhism there is no explicit body of social and political theory comparable to its psychology or metaphysics. Nevertheless, a Buddhist political theory can be deduced primarily from basic Buddhism, i.e. from *dharma*. Buddhism is of the view that political power is essential to fashion and sustain a society whose citizens are free to live in dignity, harmony and mutual respect, free of the degradation of poverty and war. In such a society of good heart, all men and women find encouragement and support in making the best use of their human condition in the practice of wisdom and compassion.

Political action, thus, involves the Buddhist ideal of approaching each situation without prejudice, but with deserved circumspection in questions of power and conflict, social oppression and justice. These social and political conflicts are the great public sāṁsāric driving energies of our life to which an individual responds with both aggression and self-repression. The

Buddha Dharma offers the possibility of transmuting the energies of the individual into wisdom and compassion.

This may indicate that Buddhist movement was mainly concerned with ethical advancement and psychic illumination and not with political affairs. Nevertheless, political repercussions did ensue from Buddhism. In the *Brahmajāla Sutta,* Gautama Buddha emphatically states that he is vitally interested in social cohesion and co-operation and in the act of reconciling those people who are divided. Early Buddhism did have significant political consequences. From the evidence of the Buddha's discourses, or *sutta*s in the *Dīgha Nikāya,*[13] it is clear that early Buddhists were very much concerned with the creation of political conditions favourable to the individual cultivation of Buddhist values. An outstanding example of this, in later times, is the remarkable "welfare state" created by the Buddhist emperor, Aśoka (274-236 BCE).

The Buddhist political justice enjoins special responsibility to the king. As the head of state he must adhere to specific code of conduct, as he is at the helm of affairs of the state. Buddha felt that the personal moral conduct of the king, along with his officials, would be expressed in the political affairs of the state. Thus, the righteous character of the state would help to prevail universal righteousness on earth. Hence, deliverance through peaceful co-existence would become easily attainable for all. In some passages of the Pāli texts a parallel has been drawn between a Buddha and a monarch, as both held the same esteemed place in the eyes of the people. The two have the same objective, i.e. the well-being of people. Both are also an integral part of the ordinary empirical existence, and the political good and well-being is assured through them. The Kūṭadanta sutta of the *Dīgha Nikāya* explains that the safety of the people and their economic as well as material prosperity should be of special concern for the state and the government. Political power may manifest and sustain social and

13. Mahaparinibbana-sutta, in *Dīgha-Nikāya,* cited in G.S.P. Misra, *Development of Buddhist Ethics,* p. 110.

economic structures, which breed both material deprivation and spiritual degradation for millions of people.

Buddhists are, thus, concerned with political action, first, in the direct relief of non-volitionally caused suffering now and in the future, and, secondly, with the creation of social kārmic conditions favourable to the following of the way that leads to the cessation of volitionally caused suffering, the creation of a society which tends to the ripening of wisdom and compassion rather than the withering of them.

ECONOMIC JUSTICE

The basis of economic justice is that although people differ in mental and physical capabilities, still everyone must have enough.

Buddhist economic justice[14] follows from the precept of non-stealing — "'I will not steal." Buddha spoke against individual stealing as he felt that it causes suffering. Similarly, stealing (or exploitation), which a powerful group or society practises against less powerful group or society, would cause suffering and, thus, is antithetical to the basic Buddhist principle. Buddha felt that it is not right for some to feast while many starve. Buddhism is the middle path between luxury and need; hence all people must have sufficient for health and well-being, and in order to support efforts to fulfil higher needs. Inequality fuels resentment, anger and, ultimately, violence. In order to prevent violence there must be rough equity.

As the attitude of Buddhists was inclined towards ethical quests and psychological perfections, its philosophy did not provide any exclusive programme for the economic betterment of the masses. If any person was economically thwarted then he could join the *Saṁgha* and, thus, escape the stigma and privations of the economic world. But there was no relief provided by Buddhism to him if he continued to remain in active social life.

---

14. Sallie B. King's article, *Journal of Dharma*, vol. XX, no.1, January-March 1995, pp. 131-32.

At the time of Buddha the economy was not industrial. The trade and commerce was in agricultural products and not in industrial commodities. There was no large-scale manufacturing system prevalent at that time in spite of the mention of *śreṣṭhis*. The prevailing economy of the time was rural.[15]

Nevertheless, Buddhist scripture for economic mores can be classified in to two, one for the house holder and the other for monarch or king. While preaching to the house holder, need of hard work with righteous duties without any speculations was emphasized. Stressing upon economic order to be cultivated by the monarch, Buddha held that the root of social evil was poverty and employment. This was not to be bribed by charity and donations, which would only further stimulate evil action. The correct way was to supply food and seed to those who lived by agriculture and cattle breeding. Those who lived by trade should be furnished with the necessary capital. Servants of the state should be paid properly and regularly so that they should not find ways to squeeze the *janapadas*. New wealth would, thus, be generated and the *janapadas* liberated from robbers and cheats. A citizen could bring up his children in comfort and happiness, free from want and fear in such a productive and contented environment. The best way of spending surplus accumulation, whether in treasury or voluntary private donations, would be in public works, such as digging of wells and water ponds, and planting groves, along the trade routes.[16]

This is a startling modern view of political economy. To have propounded it at a time of Vedic *yajña* to a society that had just begun to conquer the primeval jungle was an intellectual achievement of the higher order. Schumacher puts the essence of Buddhist economics as follows:

15. C.A.F. Rhys Davids, "Economic conditions according to early Buddhist Literature", in *The Cambridge History of India*, ed. E.J. Rapson, vol. I, p. 176.

16. P.T. Barole, "Buddhism's Contribution to the world civilization", in *Contribution of Buddhism to World Civilization and Culture*, p. 32.

> While the materialist is mainly interested in goods, the Buddhist is mainly interested in liberation. But Buddhism is "The Middle Way" and therefore in no way antagonistic to physical well-being. . . . The keynote of Buddhist economics is simplicity and non-violence. From an economist's point of view, the marvel of the Buddhist way of life is the utter rationality of its pattern — amazingly small means leading to extraordinarily satisfying results.[17]

Buddhists lay emphasis on the purification of human character. Character necessarily is formed by, besides other social influences, the nature of a man's work. And work properly conducted in conditions of human dignity and freedom, is beneficial both for the worker and his products. From the Buddhist point of view, the function of work is at least threefold:

(i) To give a man a chance to utilize and develop his faculties,

(ii) To enable him to overcome his ego-centredness by joining with other people in a common task; and

(iii) To bring forth the goods and services needed for existence

This attitude has in itself the grains of distinctly far–reaching consequences. If one goes by this view of labour, it will impl that any organization or management of work in a manner tha becomes "meaningless, boring, stultifying and nerve-racking," fo the worker would tantamount to being both asocial for huma beings and an inhuman lack of compassion coupled with the bases form of profit motive. At the same time, any comprehension c leisure as an alternative to work would tantamount to a complet misunderstanding of one of the basic truths of human existenc i.e. work and leisure complement each other, and any lopside emphasis will destroy either the joy of work or the bliss of leisur

The Buddhist concept of labour, which aims at enabling th individual to overcome his ego-centredness by joining him wit

17. E.F. Schumacher, *Small is Beautiful: A Study of Economics as if Peop mattered* (Blond & Briggs, 1973), p. 52.

others in a common task, finds fulfilment in a Marxist economic system. In a communist society also the whole community works for the common good and not for the good of any individual. In the process it gives every individual a chance to utilize and develop his faculties. The Marxist motto, "From each according to his capacity, to each according to his need," underlines the dignity of human labour and common good which is really a momentous fact of any economic system. Once the whole human community accepts this principle of common good the society will restructure itself, address itself to the welfare of the people and pave the way for social justice. Thus, collective co-operative system was for the first time introduced through Buddhist *Saṁgha*, which can be said to be an ancient socialism.

Conclusion

Lord Buddha opposed the Brāhmanical social system, their dogmatism and superstition and priesthood. He taught people to exercise reason and not to be led like dumb cattle. He brought about many-sided advance in the culture and civilization of different countries by his social order and his humanistic movement. Buddha did not limit himself to curing Indian society; his aim was to cure mankind as he sought to deliver man from his bondage. An important Buddhist contribution to Indian and world culture as well is the idea of social and religious equality.

Buddha carried out a vigorous campaign against social discrimination. Throughout Buddhist literature, we find him leading debates and discussions with the brāhmaṇas, always maintaining equal claims of all classes to purity. He declared that the purity of a man does not depend upon his birth, but upon his actions. He destroyed the fundamental basis of the Brāhmanic society. Buddha knew that if all men are equal in suffering, they ought also to be equal in deliverance. He endeavours to teach them to free themselves from disease, old-age and death; and, as all beings are exposed to these necessary evils, they all have a right to the teaching, which by enlightening them is to free them.

In presence of same type of suffering, he perceives no social distinction; the slave is for him as great as a king's son. He is stuck, not so much by the abuses and the evils of the society in which he lives, as by those which are inseparable from humanity itself, and it is to the suppression of these that he devotes himself, the others appearing to him very insignificant in comparison.

Although Buddha was a spiritual and moral teacher and reformer, social, economic, political and legal implications do follow from his teachings.[18] He construed every human individual as being invested with certain duties, and the excellence and salvation of individuals depend upon ideal performance of their given duties. In other words, individual rights and dignities are strongly intertwined with corresponding duties. Rather duty is more important than right, and the individual is responsible for the society as well as for himself. Therefore, one has to play one's role well, as one's internal change, personal perfection and spiritual excellence are primary. The foundation of Buddhist path is the understanding of one's moral responsibilities towards others. Buddhists never entertained the possibility of limiting man to his physical frame and, thereupon, to one life. Buddha held that each and every man was a potential Buddha, therefore every one must enjoy equal rights and freedom. Only in a free society one can pursue one's goal. As the goal is same for everyone, as far as the quest for the highest goal is concerned, all are equal. Thus, the concept of social justice is quite in tune with Buddhist philosophy. Apparently taking a cue from it, the principles of equality, fraternity and liberty are the most important ideals and guidelines in the Constitutions of most of the countries across the globe and people are striving to attain this ideal.

---

18. V.P. Varma, *Early Buddhism and its Origins* (New Delhi, 1973), p. 367.

CHAPTER 29

Early Buddhism and its Ethics

Saraswati Mishra

EARLY Buddhism refers to the original teachings of Buddha recorded by his disciples. It is handed down to us through the Tripiṭaka in Pāli language. It is also called Sthaviravāda or Theravāda, because soon after the death of Buddha, 500 elders of the order organized the teaching of Buddha. All the teachings of Buddha can be summarized in terms of the four Noble Truths such as suffering, its cause, its cessation and the way to its cessation. The first three constitute it and the last one embraces its ethical system.

The very first sermon of the Buddha at Sārnāth is known as *Dharma-cakra Parivartana Sūtra*. In it the middle path was taught as the leading way of life. It condemns the two extreme and opposite attitudes to lisfe, that of sensual indulgence on the one hand, and of self-mortification and extreme asceticism on the other. It seeks to promote a balanced and rational attitude to life.

Buddha felt it was necessary that natural law should triumph over the supernatural and he preached that it was possible for every man to seek his salvation without assistance of any god or gods. Buddha asked his disciples never to seek refuge in or help from anyone else, but to work out their own salvation. According to him, man has the power to liberate himself from every type of bondage through his own personal effort.

After this Buddha described the 'Four Noble Truths' as his explanation and solution to the problems of life.

The first Noble Truth or *Duḥkha Satya* is the crux of Buddhism. Without understanding it the meaning and purpose of other three Truths cannot be appreciated. The truth of suffering is stated first because of its grossness and universality and is the easiest to realize. A superficial knowledge of the concept of *duḥkha* results in a tendency to think that Buddha was a pessimist and his philosophy is a message of pessimism. But this is not so. It is important to remember that according to Buddhism there is a difference between *duḥkha* as a painful feeling and the *Duḥkha Satya* as first Noble Truth.

To understand the first Noble Truth we have to understand the universal characteristic of all things. The term *duḥkha* is a compound of *dur*, meaning bad, disgraceful or lowly, and *kha* meaning "state," and *duḥkha* means unsubstantial or empty.

Duḥkha includes all physical and mental suffering, all the meanness and agony, all evils and imperfections whatsoever to which humanity and all living beings are subject. It might appear that in our life pain is compensated by pleasure but as soon as we reflect we find that pleasure itself is the root of pain. Schopenhauer has the same idea. Young also has said "a man of pleasures is a man of pain," for sorrow springs from the blood of one such pleasure as soon as the feel of pleasure is removed. The Naiyāyikas and Vedāntins too have attached little importance to sensual pleasure.[1]

The existence of this fivefold mass is disgraceful because it assists the occurrence of many harmful events. It is unsubstantial because of absence of permanence, wholesomeness, happiness and of self.

According to Buddha everything is in a flux; the existence of world is temporary. Buddha believes in the doctrine of "*anitya*" the world is a process of becoming. It is a process of incessant changes of arising and passing away. This is true of external world as well as mind which are a flowing stream of changing mental states. That transient nature of everything constituent is: *yad anicham tad duḥkham* and that which is *anichā* and *duḥkha* therefore

1. W.F. Jayasuriya, *The Psychology and Philosphy of Buddhism* (Colombo: YMBA. Press), pp. 135-48.

can't be self or belong to self. Thus the Buddhist psychology does not admit any permanent unchanging substratum.[2]

The second Noble Truth determines the cause of suffering. Suffering is conditioned by *tṛṣṇā* and *avidyā*. The theory of dependent origination shows how beings continue to be in the endless process of *saṁsāra* due to *tṛṣṇā*. It explains rebirth without accepting an unverified and unverifiable truth. By analysing an individual in his constituents and showing the dependent nature of these constituents, *Pratītyasamutpādavāda* disapprove any substantial entity behind our personality. It further explains how there can be suffering without a sufferer; the bliss of *nirvāṇa* without someone to enjoy it. This teaching is summarized by Buddhaghoṣa thus:

> Mere suffering exists, no sufferer in found;
> Nirvāṇa is, but not the man that enters it;
> The path is, but no travellers on it are seen.

The *Pratītyasamutpādavāda* is the most unique contribution of Buddha. Buddha says that a person who sees *Pratītyasamutpādavāda* sees the *dhamma* and vice versa.

The second Noble Truth is identified as craving or desire. Though the craving is the dynamic cause, ignorance and volitional activities also work together. Craving is of three kinds:

1. Sensuous desires (*kāma tanhā*),
2. Craving with Externalism (*bhāva tanhā*), and
3. Craving with Nihilism (*vibhāva tanhā*).[3]

The term sensuous (*kāma*) means the sense object and the desires in that sense object. The desires in sense objects include desires towards the bodies of living beings. The greatest of the desires is that in regard to one's own body.

Craving may also exist with desires for that particular kind of

---

2. A. Keith, *A Buddhist Philosophy*, p. 63.

3. S. Radhakrishnan, *The Dhammapada*, S-ii-26, A.9-149.

existence. By desires for life eternal is meant thoughts such as "may I and my dear ones be born to the enjoyment of eternal happiness."[4]

Desires with nihilism or wishes for annihilation means the wish for life to cease at death. Thus a person thinks this body is composed of the primary elements. The earth element unites with the earth, the fluid element with water, and so on.

This craving has four natures. The nature of getting the fivefold mass which has been taken to be ill, of causing a new fivefold mass of being no sooner the old one perished at death, of binding to *saṁsāra* and of being an obstruction to securing a release by the practice of path to deliverance. It will be found that this theory gives a sound philosophical foundation for the ethical system of Buddhism.

The third Noble Truth is the *duḥkha-nirodha* or cessation of suffering. If selfish craving is the cause of suffering, it follows that the cure for suffering must lie in the eradication of self-craving or *tanhā*. When *tanhā* is eliminated we enter the vast expanse of universal life known as *nirvāṇa*. *Nirvāṇa* is indescribable. But it does not mean nihilism nor does it mean the existence of any transcendental soul. It is called *duḥkha-nirodha* which means the absence (*ni*) of the prison house of *saṁsāra* (*rodha*).

It has the nature of release from the defilements and the suffering of the fivefold mass. The relief from the defilements means relief from the burning of lusts and other passions and also from great fires of birth, death, etc. The absence of defilements means the freedom from even the possibility of them and so it is an absolute peace. The unconditioned nature means the absence of causal influence and to be in such a state of mind which is in singleness. It is a state of *nibbāna*.

The fourth Noble Truth deals with the means of attaining *nirvāṇa*. The way to the cessation of suffering, the Buddha advocates a method which is called the Noble Eightfold Path

---

4. Nyanatiloka, *The Buddha's Path to Deliverance* (Colombo: The Bauddha Sahitya Sabha), pp. 40-49.

because it consists of eight parts. They are Right Views, Right Aspiration, Right Speech, Right Livelihood, Right Effort, Right Action, Right Mindfulness and Right Concentration. The development of wisdom and extinction of desire is made possible by this path. It is significant that the eight parts of the path may be grouped in a threefold way as moral conduct, concentration and wisdom, (*śīla, samādhi* and *prajñā*). It is an order of fulfilment. Concentration occurs only when conduct is right and firm. The fulfilment of moral conduct which comes first comprises right speech, right action and right livelihood. This means that the individual is pure in speech and action and search for food and other activities are influenced by right views and noble ideals. At the same time he strives to secure peace of mind, ease, and joy with meditation. Finally, there is wisdom made up of right aspirations and right views.

Without the practice and perfection of *śīla* the training of the mind, i.e. *samādhi* is not possible and without the perfection of *śīla* the insight of *prajñā* is not possible. Without *prajñā* the true nature of things cannot be understood. The *prajñā* cuts the root of *avidyā* and *tṛṣṇā.*

It should be noted that Buddhist training in this respect is much more comprehensive than what is understood by our modern concept of ethics. Only *śīla* covers all the aspects of morality which is usually indicated by ethics. The respective functions of *śīla, samādhi* and *prajñā,* as means of attaining *nirvāṇa,* are to be thoroughly understood in order to understand the fourth Noble Truth, which shows how *nirvāṇa,* the *summum bonum* of Buddhism can be finally realized.

The constituents of the unique path should be practised from the loftiest ideals stated as right aspiration and right views and not from any expectation of gains. Right speech, right action and right livelihood are essential factors for the attainment of higher living, the Trances and the Paths. Thus transformation of character must precede transformation of thought.

- Right speech is the expulsion of the four forms of wrong speech, i.e. lying, talk bearing use of harsh words and idle talk. Positively, it demands the utterance of Truth. The relation of right speech to right action is that it helps in controlling action through the avenue of speech.
- Right action is the expulsion of the three kinds of wrong action by of the body, namely, (i) killing, (ii) stealing and (iii) adultery. Not to kill any living and breathing thing, the moral prohibition on stealing, and not to go beyond bounds by transgressing upon the marital rights of husband and wife are the three important aspects of right action.
- Right livelihood is expulsion of wrong acts as means of earning a living. A person will not act as butcher, liar and setup houses of ill fame, and so on.

Once one has attained this path, he will no longer do evil or think evil, but is bent on doing moral acts and in perfecting the rest of the paths before he can arrive at the state of a*rhat*.[5]

The second category to achieve the state of *nibbāna* is of mental training which includes right effort, right mindfulness and right concentration.

1. Right effort is to suppress the evil and develop the morals. It is of four kinds: (a) the effort to prevent the arising of unrisen evil; (b) the effort to suppress the risen evil; (c) the effort to arouse the unrisen moral, and (d) the effort to develop the risen moral.
2. Right mindfulness is a state of calling to mind and comprehending the real worth of things which come as objects of thought. Right mindfulness may be defined as the living with strong determination to get rid of defilements, with complete awareness to overcome attachment and ill-will contemplating the body that is

---

5. Aldous Huxley, *End And Means*, pp. 3-6.

composed of the physical elements in respect of impermanence, infelicity and impersonality.

3. Meditation is to fix thought on the object which is in the mind. Concentration and wisdom follow this fixation because the mind is then rendered calm and sees the object in its true nature. This wisdom is known as "seeing things as they really are."

These insight meditations are the methods for getting rid of the twelve illusions which are the cause of ignorance. Through meditation one can attain the goal of *nibbāna*. When meditation persists to the stage that one gets completely absorbed in the object of thought and all the hindrances are suppressed, it is called *samādhi*, the highest of moral act. It is possible only for them who have purified themselves of the practice of evil words and action to a high degree by the practice of moral conduct (*śīla*).

In the third category of wisdom right aspiration is a must. It is of three kinds. The first one is the aspiration to renounce, which means renunciation from sense pleasures. Sensuality is an obstacle in the attainment of Higher Truth. Aldous Huxley also believes that the person non-attached to his bodily sensation and lusts is the ideal man. This ideal of renunciation is achieved by the ascetic practices and insight meditation. The second ideal of non-hatred means to have thoughts free from hatred to be full of friendliness or love to all living beings. The third ideal of non-harming means to have kindness and compassion to the beings in distress. These three ideals of Buddhist are known as the denial of sense pleasure, universal love and compassion. Right view is also an important category of wisdom. The aim of ethics in Buddhism is the performance of duty rightly conceived. Buddha has been able to show what is right and wrong views and what is right and wrong speech. At the highest level of the noble eightfold path, right views represent the knowledge or wisdom of four noble truths at enlightenment (*bodhi*) that has been obtained by the cultivation of insight wisdom. Right views are the founts or springs of all our action and if they get fouled then all our actions would be vitiated.

CHAPTER 30

The Central Elements of Social Morality in the Jain Perspective

Vijaya Kumar

MORALITY is an indispensable part of social life. None can deny its essential character in all ages and in all societies. So we find its interpretation among the three streams of sociology, ethics and religion. The notions of spirituality, morality and society are recognized together in Indian thought. They are inseparable because religion and ethics are twins and society is the home of both. But the value of morality is more social than individual. Individually anyone may be moral, till his morality is not expressed on social level.

There are two reasons for instability of social and individual equalities — delusion (*moha*) and disturbance (*kṣobha*). Delusion is the internal cause of instability and disturbance is the external reason. But they are interrelated and also influence each other. Delusion which is the internal cause expresses itself in the form of attachment (*rāga*), enmity (*dveṣa*), anger (*krodha*), pride (*māna*), deceit (*māyā*) and greed (*lobha*). The external reason for instability expresses itself in the form of violence, exploitation, disregard and injustice. In this way delusion is an individual evil and disturbance is a social evil. The central force of delusion is found in attachment while that of disturbance in violence. The first pollutes an individual's life and the other misguides the society. To remove this evil, the Jain philosophy has prescribed non-violence and non-attachment in the society. Non-violence that establishes equanimity in one's social life and non-attachment does the same in one's economic life. The non-absolutism of ideological world exists in non-violence and non-attachment. In this way

Jainism represents non-violence, non-absolutism and non-possession as the fundamental elements of social morality. Non-violence, non-absolutism and non-possession are main pillars of Jain philosophy and religion. Jainism represents non-violence in conduct, non-absolutism in thought and non-possession in the economic affairs.

Non-violence (*Ahiṁsā*)

All religions of the world recognize non-violence but in different forms. Some religions have adopted the principle of non-violence in a partial form while others in full form. Despite universal acceptance of the doctrine of *ahiṁsā* (non-violence), there is no uniformity regarding its meaning. All draw separate lines between non-violence (*ahiṁsā*) and violence (*hiṁsā*) in different ways. Some persons don't put even animal slaughter in the category of violence while others believe even agonizing (hurting) plants as violence.

Generally the absence of violence is known as non-violence. Non-violence has been discussed since long past, but yet its relevance is not accepted even today. In other words it may be said that if one writes thousands of pages in appreciation of non-violence that will not be sufficient. Violence is as widespread as non-violence. So before discussing the nature of non-violence one must understand the nature and form of violence because without knowing violence one can't throw light upon the universality of non-violence.

Entire tendencies or intentions of injustice are also supposed to be violence. To exploit someone, to take much work and give a little money or not at all, to usurp others' wealth or anything, to interrupt in others' happiness and to agonize beings, all come in the category of injustice. An injudicious man never cares that he is taking advantage of doing excesses or wrong upon weaker, needy, incapable and retarded — that is injustice.

Violence (*hiṁsā*) has been interpreted in two ways or forms in the Jain literatures — psychical violence (*bhāva hiṁsā*) and physical violence (*dravya hiṁsā*). Four types of passions have been accepted (*kaṣāya*) in Jainism — anger, pride, deceit and greed. Arising out of these passions in mind is psychical violence and if these intentions are brought into words and action then they become physical violence. First of all, a violent person victimizes himself in psychical violence. As anger comes into mind violence occurs. Whether the person afflicted with psychical violence assaults others or not, his power is exhausted. For instance, some children in a school vex a fellow student. The irritated child takes up some clay in his hand and rushes to throw it upon his companions. Teasers run away fast. The irritated child running speedily may or may not throw mud on his fellow children; in both the cases he makes his hand dirty. Similarly, whether a person does violence or not, he burns himself in the fire of anger that is psychical violence. It is apparent that psychical violence hurts the virtues of soul and makes its expression in physical violence.

The Fundamental Causes of Violence

Psychical passion is the root of violence. Passion leads to violence. It is said that if a being is injured by someone without any intention, i.e. unknowingly, it is not violence in itself. But, if one's life is taken due to passions, i.e. anger, pride, deceit and greed, it is violence. It means that killing or violence happens due to being afflicted with bad intention, attachment and aversion that is violence in the true sense. If someone is not afflicted with psychical passion and even then violence happens that is only physical violence. Despite being fatal to life; physical violence is not considered as violence.[1] It is obvious that the fundamental base of violence is psychical passion.

If we think from a practical point of view we can see the following reasons for violence:

1. Imbalance in social system.
2. Imbalance in social structure.

---

1. *Tattvārtharājavārttika*, 7/13.

3. Problem of armament.
4. Communalism.
5. Imbalance among human relations.
6. Problem of caste.
7. Economic rivalry and scarcity.
8. Mental tension.
9. Ideological differences.
10. Intentional imbalances and individual chemical imbalance.

Self-Violence and Other's Violence

Hiṁsā, generally denotes hurt or injury to others. It is related to the killer and the killed. One who injures commits the violence, and the other is injured. The victim feels physical sufferings and, thereafter, his soul also gets a lot of pain. In this way the victim feels both mental and physical pain, and the aggressor is considered to be relieved from all sufferings, but it is paradoxical. When attachment and enmity affects our heart (soul), we are gripped by anger and it is expressed in violent actions. At this juncture one loses one's peace of mind and gets tension in the body. Consequently, he hurts others. We find *hiṁsā* to happen in both conditions — first due to mental transition victim's soul is hurt and later it injures others.[2]

The level of *hiṁsā* depends on the high and the low degree of passions. If *hiṁsā* is committed with high intensity the degree of *hiṁsā* becomes high and if it is done with low intensity the degree of the *hiṁsā* becomes low. If a being with one sense is killed there is no feeling of sorrow in the heart of a killer. But in the killing of beings having two senses to five senses the degree of passion increases and the person interested takes stern steps against someone. In the case of one sensed, he expresses neither sorrow nor any kind of revenge. He resists cries and looks restless in killing multi sensed.

---

2. *Puruṣārthasiddhyupāya*, 47.

Meaning of Ahiṁsā and Definition

Generally *ahiṁsā* means "no *hiṁsā,*" *hiṁsā virodhinī ahiṁsā*. It means not to do *hiṁsā,* but scholars express different opinions regarding its meaning. *Ahiṁsā* is a negative term. A layman also falls in illusion that non-violence is only non-inclination. There is nothing like inclination within it. But *ahiṁsā* inherits both inclination and declination. Affirmation (*vidhi*) and negation (*niṣedha*) are two sides of one coin. Non-killing any *jīva* or to protest inclination is negative non-violence, and self-study, spiritual service to give sermon, discussion about knowledge and self-well wishing (*ātmahitakārī*) are affirmative non-violence (*vidheyātmaka ahiṁsā*). If we discuss only negative aspect of non-violence that will be incomplete analysis of non-violence. The complete analysis of non-violence will be possible only in both negative and positive aspects of non-violence.

According to the *Ācārāṅgasūtra,*

> All *jīva*s and all elements should not be hurt, nor should not be got killed, nor to be caught by force, should not be agonized, should not be hurt fatally — this kind of non-violence (*ahiṁsā dharma*) is true religion.[3]

Although in this statement, *ahiṁsā* has not been used, the interpreter has presented here *ahiṁsā* for the clarity of the subject matter. In the said statement true *dharma* has been presented as *ahiṁsā.* In this way, *Sūtrakṛtāṅga* says that the meaning of learned man is that man who does not hurt anyone. Non-violence-based equality is the centre of religion.[4] One should keep in mind that a wise man should know all about the living beings because all beings love life, but agony or suffering is not dear to anyone. Knowing these two facts one should not indulge in *hiṁsā.* We find a perfect definition of *ahiṁsā* in *Daśavikālika Sūtra.* According to it, nobody

---

3. *Ācārāṅga-Sūtra,* 1.4.1.
4. *Sūtrakṛtāṅga,* 1.1.4.10.

should be hurt by *triyoga,* i.e. mind (*mana*), speech (*vacana*) and deed (*karma*), and *trikaraṇa,* i.e. by doing it himself, by getting it done through others and by feeling pleasure in violence.[5] In this way, expounders have interpreted *ahiṁsā* with different views. Some persons have given emphasis on the cause of violence on human being and others on different kinds of *jīvas*, and to protect them. This has been the central point of their ideas or thoughts relating to *ahiṁsā*. To be different is human nature, so everybody has expressed different point of views regarding *ahiṁsā*.

Kinds of Ahiṁsā (Non-Violence)

There are two kinds of *ahiṁsā* — psychic (*bhāva*) *ahiṁsā* and physical (*dravya*) *ahiṁsā*. If a person takes a vow not to assault any being it is psychic non-violence (*bhāva ahiṁsā*). In this way a person who vows not to kill anyone and neither he kills any being nor approves killing, is a physical non-violence (*dravya ahiṁsā*). There are two more forms of psychic non-violence (*bhāva ahiṁsā*) and two of physical non-violence (*dravya ahiṁsā*) as well. They are as under:

Psychic non-violence (*bhāva ahiṁsā*):

1. *Svabhāva ahiṁsā* — not to indulge in any attachment and aversion, not to be dipped unto sexual pleasure are *svabhāva ahiṁsā*.

2. *Parabhāva ahiṁsā* — not to harm other's soul, peace or nature or individual qualities.

Physical non-violence (*dravya ahiṁsā*)

1. *Svadravya ahiṁsā* — not to harm one's own body senses under the influence of anger.

2. *Paradravya ahiṁsā* — not to destroy others' lives due to anger.

---

5. *Āvaśyaka-Sūtra*, 1.3.

Non-absolutism (*Anekāntavāda*)

Anekānta has been derived from two words *aneka* and *anta*. From the viewpoint of origin *anta* it refers to fusion of many religions and thoughts, which is called *anekāntavāda*.[6] *Anekānta* is that doctrine which believes in many characteristics. According to Upādhyāya Amaramuni, *anekānta* means to consider, to observe and to watch upon anything with different views. The non-absolutism is also called *apekṣāvāda*. The method of viewing a thing from one point of view is ever supposed to be incomplete and not evident in Jainism. And observing a thing from different points of view is supposed to be complete and evident. This doctrine is known as *anekāntavāda*.[7]

There is nothing in this world that is either bad or good in itself. Even souls of ruffians, impertinent and adulterer are full of infinite virtues, because each soul inherits infinite qualities. Static things are infinite in the world. Truth is infinite and untruth is also infinite. *Dharma* is infinite and sin is also infinite. Light is infinite and darkness is also infinite. A little particle is full of infinite qualities. Infinite moral virtues are of two kinds — attributes and modes. The characteristic determines the nature of a thing that is called attribute (*guṇa*). Without it a thing cannot exist, for example, manhood in human being, brightness in gold, etc. If a being is without humanity, he may be something else not a human being. Similarly, if gold does not contain quality of brightness, certainly it may be something else, not gold. Attribute lives in a thing and it is neither destroyed nor changed because with the destruction of attribute that thing is destroyed and similarly with the change of mode that thing also changes. Attribute is the inner property of a thing. The mode that determines the external form of a thing changes, burns and exhausts, for instance, a stage of childhood, youth and old, bulky or thin, etc.

---

6. *Ratnākarvatārikā*, p. 89.
7. *Cintana kī Manobhūmi*, p. 106.

Hīism (*Haivāda*) and *Bhīism* (*Bhivāda*)

There are two isms in the world — "Hīism" and "Bhīism." The upholder of "Hīism" says that "I am true," i.e. my statement is true and the statement of other is not true. On the contrary, one who believes in "Bhīism" says "I am also true," i.e. other's statements are also true like that of mine. They are also truthful from their own angles. In other words, the believers of "Hīism" says it is day and upholders of "Bhīism" say that it is also day, i.e. where there is no sun there is night also. "Hī" and "Bhī" differ widely in meaning also. In the use of "Hī" the statement is bound in one view which misleads people for accepting imperfect knowledge as perfect. The "Bhī" upholders welcome other's views along with their own. In this way, we see that "Hī" thought creates disparity of thoughts and paves way of conflict. The "Bhī" thought diminishes all sorts of inequality and struggle.

Non-possession (*Aparigraha*)

Muccha parigahha, i.e. possession is *parigraha*. In other words, it may be said that possession is *āsakti* and non-possession is *anāsakti*. It is *anāsakti* that becomes *aparigraha* in the field of social morality. In fact, possession appears in two forms — collection (*saṁgraha*) and contemplation of enjoyment (*bhoga bhāvanā*). A man snatches away other's rights after being motivated by the feeling of possession and enjoyment of things. To encroach others' rights or to exploit anyone is also a kind of violence. *Uttarādhyayana-Sūtra* speaks that desire is the cause of entire sufferings of the world. As desire ends delusion ends, and as delusion ends suffering ends.[8] Desire and delusion are the roots of possession (*parigraha*). Thus attachment is possession (*parigraha*).[9] In fact, attachment is a mental fact, it is transition of soul but its expression is external and is related directly with external things. Any thing or substance in all conditions or consumptions, or adoptions is not a *parigraha* —

---

8. *Uttarādhyayana-Sūtra*, 32.8.
9. *Daśvaikālika-Sūtra*, 6.21.

as roads, mountains, forests, ponds and public places are used easily by all and neither anyone is individually attached with these nor anyone's right is encroached upon by appropriate use of these things, nor there is created any nuisance in the society. So this is not *parigraha*. In this way, public trusts which have been opened for sufferers do not come under *parigraha*. In other words, the things which do not create feeling of attachment or detachment cannot be defined as *parigraha*. It is clear that *aparigraha* does not prevent a person entirely to have anything, but it says to have things as required with any transition in the soul. Anger, arrogance, deceit, temptation, aversion, attachment and pride, all these inner transitions take shelter in external substances and strike on our personality, so proper restraint on substance is necessary.

But a question arises regarding the limitation of *parigraha*. How much *parigraha* is proper and how much is improper? Who will determine this limitation, whether society or individual? It is not an easy question to reply. That is why Jain scholars, viewing human needs and discretions have left this question open to all to be discussed, because needs depend on time, space, individual and circumstances. If a person is wise he will take proper decision, if he is impressionist his right will have to be taken and given to the society. Despite equal distribution of matters disturbance of mind will remain intact. Thus peace of mind is possible only when human desire would be appeased and *aparigraha* would be maintained on the basis of detachment and circumstances.

Conclusion

One may, therefore, safely say that a prosperous, pleasant and peaceful society needs correct thinking, sympathetic behaviour with one another among its members and proper economic management, which are provided to its members by pluralistic realism (*anekāntavāda*), non-violence (*ahiṁsā*) and non-hoarding (*aparigraha*). These elements constitute the social ethics of a society. Therefore, it may be concluded that Jainism presents basic principle of social morality.

Part VI

Niṣkāma-Karma, Development and Education

CHAPTER 31

Niṣkāma-Karma

B.R. Shanta Kumari

A HUMAN being is not only a rational animal, but also a social being. This gregarious nature is not unique to human beings alone, for it can be seen even among animals. Hence, for a person to become "human" there must be the integration of one's rational faculty and one's social nature. One's instinctive senses must be tamed, and base behaviour regulated to accord with the approved and accepted norms and conventions of society, because one does not live in isolation from society — for individual welfare contributes to social welfare and social progress influences individual well-being. Therefore, the welfare of the individual, both material and spiritual, can be attained simultaneously with the welfare of the society. This interrelation and mutual dependence between (wo)man and society has been recognized by Indian philosophers in their emphasis on selfless service, *niṣkāma-karma*, which forms the key concept of the *Bhagavad-Gītā*. In fact, all the schools of Vedānta assign to it the foremost place among the preliminaries to liberation. The ideal of *niṣkāma-karma* otherwise called *karma-yoga* has inspired contemporary neo-Vedāntins like Swami Vivekananda and others.

Meaning of Niṣkāma-Karma

In the *Bhagavad-Gītā*, Śrī Kṛṣṇa tells a confused Arjuna that in the days of yore, after creating the world and mankind, He propounded two paths:

1. The path of activism (*pravṛtti-mārga*), leading to worldly prosperity (*abhyudaya*), and

2. The path of asceticism (*nivṛtti-mārga*), leading to liberation (*niḥśreyasa*).

To effect a *via media* between these two extreme paths, leading to divergent goals is the aim of the *Bhagavad-Gītā*. This is attained in *niṣkāma-karma-yoga*, wherein there is a harmonious synthesis of knowledge, devotion and action pertaining to the intellectual, the emotive, and the conative aspects of man. *Yoga* is perfection in action (*karmasu kauśalam*). It has to be borne in mind that *niṣkāma-karma* is not *un-interested activity* but *dis-interested activity*. In detachment or selfless action we do not suppress the senses and their activities, but sublimate them for spiritual purposes.

Let us now see whether *niṣkāma-karma* is possible, and what benefits accrue to the individual and the society, when it is adopted and practised by the individuals constituting the society. We shall, therefore, discuss the psychological, the sociological and the philosophical aspects of disinterested or selfless work.

Psychological Aspect

In the *Bhagavad-Gītā* (III.5), Kṛṣṇa tells Arjuna that no one can remain quiet without doing any work even for a moment and that one is impelled to act by the constituents of *prakṛti*. But a life of ceaseless desire-impelled activity is unfavourable for spiritual progress. For, while engaged in action, an individual considers oneself as the agent or doer (*karttā*) and enjoyer (*bhoktā*). Inevitably, one comes across failure or success. When one's efforts fail to produce the desired result, a discontented individual is overtaken by depression and anger, leading to non-discrimination between the bad and good. Ultimately, one loses one's mental equipoise and perishes, unfit to realise the higher values of life (*Bhagavad-Gītā*, II.63).

Scriptures recognize the psychological weakness inherent in man, when they affirm that no individual ever acts without a motive behind the act, i.e. all the actions of an individual are desire-driven. And desires, usually being self-centred or ego-centric, are non-conducive to liberation, because liberation (*mokṣa*) demands the total annihilation of the ego (*ahaṁkāra*) and a complete loss of self-identity.

In the hierarchy of values (*puruṣārthas*), wealth (*artha*) and pleasure (*kāma*) are regarded as lower values, whereas righteous action (*dharma*) and liberation (*mokṣa*) are considered as higher values. *Artha* and *kāma* are called lower values, because these are common to human beings as well as beasts, and they are also selfish. Through *dharma* one strives to rise above one's base and impulsive behaviour and become divine by attaining *mokṣa*. Thus *dharma* becomes the means for attaining salvation, which is foremost among the values (*parama puruṣārtha*). *Mokṣa* is the highest value because in it there is a total absence of the ego. In *dharma*, an individual who practises one's duty (*svadharma*) with a detached attitude, subordinates one's selfish desires to those which promote the welfare and progress of the family and the society at large.

Actions are unavoidable in life; because one has to act even to sustain one's life. The actions of the realized (*jñānīs*) are desireless, whereas those of the bound (*baddhas*) are tainted with desires. Desire is the source of all misery and bondage. Desires lurking in the senses confound the mind and lead it astray, just as wind sweeps a boat off its course at sea. Hence, the emphasis on the need to mentally renounce the desire for the fruit (*phala*) of one's effort. A fried seed can only be eaten, it is incapable of sprouting, whereas a seed which is not fried is potent. It can germinate, grow into a plant, put forth flowers, bear fruits, and perpetuate the life cycle. Similarly, desireless action liberates an individual, whereas actions performed with a selfish motive bind the individual and lead to endless transmigration (*saṁsāra*). Hence the *Bhagavad-Gītā* exhorts one to renounce desire and not the deed. One is asked to renounce the fruit of one's action and not the action itself, i.e. it teaches *karma-phala-tyāga* and not *karma-tyāga*. Disinterested work involves sacrificing the agency and not the act. Therefore, "duty for one's own sake" is transformed into "duty for duty's sake," in the words of Kant. Through *niṣkāma-*

karma-yoga, one attains freedom *in* action and not freedom *from* action.

Niṣkāma-karma does not mean just desireless or detached action. It also includes acting in accordance with God's will, as an instrument in His hands, for the fulfilment of a divine purpose. And acting in accordance with God's will requires devotion (*bhakti*) and self-surrender (*prapatti*). One, therefore, dedicates one's actions to God. "Duty for duty's sake," now, becomes "duty for God's sake." With this spiritualization and enrichment of action, *karma* gets transformed into service (*kaiṅkarya*).

Thus, we see that in *niṣkāma-karma* which forms the core of the *Bhagavad-Gītā*, there is a harmonious blend of knowledge (*jñāna*), devotion (*bhakti*) and action (*karma*) pertaining to the intellectual, the emotive and the creative aspects of a human being.

Sociological Aspect

An oft-repeated criticism is that Indian philosophy is other-wordly, *mokṣa*-oriented, self-centred, preaches renunciation and is therefore negative, places more emphasis on the liberation of the individual than on society, etc. But this is wrong or only partially right. Its initial pessimism promises a more worthier goal. Just as little drops of water make a mighty ocean, integrated individuals ensure an integrated society. This results when every individual adheres to what Bradley calls "my station . . ." (*āśrama*), and performs "its duties" (*dharma*). A detached performance of one's duties assures the welfare of an individual, here and hereafter, as well as that of the society both materially and spiritually. It has to be remembered that in the enunciation of the ideal of one's duties, the criterion is psychological, since the "nature" of the individual is taken into consideration. Kṛṣṇa tells, *cātur-varṇyaṁ mayā sṛṣṭaṁ guṇa-karma-vibhāgaśaḥ*.

Presuming that a human being lives for a hundred years in one's journey from the womb to the grave, we can discern four stages (*āśramas*) in a person's life.

1. In the first stage of celibacy (*brahmacarya*), an individual after initiation (*upanayana*) stays in the house of one's teacher (*guru*), serves the teacher and acquires knowledge, both sacred and secular. The student lives a disciplined life, develops respect for elders, learns to become independent, gains control over one's senses and cultivates fellow-feeling.

2. On completing one's studies, an individual enters the stage of a householder (*gṛhasthāśrama*). The individual's pursuit of *artha* and *kāma* is guided by *dharma*. A householder is under the obligation of three debts (*ṛṇa*s) — (a) debt to God (*deva-ṛṇa*), (b) debt to sages (*ṛṣi-ṛṇa*), and (c) debt to the ancestors (*pitṛ-ṛṇa*). To repay these three debts, one performs the five great sacrifices (*pañca-mahāyajñas*) — (a) sacrifice to God (*deva-yajña*), (b) sacrifice to sages (*ṛṣi-yajña*), (c) sacrifice to the ancestors (*pitṛ-yajña*), (d) sacrifice to human beings (*nṛ*- or *manuṣya-yajña*), and (e) sacrifice to the birds and beasts (*bhūta-yajña*). An individual's daily worship of God is a token repayment of *deva-ṛṇa*, and an acknowledgement of one's indebtedness to God for the bountiful blessings showered on one. By studying scriptures (*svādhyāya*), a person repays the seers for having shown the way to live a wholesome, happy, and righteous life, which caters not only to one's material welfare but also to one's spiritual welfare, here and hereafter. By begetting progeny, to continue the family and by offering oblations to the departed, one redeems oneself of the obligation towards one's forefathers and ancestors. In *nṛ-yajña*, a householder entertains and hosts guests. This fosters cordial human relationships. In *bhūta-yajña*, one feeds birds and beasts to acquit oneself of the five great sins (*pañca-mahā-pātaka*s) incurred by one unknowingly in the kitchen, while walking, sweeping, etc. This helps one develop compassion even for the low forms of life, while the deification of non-sentient phenomena, e.g. rivers,

mountains, etc. instils reverence for nature and helps curb its abuse.

Of all the four *āśramas*, *gṛhasthāśrama* is the most important, because it sustains the other three *āśramas*. Tradition and culture are nurtured in this *āśrama*. A householder not only begets children, but also ensures that they grow to become responsible, integrated and "cultured" citizens of the society in which they live.

3. In the third stage of *vānaprastha*, an individual retires from active life after handing over one's household and other responsibilities to one's children. One spends one's life practising *dharma*, and strives for attaining *mokṣa*.

4. In the final stage of *saṁnyāsa*, an individual on attaining realization renounces all duties towards one's family and society and becomes an ascetic. Such a person helps the spiritually fallen and the worldly-minded to arise and reach the supreme goal of life.

Thus it can be seen that when one performs the duties of one's station in life with detachment, it leads to a double benefit — (a) it results in social welfare or *abhyudaya* by ensuring the smooth functioning of the society, and (b) it bestows individual liberation (*niḥśreyasa*). An individual is gradually, unconsciously and gently weaned away from the pleasant (*preyas*), by placing before one a higher and more desirable good (*śreyas*). Detached action favours spiritual progress and liberates an individual. In this way, when everyone follows the ideal of selfless service, it leads to social welfare with which the welfare of the individual is connected. It means that the problem starts at the individual level. "If you take care of the pennies, the shillings will take care of themselves." Likewise, if one takes care of the individuals, society will take care of itself. This is the simple and ancient wisdom of the Indian philosophers. Therefore, the criticism that Indian philosophy is negative, that it preaches asceticism and overlooks society, etc. is baseless and arbitrary, revealing incomplete and superficial understanding of the glorious philosophy.

Philosophical Aspect

All activity is aimed at happiness, because happiness alone has intrinsic value. The desire for *mokṣa* too is motivated by one's desire to overcome the finitude and miseries of life and enjoy happiness permanently. In *mokṣa*, a person (*jīva*) enjoys bliss which is the Self's (*Brahman*) true nature. *Artha*, *kāma*, and *dharma* are instrumental values in attaining *mokṣa*. Hence the reason why Yājñavalkya tells his wife Maitreyī in the *Bṛhadāraṇyaka Upaniṣad* that all objects are desired for the sake of the Self.

Suffering is due to ignorance of one's real nature (*svarūpa-ajñāna*). Due to ignorance (*avidyā*), there is false identification (*adhyāsa*) with the body-sense-mind complex. An individual thinks that one is the knower (*jñātā*), doer (*karttā*) and enjoyer (*bhoktā*). Seeking pleasure one is engaged in activities, lawful and unlawful. A major part of one's life is preoccupied in accumulating wealth under the illusion that wealth confers happiness. But the happiness which wealth affords also brings misery along with it. In the *Bhajagovindam*, Śaṅkara tells that a wealthy man fears even his own children. Therefore, there is much pain and agony involved not only in amassing wealth but also in ensuring its safety.

It is said that God, after creating the world and human beings, did not know where to hide happiness. He, therefore, placed it within (wo)man. In one's quest for happiness, the ignorant grope, in vain, in the jungle of external objects of the physical world. One acts to enjoy and enjoys to act, while happiness keeps evading one — like a butterfly which flits from one flower to another as soon as one nears it, or like water in a mirage. Thus there is endless transmigration (*saṁsāra*), because desires remain unsatisfied and the Self unrealized. But the nature of desire is such that it cannot be quelled by sense-satisfaction. Like fire fed by ghee, desires only increase in number and strength with their gratification. The degree of pain or pleasure experienced by an individual through the gratification of one's desires is directly proportional to the intensity of the desire gratified. All desires vanish and cease to exist only when one attains knowledge of the Self. It is only a person of discrimination who through right knowledge is able to discern the Self and experience the "real" happiness which is within oneself.

According to scriptures (*śruti*), the Self is essentially existence (*sat*), knowledge (*cit*) and bliss (*ānanda*). In living beings (*jīva*s), *sat* and *cit* are manifest whereas *ānanda* is only partially manifest due to its obscuration by *avidyā*. When an individual desires an object; the mind gets agitated and there is no peace. But when the desire is satisfied, an individual feels happy. It must be noted that the pleasure enjoyed is not conferred by the object — the object only serves as an avenue to enable the blissful nature of the Self to reveal itself temporarily.

All objects of the world possess five qualities — (a) existence (*asti*), (b) manifestedness (*bhāti*), (c) desirability (*priyam*), (d) name (*nāma*), and (e) form (*rūpa*). Among these *asti, bhāti,* and *priyam* belong to the Self, whereas *nāma* and *rūpa* belong to objects which are the evolutes of the five great elements (*pañca-mahābhūta*s). Due to *avidyā* or ignorance of the Self's true nature, an individual ascribes the bliss of the Self to objects. Thus deluded one thinks that happiness is bestowed by objects.

The common (wo)man not only does not know one's own nature, but is also unaware of the supreme truth that it is one and the same Self which pervades the world of varied beings — from Brahmā to a blade of grass. One, therefore, perceives diversity — plurality in terms of caste, creed, race and religion. These differences, in turn, influence inter-personal relationships. But, in fact, there is no friend or foe other than one's own Self. The whole world is one universal family (*vasudhaiva kuṭumbakam*). The wise perceive the same non-dual Self in a brāhmaṇa, a cow, an elephant, a dog and an outcaste. There is no plurality for the enlightened (*jñāte dvaitam na vidyate*), because they perceive the same Self everywhere.

When an individual acts, dedicating one's actions to God and renouncing one's desires, one becomes mentally immune and indifferent to the outcome of one's actions. Such a person remains unaffected by failure and success, pain and pleasure, etc. since one does not consider oneself as the doer and the enjoyer. This detachment towards the fruit of one's work coupled with non-identification with the psycho-physical complex helps a still and pure mind to reflect the bliss of the Self. When the individual gets established in the knowledge of the Self, i.e. that the Self is actionless because it is perfect (*pūrṇa*), and that it is only a witness (*sākṣin*) to the activities of the body, the senses and the mind, one attains liberation-in-life (*jīvanmukti*) and overcomes transmigration because one has accomplished and attained that by which everything else is accomplished and attained (*kṛta-kṛtya*). For, other than It there is nothing else to be known or achieved. A knower of *Brahman* becomes *Brahman* (*brahmaveda brahmaiva bhavati*), and delights in the bliss of *Brahman* (*brahmānanda*).

CHAPTER 32

Social Justice and Development

S.C. Panigrahi

MAN is a social being. The gregarious instinct, though found in some birds and animals, is consciously pursued by man. Formation of clans, tribes, community, state and nation refer to different levels of socialization and corresponding complexity in the social structure. The fact remains that in the state of nature, no two individuals are identical. Diversity is the law of nature. Individuals differ from one another in respect of physiognomy, predispositions, values, ideals, strength and weakness, language, nationality, religion, etc. Nonetheless, because of innate social disposition as well as circumstantial compulsions, man opts for group living, be it a family (the minimal unit of group living) or a nation (the maximal unit of co-existence). Besides the nature-made difference in respect of the bodily features and the mindset or the fundamental traits which man owes to factors beyond his control, there are differences that are man-made. For example, the difference in respect of language one speaks, the community one belongs to, religion one professes and the economic status that one has are man's own making. It is to be kept in mind that society is not a mere juxtaposition of individual. Physical togetherness or geographical proximity is not a defining criterion of a society. Man is predominantly a psychic being. A herd of animals or flock of birds characterizes spatial togetherness, but living together is not a sufficient condition for human beings to make a society. In order to constitute society, its members need to have certain common values and shared modes of life. Formation of society calls for efforts in the direction of finding unity or commonality, beneath nature-made or man-made differences. Here comes the role of the state which plays its obligatory role as the regulative authority. Thus, man, society and state constitute a triune. The rationale behind formation of society has been differently conceived by different thinkers. Contractualists opine that the "state" as a social entity comes into being as a result of implicit or explicit contract among individuals who, otherwise, have diverse interests. They construe state of nature as one of anarchy characterized by perpetual conflict of interests of the individuals. Since self-love overrides other considerations, given the absolute freedom, the individual would seek to maximize his own interest at the cost of others. This would set in constant conflict or warfare among individuals, groups or vested interests, making social harmony an impossibility. Survival of the fittest, the rule of the jungle, would reign supreme. In social living, in order to be an enduring phenomenon, it is necessary that the self-regarding considerations are sacrificed in favour of other-regarding considerations on the part of every individual, group or social entity. There are certain basic things to which the individual is entitled, irrespective of his place in the social hierarchy, and there are certain obligations which an individual or group owes in relation to others. This introduces one to the concept of rights and obligations. A harmonious social order is one where the basic interests of its people are safeguarded without prejudice to the interest of others. Here comes the notion of "social justice."

A just society is one where no one is discriminated against. Rather everyone gets his due which is beneficial for the good of the society. Society has been conceived as an organism, with individuals constituting its integral part. Disharmony, disequilibrium or injustice in any given part, has its necessary bearing on the health of the whole. Since individual and society are integrally related, the good of one presupposes good of the other. The state justifies its existence by enforcing the canons of justice. A citizen has a right not to be discriminated against. Therefore, the state has a corresponding obligation to enforce justice. Principles of justice help in resolving considerations, reconciling differences, and thereby ensure stability and harmony in the collective body whereas injustice has its necessary aftermath in the form of social anarchy and discord.

There are some who subscribe to the view that justice is intrinsically good. They adduce ontological definition of "justice" by appealing to the nature of reality.

> Justice is the virtue of the soul. Justice is good because it is indispensable. Justice is not only the attribute of an individual but also of a whole society.[1]

Every individual is inherently good, and reality as a whole is also orderly. It is a cosmos, not a chaos. The reality is a whole of which the animate and inanimate, mobile and immobile constitute the integral parts. So, the well-being of the part depends on the well-being of the whole and vice versa. The ultimate good of man and society consists in cultivating the virtues of love, friendship, wisdom and sacrifice. Social justice is best ensured when every citizen seeks to maximize and harness the goodness latent within the well-being of the collective body. On the other hand, when the evil propensities are allowed to flourish it brings ruin not only to the individual but also to the collective body. The Protagorians and the Sophists subscribe to the other extreme view that there is nothing like an absolute or objective "justice." Since man is the measure of things, notions of "right" and "wrong," "justice" and "injustice" are parasitic on the interest of the individual. The utilitarians, on the other hand, plead for the cause of 'justice' on the ground that "justice" pays in the long run. The society where the rules of justice reign supreme witnesses peaceful social harmony, political stability, religious tolerance and economic parity. Laws and institutions are just insofar as they pave the way for the security and well-being of the individual.

- Justice is a virtue implying a relation to others for it promotes the interest of another whether he be a ruler or simply a fellow çitizen.[2]

---

1. A.D. Lindsay (ed.), *Plato's Republic* (1954).
2. Aristotle, *Politics*.

- The social order can exist only when there are rules of law and justice with objective and universal validity and independent of the subjective individual will.[3]

The concept of "equality" is integral to the notion of social justice. Equality means equality of opportunities, i.e. fair share of the individual in opportunities and pursuits. In the state of nature no two individuals are equal in respect of their ability and predilection. But beneath the differences there are certain communalities which cut across groups, communities, states and nations. It pertains to man's interest in securing his existence and opportunities for unfoldment of his potentialities. The five necessities like food, clothing, shelter, education and medicine are the fundamental needs of every individual, irrespective of his capacity, vocation and station in life. Social harmony and stability remain a distant cry when a section of its people remain deprived of the basic essentials of existence. Man is more psychic than physical. Even if the fundamental prerequisites of existence are ensured for one and all, there remains the need for opportunities for its people to grow and expand psychically. Peace and contentment of the individual cannot be surely ensured by granting amenities and affluence to its people. Individuals, at large, should be made to cultivate the virtues of head and heart so that the differences and inequalities in the state of nature do not stand on the way of living and growing together. Justice in physical, therefore, minimally means that each individual should have his legitimate share in the natural bounty, social dividends and benefits.

> Each should have a fair share and a fair share means that unless there is some justification for acting otherwise share should be approximately the same . . . that justice demands the same treatment for the same differences.[4]

---

3. J. Messenger, *Social Ethics* (1973), p. 213.
4. G. Sartori, *Democratic Theory* (1965), p. 330.

The notion of social justice is based on the golden rule that "like should be treated alike." This is elucidated by Hart as follows:

> Individuals are entitled in respect of each other to a certain relative position of quality and inequality. This is something to be respected for the vicissitudes of social life when burdens and benefits are to be distributed. It is also something to be restored when it is disturbed. Hence justice is traditionally thought of as maintaning or restoring a balance or proportion, and its leading precept is often formulated as "treat like cases alike," though we need to add, "and treat different cases differently."[5]

Development is always a goal specific. In Indian system, the concept of "justice" has been discussed from a broader perspective. Human beings have been classified into four classes (*varṇa*s), according to their disposition (*guṇa*) and ability (*karma*), namely, *vipra* the enlightened class who are bearers of enlightenment and are predisposed to guide others along the path of righteousness; warriors who have the ability to serve the society by their physical strength or prowess; *vaiśya*s who have the special knack to undertake trade and commerce and thereby help in the society to attain equilibrium on physico-economic front, and the śūdras who can serve the society by lending their physical strength. Besides *varṇa-dharma*, *āśrama-dharma* refers to rights and duties of the individual according to the four different stages of life such as *brahmạcarya*, *grahastha*, *vānaprastha*, and *saṁnyāsa*. People belonging to the four *varṇa*s serve the cause of collective good, i.e. the cause of social justice, only when they perform action enjoined by the class (*varṇa-dharma*) they belong to. On the other hand, the individual good is maximized when every person discharges his obligations according to his *āśrama-dharma*. Needless to say that the individuals constitute the bedrock of social justice. Social norms, political enactments, religious degrees, and legal dispensations serve as the facilitating agencies in translating the principle of "social justice" into a living reality.

---

5. H.L.A. Hart, *The Concept of Law* (1970), p. 155.

Development is goal centric. Movement, as such, does not amount to development. In other words, the success and viability of the development strategy is to be defined in terms of the social goal at hand. By and large, pace and degree of development is determined in terms of scientific technological progress, Gross National Product (GNP) and per capita income. Needless to say that GNP and per capita income are predominantly statistical. Besides, they do not reflect the interest of those who stand marginalized in the developmental spectrum. The so-called dividends do trickle down to the mass. Developmental strategies are mostly tampered with by class interest and the interest of the ruling polity. Hence, it is imperative that while defining the goal and parameters of development, the interests of all the sections of the society be taken into account. "Development" in the real sense of the term remains an unattainable ideal, unless it is motivated by and integrated with the fundamental principles of "social justice."

CHAPTER 33

Social Justice and Development on Plato's Radar

Madhubala Kumari

THE concept of "justice" can be studied from various standpoints. One can make an empirical study of it. One can raise such questions as how did the concept of justice originate in human society, what is the impact of other allied and related concepts, and how has the concept influenced life and society?

We come across the earliest account of justice in the *Ṛgveda* and in the writings of ancient Greek philosophers. *Ṛta* in the *Ṛgveda* has been treated as the cosmic moral principle which controls and pervades the universe. Universe functions on a set pattern, the nature functions harmoniously, and the human beings behave morally and justly or else are punished only because of the principle of *ṛta*.

It is to be remembered that "justice" is a value-concept, hence related to ideologies. Like equality, liberty and right, justice is also regarded as a social value. The contractualists like Hobbes, Locke and Rousseau maintain that a society logically presupposes the concept of justice. It is debatable whether the civil society evolved out of the state of nature. But the fact remains that the concept of society can't be explained without the concept of justice. Thus justice and society are interlinked. But justice is meaningful only in the context of society. Justice has no meaning to men living in a state of nature. The idea of contract to form a society portrays the limits to human liberty and right which reflect a sense of justice. Thus the concepts of justice and civil society go together. To quote John Rawls:

> The various conceptions of justice are the outgrowth of different notions of society against the background of opposing views of the natural necessities and opportunities of human life.[1]

The conception of social justice provides a standard of distribution. It determines the shares of different individuals in the distributive aspect of the society. It keeps a balance between the competing claims of individuals in the society. Thus it tends to harmonize the different conflicting claims, interests, rights, etc. and lead to a healthy social progress.

Social justice infuses a sense of morality into different individuals of society to honour the rights of one another and dispense their duties properly as per their station or position in society. "Live" and "let live" should be the foundation of any society to run smoothly. Next comes the principle of "right" and "duty." In fact, moral values are a must for any society to function properly. When individuals of any society tend to be immoral and do not honour the basic values, society gives birth to violence, chaos and conflict leading to the disruption of normal life. In this way, the concept of social justice is essential for proper functioning of any society.

What we want to assert is that justice is treated as a moral ideal. Morality is concerned with the question as to what is good and bad, right and wrong, in the conduct of human beings. A moral standard approves or disapproves human actions according to a particular narrative standard. The principle of justice also evaluates the conduct of man and it also approves or disapproves human actions. This shows that justice and morality are connected in some way or other. For instance, when we say that a given law or any judicial decision is not good, we naturally refer to morality. Therefore, the justification of any law or government actions lies in morality.

Justice in ancient Greek philosophy is treated as a moral ideal. Plato and Aristotle have treated justice as co-extensive with

1. Dibakar Sahoo, *The Concept of Justice* (Delhi: Atlantic Publishers and Distributors), p. 2.

morality. To them, justice is nothing but morality itself. Justice without morality or righteousness is inconceivable.

> No one can fail to recognize the breadth and profundity of this doctrine which makes justice one with harmony, with perfection and with beauty.[2]

Indeed, the Platonic conception of justice has been construed as controlling all the walks of life and acting as the regulative principle of the whole life. In fact, Plato has not distinguished politics from ethics, rather both are fused together to eulogize the concept of justice. The concept of justice takes into account the inner life of individual and his social interconnections. In corollary to this assertion, we may focus on the ideas contained in Plato's work *Republic*.

Plato, in fact, wants politics to stand on the sound foundation of philosophy. It is because philosophy is believed to promote reasoning and rational virtues. It somehow or the other teaches us values which are essential for smooth sailing of society and state, both. It has tremendous potential to contribute a lot in the task of nation building and promoting justice in day-to-day life of individuals and society as well.

Plato opines that the ends or objectives of all life are wisdom, virtue and knowledge. The individuals can realize these ends only when state administration (working on reason or philosophy) provides them cordial atmosphere and suitable equal opportunities. The end of the state thus is the virtue and happiness of the citizens. And since this is only possible through education, the state's primary function is educational.[3] Since the state is to be founded upon reason, its laws must be rational, and rational laws can only be made by rational men, philosophers. So, the rulers must be philosophers. Plato, therefore, asserts that the first operative principle of the state is *reason*, the second is *force* and third is *labour*. Plato believes that *force* is used to control the

---

2. Dibakar, Sahoo, op. cit., p. 7.
3. W.T. Stace, *A Critical History of Greek Philosophy* (Delhi: Macmillan, India Ltd.) p. 227.

irrational masses who never willingly submit to the rational laws. And since the work of the world must go on, the third operative principle will be *labour*. The three operative principles correspond to the three classes (castes or professions). Reason is embodied in the philosopher rulers, force in the warriors, and labour in the masses. In this way there are three classes in the society:

	Classes	**Operative Principle**	**Virtue**	**Hindu equivalents**
1.	The Philosopher rulers (The most wise class)	Reason	Wisdom	Brāhmaṇa
2.	The warriors (The most valiant class)	Force/Spirit	Courage	Kṣatriya
3.	The masses (The most appetitive class)	Labour	Temperance	Vaiśya and Śūdra

Plato also considers the soul of man as the abode of three qualities: *reason, spirit* and *appetite*. Men whose souls are dominated by reason are regarded as *the most rational and wise class,* those whose souls are dominated by spirit are regarded as the *most spirited and valiant class,* and those whose souls are dominated by appetite or desire are regarded as *the most appetitive class.* The virtue of the philosopher rulers is *wisdom,* of the warriors *courage,* of the masses *temperance.* The harmonious co-operation of all three produces justice.[4]

The division of society, therefore, operates according to the nature of man. Moreover, the division of the society is regulated as per the dictates of the soul of man. Men are stationed in the society according to their inborn nature and potentialities. Society should not put an individual to the class which is not compatible to his innate nature.

Let us now throw a brief light on the *function* of the three classes:

1. Plato wants philosophers to rule the state as their own life is a hallmark of reason and virtues. They can restore values

---

4. W.T. Stace, op. cit., p. 227.

to the society and polity, both. But they must not cease to be philosophers rather continue with their philosophical enterprise through leading a contemplative life. They can spend their leisurely hours only in governance.

2. The warrior class enforces the decrees of the philosopher-rulers. However, their primary duty is to protect the nation and society from internal and external disturbances.

3. The masses will engage themselves in trade, commerce and agriculture. Both the other ranks are prohibited from doing the business of the masses.

Contemporary Relevance of Plato's Idea of Justice

Plato's ideas regarding division of society reminds us of the concepts *varṇāśrama-dharma* and *sva-dharma* enshrined in *Bhagavad-Gītā*. These concepts give us a message to perform our duty honestly as per our position in the society along with least meddling into the affairs of others — only then justice will be done to the individuals and society. We observe that Platonic conception of justice carries the similar sense and message. It is an irony that people often do not dispense their assigned duty sincerely and meddle into the business of others which create lots of troubles in public life. We notice in our day-to-day life the public blockade of rail-road traffic and the like disturbances which disrupt the normal life. This is because the public servants don't dispense their assigned duty properly. Also the district administration does not act properly in time in most of the cases of the sensitive issues. It is to be mentioned that besides bad governance, different kinds of rallies to gain political mileage further add to the public woes. Thus the entire socio-political scenario in states like Bihar presents a dismal picture of sheer violation of the principle of social justice.

In corrollary to this idea, it is not out of place to mention that "justice delayed is justice denied" which is but the harsh reality of our judicial system. The poor and lower middle-class people in India suffer a lot due to this delayed justice and hence most of the youngsters of this class sometimes join the bandwagon of MCC and other terrorist outfits or indulge in some anti-social activities. As students of philosophy we must ponder over the issues as to why the common mass in India doesn't believe in police and judiciary. Why the law enforcing agency has a dismal performance in our country? We have to contemplate over the issues since law enforcing agency and judiciary are the major sources of propagating justice in society. In the interest of social justice, we have to see that executive, legislature and judiciary should function properly in a harmonious manner. Unfortunately, these three powers don't seem to be functioning in unison. Sometimes, judiciary reminds the executive of its duty, and judiciary too in India is not trouble-free. The highest governing body, i.e. the parliament never appears to be accountable to the public grievances. This is why proceedings in parliament are often marked by chaos, confusion and some sort of verbal conflict among its members; thus major parts of precious time of parliament are simply wasted on small matters without transaction of any business. We are aware that sessions in parliament are held at the expense of public money. Thus parliament too is not working as per the principle of justice.

Let us now shift our attention to the plight of small children in India who in the ripe age of getting primary education become child-labour, and are seen cleaning utensils in hotels, homes and elsewhere. Some of them work in automobile centres and some factories. Special provision for the protection of children is made in Article 24 of the Indian Constitution, which says —

> No child below the age of fourteen years shall be employed to work in any factory or mines or engaged in any other hazardous employment.

We know according to Plato that the primary duty of state is to provide education to its would-be citizens so that they could learn and cultivate virtues in their conduct. But how can we make our children virtuous and responsible citizens when a large percentage of them become child-labour and don't get primary education owing to government apathy and poor management of government schools and also non-availability of such schools in remote rural areas? It is a shame that after six decades of its Independence a nation is not able to provide free, fair and compulsory education to the small children who are but the future of the country. The society simply uses the children and leaves them uncared. Are we not preparing a whole generation of ruffians and anti-socials by neglecting these children? In the absence of education and care, they are not expected to be responsible citizens of the nation. Imagine also the destiny of those children who beg alms on roads, at railway platforms and on running trains! Thus we see that the principle of social justice is not working in most of the states of India partly because of government apathy and partly because of the well-off people not fulfilling their social moral obligations towards the deprived lot of society.

Plato has talked a lot about the education and care of children which may not seem very appealing in the present context. According to Plato, sick and feeble children and also children of bad parents or any offspring not sanctioned by the state should not be allowed to survive. People will have no family life and no private property. Children from their earliest years do not belong to their parents, but to the state. They are, therefore, at once removed from the custody of their parents and transferred to state nurseries. The state machinery must see that parents shall never again be able to recognize their own children once they have gone out of their custody.[5] The state should take total responsibility of the education of the children.

Plato opines that all the details of the educational curriculum are decreed by the state. In no case, the state should allow epic, play (drama) and poetry as they appeal to the baser needs. It should only allow such poetry which helps in inculcating virtues and motivating young brains for nobler things. All poems, therefore, must inculcate virtues.

5. W.T. Stace, op. cit., p. 228.

It is, in Plato's opinion, intolerable that the individual should have any interest apart from the interests of the state. Private interests clash with those of the community, and must therefore be abolished.

Besides state ownership of children, Plato talks about the community of wives and community of goods which may not suit to Indian social conditioning. Nevertheless, the principle of justice as propounded by Plato has several ingredients to benefit our social life. We can mention them in the following manner:

- The philosophers (students and teachers of philosophy) and noble people should come forward and involve themselves in active politics and different social activities in order to serve the nation in the larger interest of the principle of justice.

- The philosophers can restore values in socio-political and economic streams of national life.

- People of different walks of life, administrators, judges and others should dispense their own duties sincerely least bothering to meddle into the business of others.

- Philosophers (in the capacity of holding high offices) may help creating a work culture and cordial atmosphere in which citizens will develop their potentials to the full.

- State should try its level best to provide free, fair and compulsory education to the children. These Constitutional obligations should be complied with at all costs.

- States should try to see that its citizens are secured and inculcate good virtues into them. Quite akin to Plato's view we should always keep in mind that the objectives of human life are wisdom, virtue and knowledge. This necessitates the role of philosophers who can transform the society through their sincere efforts and noble ideas.

CHAPTER 34

Education through the Prism of Social Justice

Priti Kumari

EDUCATION is that which makes man a person. It helps him to cherish some ability, belief, knowledge, habit, skill, trait of character or value and creative orientation for attainment of deep-level traits which is ideal and actually consists in overcoming self-sense and egoism. It helps in abreacting the beast in man and elevating the best in him. It is an enterprise, a kind of action, a discipline. It also combines different disciplines supporting it. It exudes its hidden force that determines the destiny of man. It reflects the triumvirate of educating, educated and education. It marks man's reality rooted in his lived-through experience of which value awareness is the case. It conveys encomium, accepted excellences, cultivation of which is desirable, appreciable and morally justifiable. It is always a gain and is worth getable. It is deeply connected with social justice, the most important concern of the society.

The sense of social justice and equality is one of the important factors and talked of topics not only in Indian society but also in the global community. In ancient period, Indian society was divided into different castes. Social discrimination based on caste had crept into life and introduced a strong feeling of superiority and inferiority. As a result, one particular class/caste came to be identified as the oppressed and exploited class, and it became impossible for this class even to dream of social justice. The exploited classes were deprived of their natural rights. This is why the contemporary Indian social system has made special provisions for ensuring social justice.

Meaning of Social Justice

Social justice means no discrimination on the basis of class, caste, birth, sex, place, etc. in a social order. The present-day Indian society is based on social justice which is free from all the discriminations, a fact already in theory, but to some extent in practice. Since we have inherited many kinds of social discrimination from the traditional Indian society in which a large section of the population was classified as weak and backward many provisions have been made for the upliftment of these sections of the society because no society can be said to be upholding the principle of social justice as long as it makes no effort to raise the backward and weaker sections of the society to the equal level.

Nowadays wealth has become the status symbol for respect in the society. Consequently, efforts have been made for the economic upliftment of the traditionally exploited weaker and backward section of the society so as to procure social justice for them. Article 23 of our Constitution is concerned with the prohibition of trade and traffic in human beings and forced labour as (i) trade in girls and women, (ii) the custom of bonded labour and beggar or forced labour and (iii) the custom of slavery. Not only women, even children fall into the category of "weaker section" of the society, even children had been deprived of social justice in traditional Indian society. With regard to it, Article 24 places a prohibition upon the employment of children below fourteen years of age in factories and other places of work. The purpose of this provision is to protect the health of young children, to ensure the growth of leading citizens and to provide for the establishment of healthy and just social order for the future. Article 15 directs the state to make special provisions for women and children. It empowers the state for making special provisions for the advancement of any socially and educationally backward class of citizens or for the scheduled castes (SCs) and scheduled tribes (STs). Our Constitution provides for reservation of seats in the parliament and state assemblies, seats in educational institutions/

courses and posts in government/quasi government services for SCs and STs for a specified period. Such provisions for certain minorities and backward communities are also indicated.

The educational corollary of these constitutional guarantees are equality of educational opportunity, the provision of opportunities for every child to obtain education suited to his ability and interest irrespective of caste, colour, creed, sex, or the financial ability of his parents.

The very foundation of social justice must necessarily be non-existent in a society in which a particular class in society is regarded as being unworthy of being touched by other members of society. In traditional Indian society, śūdras came to be regarded as untouchables. This is clearly the anti-thesis of any concept of social justice. Hence, accepting social justice as one of the fundamental principles of a healthy social order, according to Article 17 untouchability is abolished and its practice in any form is prohibited. The Parliament has passed a law defining offences arising from this practice and prescribing penalties thereof. To strengthen the provisions in social justice, a provision has been made for the directive principles, which have assumed great significance as the result of the 42nd Amendment. These directive principles help to throw light upon the nature of social system we wish to evolve by basing it on social justice. These lay down that the state shall strive to promote the welfare of the people by securing and protecting effectively, as it may, a social order in which justice — social, economic and political — shall inform all the institutions of social life.

While typifying democracy, we find that it is of ethical, political, social and economic types. In contemporary society, economic element is the basis of society and justice and hence the following provisions have been made for economic justice:

- The citizens (men and women) equally have the right to an adequate means of livelihood (Article 39a).

- The ownership and control of the material resources of the community are so distributed that they subserve the best of common good (Article 39b).
- The operation of the economic system does not result in the concentration of wealth and means of production to the common detriment. (Article 39c).
- Equal pay for equal work (Article 39d).
- The health and strength of workers (men and women) and the tender age of children are not abused and that citizens are not forced by economic necessity to enter a vocation unsuited to their age or strength (Article 39e).
- The childhood and youth are protected against exploitation and against moral and material advancement (Article 39f).
- The state shall, within the limits of its economic capacity and development, make effective provision to secure the right to work and education to public assistance in cases of unemployment, old age, sickness or disablement (Article 41).
- The state shall make provisions to secure just and humane conditions of work and maternity relief (Article 43).
- The state shall promote the educational and economic interests of SCs, STs and other weaker sections and shall protect them from social injustice and all forms of exploitation (Article 46).
- Efforts will be made to organize agriculture and animal husbandry on the basis of modern scientific laws (Article 48).

It is evident from the economic provisions explained above that B.R. Ambedkar, laid a firm foundation for social justice in present-day Indian society.

In Article 19 (in which the rights of citizens are enshrined) attempts have been made to harmonize individual and social interests for achieving social justice. By the 42nd Constitutional Amendment of 1976, a new part (4a) has been added to part 4 of the Constitution, by which basic duties of citizens have been incorporated in the Constitution. Observance of duties is a prime necessity from the viewpoint of contemporary democratic arrangements and social justice. Thus in the Constitution the provision has been made for a balanced and just social order. Promising growth with equity and social justice, the Indian Prime Minister Manmohan Singh in his addresses to the nation on 24 June 2004 reaffirmed his government's resolve to generate employment and promote distribution of justice.

Social Justice and Aims of Education

It is on the basis of what have been given above about education and social justice that we can very well see the role of education in eradication of injustices in a society. The basis of social justice is economic justice. Real social justice can be available to all our citizens only when there are suitable opportunities available for economic development of all our citizens. As such, we can see education playing its pivotal role in social justice and its realization. Some important principles may be laid down as follows for activating social justice through promotion of education.

TO ENCOURAGE THE FEELING OF SOCIAL JUSTICE

Indian society has become highly stratified since many classes, levels and steps have come into existence within it. Consequently, a large section of society remains deprived of social justice. It is essential that the young men and women of today, forgetting all differences of caste, class, colour, sex or religion, learn to demand for others whatever they want for themselves. It is essential that, as a result of education, our younger generation becomes more sympathetic and sensitive. The qualities of co-operation, discipline, leadership and sharing other's burden, develop in them. Our new generation must develop the courage and strength to fight the existing differences, injustice and discrimination prevalent in our society. It is only through the evolution of this kind of awareness that the goal of social justice can be achieved.

TO CREATE EQUAL EDUCATION OPPORTUNITIES FOR ENLARGEMENT OF SCOPE FOR SOCIAL JUSTICE

(a) *Provision of Free and Compulsory Education*: It is essential to provide free and compulsory education for all children between the age of 6 and 14 irrespective of class, caste, religion and sex. In the event of failing to achieve this objective, which is stated in our Constitution, we cannot even dream of creating a social order based upon social justice.

(b) *Common School System*: At present, different types of schools in India are encouraging class differences. The inevitable result is a diminution in the sense of social justice. Hence, it is desirable that there should be similar schools for all students. For this, provision must be made for creating a common school system.

(c) *Encouraging Adult Education Programme*: At present a very large portion of the country's population is illiterate and adults form a big chunk of this illiterate mass. In such a situation, it will be essential that this section of society must be encouraged to receive education for achieving social justice

ECONOMIC DEVELOPMENT FOR SOCIAL JUSTICE

Mahatma Gandhi expressed the profoundly truthful thought that if God were to incarnate in India, He would have to assume the form of a piece of bread. Swami Vivekananda too in his concept of Daridra Narayana as God visualizes a similar situation. This striking statement directs our attention powerfully towards our economic condition. Social democracy is not possible without economic democracy. Thus the major aim of Indian education must be economic development and this implies that —

- education must develop human resources;
- education must feel the development of natural resources;
- education must create devotion to labour and work;
- education must bring about an increase in opportunities for employment.

To achieve these aims for social justice, the environment of school should be free from prejudices, and should be based on equality. The curriculum should be the same for all the children. Methods of teaching should be used according to the potentialities and abilities of the child. Different co-curricular activities should be organized for the development of feeling of co-operation and service. Teachers should have faith in social, political and economic justice, and faith in child's talent and abilities as well.

Contributors

Sajida Adeeb is Professor of Philosophy and the Director, Centre for Women's Studies at Osmania University, Hyderabad. She has been teaching Moral Philosophy and Philosophy of Religion for more than twenty-seven years. She is currently editor of the journal, Osmania Journal of Women's Studies. She is the author of a couple of books, Iqbal as a Philosopher and Moral Philosophy, Adeeb has participated in a number of national and international seminars and published nearly 30 research articles as well. She is presently serving as a member of the Academic Boards and Selection Committees of Osmania University, Hyderabad. She may be contacted at sajidaadeeb@hotmail.com

Binod Kumar Agarwal is currently working as a Professor of Philosophy at North-Eastern Hill University, Shillong, after teaching for more than two decades at Lucknow University, Lucknow. He began his academic career with a brief stint at Visva Bharati, Śāntiniketan. He graduated with first class honours from Hans Raj College, University of Delhi. With M.A. and M.Phil. from University of Delhi and Ph.D. from Lucknow University, Agarwala is actively engaged in research in Critical Philosophy of Kant. Political Philosophy and Philosophical Hermeneutics are also major areas of his interest. He has published scholarly essays in political philosophy and Kant's Critical Philosophy in national and international journals, and in books edited by eminent scholars. He may be contacted at binodagarwala@rediffmail.com

Girish Baruah is a retired Professor of Philosophy. At present he is living in Chandan Nagar, Golaghat, Assam. He is actively engaged in research work. His writings address the questions of social philosophy, human rights and metaphysics. His most recent book is Metaphysics: Problems and Prospects (2008).

M.P. Chaurasia is Reader in the Department of Philosophy, J.P. University, Chapra (Bihar). He has earned his M.A. in Philosophy specializing in Ethics (1980), a Ph.D. (1985) and a D.Litt. (2000), all from B.R.A. Bihar University, Muzaffarpur. Chaurasia completed a minor research project sponsored by the UGC on "Problem of Extremism in

North West Bihar — Its Causes and Remedy" in 2006. He has authored Anupyukta Nītiśāstra in 2007 and Astitvavadi aum Abhasaki (in press) and has published twenty-nine research papers as well.

S.P. Dubey is distinguished Professor and Head (retired), Department of Philosophy, at R.D. University, Jabalpur. He is a Gold Medalist in M.A. Philosophy (1963), and got his doctorate on "Treatment of Appearances In Ṣankara and Bradley" from Banaras Hindu University, Varanasi. He was awarded Graduate Teaching Fellow at McMaster University, Hamilton, Canada, for about two years (1966-68). In connection with academic pursuits, Professor Dubey has travelled to several countries, including U.S.A., U.K., France, West Germany, Switzerland, Italy, Japan, Hong Kong, U.S.S.R. and South Korea. Formerly a member of Indian Council of Philosophical Research as well as President of Federation of Madhya Pradesh Universities Teachers Association, he is at present Chairman, Akhila Bhāratīya Darśana Pariṣad. He has published several books, including Rudolf Otto and Hinduism and Idealism: East and West, and more than fifty research papers and articles in national and international journals and anthologies. He has, moreover, edited the third volume (Problems of Indian Philosophy) of the ICPR sponsored series entitled Facets of Recent Indian Philosophy, and translated into Hindi Burner's Greek Philosophy. He may be contacted at sp_dubey@rediffmail.com

D.A. Gangadhar is Professor in the Department of Philosophy and Religion, Banaras Hindu University, Varanasi. He has lectured at conferences/seminars all over India and abroad as well. He may be contacted at dagangadhar@gmail.com

Debashis Guha teaches Ethics and Phenomenology and Existentialism in the Postgraduate Department of Philosophy, Ranchi University, Ranchi. Guha takes interest in Philosophy of Religion, Social and Political Philosophy, Philosophy of Science and Analytic Philosophy. He was awarded Visiting Associateship (1994-96) by the UGC, New Delhi, in Jadavpur University, Kolkata, where he worked out An Inquiry into the Cases of Pain and Suffering, which has been published recently. He has completed a Major Research Project (1997-2000) duly sponsored by the UGC on Applied Ethics in Indian Context, which has been shaped into six volumes under the series: Practical and Professional Ethics. Guha has fifteen papers to his credit. He has presented philosophical papers in several national/international seminars, symposia and conferences.

He envisions peoples' participation in practical and professional ethics. He may be contacted at reejuguha007@gmail.com

S. Imtiaz Husnain is Professor of Sociolinguistics in the Department of Linguistics at Aligarh Muslim University, Aligarh. He is a graduate of Jawharlal Nehru University, New Delhi. He has held East West Center Fulbright Fellowship and was a Fellow of Central Institute of Indian Languages, (MHRD, Government of India), Mysore as well. He has several publications, including a co-edited book Globalization, Language, Culture and Media in 2006. He may be contacted at imtiaz.husnain@gmail. com

Md. Sirajul Islam is Reader of Philosophy and Religion at Visva Bharati University, Santiniketan. He is associated with twelve learned bodies, and has served four administrative posts of the university as well. He has authored Sufism and Bhaktī in 2004 and Raja Rammohun Roy and Islam (in press), as well as edited Social Philosophy for the New Millennium and translated in Bengali six books. He has, moreover, published twenty-two articles in research journals and anthologies. Islam has completed three post-doctoral research works and has presented research papers at seventy-two seminars/conferences/symposia (30 international and 42 national). His areas of interest are Sufism, Islam, Comparative Religion, Environmental Ethics (Indian, Western & Islamic), Civil Society, Baul-Faqir Cult and Bhakti Philosophy (India). He has organized 7th International Congress of Social Philosophy (ICSP-2008) at Visva Bharati as a General and Local Secretary in 2008. He may be contacted at siraj_tuli@yahoo.co.in

Tariq Islam is presently Senior Reader in the Department of Philosophy at the Aligarh Muslim University. He did his schooling at Oxford and B.A. (Honours) from London. He joined the Department of Philosophy and Religion at Aligarh Muslim University, Aligarh, as a faculty in 1981. He completed his M. Phil on "Gilbert Ryle's Analysis of Thinking as Activity" in 1986 and Ph.D. on "Ryle's Concept of Thinking" in 1991. He authored "The Concept of Thinking" in 1996, and got published several papers on political philosophy concentrating on "Political Islam" in national and international journals. He may be contacted at tariq43@gmail.com

Ameeta Jaiswal is Head of the Department of Philosophy, Patna Women's College, Patna University, Patna. She has been an enthusiastic teacher of philosophy since 1986. She is a recipient of a Fellowship of

ICPR, New Delhi, and Research Associateship of UGC as well. Jaiswal is actively involved in various research and academic activities in college. She has attended several workshops and seminars in philosophy and presented research papers therein. Presently she is actively engaged in guiding several research scholars in philosophy.

Md. Imteyazul Haque Khan is Reader in the Depatment of History, Oriental college, Patna City, Patna. He completed his postgraduation in History — with specialization in Medieval Indian History — from Patna University. He has been teaching since last twenty-four years. Khan has several articles published in journals and newspapers as well. Since the last several years he is associated with media, and is Newscaster on All India Radio Patna (Hindi) and Doordarshan, Patna, (Urdu) as well.

Indoo Pandey Khanduri is Reader in the Department of Philosophy, HNB Garhwal University, Srinagar (Garhwal) Uttarakhand. She has to her credit a book Hume and Kant on Knowledge and edited a book Environment and Ecology: Problems and Perspectives. She has translated Kant's Critique of Practical Reason in Hindi with financial assistance of ICPR. She has completed two research projects sponsored by the Department of Culture, Ministry of Human Resource Development, Govt. of India, and at present she is working on a Major Research Project grant provided by University Grants Commission. Besides, she has a number of research papers, book reviews, and critical comments published in national and international academic journals. She has participated and presented a number of research papers in national/international seminars and conferences. Pursuing her urge for creative writing she had been associated with the national daily English newspaper Hindustan Times as freelance contributor. She may be contacted at indoo_khanduri@rediffmail.com

Rajjan Kumar is Reader in the Faculty of Applied Philosophy at M.J.P. Rohilkhand University, Bareilly. He completed his Ph.D thesis, Jaina Dharma Mein Samadhimarana ki Avadharana and D Litt., A Critical Survey of Different Aspect of Jainism. He has authored four books, Jivana Vijnana and Jain Vidya (1993), Preksa Dhyana and Jain Vidya (1994), Samadhimarana (2001), and Different Aspects of Jainism (2006) and has published eighty-five research papers as well. Recently, he edited a book *Kautilya ke Arthasastra ke Paripreksha mein Sasana Vyavastha*. He has completed one major research project funded by UGC on "Applicability of Indian Philosophical Conceptions to the Society" and two research projects sponsored by ICPR on "Samthara: An Art of Pursuing Death" and "Relevance of Socio-Ethical conceptions of Mahabharata and Republic of Plato to the Modern Society." A participant of thirty-seven seminars/confererences, he has conducted seven seminars as well. His research and publications focus on Jain philosophy and Indian philosophy. He may be contacted at rajjan.k@rediffmail.com

Vijaya Kumar is Lecturer in the Department of Philosophy at Parshwanath Vidyapith, Varanasi (recognized by Banaras Hindu University, Varanasi, as external research centre). He has a doctorate from Banaras Hindu University, Varanasi in 1989. He is currently the editor of a quarterly research journal on Jainology, Shramana. Kumar has edited six books. He is the author of five books and forty-five research papers published in scholarly national and international journals. The recent focus of his work has been Jain philosophy. He may be contacted at vijaya_2009@india.com

Prabhu Narayan Mandal is Professor, Department of Philosophy, T.M. Bhagalpur University, Bhagalpur. He served as Head of the said department for about six years (2002–2008). Prior to it, he was Head of the Department of Gandhian Thought in the same university for about a couple of years. He was Sectional President in the annual session of Indian Philosophical Congress held at Tirupati in 2007. Mandal authored a book The Rise and Fall of Phenomenology, with Reference to A. J. Ayer in 1996. He has more than a dozen aricles published in national journals. His research interests include philosophy of religion, contemporary Western philosophy, Gandian thought and social philosophy. Presently he is the President of Bihar Darśana Pariṣad.

Madhubala Mishra is Head, Department of Philosophy at Z.A Islamia College, Siwan. She has participated in a number of national and international seminars and conferences, and published many research articles as well. Besides her active academic pursuits, she is also engaged in social and political activities.

Nityananda Mishra is Disinguished Professor & Head (retired), Department of Philosophy, T.M. Bhagalpur University, Bhagalpur. He graduated and postgraduated from Patna in 1938 and 1940 respectively. He also obtained B. Litt. from Oxford in 1959. He has served under Bihar Educational Services. He was associated with the Patna University for long years as Lecturer and Reader. He was also a Visiting Professor in the Magadh University at Bodh Gaya. Prof. Mishra was invited to deliver the General Presidential Address at Agra in 1989 session of the Akhila

Bhāratīya Darśana Pariṣad. His published works include *Sence Data and Perception and Samakālīna Pāścātya Darśana*. He has dedicated his life to the cause of philosophy. Even at the age of ninety-two he is a voracious reader and writer of repute.

Saraswati Mishra is Professor of Philosophy at Ranchi University, Ranchi. Her research and publications are focused on Indian philosophy and Buddhist studies.

Asha Mukherjee is Professor in the Department of Philosophy at Visva Bharati University, Santiniketan. She is the author of several books, articles and book chapters. One of her recent works is a co-edited book Conditioning and Empowerment of Women: A Multidimensional Approach. The current focus of her work has been on gender studies. She may be contacted at ashamukh@gmail.com

Sharat Chandra Panigrahi is Professor in the P.G. Dept. of Philosophy, Utkal University, Bhubaneshwar. He is the author of The Concept of Yoga in the Gita. Panigrahi's articles have been published in journals of philosophy with national and international circulation. He has lectured at several conferences and seminars. He may be contacted at philosophybhu@rediffmail.com

Priti Kumari is presently Lecturer in B.Ed. at Government Postgraduate College, Ranikhet (Uttarakhand). Previously she worked as Lecturer of Elementary Teacher Education at Trinity Institute of Professional Studies (TIPS), New Delhi. She is the author of Development of Learner and Teaching — Learning Progress and co-edited with Dr Geeta Tewari A Text Book on Environmental Studies as well. She may be contacted at pritiksingh78@yahoo.com.

Y.V. Satnarayana is Professor, Department of Philosophy, Andhra University, Vishakhapatnam. He has been sectional president in several sessions of Indian Philosophical Congress and has organized six national seminars as well. He has authored Marx and Gandhi. He is currently writing a book on applied philosophy. Prof. Satnarayana's research and publications have focussed on Indian philosophy, social philosophy, Western philosophy and ethics. He is currently serving as a member of ICPR, New Delhi. He may be contacted at satyanarayana48@gmail.com.

B.R. Shanta Kumari is Reader & Head, Department of Philosophy, Pondicherry University, Pondicherry. Her Ph.D. Thesis was on Advaita as Transformative Metaphysics and her areas of specialization are advaita, aesthetics, and classical Indian philosophy. A recipient of the UGC Junior and Senior Research Fellowships (1989-92), she completed a Minor Research Project funded by the UGC Unassigned Grant on The Philosophy of Professor S.S. Suryanarayana Sastri in 1997. She is also a Member of the Board of Studies in Philosophy. She has delivered many lectures in philosophy, in most of the major Universities in India and abroad. Her articles have been published in journals of philosophy having national and international circulation. She has won many prizes in sports and extra-curricular activities; has a variety of interests; travelled widely in India, and visited abroad. She may be contacted at shivapriya24@yahoo.co.uk

Abha Singh is Head, Department of Philosophy at B.S. College, Danapur, Patna (a constituent unit under Magadh University, Bodh Gaya). She has published extensively in the fields of Social Philosophy, Buddhist Studies, Metaphysics and Ethics — several of her publictions have been indexed in the Philosopher's Index, USA, as well as Bibliographique de Philosophie, Belgium. She was the Director of the ICPR's national seminar on Morality and Social Justice, which met in Patna from 27 to 29 January 2008. Singh is currently working in the area of applied philosophy. She may be contacted at abhasingh23@rediffmail.com.

Damodar Singh is Head, Department of History at B.S. College, Danapur, Patna. He has been awarded National Merit scholarship at the graduate level (history honours), as well as a gold medal in postgraduate history, and has received his Ph.D. in 1989. He is the recipient of a Visiting Fellowship from the Centre for Advance Studies, Department of History, Aligarh Muslim University, Aligarh. He has completed three research projects — two of them sponsored by the UGC and one by the ICHR, New Delhi — and has recently been awarded a research project from the ICHR. He is currently serving on the editorial board of the journal Itihas ki Khoj Mein. Singh is the author of Political Biography of Khan-i Khanan Bairam Khan (1998) and The Political Biography of a Mughal Noble Shaista Khan (in press). He has published more than two dozen research papers on medieval Indian history and Buddhist studies, and has attended over thirty national/international seminars and conferences as well. The recent focus of his work has been on regional studies (Bihar). He may be contacted at dam_singh@rediffmail.com

Mahesh Singh is Professor & Head (retd.), Department of Philosophy, V.K.S. University, Ara. He has been Sectional President of several sessions of Indian Philosophical Congress and Akhil Bhāratīya Darśana Pariṣad. His area of specialization is Indian philosophy, religious studies, theology and Hindu culture. He is an ardent student of Sanatan Dharma (Hinduism) and has given a myriad of talks on various aspects of his faith in the "Radha Swami Satsang" at Patna.

R.P. Singh is Professor at Centre for Philosophy, School of Social Sciences, Jawaharlal Nehru University, New Delhi. His academic/research interests include Modern Western Philosophy, Post-modern Philosophy and Indian Philosophy with specializations on Rene Descartes, Spinoza, Leibniz, Locke, Berkeley, Hume, Immanuel Kant, G.W.F. Hegel, Schopenhauer, Karl Marx, V.I. Lenin, Heidegger, Husserl, Bertrand Russell, Ludwig Wittgenstein, A.J. Ayer, Gilbert Ryle, Nietzsche, Ferdinand de Saussure, Michel Foucault, Jacques Derrida, Richard Rorty, Max Horkheimer, Herbert Marcuse, Jurgen Habermas, J.F. Lyotard, Upaniṣads, Buddhism and Advaita Vedānta. He has got 16 books and 95 research articles published in different academic journals in India and abroad. He has visited Harvard University, Cambridge University, University of Massachusetts and many other Universities abroad. He may be contacted at rpsinghjnu@yahoo.com, rpsingh@jnu.ac.in.

Mritunjaya Narain Sinha is Professor & Head (retired), Department of Philosophy, B.R. Ambedker Bihar University, Muzaffarpur. He was also Professor Emeritus in the same department. He has been supervisor of more than fifty Ph.D. scholars, and five D.Litt. scholars as well. He has conducted ICPR'S national seminar on "Towards Women's Empowerment." He has published numerous books, as well as research papers and articles in national research journals and anthologies. His area of interest includes analytical philosophy, contemporary Indian philosophy and philosophy of religion.

Ramesh Chandra Sinha is former Professor and Head, Department of Philosophy, Patna University, Patna. His publications include three books, namely Concepts of Reason and Intuition, Samkālīn Bhāratīya Cintak and Samāj Evam Rājnīti Darśana kī Rūparekhā, and several research papers in national and international journals/ books. He also edited the third volume of Samkālīn Bhāratīya Cintan (published by Akhil Bhāratīya Darśana Pariṣad). He presented papers in several national and international conferences/seminars, as well as delivered several Endowment Lectures. Sinha has been sectional president at several annual conferences of Indian Philosophical Congress and Akhil Bhāratīya Darśana Pariṣad as well. He was the Guest Fellow of Indian

Institute of Advanced Study, Shimla, and was awarded Short Term Fellowship by the UGC, as well as Resident Fellowship of ICPR. He may be contacted at ramesh_chandra22@yahoo.co.in

Alok Tandon graduated in science from Lucknow University and obtained postgraduate degrees in economics, sociology and philosophy. As a general fellow of ICSSR, he worked on "Religion and Violence". He is currently pursuing his career as a bank officer. He has published a couple of books, namely Man and his Destiny with Special Reference to Marx and Sartre and Vikalpa and Vimarsha [Hindi] and several papers in reputed journals as well. Tandon's published work encompasses the diverse areas of ethics and his special field of interest is social philosophy. An active participant in conferences and seminars, he is known for his critical acumen. He may be contacted at dralokboi@yahoo.com

Ashok Kumar Varma is former Professor and Head Department of Philosophy B.R.A. Bihar University, Muzaffarpur. He has served the department for about thirty-five years. His research work is focused on analytic philosophy, ethics and symbolic logic.

Vinod Kumari is Head, Department of Philosophy at M.M.H. College, Ghaziabad (UP). She has conducted two ICPR sponsored national seminars. She has numerous publications to her credit. Recently she edited The Philosophy of M.N. Roy and Narendra Deva. Her areas of interest include social philosophy, contemporary Indian philosophy, philosophy of ethics and gender studies. She may be contacted at shubhra1000@hotmail.com.

Index